Gabon

the Bradt Travel Guide

Sean Connolly

edition
2

www.bradtguides.com

Bradt Travel Guides Ltd, UK
The Globe Pequot Press Inc, USA

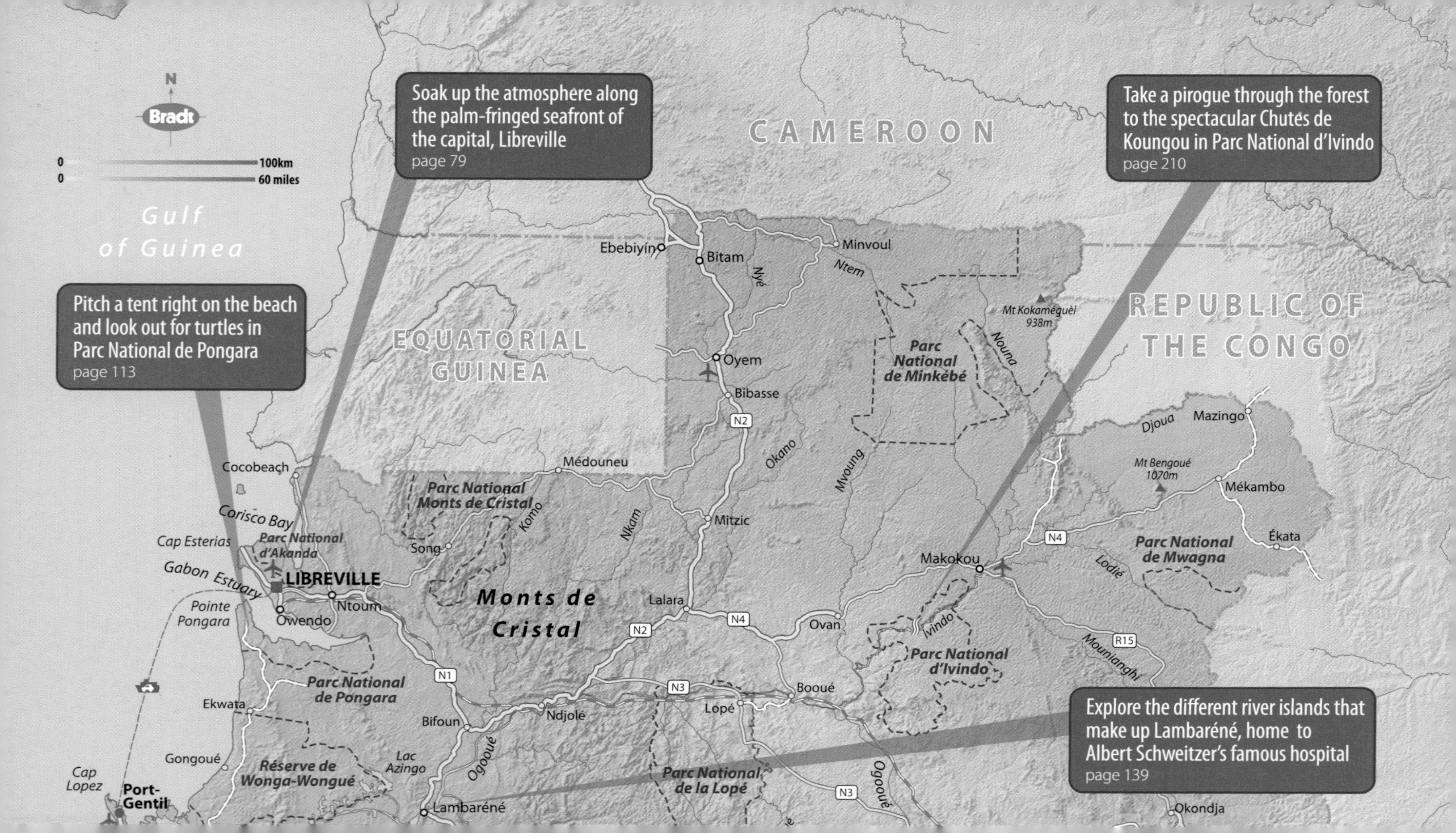

Take a pirogue through the forest to the spectacular Chutés de Koungou in Parc National d'Ivindo page 210

Explore the different river islands that make up Lambaréné, home to Albert Schweitzer's famous hospital page 139

Soak up the atmosphere along the palm-fringed seafront of the capital, Libreville page 79

Pitch a tent right on the beach and look out for turtles in Parc National de Pongara page 113

REPUBLIC OF THE CONGO

CAMEROON

EQUATORIAL GUINEA

Gulf of Guinea

Monts de Cristal

LIBREVILLE

Parc National de Mwagna

Parc National de Minkébé

Parc National d'Ivindo

Parc National Monts de Cristal

Parc National de la Lopé

Parc National de Pongara

Parc National d'Akanda

Réserve de Wonga-Wongué

Gabon Estuary

Mékambo
Ékata
Djouà
Mazingo
Mt Bengoué 1070m
Lodié
Mounionghi
Makokou
Mt Kokaméguel 938m
Nouna
Minvoul
Ntem
Nyé
Bitam
Oyem
Bibasse
Mitzic
Ovan
Booué
Okano
Mvoung
Médouneu
Lalara
Lopé
Okondja
Ogooué
Ndjolé
Song
Ntoum
Ovendo
Bifoun
Lac Azingo
Lambaréné
Ekwata
Gongoué
Port-Gentil
Cap Lopez
Cap Esterias
Corisco Bay
Cocobeach
Ebebiyin
Pointe Pongara

N2
N4
N3
N1
R15

Bradt

N

0   100km
0   60 miles

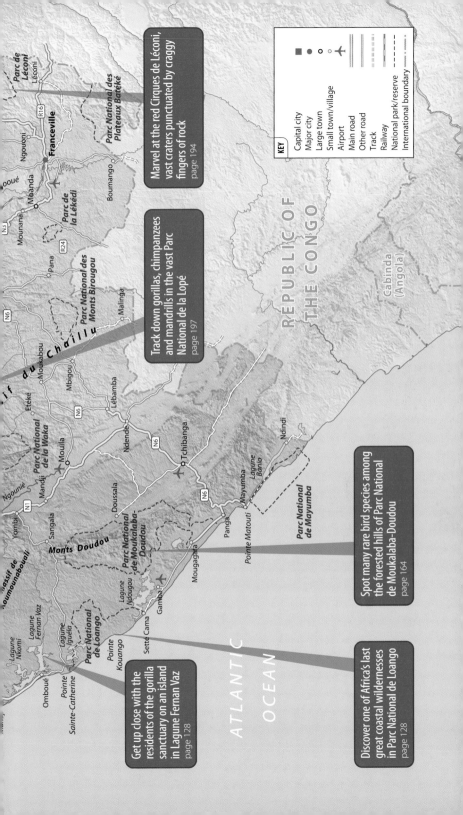

Marvel at the red Cirques de Léconi, vast craters punctuated by craggy fingers of rock
page 194

Track down gorillas, chimpanzees and mandrills in the vast Parc National de la Lopé page 197

Spot many rare bird species among the forested hills of Parc National de Moukalaba-Doudou
page 164

Get up close with the residents of the gorilla sanctuary on an island in Lagune Fernan Vaz
page 128

Discover one of Africa's last great coastal wildernesses in Parc National de Loango
page 128

KEY

Capital city
Major city
Large town
Small town/village
Airport
Main road
Other road
Track
Railway
National park/reserve
International boundary

REPUBLIC OF THE CONGO

Cabinda (Angola)

ATLANTIC OCEAN

Parc de Léconi
Léconi
Franceville
R16
Ngouoni
Ngouoni
Mbanda
Mounana
Parc National des Plateaux Batéké
Boumango
Parc de la Lékédi
N3
Pana
R24
Parc National des Monts Birougou
Malinga
Moukabou
Mbigou
Lébamba
lif du Chaillu
N6
N6
Etéké
Parc National de la Waka
Mouila
Mandji
N6
Ndendé
Tchibanga
N6
Ngounié
N1
Sangala
Yombi
Doussala
Monts Doudou
Parc National de Moukalaba-Doudou
Panga
Mayumba
Lagune Banio
Ndindi
Pointe Matouti
Parc National de Mayumba
Massif de Koumounabouali
Lagune Nkomi
Lagune Fernan Vaz
Lagune Iguéla
Parc National de Loango
Pointe Kouango
Setté Cama
Lagune Ndougou
Mougagara
Gamba
Omboué
Pointe Sainte-Catherine

Gabon
Don't
miss...

Parc National de Loango
Gabon's flagship park offers forests, savannahs and wetlands, along with wildlife including foraging lowland gorillas (SS) page 128

Parc National d'Ivindo
The spectacular Chutes de Koungou have a drop of over 60m, making them the highest falls in equatorial Africa (SJ) page 207

Cirques de Léconi

These eroded craters, punctuated by craggy fingers of rock festooned with greenery, are believed to be the home of rapacious spirits (BK) page 194

Lambaréné

Founded in 1924, Lambaréné's Hôpital Albert-Schweitzer now treats around 30,000 patients every year, while Albert Schweitzer's former lodgings are open to visitors (SS) page 143

Libreville and the Gabon Estuary

Gabon's capital is surrounded by palm-fringed beaches where it's possible to walk for miles along the shore at high tide (SW) page 106

Gabon in colour

above   Though poaching remains an acute risk, Gabon is home to Africa's largest population of forest elephant (BG/D) page 41

above left   The bongo is the largest of Gabon's forest antelope (KB/S) page 40

left   Leopards prowl many of Gabon's forests and are spotted by the occasional lucky visitor (SS) page 41

below left   Hippos are most commonly found in still pools or slow-running water (SS) page 41

below   The charismatic red river hog forages in groups on the shores of Parc National de Loango (SS) page 42

above   Parc National de Moukalaba-Doudou is known for its large population of chimpanzee (SS) page 37

right   Visitors can track mandrill in Parc National de la Lopé, where they live in troops of over 1,000 (SS) page 37

below right   De Brazza's monkey is often spotted in riverside forests (SS) page 38

below   Red-capped mangabey can be found in large arboreal groups along Gabon's coast (SS) page 38

above   The Parc National de la Lopé is a striking mosaic of open savannah and dense rainforest (SS) page 197

left   The coffee-dark waters and intensely verdant shores of the Lagune Fernan Vaz form one of Gabon's most fascinating landscapes (SS) page 127

below   Nyonié Camp offers a taste of the rolling savannahs that lie within the presidential Réserve du Wonga-Wongué (BK) page 115

AUTHOR

Sean Connolly (☐ @shanboqol) first travelled to Africa as a student in 2008 and has been returning to the continent regularly to research, teach English or simply soak up the ambiance in Africa's countless little-visited corners (of which Gabon has many) ever since. He's been poring over maps since before he could read them, and working with Bradt Guides since 2011. Along with authoring Bradt's *Senegal*, he's also updated or contributed to the Bradt guides to Somaliland, Malawi, Mozambique, Ghana, Uruguay, Sierra Leone and Rwanda. When he's not updating guides or  discussing the many merits of camel meat, you may find him hitching a lift on a grain truck, sampling questionable local delicacies (though he's recently had to draw a few lines, as Gabon truly excels when it comes to hair-raising foods!), or seeking out a country's funkiest records. Raised in Chicago, Sean stays on the move whenever possible, though lately you'll find him most often in Berlin.

CONTRIBUTOR

Annelies Hickendorff first set foot in Gabon in 2006 during a 25,000km overland journey. The fact that not many people in the West seemed to know this Central African country enormously triggered her curiosity and sense of adventure. The desire to explore lured her deep into Gabon's majestic rainforest. Captivated by nature's stunning beauty and its amazing inhabitants, she has been returning ever since, including once to update the previous edition of this guide.

Annelies lives in Brussels with her husband and daughter but travels whenever she can, and keeps dreaming of that beachside cottage where the rainforest meets the sea.

FEEDBACK REQUEST AND UPDATES WEBSITE

At Bradt Travel Guides we're aware that guidebooks start to go out of date on the day they're published – and that you, our readers, are out there in the field doing research of your own. You'll find out before us when a fine new family-run hotel opens or a favourite restaurant changes hands and goes downhill. So why not write and tell us about your experiences? Contact us on ☎ 01753 893444 or e info@bradtguides.com. We will forward emails to the author who may post updates on the Bradt website at w bradtupdates.com/gabon. Alternatively, you can add a review of the book to w bradtguides.com or Amazon.

PUBLISHER'S FOREWORD *Adrian Phillips, Managing Director*

Gabon has long seemed on the brink of becoming a magnet for eco-tourists. We first published a guide to the country well over a decade ago, following the then-president's announcement that 11% of the country would be made into national parks. As its oil reserves diminish and ecotourism rises up the government agenda, Gabon is finally starting to fulfil its early promise. Sean Connolly has done a great job of updating the material, keeping alive the spirit of the book following the tragic death of Sophie Warne, author of the acclaimed original edition.

Second edition published January 2020
First published 2014
Bradt Travel Guides Ltd
31a High Street, Chesham, Buckinghamshire, HP5 1BW, England
www.bradtguides.com
Print edition published in the USA by The Globe Pequot Press Inc,
PO Box 480, Guilford, Connecticut 06437-0480

ISBN: 978 1 78477 601 5

British Library Cataloguing in Publication Data
A catalogue record for this book is available from the British Library

Photographs Alamy.com: Arterra Picture Library (APL/A), Greenshoots Communications (GC/A), Hemis (H/A), National Geographic Image Collection (NGIC/A), Nick Greaves (NG/A), Portis Imaging (PI/A); Boris Kester (BK); Dreamstime.com: Beat Germann (BG/D); Flpa-images. co.uk: Sebastian Kennerknecht, Minden Pictures (SK/MP/FLPA), Thomas Marent (TM/FLPA); istockphoto.com: tropicalpixsingapore (t/i); naturepl.com: Enrique Lopez-Tapia (EL/NPL); Sean Connolly (SC); Shutterstock.com: Anton_Ivanov (AI/S), Bogdan Skaskiv (BS/S), Kapuska (K/S), Karel Bartik (KB/S), mbrand85 (m/S), PicksArt (P/S), Vladimir Wrangel (VW/S), William Farah (WF/S); Stuart Jarvis stujarvis.com (SJ); Superstock (SS); Sven Watterreus (SW)

Front cover Sunny-tailed monkey (TM/FLPA)
Back cover Lopé National Park (SS)
Title page Forest buffalo (m/S); Traditional masks (SS); Mandrill (SS)

Maps David McCutcheon FBCart.S. Colour map relief base by Nick Rowland FRGS

Typeset by Ian Spick, Bradt Travel Guides Ltd, D & N Publishing, Baydon, Wiltshire & www.dataworks.co.in
Production managed by Jellyfish Print Solutions; printed in India
Digital conversion by www.dataworks.co.in

The research trip for this guide started out with dropping my phone on the way out the door en route to the airport and smashing the screen to bits. That was – literally and figuratively – just the beginning. Landing in Gabon, my luggage was nowhere to be found, and it took several days and many fruitless trips to the airport's hopeless scrum of a lost-luggage room before it appeared – in one piece at least. Finally armed with my luggage and a new phone, I set out to take care of the sort of errands familiar to any traveller starting a long trip.

Unfortunately, there was a shortage of SIM cards, so getting connected turned out to be a non-starter. Undeterred, I went to draw cash, only to be inexplicably rejected by one ATM after another. Worse still, my account was almost entirely drained when I checked it – it had been charged for each attempted withdrawal, for money I'd never received! After picking myself up off the floor, uttering a long streak of unprintable words, and perhaps taking refuge in a cold Régab, I spent several stressful hours on the phone (not *my* phone, mind you, as I couldn't get a SIM) to the bank. Suffice to say, Gabon was not getting on my good side.

Nonetheless, there was a job to do and it was time to get on with it. I eventually managed to draw cash, get a SIM and get moving, and ever so slowly my luck began to change. Leaving Libreville with a window seat on the minibus gave me my first look at the otherworldly greenery that characterises so much of the country. We sped past tiny timber-built hamlets that seemed to me like boats on a green sea with residents perpetually tasked with bailing out their collective vessel to keep the forest at bay. Indeed, Gabon's interior – by turns bounteous and baleful – left me feeling small in the exhilarating, intimidating way of the ocean. It also left me gobsmacked – again whispering a few unprintable words – with its natural riches: a surfeit of wonders that seemed so normal and natural that it was easy to forget just how unique it is, and how it becomes more so by the day as our global environment continues to degrade.

Getting within metres of a forest elephant family grazing on a riverbank, spotting a lowland gorilla simply crossing the road and marvelling at breaching whales and nesting turtles along hundreds of kilometres of wild, windswept, undeveloped coast are increasingly rare privileges in today's world, and I somehow began to feel it appropriate that I couldn't just walk into this hidden, halcyon realm without letting go of a few of my worldly concerns along the way. While I knew the world of bank cards, SIM cards and lost luggage would be waiting for me upon my return, for many happy moments I was both lost and liberated in the wilds of Gabon – I hope this book can help you get there, too.

Acknowledgements

As ever, my deepest thanks go first to my partner Imke Rueben, whose deep wellspring of support, patience, and compassion in navigating what has been a year's worth of personal and professional change as I wrote this guide is more than I could ever ask for.

To Rachel Fielding, Anna Moores and everyone at Bradt for the opportunity, and especially to Carys Homer for her impressively meticulous editing, without which this would have undoubtedly been a much poorer guide.

My gratitude also, of course, goes out to everyone who shared their expertise with me in Gabon and helped me along the way as this book slowly came to fruition, including: Antonio Anoro (Gabon Untouched); Karolien Pieters and Jacques Régnault Zico Ibamba (Cooperative Abiétu); Mathieu Msellati and Jan Fourie (Loango Lodge); Lee White and Christian Johnson-Ogoula (ANPN); Grace Ntahinta (Gabon Wildlife Camps); Hugo, Chris and Emilie Fairet (WCS Congo); Philippe Robin and Nathalie Carrière (Eco-Village d'Enamino); Sylvie Duplessis (Le Bougainvillier); Heather Arrowood (OELO/Tsam-Tsam); Goody (Pico Mocambo); Carole Degioanni (Nomad Suites Résidence); Arshenne Lembouma (Afrijet); Sylvia Dirabou (Radisson); Ghislain Bouassa (Back to Roots Tours); Remy Nkombe (Nkombe Remy Tour); Leina Yangari (Lopé Hotel); Yannick Lindzondzo Dinah (Les Guides de l'Ogooué); Marie (Pongara Lodge); Joseph Okouyi Okouyi (Ivindo National Park); Pierre Amiet; Titus Drummond; George Vlad; Andrea Brum and Jean-Louis Albert.

ACKNOWLEDGEMENTS FOR THE FIRST EDITION *Annelies Hickendorff*

The first edition took shape with the valued input of many people in Gabon and beyond. I'm particularly grateful to Paul Mombey Indaki and the staff of Ngondetour, who provided me with advice, information and practical support in Gabon. Thanks go to Romain Beville (PROGRAM) for showing me Moukalaba-Doudou, to David Nzokou for his help in Port-Gentil, to Bas Verhage (WWF) and Mathon van Wijk (Transjungle) and Sven Watterreus for sharing their knowledge on the country. It's not easy to write about a destination so far from its own cultural experience without falling into the trap of stereotyping, and I'd like to thank Rivke and Wayne for their help in keeping an open mind.

I owe much to many people whose names I never learned, including the bus driver from Benin, who graciously saved me from some overenthusiastic policemen, and my fellow bus passengers who did all they could to cheer me up. I'm grateful to some wonderful hotel staff that took care of baby Lina, and to the guests and manager of Lékédi Park, who generously offered me a wonderful Christmas dinner. The assistance of Thomas Balmelle of the Radisson Blu was greatly appreciated.

Finally, I'm indebted to Sophie Warne, the author of the original *Gabon, São Tomé and Príncipe* guide. It was impressive to hear how Sophie is still remembered by the people she met during her time in Gabon.

NEW TELEPHONE NUMBERING PLAN

At the time this guide went to print, the Autorité de régulation des communications électroniques et des postes (ARCEP; Regulatory Authority for Electronic Communication and Post; w arcep.ga) was in the process of changing the Gabonese telephone numbering plan (Plan de numération téléphonique) from eight digits to nine. The move was originally scheduled for July 2019, but had been pushed back by several months. It was unclear as to whether or not it would be pushed back again, but it nonetheless seemed likely to happen during the lifetime of this edition.

The move will impact how you dial every telephone number in the country (including all numbers listed in this guide). Under the old system, numbers are eight digits long, with the type of number (fixed or mobile, and service provider) indicated by the first two digits – different service providers may have different leading digits. Under the new system each will be harmonised under one two-digit prefix. A further explanation of the planned changes is included below.

OLD NUMBERING
Fixed/landline: 01 XX XX XX
Airtel (old prefixes of 04 & 07): 04 XX XX XX, 07 XX XX XX
Gabon Telecom (Libertis) & Moov (old prefixes of 02, 05, & 06): 02 XX XX XX, 05 XX XX XX, 06 XX XX XX

NEW NUMBERING
Fixed/landline: 011 XX XX XX
Airtel (new prefix of 07): 074 XX XX XX, 077 XX XX XX
Gabon Telecom (Libertis) & Moov (new prefix of 06): 062 XX XX XX, 065 XX XX XX, 066 XX XX XX

The changes will also see the leading zero on Gabonese numbers dropped when dialling from abroad. Landlines dialling from abroad will follow the format (+241) 11 XX XX XX, Airtel numbers from abroad will follow the format (+241) 74 XX XX XX, and Gabon Telecom numbers from abroad will follow the format (+241) 62 XX XX XX.

FOLLOW US

Tag us in your posts to share your adventures using this guide with us – we'd love to hear from you.

🅕 BradtGuides
🐦 @BradtGuides & @shanboqol
📷 @bradtguides & @shanboqol
ⓟ bradtguides
▶ bradtguides

Contents

Introduction

When I mentioned to relatives and friends that I would be writing a travel guide to Gabon, some gingerly asked just how many travellers there are to write that guide for (and these were the ones who didn't scrunch up their faces and ask 'where?'). And while it's true that until now foreign appreciation has been predominantly confined to oil workers and people travelling Africa overland, Gabon is slowly but surely getting serious about unlocking its ecotourism potential. Dubbed 'the land of the surfing hippo' or 'Africa's Eden', the country aimed to attract 100,000 high- and middle-end visitors by 2020. They'll miss this figure by a mile, but the national parks bureau is making a commendable effort to both safeguard and share the country's staggering ecological heritage. Gabon's national parks protect over 12% of the country and the government has taken up the battle against poaching by creating well-trained and well-funded anti-poaching brigades. In 2012 the president publicly destroyed the country's ivory stocks, and it's hoped that ecotourism can be the key to sustainable nature and wildlife conservation.

In fact, little-visited Gabon has everything to become Africa's next big ecotourism destination, while the fact that it isn't a mainstream holiday location yet only adds to its attraction. Not only is it exciting to travel in this pristine region off the tourist radar, but also the hassle of other safari destinations is totally lacking. Without a dozen minibuses crowding around one lion, there's actually something left to explore.

The main part of the country, over 80%, is covered in dense rainforest, and the remainder is savannah and coastline, and for each of these habitats Gabon has the wildlife to match. This is a country where gorilla and elephant can be caught on camera on the same stretch of beach – although a healthy dose of patience is obligatory. At the same time, birders are guaranteed to leave satisfied, as they will surely spot many of the almost 700 species recorded in the country.

Despite a difficult few years of plummeting oil prices, a deeply controversial election, and even a putative coup d'état, Gabon remains a comparative oasis of stability and prosperity in a region that has had more than its fair share of tension and violence. The discovery of oil boosted the economy and its main cities are modern with high rises. The country enjoys one of the highest GDP per capita in sub-Saharan Africa (although far from equally divided) and you will notice more fancy cars on the streets of Libreville than in a European capital.

Gabon not only possesses a huge wealth of natural treasures, it also maintains a rich tradition of pre-Christian animist culture, including mystical ceremonies and initiation rites. One of the secret societies that appeals most to the imagination is Bwiti, whose initiates eat the hallucinogenic shrub of the *iboga* plant to facilitate contact with their ancestors and deepen their understanding of life.

All that being said, getting around Gabon isn't exactly a stroll in the park. It is an expensive country, and the infrastructure and tourist facilities are basic (and, in more remote places, simply non-existent). While travelling here can occasionally feel like hard work, the rewards are worth the effort. The Gabonese travel around a lot to see friends and family, particularly during the holidays, and the atmosphere is invariably fun and friendly.

This is Africa at its purest, where you can still enjoy wildlife and breathtaking natural beauty while having the place to yourself. That's why now is the perfect time to go – before the 100,000 tourists actually *do* arrive.

HOW TO USE THIS GUIDE

AUTHOR'S FAVOURITES Finding genuinely characterful accommodation or that unmissable off-the-beaten-track café can be difficult, so the author has chosen a few of his favourite places throughout the country to point you in the right direction. These 'author's favourites' are marked with a ✳.

MAPS
Keys and symbols Maps include alphabetical keys covering the locations of those places to stay, eat or drink that are featured in the book. Note that regional maps may not show all hotels and restaurants in the area: other establishments may be located in towns shown on the map.

Grids and grid references Some maps use gridlines to allow easy location of sites. Map grid references are listed in square brackets after the name of the place or site of interest in the text, with page number followed by grid number, eg: [95 C3].

PRICE CODES Throughout this guide we have used price codes to indicate the cost of those places to stay and eat that are listed; please note that codes are reflective of price only, they are not an indication of quality or star rating. For a key to these price codes, see page 69 for accommodation and page 71 for restaurants.

STREET NAMES Rather than street names, landmarks and key road junctions are the primary means of navigation in Gabon. Local street names are often unrecognised by the public or, more often, are simply absent in the first place.

Part One

GENERAL INFORMATION

GABON AT A GLANCE

Location West coast of Central Africa
Neighbouring countries Republic of the Congo, Cameroon and Equatorial Guinea
Size 267,670km²
Climate Tropical; always hot and humid
Capital Libreville
Provinces Estuaire, Moyen-Ogooué, Ngounié, Ogooué-Maritime, Nyanga, Woleu-Ntem, Ogooué-Ivindo, Haut-Ogooué and Ogooué-Lolo
Main towns Port-Gentil and Franceville
Status Republic; multi-party presidential regime
Population 2.1 million (2018)
Urbanisation 89.5% (2018)
Life expectancy 68 (2018)
Languages French (official language) and some 40 African languages, including Fang, Myènè, Nzebi, Bapounou, Eshira, and Bandjabi
Ethnic diversity 80% of the population is Gabonese-born, among which the largest groups are Fang (23.2%), Shira-Punu/Vili (18.9%), Nzabi-Duma (11.3%), Mbede-Teke (6.9%), Myènè (5%), Kota-Kele (4.9%) and Okande-Tsogo (2.1%)
Religion Largest denominations are Roman Catholic (42.3%), Protestant (12.3%), other Christian beliefs (27.4%) and Muslim (9.8%)
Currency CFA franc
Exchange rate £1 = 737CFA; US$1 = 597CFA; €1 = 656CFA (fixed) (October 2019)
GDP US$36.66 billion (2017); GDP per capita US$18,100 (2018); GDP growth 0.5% (2017)
Poverty 34.3% living below the poverty line (2015)
Inflation 2.7% (2017)
Independence 17 August 1960 (from France)
Flag Three horizontal stripes: green, yellow and blue
Time GMT +1
International telephone code +241
Internet top-level domain .ga
Electrical voltage 220V
Weights and measures Metric
Public holidays 1 January, 12 March, Easter, 1 May, Pentecost weekend, 17 August, 19 August, 1 November, 25 December

1

Background Information

GEOGRAPHY

Gabon straddles the Equator on the west coast of Central Africa. Its capital, Libreville, has a latitude of 0°25'N. Equatorial Guinea and Cameroon border Gabon to the north, Republic of the Congo to the east and south, and to the west is the Atlantic Ocean.

The country covers an area of 267,670km². To put this in context, Gabon could fit into the USA 35 times, into France twice and into Zimbabwe once.

Gabon's coast stretches for 855km, so it is hardly surprising that it is not uniform. Just by looking at a map, you can see how craggy it is to the north of Cap Lopez, while to the south the coastline becomes much smoother, straighter and sandier. At its deepest, the coastal region encroaches some 200km inland. In parts it is very swampy and the only way to get around is by pirogue.

Inland from the low-lying coastal plain lie elevated plateaux of up to 500m in height. Rising above these plateaux is the occasional mountain range reaching around 1,000m, notably the Crystal Mountains and the du Chaillu range – the location of what's often touted as the highest point in Gabon, Mount Iboundji (see box, page 30). In fact, the 1,575m figure often attributed to this mountain is false; it actually tops out at 972m, making Mount Bengoué near Mékambo the country's highest at 1,070m.

Of Gabon's many rivers, the largest is the Ogooué River, which flows between Cap Lopez on the Atlantic to its source in the Congo 1,200km away, fed by many tributaries on the way. Just beyond Lambaréné, the absence of mountains enables it to open out into an enormous delta of lakes.

Over 80% of Gabon is covered in dense tropical forest. Ancient forest dominates the mountain ranges and remote areas, while post-agricultural forest grows in areas that were once cultivated. Compared with the forest, savannahs are a minute proportion of the landscape, but they're nonetheless found in parts of the Ogooué-Maritime, Ngounié, Nyanga and Haut-Ogooué provinces, particularly dominating the latter.

CLIMATE

Like all equatorial regions, Gabon's is a tropical climate. It's hot and humid all year-round, averaging 26°C and 85% humidity, with a typical annual rainfall of 2.51m. The climate does of course vary slightly depending on where you are. Thanks to the trade winds, the humidity on the coast is less intense, and there is less rain the further south you head. Broadly speaking, Gabon has two main seasons: a long rainy season between February and May, followed by a long dry season from late May to mid-September. The rest of the year is made up of two shorter seasons: a rainy season from late September to November (the month with the highest average rainfall) and a dry season from December to January.

Archaeological research has uncovered a handful of artefacts in the Ogooué Valley, particularly around La Lopé, testifying that human life here dates as far back as 400,000 years. These prehistoric peoples probably came to the area from the Congo or Cameroon. Of the people living in Gabon today, the earliest inhabitants are the 'Pygmies' (see box, page 17), who can be traced back to AD1100. These forest-based communities came from elsewhere in Central Africa, driven by the spread of the Bantu to find alternative areas to support their nomadic forest existence. Unfortunately for them, the Bantu kept on coming. In fact, the Bantu migration into western Africa was to continue for several centuries. As late as the 19th century, Fang migration into southwestern Gabon from the northeast caused massive instability and intertribal fighting.

THE ARRIVAL OF THE EUROPEANS Little is known with much certainty about Gabon before the Europeans arrived and started making notes, though these sources tell us just as much about European attitudes – invariably exploitative, patronising and prejudiced – as they do about the damage they wreaked. European attempts to replace traditional societies and their practices with European models of civilisation and spiritual fulfilment have since been well documented.

Gabon's European history starts with a Portuguese sailor, Lopes Gonçalves, who trawled Africa's west coast in 1474 and entered the Gabon Estuary. There is a story that he named the estuary *gabão* because its shape reminded him of a gabão, or sailor's cloak, and that later gabão was transformed to become Gabon. It's not a very popular story, because the estuary's shape doesn't, in fact, look much like a cloak. An alternative idea is that the name Gabon was derived from the name of an important local ruler.

Slave traders What we know of the history of Africa's west coast, from the arrival of the first Europeans up to the 18th century, is all trade-related. The Portuguese struggled to fend off the Dutch but by the mid 17th century had effectively lost the fight for trading supremacy, leaving the Dutch traders to ply the coast, buying gold, ivory and slaves. A century later much of the Dutch-controlled coast had passed into the hands of the English and French, who took more than one million Africans from the Loango coast between 1700 and 1807 – an enormous figure in an already sparsely populated area. There were known slave depots and embarkation points along the coast, and also at Lopé, Cap Lopez. Slavery was banned in Britain in 1838, in France in 1854 and in the United States in 1865, but trade continued illegally. From the late 1820s French anti-slavery naval patrols were operating – with the underlying agenda of finding suitable areas to establish trading posts – but the coast was too large and the number of vessels too small for their efforts to definitively halt trade.

In 1839 the French naval lieutenant Bouët-Willaumez obtained territory on the Gabon Estuary from the Mpongwé king Antchouwé Kowe Rapontchombo. (The French called him Denis, as Antchouwé Kowe Rapontchombo was too much of an effort.) The French now had a base from which to combat slave traders and spread French control. In return, Rapontchombo was given a few goods, including two sacks of tobacco, ten white hats and 20 guns. This was the first of many such treaties the French were to sign with local chiefs.

Missionaries and traders Not long afterwards, in 1842, the first missionaries – Protestants from the American Board of Commissioners for Foreign Missions

(ABCFM) – descended on the estuary. They chose to build their mission at Glass, immediately south of the spot that would be chosen for Libreville seven years later (page 79). They built a handful of mission schools in Mpongwé villages around the estuary in an attempt to outflank the Roman Catholic Holy Ghost Fathers, who arrived soon after them, from France in 1844. As was the case in much of Africa, the newly arrived missionaries of each denomination were fixated on suppressing traditional spiritual practices, including Bwiti (see box, page 18), in favour of Christian rites.

Alongside the missionaries, the great trading firms of Europe also set up shop in Glass, with the intention of trading with the interior. A first-hand, if exaggerated, account of life for one European trader is described in *Trader Horn*, a record of tales Aloysius 'Trader' Horn told to a South African writer in 1926. Trader Horn arrived in Africa around 1871 as an employee of the British trading company Hatton and Cookson, of Liverpool. He was based at the first factory in Lambaréné, on Adolinanongo Hill (now home to the Schweitzer Hospital), and made frequent forages into the unexplored interior in search of new trading routes and treaties. Trade at that time consisted of exchanging cloth, cooking pots, brandy, guns, gunpowder and salt, for ivory, rubber, ebony and padouk wood.

Explorers Along with the traders and missionaries came European explorers. While the traders were keen to exploit Africa's riches as cheaply as possible, the explorers were motivated predominantly by curiosity and the desire for glory. Their accounts are peppered to varying degrees with tales of tribal skirmishes, light-fingered porters and reports of the constant haggling and bribing necessary to progress further into the interior. A large number of the crates on any expedition were crammed with necessary bribes – above all cloth and alcohol.

Paul Belloni du Chaillu undertook an expedition in 1855 with the intention of finding animals and tribes never before seen by outsiders, as well as to locate any healthy places in the interior where missionaries could do their work without dying in such great numbers as they were on the coast, thanks to the difficult climate. An ambitious agenda by anyone's standards, but he was better equipped than most for the task in hand. Having lived for several years on the coast, where his father had owned a trading post, du Chaillu was fluent in the languages and customs of the coastal people at least. There can be no doubt that this knowledge, coupled with an iron constitution, was a decisive factor in his return alive. He journeyed 'always on foot, and unaccompanied by other white men' across 12,000km of jungle, withstanding relentless tropical rains, unrelenting insect bites and 50 attacks of fever, on an uncertain diet and masses of quinine.

Unfortunately for du Chaillu, when his books were published in England – most famously his *Explorations and Adventures in Equatorial Africa* in 1861 – they were heavily criticised as being far-fetched and unscientific, little more than flights of fancy. He had shot, stuffed and carted home 2,000 birds and 200 quadrupeds, of which 60 and 20 respectively were identified as new species. He was probably the first outsider to have come face to face with a gorilla, to have met Pygmies, and to have eaten with (and not been eaten by) the Fang, and yet his encounters were dismissed as overblown storytelling. An angry du Chaillu undertook a second expedition in 1863. His account of that trip – *A Journey to Ashango-Land* – was more kindly received, but nonetheless he vowed never to do another.

Du Chaillu's stories struck a chord with a naturalised Frenchman born in Italy. **Savorgnan de Brazza** obtained sponsorship from the French navy and threw himself into exploring Gabon's forest interior in 1875. Three years later he re-emerged, a barefoot, feverish, starving wreck. He had got as far as the Poubara waterfall (page 183) and was able to report that the Ogooué River was neither a tributary of the Congo nor a suitable trading river, on account of its numerous rapids. Believing that with trade would come 'civilisation', he suggested that a railroad be built into the interior along the river instead.

By this time the American **Henry Morton Stanley** had just succeeded in crossing Africa from east to west, and had written up his achievement in a book entitled *Through the Dark Continent* (1878). De Brazza immediately set about preparing another trip. In 1879, they were both setting off again. The race for territory was on between de Brazza (for the French team) and Stanley (hired to work for the Belgians). De Brazza came up trumps. He founded Franceville and Brazzaville, and in between made a treaty with the king of the Batéké, who agreed to place his land west of the Congo River under French protection.

Of all the explorers, de Brazza was probably the least aggressive but the most dissembling. (His defenders claim he conquered an empire without firing a single shot, which is not quite true, but he was certainly a tireless campaigner against slavery.) He won the trust of local peoples with patience and artful persuasion. He waxed lyrical about the benefits of free trade in order to extract treaties from the chiefs in which they committed their kingdoms to French protection. It is because of his efforts that the land between the coast and the Congo River was recognised as being under French control, firstly at the Berlin Conference in 1885, and again in 1888 with the creation of the Congo Français, with Libreville as its capital and de Brazza as its governor.

FRENCH RULE When formidable Victorian Mary Kingsley (see box, page 146) set off on her travels in 1893, the area known today as Gabon was an administrative district within the Congo Français, referred to as the Gaboon. By this time there were already a number of foreigners living in the territory, not only on the coast, but also strung along the Ogooué River into the interior. There were government posts (French), trading posts (mostly British) and mission houses (American Protestants and French Catholics).

By the turn of the century, de Brazza had been fired from his position as governor, in part thanks to a dispute with higher-ups in the colonial administration, where he opposed expanding the use of forced labour concessions. When he saw the reality of colonisation, de Brazza seriously regretted the role he had played, but by then it was too late. French attempts to monopolise trade and levy taxes had naturally been fiercely resented by the local peoples. Direct attacks on Europeans became much more frequent and there were violent rebellions across the colony. The French government invested nothing in its newly acquired colony, and instead simply sold large concessions to rubber companies. They used forced labour to meet unrealistic quotas, and then punished the labourers severely when they failed to meet them. Death and disease were rife, as was the spirit of rebellion, but this alone could not overcome the superior training and equipment of the French, and within a couple of decades the French had quashed all opposition.

In 1910, the Congo Français was replaced by the Federation of French Equatorial Africa, which united Gabon, Chad, the Central African Republic and Congo under a governor general based in Brazzaville. In 1913 another formidable European arrived on the scene for the first time, **Doctor Albert Schweitzer**. Though overflowing with the usual paternalistic attitudes of the time, he did at least put his energies into doing something of practical importance (see box, page 144). He was still there in 1958, when the Federation of French Equatorial Africa broke down and a Gabonese Republic within the French Community was proclaimed. With legal and government systems based on the French model, Gabon was finally granted independence from France on 17 August 1960. However, of all the Western powers, the French have proved the most reluctant to withdraw from the affairs of their former colonies, and perhaps nowhere more so than in Gabon.

INDEPENDENCE AND THE RULE OF OMAR BONGO The first president of the Gabonese Republic, **Léon Mba**, presided over a multi-party system, but not without some difficulty. In early 1964 the tension culminated in an opposition attempt to seize power. It was quashed by French troops and Mba was reinstated, only to lose the election in April. He made a comeback in the March 1967 election, where he took 99% of the vote, but wasn't destined to enjoy his success for very long.

The man who was then known as **Albert-Bernard Bongo** (see box, page 8) became vice-president on 12 November 1966. As a result of Mba's illness, Bongo was acting as president weeks before Mba actually died on 28 November 1967. He was officially confirmed president on 2 December, and wasted no time in founding the Gabonese Democratic Party, claiming that one-party rule meant national unity while a multi-party system could only foster divisions. Bongo's one-party state was to survive unchallenged for 22 years, with Bongo being re-elected president in 1972, 1979 and 1986 to seven-year terms. In April 1975, the office of vice-president was abolished and replaced by the office of prime minister, with no provision for automatic succession. Successive French governments strongly supported the elder Bongo, even coming to his aid with troops after protests in 1990.

Bongo maintained that while not opposed to the multi-party system in principle (the West was living proof that it could work well), it was 'ill-suited' to Gabon. He described Gabon as a country where voters always chose the man from their province, irrespective of ideas or issues. Bongo's avowed primary concern was to suppress old tribal divisions in the move towards national unity, a necessary precursor of the stable, successful Gabonese nation he envisaged. From the start, Bongo's single-party system was met with criticism, and not only from the Western democracies. The Mouvement de Redressement National (Movement for National Rectification; MORENA) – an opposition group made up of nationalist intellectuals and students – claimed that the interests of several ethnic groups were not being addressed. Other opponents, some in voluntary exile, made allegations of electoral rigging and corruption. Some even accused the president of being involved in drug trafficking.

Until oil was found in Gabon, the country depended heavily on manganese and timber. With the discovery of oil offshore in the early 1960s, Gabon was catapulted into the limelight as the smallest country to be a member of OPEC and the country with the highest per-capita earnings in Africa.

With *les petrodollars* came change. Many exchanged a life of rural subsistence for an urban existence. Almost every Gabonese family has at least one member working in some kind of civil service, providing for the whole family, and you'll often hear foreigners lamenting that the Gabonese do not need to work and prefer to leave their jobs to immigrants.

Gabon quickly became dependent on imports. More than 80% of the food and goods required by Gabon's urban populations are now imported – mangoes from Mali, pineapples from Cameroon and so on – a costly reflection of the underdeveloped state of the country's farming, fishing and manufacturing resources. Agricultural projects existed – cultivating manioc, tomatoes, taro, cucumbers and coffee – but yields were insufficient and transport unreliable. By the late 1970s the country was in financial difficulties, thanks in part to the opulent renovation of the

Albert-Bernard Bongo was born in Lewai (now Bongoville) in Haut-Ogooué on 30 December 1935. Although the Bongos are now among the world's wealthiest families, his childhood was a humble one. He said, 'I do not forget my peasant origins. I was not born in a hospital bed or a cradle and never had a nanny. I was born in the grass. Despite honours, power and all its attendant advantages, that is a fact I have never forgotten.' He was ten years old when he attended school for the first time, but quickly made up for this late start with his ambition. He defied his guardian (his father died when he was just seven years old) to attend technical school in Brazzaville. He started work there as a civil servant in the post office and was a supporter of the Mouvement Socialiste Africain (African Socialist Movement; MSA). Before independence, he had worked his way up to the French rank of lieutenant in the air force.

After independence, his political rise was rapid. In the 1961 elections for the National Assembly, Bongo took an active role in the campaign in Haut-Ogooué. A year later he became assistant director of the Cabinet that supported the president, and just months after that appointment he was promoted to be its director. President Léon Mba nominated him vice-president in 1966. The following year, Bongo was president himself.

Bongo was motivated by ambitions that upped the country's international profile in conjunction with his own. He wanted to build a country that looked modern and wealthy, and a people that were superior to their neighbours. For him the Trans-Gabon Railway (page 66) was a symbol of Gabon as a modern, progressive state. Bongo was not the first man to visualise a railway that would transport raw materials from Gabon's interior to the coast – Savorgnan de Brazza drew up plans back in 1885 – but he was the most determined. The stories about how he financed it smack of political opportunism. Supposedly, having been turned down for financing by the World Bank and the West, Bongo turned his attentions elsewhere. He is reported as saying about the Trans-Gabon Railway: 'It will be built by one means or another with the help of this country or that country.' In the end the money came from Abu Dhabi. Bongo ditched Catholicism as a poor investment and made a calculated conversion to Islam. On his way back from Mecca he dropped in on Sheikh Zayd of Abu Dhabi. When his plane left the following morning it was full to bursting with French francs.

Work on the railway started at Owendo, 20km south of Libreville, in December 1973. The final section was finished in December 1987, not at the iron deposits in

Presidential Palace in Libreville. What little was left in the coffers, plus some, was devoured by the massive cost of the Trans-Gabon Railway (see box, above). The 1980s saw a fall in the price of oil paralleled by a drastic drop in worldwide demand for timber. To make matters worse, by 1991 the production of both manganese and uranium would also have sharply declined. Alongside all this the cost of imported goods rose, while, predictably, salaries did not. These economic problems came at a time when resentment towards the way Bongo squandered Gabon's income could no longer be contained. Violent protests in the early 1980s led to MORENA leaders being imprisoned, but violence in 1989 was to force Bongo to amend the constitution and legalise opposition parties.

However, in May 1990 **Joseph Redjambe**, president of the opposition Gabonese Progressive Party, was killed in a fire in a Libreville hotel. Anti-governmental the northeast as had originally been planned, but in the southeast, at Franceville. The official reason why Bongo had changed the route was to transport the Haut-Ogooué's manganese and uranium to the coast. To many it looked more like a thinly veiled attempt to contain the power of the Fang, the prominent ethnic group in the north, while favouring the Batéké, Bongo's own people, in the southeast. The Trans-Gabon Railway stretches from west to east for 660km through the forest. It far surpassed the original budget, costing approximately 20 million French francs per kilometre, leaving Gabon teetering on the brink of bankruptcy.

From 1959 to 1988 Bongo was married to the singer and drummer Patience Dabany, a Batéké from the Central African Republic. After their divorce Bongo married his second wife, the daughter of Denis Sassou-Nguesso, thereby becoming son-in-law to the President of the Republic of the Congo. Patience Dabany is the mother of Bongo's eldest son, Ali Bongo Ondimba, who was born Alain Bernard Bongo in the capital of the neighbouring Republic of the Congo on 9 February 1959. Like his father who became Omar Bongo in 1973, Alain Bernard also changed his name when they both converted to Islam. Ali received a privileged education in France, going to a private Christian secondary school in the upmarket town of Neuilly, west of Paris, and to the Sorbonne, where he graduated with a PhD in law. While Ali thanks his father for 'giving him the genes of responsibility, dignity and honour', he is said to have inherited his mother's talent for music. He even released a disco-funk album, *A Brand New Man*, in 1977 under his former name.

Ali Bongo made his political debut by joining his father's Parti Démocratique Gabonais (PDG; Gabonese Democratic Party) in 1981. His rapid political rise, which saw him occupy the posts of foreign minister and defence minister, successfully prepared him to succeed his father as president after his death in 2009. The elections in which Ali Bongo was chosen with an overwhelming majority were controversial and the opposition denounced the elections as corrupt. Generous payoffs and the threat of prison would have silenced political opponents. Bongo went on to be re-elected in 2016 under even more dubious circumstances, and no amount of payoffs were able to keep a lid on the furious opposition. Protestors torched the National Assembly after results were announced; however, the Constitutional Court would go on to certify Bongo's victory some weeks later.

Ali Bongo is married to the Frenchwoman Sylvia Bongo Odimba (née Valentin), his second wife, with whom he has four children.

feeling reached new heights in a ten-day demonstration that was the most violent yet, to the extent that 5,000 French residents were evacuated. In June 1990 it was agreed that presidential elections would be held in 1992, but Bongo then brought the date forward to the end of the year. In doing so, he was safeguarding his own success by depriving the opposition of any fair chance of gathering support. The French came to Bongo's aid and a new constitution was introduced in March 1991, confirming a multi-party system and stipulating that the president, to be elected for a seven-year term, would appoint a Council of Ministers headed by a prime minister. The constitution also granted real power to the National Assembly and the Senate, both of which are directly elected for five and six years respectively. In the event of the president's death, the prime minister, National Assembly president and defence minister should share powers until new elections are held.

Bongo once again won the elections of 1993, the first under a multi-party system, but the word on the street was that he had shuffled the figures. Protests broke out and were quashed, leaving 30 people dead. The 'Paris Accords' negotiated in Paris in 1994 between majority and government representatives agreed to a more transparent electoral process and reforms of government institutions. In the parliamentary elections of December 1996 – Gabon's peak year of oil production – Bongo's PDG gained a clear majority, but in many towns the opposition carried away the municipal elections. This was the case in Libreville, where **Paul Mba Abessole** of the opposition party Rassemblement des Bûcherons, or the Association of Woodcutters, stormed to victory and became mayor of Libreville. Abessole immediately requested the UN to supervise the presidential elections to be held in 1998. Once again, the elections confirmed Bongo as president, with a landslide victory, for another seven years. In early 1999 there were more protests. Bongo retaliated by closing schools and universities, which he identified as hotbeds for demonstrators.

The parliamentary elections of December 2001 were a replay of the same, tired old story. The ruling PDG retained a convincing majority. Once again there were murmurs of electoral fraud and accusations that multi-party elections were nothing but a sham in what was to all intents and purposes a single-party state. The public made their feelings clear by abstaining in large numbers, up to 80% in the larger towns. Bongo responded by appointing four opposition members as ministers in his new government, including Paul Mba Abessole and Pierre Claver Maganga Moussavou, president of the Parti Social Démocrate (PSD; Social Democratic Party). People started joking that the fastest way to become a minister in Gabon was to enter the opposition.

In 2003, constitutional restrictions on how many terms a president may serve were abolished, and in the elections of 2005 Bongo was re-elected president again. According to Gabon's election commission the poll was fair. Protests and barricades in Port-Gentil were responded to with tear gas.

On 8 June 2009, at the age of 73, the (at that time) longest-serving president in Africa died of cardiac arrest in a hospital in Barcelona, Spain. The government immediately responded to the news of Bongo's death by closing the borders and securing government buildings and strategic targets. The president of the Senate, **Rose Francine Rogombé**, took over as interim president and was charged with the organisation of elections. Bongo was buried in Franceville, in his native province, in the presence of a large French delegation.

ALI BONGO TAKES THE REINS Nobody seemed very surprised when the president's son and former defence minister Ali Bongo Ondimba (see box, page 8) was the declared winner of the 2009 elections. He received 42% of the vote, far ahead of former interior minister and leader of the National Union Andre Mba Obame (26%) and Pierre Mamboundou (25%), a long-time opponent of the Bongos. Voters complained about problems with voter lists and registration, polls that opened late, improperly secured ballot boxes and armed security personnel in or near voting sites. Authorities were said to censor news coverage and harass the press.

Upon the announcement of the results, there were several outbreaks of violence, particularly in Port-Gentil where angry inhabitants set the French Consulate alight. Mba Obame claimed to be the rightful winner of the elections, but the Constitutional Court, widely seen as packed with PDG allies, validated the outcome and on 16 October 2009 Ali Bongo succeeded his father and was officially installed as president.

Ali Bongo sought re-election in 2016, and this election would prove even more controversial than the last. This time, Bongo's main opponent was Jean Ping, a former

PDG member and one of Gabon's most powerful ministers under Omar Bongo's government. He left the party in 2014, forming the Front Uni de l'Opposition pour l'Alternance (Opposition Front for Political Change; FOPA), an alliance of opposition parties aiming to unseat Ali Bongo. Their strategy was nearly to prove effective, save for some dubious voter totals in Bongo's home province of Haut-Ogooué.

While the national voter turnout in August 2016 was 59.5%, and participation in all other provinces sat somewhere between 45 and 71%, official results declared that the admirably civic-minded voters in Haut-Ogooué came out in droves, clocking a rather hard to stomach 99.93% turnout, with 95.46% of them plumping for Ali Bongo. He was duly declared the winner, 49.8% to 48.2%, for a difference of barely 5,500 votes. International observers lamented the irregularities, and Jean Ping also cried foul, demanding a recount and declaring himself to be the rightful president of Gabon.

Protests broke out immediately, with security forces storming Ping's headquarters, and demonstrators setting the National Assembly in Libreville alight on the night of 31 August. More than 1,000 people were arrested, and between five and 50 people were killed. Ping filed an appeal with the Constitutional Court, but the results were upheld the next month and Ali Bongo was sworn in as president once again, having even gained a few additional votes thanks to the constitutional court's recalculations. Ping continues to claim the election was stolen, but the protest movement behind him proved unsustainable.

After being postponed three times, legislative elections took place in October 2018. Despite losing 15 seats, the PDG won a substantial majority, taking 98 of the 143 seats at stake. Jean Ping boycotted the election, leaving Les Démocrates, led by Guy Nzouba Ndama, as the largest opposition party with 11 seats.

The same month was to see Gabon's ruling house teeter once again when Ali Bongo fell ill during a trip to Saudi Arabia, triggering a period of intense speculation as to the nature and severity of his illness, or whether he was even alive. (Memories of a brief cover-up of Omar Bongo's death in 2009 live on in Gabon.) It emerged some weeks later that Ali Bongo had suffered a stroke and would spend his recuperation in Saudi Arabia and Morocco. He was not seen or heard from until New Year's Day 2019, when a short, pre-recorded message to the nation was released, though this did little to quell speculation over his fitness to rule.

Indeed, just a week later, disgruntled army officers took advantage of Bongo's prolonged absence, launching an attempted coup d'état. On the morning of 7 January, a handful of officers took over the national broadcaster, Radio Télévision Gabonaise, and read out a message that encouraged Gabonese people to rise up against the regime. The rest of the military remained loyal, however, and the putative putsch was quashed before the day was over; two soldiers were killed and eight arrested. Bongo finally returned to Gabon in March 2019.

In spite of all controversy, Ali Bongo's government has been credited for heavily investing in public works as part of the Gabon Émergent development programme (see box, page 14), and has surfaced more kilometres of road in the last decade than in Omar Bongo's entire 41-year reign. The next elections are planned for 2023.

FRANCO-GABONESE RELATIONS France has often been accused of maintaining a paternalistic attitude towards its former colonies. In the former African colonies, this attitude is embodied in the term Françafrique. Irrespective of their politics and ideologies on the home front, presidents from François Mitterrand to Nicolas Sarkozy have been equally committed to safeguarding their economic and cultural hegemony in the region.

Like many other francophone African nations, Gabon has retained strong political, military, economic, legal and cultural ties with its former coloniser. In fact, a neo-colonialist system was sealed at independence with a military treaty signed between Libreville and Paris: in return for French military support, Gabon would serve as a French military base in Africa. In economic terms, France continues to view former African colonies not only as an invaluable source of cheap raw materials, but also as a useful market for surplus French goods. Until not so long ago, French corporations that bribed officials abroad were allowed to deduct the cost of their bribes as 'business expenses'.

For Gabon's political leaders, the trade-offs of French patronage have been regime stability and financial aid. Both president Mba and the Bongo family have relied on a French military presence to sustain their regimes more than once.

Since the mid-2000s, successive French governments have indicated that they increasingly see the entanglement of French commercial interests and French foreign policy as problematic. During his presidential campaign in 2007, Nicolas Sarkozy vowed to put an end to Françafrique and advocated for more transparent French–African ties. He promised to diminish France's complicity with undemocratic African leaders, referring to 'networks of a bygone era'. Notwithstanding, he and former president Jacques Chirac were openly accused of shadowy dealings and receiving campaign financing from the late president Bongo. Several investigative journalists published on the matter, with *The Scandal of the Ill-gotten Gains* by Thomas Hofnung and Xavier Harel and *The Briefcase Republic* by Pierre Pean attracting the most attention. These studies suggest that France's former presidents accepted tens of millions of dollars from Gabon in secret cash payments. Both Sarkozy and Chirac continue to deny these charges.

In addition to these journalists' allegations, the French branch of anti-corruption group Transparency International filed a complaint against the presidents of Gabon, Equatorial Guinea and Congo, involving charges of embezzlement and the misuse of public money. An inquiry tracing their expenditures showed that the Bongo family had acquired no fewer than 39 luxurious properties, 183 cars and 70 bank accounts in France. Their acquisitions in Paris include the Hotel Soyecourt in the 7th arrondissement, bought by the family in 2010 for €98 million. Although President Sarkozy awarded Ali Bongo the Légion d'honneur (France's highest honour) in 2010, the shift in the Franco–Gabonese relationship became evident in 2012 as French judges froze nine of Bongo's bank accounts and seized the whole fleet of luxury cars.

Claiming that Gabon needed diversification, Ali Bongo brought new business partners from the United States, Australia and China. The last quickly overtook France as Gabon's top trading partner. On the eve of the 14th Francophonie Summit in Kinshasa, Bongo announced that Gabon had decided to abolish French as its official language. He later softened this statement by clarifying that the country intended to introduce English as a first foreign language in schools, while keeping French as the general medium of instruction; nowadays you'll find little evidence there was anything behind the threat at all. Thus, despite occasional tough talk from Gabon and some lofty rhetoric from Emmanuel Macron about a 'new, balanced relationship', popular belief on the streets (and in the boardrooms) of Libreville is that Paris is still pulling the strings.

GOVERNMENT AND POLITICS

Since the Republic of Gabon achieved independence from France in 1960, and despite occasional bouts of protest, notably in 2016 (page 11), it has enjoyed relative political stability, especially by regional standards. The head of state is the president, elected for a renewable seven-year term. The president is the supreme holder of executive power, which he shares with the prime minister, the head of the government. The government is accountable to both the president and the National Assembly, but the latter can be dissolved by the president.

Gabon's highest courts are the Constitutional Court, the Court of Cassation, the Council of State, the Court of Accounts, the Courts of Appeal, the Provincial Courts, the High Court and the other special courts of law. Theoretically, the courts are independent of the executive power and the legislative power.

The Parliament of Gabon is represented by two chambers: the National Assembly (120 deputies) and the Senate (102 senators). In cases where the two chambers disagree on a piece of legislation, the National Assembly may be called to rule alone. In addition, only the National Assembly has the power to pass a vote of no confidence in the government.

The administrative system is bloated and highly decentralised with many levels of authority. There are over 40 ministers, each of them leading enormous institutions. The country is divided into nine provinces or administrative districts: Estuaire, Moyen-Ogooué, Ngounié, Ogooué-Maritime, Nyanga, Woleu-Ntem, Ogooué-Ivindo, Haut-Ogooué and Ogooué-Lolo, each with its own capital. Each province is split into departments, each department into districts and communes, each district into cantons, and finally at the lowest level there is a multitude of villages.

With over 75,000 civil servants for only 2.1 million people, almost every Gabonese family has at least one family member working in the civil service and earning a decent salary (with which they often have to provide for the rest of their relatives). Besides this staggering amount of civil servants, there are also a huge number of fake employees on the payrolls. In 2009 the country paid up to 10,000 fraudulent state employees, costing the state about US$50 million. Since his inauguration, President Ali Bongo has taken up the fight against these fake officers, and by 2013 their number had been reduced to 3,000. Efforts were still underway to root out fraudsters in 2018, with workers required to physically present special vouchers in exchange for salary payments.

ECONOMY

There is a lot of money in Gabon. **Oil** is the backbone of the economy and accounts for half the state's revenues. In addition, the country is also the third-biggest manganese producer in the world and an important exporter of timber. Having only been exploited since independence, Gabon's underground still holds considerable resources, such as iron, where untapped reserves are deemed the world's largest. Gold, diamonds, phosphates, mercury, niobium, potash and others complement the considerable mineral potential.

The combination of abundant natural resources, a comparatively small population and foreign private investment has made Gabon the envy of its neighbours. Gabon's annual revenue per inhabitant of US$18,100 (2018) stands several times higher than that of most nations in sub-Saharan Africa, and it is classed as an upper middle-income country.

In spite of money pouring in, Gabon's economy is not without its problems. Rating agencies Fitch Group and Standard and Poor's rate the country 'B', meaning that 'financial commitments are currently being met; however, capacity for continued payment is contingent upon a sustained, favourable business and economic environment' (2018).

Owing to high income inequality, a vast majority of the population remains poor and there is virtually no middle class. Although the minimum wage was increased from 80,000CFA to 150,000CFA in 2011, a significant proportion of the population lives in extreme poverty (on less than US$1.25 a day). Unemployment is high among young people, as a large number of them enter the labour market every year. On the United Nations Human Development Index 2018, Gabon comes in at 110 out of 187 countries.

The economy is heavily dependent on oil and is relatively undiversified, meaning the 2014 drop in global oil prices remains a huge problem for Gabon. Previously trading at around US$100, the price for a barrel of crude oil has hovered close to US$50 ever since, severely impacting the national budget, and all this without mentioning the fact that the oil supplies are slowly but surely running out. Proven oil reserves are estimated at 2bn barrels. Total Gabon and Assala Energy (who bought the recently departed Gabonese branch of Royal Dutch Shell) currently

GABON ÉMERGENT

Realising that in the absence of a major discovery, oil production will decline and eventually run out, the Gabonese government launched an ambitious development programme in 2009, under the name of Gabon Émergent (Emerging Gabon).

Emerging Gabon seeks, by the year 2025, to strengthen and diversify Gabon's economy around three pillars: Green Gabon seeks to sustainably develop the country's parks and natural resources; Industrial Gabon seeks to develop local processing of primary materials and subsequently promote the export of high-value-added products; and Services of Gabon seeks to develop the Gabonese workforce to become a regional leader in financial services, IT, green growth, tertiary education and health. Furthermore, increasing transparency and reducing red tape should make Gabon a more interesting destination for foreign investors. In large part thanks to governmental belt-tightening necessitated by the global drop in oil prices since 2014 – known locally in Gabon as *la crise* (the crisis) – many of the initiatives remain unfulfilled, though there's still time before the programme's scheduled culmination.

GABON VERT (Green Gabon) 'Gabon, designed by nature' is the slogan of the ambitious Green Gabon programme that aims to diversify sources of growth and sustainable development by developing the country's 'green oil' through a focus on **ecotourism**. Seeing conservation as an essential part of economic development, Gabon aims to become the gateway to equatorial Africa.

Though the country has missed its target to attract 100,000 tourists per year by 2020 (according to the Ministry of Investment Promotion, Public Works, Transport, Housing and Tourism, most tourists are expats already living in Gabon – often accompanied by visiting family and friends), the World Travel and Tourism Council (WTTC) still predicts consistent growth of tourism's contribution to GDP over the coming years.

GABON INDUSTRIEL Industrial Gabon encourages the domestic processing of primary resources and the export of high-value procesed goods, rather than raw materials. In January 2010, the president banned all **unprocessed log exports** (which previously made up to 60% of the country's exports). The final aim is to process timber entirely at the local level by creating a dynamic artisanal industry, pump up to 243,000 barrels per day and while some near-term gains are expected, the long-term trend is for decline.

Besides the extractive industries, the country produces next to nothing. Almost everything is imported, which makes Gabon one of the most expensive countries in the world. Lack of competition pushes up the prices even further, while the artificially high rate of the CFA (it is tied to the euro) makes Libreville more expensive for visitors than most leading cities in the West. The wealthy – including some Gabonese as well as foreigners – patronise the pricey Western-style shops, but most Gabonese will never be able to afford a US$10 Coca-Cola on a nice terrace overlooking the sea. Petrodollars only change hands among the lucky few and the government doesn't fancy making the game more transparent.

In 2007, Gabon joined the Extractive Industries Transparency Initiative but it lost its candidacy status in 2013, having failed to provide the required documentation – it hasn't reapplied since. Oil contracts are often the product of direct negotiations while improving the living conditions of the local population at the same time. To that end, the **Gabon Wood Show** (w gabonwoodshow.com) has become an important annual event in timber processing. Beyond timber, the government has similar plans (in various stages of completion) to boost the domestic refining capacity for manganese, iron and oil.

This is the motivation behind the proposed (but currently shelved) construction of a new oil refinery in Port-Gentil. The country has long had one refinery located here, the Société Raffinage du Gabon (SOGARA). It was the first refinery in Central Africa and has been in production for nearly half a century, but has never reached full capacity.

Also in 2010, a US$814 million, 50-year contract was signed with the Singaporean multi-national Olam, to develop 300,000ha of **palm groves** in order to become one of Africa's leading palm oil producers. Olam started by planting 50,000ha around Kango and 42,500ha around Mouila, followed by 11,000ha near Bitam. The contracts are highly controversial. According to critical voices, who claim large-scale palm oil plantations do not improve the country's food security, the presidential family is an important shareholder of the company. Furthermore, the environmental impact of the plantations is significant. Not only does the clear-felling of forest release millions of tonnes of carbon dioxide, but it also destroys some rare, threatened or endangered ecosystems and species, and forest areas critical to water catchment.

A large public investment programme has also boosted investment in **infrastructure**, particularly expanding the nation's weak and incomplete network of roads. Here, the programme can show some demonstrable successes (page 54), but also some notable failures (such as the still-incomplete road to Franceville).

The preparation for the Africa Cup of Nations, hosted by Gabon and Equatorial Guinea in 2012 and Gabon alone in 2017, was an enormous trigger for **construction** and public works, with construction now playing a larger role in the country's economy.

GABON DES SERVICES Services of Gabon sets **human-resources development** as its top priority. The government aims to become a regional hub in the fields of financial services, IT, health care and (higher) education (page 16).

between companies and the government. Environmental and social impact assessments do not have to be published, and there is no freedom of information law.

CEMAC Together with the Republic of the Congo, the Central African Republic, Cameroon, Equatorial Guinea and Chad, Gabon is a member of the Communauté Économique et Monétaire de l'Afrique Centrale (Economic and Monetary Community of Central Africa; CEMAC). This was established with the aim of tearing down economic barriers between the six states of the region. Nevertheless, the movement of people is far from free, as Gabon fears massive immigration if it opens its borders. On the contrary, Cameroonians who cross the border in the north of the country complain of facing serious discrimination and arrogance from Gabonese officials.

EDUCATION

Gabon scores high on education: 89% of adults (over 15) and 98% of youth (15–24) are literate. These are much higher percentages than the regional averages of 59% and 69% respectively. Education is compulsory from the age of six to 16 and around 87% of the children attend primary school. Theoretically, education is free for all and up to international standard, but in reality bribes are mandatory (teachers often have to wait for months for their salaries to be paid, if they are paid at all), classrooms are often overcrowded and there's a lack of resources, teachers and facilities. For those who can afford it, there is a well-established network of private education.

The curriculum is broadly based on the French model: after six years of primary, six years of college and three years of *lycée*, the national graduation exam or *baccalaureate* follows. Those who pass can enter university. There are currently public universities in Libreville and Franceville.

In order to bridge the significant gap between the needed skilled labour and the quality of education and training currently available in Gabon, three new campuses are planned as part of the Emerging Gabon scheme (in Oyem, Port-Gentil and Mouila; page 154), though none had opened at the time of writing.

PEOPLE

The estimated population of Gabon is 2.1 million (2018). The yearly growth is 2.73%. With close to 90% of its inhabitants living in cities and towns, Gabon is one of Africa's most urbanised countries. Just shy of half the population live in the capital, while other areas of dense population include Port-Gentil, Franceville and certain parts of the Woleu-Ntem province. By comparison, the country's interior boasts some of the lowest population densities on the globe. Gabon's inhabitants are young: 37% are under the age of 15.

The vast majority of Gabon's different ethnic groups are of Bantu origin, and include the following major groupings: the Fang, the Eshira (also known as Shira or Échira), the Mbede-Teke, the Myènè and the Okande-Tsogo. The **Fang** – numerically the largest – are mostly concentrated in Woleu-Ntem, but are also found in Ogooué-Ivindo, Moyen-Ogooué and Estuaire. For the most part, the **Eshira** are found in the south of Gabon, particularly Ngounié province, the **Mbede-Teke** in the southeast, the **Myènè** and **Mpongwé** in Ogooué-Maritime and Estuaire, and the **Okande-Tsogo** in the country's central interior. Each group speaks their own language, with French serving as the *lingua franca* across the country. The most important of the remaining ethnic groups are the Bandjabi, the Bapounou, and

So-called 'Pygmies' – indigenous forest-based communities – are located throughout Gabon and include numerous ethnic groups separated by locality, language and culture. Whether the Baka of Woleu-Ntem, the Babongo of Ngounié or the Bakoya around Mékambo, these forest communities traditionally keep themselves to themselves. A rough estimate is that their number is around 30,000, but as they are often without birth certificates or identity cards, it's hard to know for certain. They are certainly a tiny minority of Gabon's total population.

Often they face severe discrimination, and to call someone a 'Pygmy', a derogatory term that emphasises short stature, is considered an insult (although the term is still commonly used throughout the country). Communities are regularly treated with derision and contempt, and are often cheated and exploited. More often than not they are paid in kind rather than money for their services, which only reinforces their marginalised position. Children often miss out on school, as their parents cannot afford uniforms, books and the necessary bribes. Those who make it risk being taunted and ostracised by their peers.

Although their nomadic hunter-gatherer lifestyle has given way to a more sedentary way of life in modern times, they often choose to live deep in the forest to a degree unparalleled by any other peoples in the interior, who for the most part have moved their villages to roadsides.

Indigenous forest communities possess superior skills in hunting, healing, polyphonic music and collecting honey. Their traditional weapon for small game is the bow and poisoned arrow, and for larger game traps and harpoons. Nowadays, though, they are just as likely to hunt with rifles. Despite these skills, Gabon's first inhabitants are ignored rather than respected by their countrymen – until they have need of a 'Pygmy' tracker or healer, that is.

Traditionally, politicians have taken no account of these communities either, until perhaps elections are on the horizon. However, since the turn of the century there has been a small change in awareness of the rights of indigenous peoples in matters concerning the conservation and development of the country.

In 2005, Gabon agreed to its own Indigenous Peoples' Plan as part of a World Bank policy loan agreement for the Forest and Environment Sector Program. This marked the government's first official recognition of the existence of and its responsibility towards indigenous peoples. In 2007, Gabon voted for the UN Declaration on the Rights of Indigenous Peoples, though there remains a long way to go in ensuring these rights are respected on the ground.

Indigenous-rights organisation **Cultural Survival** (w culturalsurvival.org) assembled a report, *Observations on the State of Indigenous Human Rights in Gabon*, in 2017, detailing some of the failings in this regard, particularly when it comes to conflicts over conservation. It can be found here: w bit.ly/culturalsurvival.

the Batéké (the president's people). Gabon is becoming an increasingly integrated population, with the exception of forest-based communities (see box, above) who remain socially and economically marginalised and often extremely poor.

Within Africa, Gabon enjoys its image as a country of peace, economic growth and low population, which explains why it attracts so many West African immigrants, particularly from Mali, the Republic of the Congo, Equatorial Guinea, Benin, Cameroon, Senegal and Mauritania. Around 20% of Gabon's population consists of immigrants, which plays right into the hands of those lamenting that the Gabonese do not need to work, but prefer to leave their jobs to immigrants instead.

However, there are not enough well-paid jobs for Gabonese (anymore), let alone for so many foreign workers. Often forced to accept menial jobs, many struggle to make ends meet, and the Gabonese police are known for their harsh treatment of illegal African immigrants.

In general, each group of foreign workers keeps to a particular field of activity, depending on their country of origin. People from Benin, Togo and Cameroon are generally in the transport business and work as taxi drivers, for example, while the Senegalese have restaurants and Nigerians dominate in hairdressing, the selling of used clothes and spare motor parts. Mauritanians and Malians are often businessmen and own local supermarkets. Particularly in rural Gabon, 'un Malien' has become synonymous with a shop. Bigger businesses are often owned by

BWITI

According to traditional beliefs in Gabon, the natural and the supernatural are inextricably linked and there are special and powerful forces at play in a person's everyday life. There are a number of different male and female religious societies in the country that share this premise. These initiation societies have traditionally played a crucial social role, determining social order, settling disputes and dispensing knowledge. The most widespread male secret society is Bwiti. Through the philosophy of Bwiti a man acquires the knowledge, discipline and strength necessary for life. He is taught to respect the powers of nature and the spirits, and to value the forest. He is also taught how to communicate with his ancestors.

It is through the cult of ancestors that the cosmic cycle of life and death operates, which is the basis of religion. The skulls of important people, and sometimes also teeth and bone fragments, are kept in baskets and bags by the Kota, and in bark receptacles by the Fang. These receptacles are usually then surmounted by small statues meant to symbolise the ancestors. They are kept under a shelter away from the village. When an event demands it – for example birth, marriage, illness, an initiation, the beginning and end of a period of mourning – the bones are brought out and the ancestors are consulted.

In each village there is a Bwiti temple called a *mbandja*, or *corps de garde* by the French. This is an open-sided hut where the ground is consecrated. Special ceremonies take place here, in which initiates seek to enter into contact with the spirits in the other world in order to further their spiritual enlightenment, their understanding of themselves and their understanding of the world. In preparation for a Bwiti ceremony, white kaolin is applied as protection from evil and as a channel to communicate with ancestors. The initiates facilitate their contact with the other world by eating the sacred wood, the root of the iboga shrub. Iboga induces hallucinations when consumed in sufficient quantities (and death when consumed in excessive quantities).

At all ceremonies there is traditional music and dancing. The sacred music includes drums, the *ngombi* (a harp with eight strings) and a musical bow, the *mongongo*, that is plucked with the mouth and tapped with a stick. Only the male dancers wear masks,

Lebanese, who have built up thriving businesses all over West and Central Africa. There are also some 15,000 French foreign workers living in the country, often employed in the petroleum industry.

LANGUAGE

The official language in Gabon is **French** – this is the language used by the government, the media and between different ethnic groups. Even people speaking in an African language generally use some French words, such as the days of the week. There are over 40 living African languages listed for Gabon, usually associated with a particular ethnic group. The most widely spoken indigenous language (and also the largest ethnic group; page 16) in Gabon is **Fang**, with some 350,000 speakers mostly concentrated in Woleu-Ntem. **Punu** is probably the second largest, with more than 150,000 speakers mostly found in Nyanga and Ngounié. Other significant indigenous languages include Njebi (among the Nzebi), Teke-Tege (among the Batéké; page 17), and Myènè (page 16). There are many more languages counting 10,000 speakers or less scattered throughout the country. For

their identity usually a secret. A mask is another tool for establishing contact between the spiritual and earthly worlds. It is a physical manifestation of a mythical concept, namely the spirits of the ancestors or the spirits of the forest. It can be in the form of a human or other animal – man, woman, snake, crocodile, gorilla or elephant – and each mask has a different expression to indicate whether it is good or bad. The style and materials of the mask depend on why and where they were made. For example, in Ogooué-Maritime masks are traditionally carved out of wood in the shape of a helmet, and are often painted white and adorned with mirrors, feathers and horns.

The *nganga* is a traditional practitioner who has spent years studying the art of healing and the links between this world and the other. It is the nganga who administers the iboga, as well as all other forest remedies. He does not have absolute power. He is a man with the weaknesses of a man. The nganga's gift lies in his ability to feel a person's illness, and his intimate knowledge of the forest enables him to prepare a remedy. A nganga will tell you that the human and the forest are one, and that everything in the forest has an important role to play, from termites and bees, to pythons and leopards. Jean-Claude Cheyssial, a French film-maker, has produced a series of fascinating documentary films since the early 1990s focusing on subjects such as the importance of the forest in Gabonese society and the role of the nganga.

Traditional beliefs and practices suffered enormously at the hands of the missionaries, who taught people to be ashamed of their culture and to destroy the instruments of their beliefs, such as the masks. The frequency of rituals has decreased enormously, and naturally there are fears for what is being lost and questions as to whether there is a future for authentic masks (meaning masks created for religious as opposed to artistic purposes). That said, the young Gabonese exhibit a growing recognition of and pride in their traditions, even if they do not all choose to participate. This home-grown interest is paralleled outside Gabon, and there is a steady trickle of foreigners who come to Gabon to be initiated into Bwiti (page 20). Indeed, as this book went to print, the first ever international forum on iboga, organised by NGOs ESAB Gabon (f) and IDRC Africa (f), was set to be held in Libreville in February 2020.

English-speakers, it can be quite a challenge to get around, so it would pay to brush up on your French before arrival. For more information on language, see page 223.

RELIGION

Religion in Gabon is usually harmoniously mixed with traditional beliefs. Roughly 82% of the population is **Christian**, of which 42% are Roman Catholic. Protestants make up about 12%. A minority of less than 10% is **Muslim**, among them President Ali Bongo Ondimba, and the rest of the population is animist.

Gabon's best-known cult is without doubt the mystical **Bwiti** initiation (see box, page 18), in which young men take the powerful root of the iboga plant to facilitate a spiritual journey that deepens their understanding of the world and enables them to communicate with their ancestors. Spiritual rebirth purifies the mind of the initiated. Other ceremonies are held to heal the sick, drive out spirits or worship the ancestors.

CULTURE

LITERATURE As in most African countries, **oral tradition** has always played a major role in Gabon. Founding narratives, fables and tales featuring animals and spirits have been told for centuries. Legends that remain vivid to this day include stories about *sirens* (mermaids) who inhabit the water. The best-known sirène must be **Mami Wata**, the omnipresent mother of the water, known to lure humans through her mesmerising singing and unparalleled beauty. Deeply rooted in folk tales all over Central and West Africa, her supernatural powers are still very much feared.

The Gabonese author, ethnographer, Catholic priest and missionary **André Raponda Walker** (1871–1968), strongly believed in the value of recording indigenous beliefs and the medicinal powers of the forest. Walker was born in 1871 as the son of a Mpongwé woman and a British trader called Bruce Walker. (Bruce Walker set up the first trading posts in Gabon for the British firm Hatton and Cookson, including the one at Lambaréné.) Walker was one of the first to study the Gabonese oral tradition, and his *Contes Gabonais* (Paris, 1967) is an extensive collection of fables, while *Rites et Croyances des Peuples du Gabon* (Paris, 1962) studies the beliefs of Gabon's different peoples.

Gabon does not have a long history of written **literary fiction**. The tradition started with Roger Zotoumbat's *Histoire d'un enfant* (1971) and includes Laurent Owondo's *Au bout du silence* (1985) and Hubert Ndong Freddy's *Les Matitis* (1992). Sandrine Bessora first arrived on the international scene with her novel *53cm* in 1999. Born in Brussels in 1968 as the daughter of a Gabonese diplomat, Bessora's work deals with the effects of French colonial history on present-day immigrants in France, particularly women. In 2007 she was the first Gabonese to win the Grand Prix Littéraire de l'Afrique Noire – a literary prize awarded annually by the Association of French Language Writers (ADELF) for a French text from sub-Saharan Africa – with her novel *Cueillez-moi jolis messieurs*. In 2008, a Gabonese writer was named the winner of Africa's leading prize again. Jean Nivassa Nyama, born in 1962 in a small village near Moabi, Nyanga, received the award for his trilogy *Vocation de dignité*.

The third time a Gabonese author won the Grand Prix was in 2013, the centennial anniversary of Albert Schweitzer (page 144). Augustin Emane's study *Docteur Schweitzer, une icône africaine* won him the prestigious award. Emane works as a senior lecturer at the University of Nantes faculty of law.

For more on Gabonese literature, see page 226.

MUSIC Traditional music is of great importance in daily life, with variations of style and subject among the 40 ethnic groups. Typical **instruments** are the *mongongo* (mouth bow), harp and *balafon* (wooden xylophone). Each specific sound of each specific instrument calls a particular spirit, and each instrument corresponds to a specific rite. Particularly famous for their music are the forest people, who use it to entice forest animals before the hunt, to cure illnesses and to overcome disputes. The characteristic complex **vocal polyphony** is a kind of non-linguistic code for communicating with the unseen world of spirits and departed relatives.

The heyday for Gabon's **contemporary music** industry was halfway through the 1980s. The formation of the popular radio station Africa No. 1 and the opening of the first Gabonese recording studio, Studion Mademba, turned Libreville into a hotspot for musicians from all over Africa.

The 'father of Gabonese music', **Pierre-Claver Akendengué**, played an important role in the diffusion of African culture and music in the world. Born on the island of Awuta (Fernan Vaz Lagoon), Akendengué studied Psychology at the University of Caen in France, where he recorded his first album *Nandipo*, sung in French and Nkomi, a dialect of Myènè (1974). His second album, *Africa my mother (Africa Obota)*, won him the Prix de la Jeune Chanson Francophone in Cannes in 1976. His album *Lambarena* (1993, with Hugues de Courson) is an example of the perfect symbiosis between French and Nkomi musical cultures. In 2013, he celebrated his 40 years of fame and success with two 'best of' concerts at Libreville's Institut Français du Gabon (page 104). His most recent album, *La Couleur de l'Afrique*, came out at the end of 2018. Akendengué also discovered another now-popular singer, Annie Flore Batchiellilys, when she took part in the TV competition *Africa Star*.

Well known as both the ex-wife of former president Omar Bongo and the mother of the current president, **Patience Dabany** (affectionately called 'La mama') is a successful singer and musician. Born as Josephine Kama Dabany in Brazzaville in 1944, she started her musical career as Patience Dabany after her divorce from Omar Bongo in 1988. Her most popular songs are *C'est pour la vie*, a throwback to independence-era Congolese music, and *On Vous Connait*. Her 2004 world music album *Obomiyia* allowed her to tour with James Brown in Europe.

Gabon has a lively **hip-hop** scene, once dominated by the group Mauvaizhaleine, but today is populated with dozens of up-and-coming rappers and groups – Ekivo'k Family and Zayox are two names to look out for.

See page 73 for an overview of Gabon's music festivals.

OTHER ARTS Like literature, art for the sake of it has existed only since colonial times. Most genuinely traditional statues and masks had a practical use. In all Gabon's ethnic groups, **masks** are used for protection from the deceased and to recruit their aid in matters of daily life. The style and materials of the mask depend on why and where they were made (see box, page 22).

There is no long tradition of **painting** just for the pleasure of the eye. In the 1960s Professor Basile Allainmat-Mahinè started a faculty of arts at the Collège Technique. It was this section, currently in the form of the independent École Nationale d'Art et Manufacture, that delivered Gabon's first generation of modern painters including Jean Prosper Ekoré, Marcellin Minzé Minkoe, Nalvad, Jean Baptiste Onewin-Walker and Maurice Mombo Mubamu. Upmarket hotels often function as galleries. Hôtel Le Cristal (page 90), for example, is decorated with works by painters/sculptors Marcellin Minzé Minkoe and Marc Obiang Nguenia. Another well-known painter is Georges Mbourou, who represented Africa at the 2005 Expo, Nature's Wisdom,

Gabon's woodcarvings and masks are world famous and have been a source of inspiration to artists worldwide. Both Picasso and Matisse were influenced by the beauty of Fang masks. The sale of a typical Fang's Ngil mask for US$7.5 million in 2007 is a clear indicator of the value the art world currently places on them.

During the colonial era, however, these particular masks terrified the French. Worn by the law-enforcing Ngil society, carriers of the masks were responsible for maintaining law and order and persecuted suspected offenders. The masked Ngil members arrived at the home of a suspect in the dead of night, performing mysterious ceremonies that often resulted in the death of the wrong-doer. After a series of ritual murders in 1910, the French ultimately forbade the Ngil to produce its masks.

Known as the white-face style, Bapounou (or Punu) masks (*mukudj*) are whitened with kaolin, the colour of death and spirits. They represent the Bapounou's female ancestors and have diamond-shaped scarification marks on their forehead. The elaborate Bapounou hairstyles suggest that the wearer is wealthy, as her hair has not been flattened by the need to carry goods. These masks are still worn by dancers during public ceremonies or funerals. The dancers perform on high stilts so they tower above their audience.

As in many African cultures, all 40 or so ethnic groups in Gabon believe ancestors to have the powers to bring good or bad fortune to their descendants. Their relics, such as skulls, teeth and certain bones, which are believed to be imbued with the powers these people had during their lives, are kept in containers. Sitting on top of the containers, wooden reliquary figures guard these enshrined relics.

With its large head, long body and short limbs, the Fang's guardian or Bieri has the proportion of a newborn, thus emphasising continuity of the 'not-yet-born', the living and the dead. Bieri figures are often embellished with elaborate coiffures, facial scarification, jewellery, horns and other emblems of spiritual power. The Bakota guardians, Mwete, are flat, more abstracted, with their oval, concave faces sheathed in metal (brass or copper), which gleam at night to protect against evil.

Every aspect of the reliquary figure, from the selection of the wood to its creation, was overseen by a priest. During the first decades of the 20th century reliquaries and the priests who controlled them were banned by the French.

in Aichi, Japan. In 2006 he undertook a creative safari in his own country to run painting workshops in isolated villages organised by the Wildlife Conservation Society (WCS).

The Congolese sculptor Bernard Konongo, son of the famous sculptor Benoit Konongo, followed in the footsteps of his father and is an internationally renowned artist with a workshop in Quartier Louis in Libreville (page 100). Minkoe made the remarkable statue **Door to Freedom** (Porte de la Liberté), on boulevard de Mer in remembrance of Libreville's first inhabitants.

Gabonese **cinema** is still in its early stages. Classics are *Les tam-tams se sont tus* (1971) by Philippe Mory, *Ayouma* (1977) and *Ilombè* (1978) by Charles Mensah, and *Demain, un jour nouveau* (1978) by Pierre Marie Dong. Since the turn of the century, a few Gabonese productions have emerged and been internationally recognised, starting with *Dôlè l'argent* (2000) by Imunga Ivanga, a film-maker from Libreville. This film offers a Gabonese perspective on the global crisis facing today's youth and has won several awards at the Carthage, Cannes and Milan film festivals. More recently, Amédée Pacôme Nkoulou's *Boxing Libreville* (2018) is set against the backdrop of the 2016 election crisis and was selected for several international festivals.

Another artist worth mentioning is cartoonist **Patrick Essono**, also known as Pahé. Pahé used to be a press cartoonist but as censorship is tight and the police do not always appreciate his talents, newspapers do not publish him anymore. His political satire appears on his blog (w pahebd.blogspot.com or f pahe2009). The 130-page series *Best of Pahé* contains a compilation of his life's work, from the first president, Léon Mba, to Ali Bongo.

SPORT

If you like **football**, you'll always have an inexhaustible conversation subject at hand as many Gabonese, particularly men, are passionate fans. The domestic premier league consists of 14 teams and is administered by the Ligue Nationale de Football (f Linaf.net). Since 1968, the two most successful teams have been FC 105 Libreville with 11 titles and AS Mangasport (based in Moanda) with nine.

The Gabon national football team, known as Les Panthères (or sometimes Les Brésiliens), has qualified for the Africa Cup of Nations seven times, but has never advanced further than the quarter finals. The team is managed by the Fédération Gabonaise de Football (w fegafoot.ga; f FEGAFOOT).

Several Gabonese footballers play for clubs abroad, including Pierre-Emerick Aubameyang, who plays for Arsenal and won the 2019 Premier League Golden Boot alongside Sadio Mané and Mo Salah. Daniel Cousin played for a variety of European clubs, including Hull City and Glasgow Rangers, until his retirement in 2014.

Gabon has competed at eight summer **Olympic Games**, and has taken home exactly one medal, when Anthony Obame took silver in heavyweight taekwondo at London 2012.

Background Information SPORT

1

2

Natural History and Conservation

Pristine rainforests, an astonishing range of wildlife and an 855km coastline dotted with idyllic beaches make Gabon one of the last remaining unspoilt natural paradises on earth. With more than 11% of the country protected in 13 national parks, Gabon is one of Africa's best places to access the untouched rainforest. Although tourism is still in its infancy, the country boasts an extraordinary biodiversity, gorillas, chimpanzees and a long list of endemic birds that attract adventurers and nature lovers from all over the world. Though it has a long way to go in terms of services, it's no exaggeration to say that Gabon has the potential to become one of the world's premier ecotourism destinations.

What's more, the forests that cover more than 80% of Gabon are critical spaces in the battle against climate change, and valorising their growth rather than their destruction is a key step in making sure they remain standing.

HABITATS AND VEGETATION

FOREST Most of Gabon – nearly 23 million hectares – is covered in dense, tropical rainforest. Along with Cameroon, Equatorial Guinea, Congo and the Central African Republic, Gabon forms part of the Congo Basin, the most heavily forested area in Africa. Parts of these Central African rainforests are among the oldest in the world, thought to be between 60 and 100 million years old.

The country is a patchwork of different forest formations. About 18,000 years ago, with the onslaught of the last Ice Age, only patches of rainforest survived in Equatorial Guinea, northeast Democratic Republic of the Congo (DRC) and Gabon. As it's generally recognised that rainforests need upwards of 2,000mm of rain a year to survive, the forest zones that hung on amid the savannah – it is thought that there were three in Gabon – were regions at altitude or alongside rivers, where rainfall patterns were less affected by the changing climate. These zones of Gabon's oldest forests are found in the Crystal Mountains (page 110), the du Chaillu Mountains (page 169) and the Doudou Mountains (page 164). By contrast, areas like Lopé National Park (page 197), where patches of savannah still survive, give us an idea of what most of the Central African landscape must have looked like between 18,000 and 12,000 years ago.

Effectively serving as refuges for the plants and animals of the rainforest, these forest strongholds would become key to recolonising the savannah of Central Africa, a process that began with the return of widespread warmth and rain about 12,000 years ago. It's thanks to the survival of these ancient rainforests that Gabon boasts such rich and varied vegetation. There are over 10,000 species of plants in the Congo Basin, 3,000 of which are endemics found nowhere else in the world.

Rainforest is characterised by very tall, very straight hardwood trees, whose branches and trunks are often entwined with vines and covered with epiphytes that take root in crevices in the bark. The average height of the trees varies between 30m and 45m, although those that do rise above the thick canopy can reach heights of up to 60m. Little light penetrates this, so there's not much on the ground in the way of bushes and foliage. Younger, post-agricultural forest is found in areas that were once cleared for cultivation, often in valleys and on the edges of large blocks of impenetrable forest. In comparison with the ancient forest, it is lighter and less dense, with a higher concentration of faster-growing trees and softwoods, such as *okoumé* and *ozigo*, and occasionally dense vegetation on the forest floor.

Gabon is also home to several forest clearings known as **baïs**, where forest animals come to eat, drink and socialise; the most significant is Langoué Baï in Ivindo National Park (page 207), where gorilla, elephant, and numerous other species regularly congregate.

The majestic **moabi** (*Baillonella toxisperma*) is found only in primary and especially old secondary forests. Given the chance, a moabi can grow up to 60m high, but this can take over 600 years. Forest elephant love to feast on the fruits of moabi trees and they can hear the ripe, heavy fruits fall from the high trees and hit the ground from miles away.

Also popular with elephant are the bark and the fruits of the **marula tree** (*Sclerocarya birrea*), belonging to the mango family. Tall and leafy, marula trees grow all across sub-Saharan Africa. In South Africa, its sweet fruit is used to make a liqueur called Amarula. There are persistent stories about forest elephants getting drunk by feasting on fermented fruit from the ground, but don't set your heart on seeing any tipsy elephants dancing around a marula tree – modern studies show they only eat the fresh fruits, and that even if they did eat the rotten ones, they would have to gorge on an impossible amount to become tipsy. As you might imagine due to their size, elephants are anything but lightweights.

The **okoumé** (*Aucoumea klaineana*), Gabon's emblematic tree (as seen on the coat of arms), is also the country's most important commercial tree, accounting for some 90% of Gabon's total timber production. It can reach up to 40m high and live for hundreds of years. New leaves appear from September to December and are bright red for about a week.

Another iconic tree is the **azobé** (*Lophira alata*), which can grow to a height of 40–50m. Like the okoumé, the azobé's new leaves colour the canopy bright red every December, and the trees are in high demand thanks to their unusually hard timber.

The **kevazingo** (*Guibourtia* spp) tree shot to prominence in March 2019 when an illegal logging scandal that would become known as 'kevazingo-gate' came to light (page 32). The trees themselves can grow up to 50m tall and 2m in diameter.

Without the seeds of the **odika** (*Irvingia gabonensis*) there wouldn't be *chocolat*, the main ingredient for Gabon's dearly loved sauce (page 70). Also called African or wild mango, the tree grows 10–40m in height and flowers after reaching maturity within 10–15 years.

Though more a shrub than a tree, **iboga** (*Tabernanthe iboga*) is considered a sacred plant and is a national treasure in Gabon. It is commonly used in traditional

ON FOOT IN THE FOREST

- Always follow the instructions of your guides and trackers.
- Dress appropriately – lightweight, long-sleeved trousers and shirts are preferable, despite the heat, as these provide proper protection against scratches and bites. Try to avoid bright colours, such as blues and whites, that aren't normally found in the jungle. Blue also attracts biting tsetse flies. Waterproof boots are preferable, though expect to get wet feet anyway. Guides and trackers may be wearing wellington boots, but many people find these uncomfortable for a long walk. Gaiters are not only good for keeping out water, but also biting ants and ticks. If you intend to try to keep dry you should take a waterproof, but anything other than the best quality will not withstand the weight of a rainforest deluge.
- Drink plenty – always take more water than you think you'll need.
- Aim to leave about 1.5m between walkers to avoid bumping into one another.
- Wear insect repellent (except if you are tracking elephants, who are sensitive to the smell).
- Always look carefully before leaning against anything or you might get a nasty surprise. Some stinging caterpillars are camouflaged against bark. Gardening gloves can be useful to protect yourself.
- Do not leave anything behind in the forest – any rubbish, including toilet paper, should be put in a plastic bag and brought back to camp with you for disposal.
- Do not pick any flowers or remove anything from the forest.
- Never touch a wild animal, dead or alive.
- Under certain circumstances, you should stand your ground if you find yourself being charged by a wild animal. This is not the case with elephants! Follow the guide's instructions and stay calm, but be prepared to run. You probably won't need to run for very long as elephants tend to lose interest quite quickly once they've made their point.
- If you find yourself dangerously close to a snake, back away very slowly, taking care to avoid making any sudden, aggressive movements.
- If you are going to be camping you will also need camping equipment, a medical kit and a second set of dry clothes to be worn after each day's walk. If it is the rainy season and there is to be any hope of a dry bed, it is a good idea to cover the tents with a tarp. Always choose a campsite with great care, bearing in mind the dangers of animals, including snakes, and falling trees.
- Finally, and most importantly, don't get lost! This may seem an obvious piece of advice but it has happened, with tragic consequences. On no account and under no circumstances should you wander off on your own in the forest – a trail may look easy to follow when a tracker is leading the way, but alone the forest can be very disorientating and dangerous.

Bwiti initiation ceremonies (see box, page 18). Recent years have also seen it gain popularity in the West as a treatment for addiction.

SAVANNAH As a general rule in Gabon, where there's no forest, there's savannah – wide, open areas of high grass, shrubs and isolated trees. Gabon's savannah is mostly found in the Ogooué-Maritime region and in the southern half of the country, for example in the Ngounié region around Mouila. The Batéké Plateaux in the far southeast – known as the 'Highlands of Gabon' – are characterised by open grasslands and valleys, and Lopé is renowned for its unique mosaic of forest and savannah.

WETLANDS Gabon is home to nine **RAMSAR** Wetlands of International Importance. There are **mangrove swamps** at Mondah Bay near Libreville (page 108), in the briny lagoons near the coast and along the banks of the Ogooué. The mangroves' unique above-ground root structure delighted Mary Kingsley when she saw them for the first time in 1894. She described them in *Travels in West Africa*: 'At high water you do not see the mangroves displaying their ankles in the way that shocked Captain Lugard. They look most respectable.'

The **Ogooué Delta** is the second largest freshwater delta on the African continent; in addition to mangroves, it is also known for its marshes, papyrus, reedbeds and floating grasses.

CONSERVATION

HISTORY Until 2002, Gabon had no national park system and so-called 'protected areas' were in actual fact not well protected at all. Lopé National Park, which had been a reserve since 1946, illustrates this point. Under laws passed in 1960 and 1982, 'rational exploitation' was allowed in protected areas. This officially meant controlled hunting and logging, but inevitably logging roads reaching previously inaccessible parts of the forest also opened the forest up to poachers. In 1996 the permissible exploitation was confined to a peripheral area of Lopé, while a core zone of about 2,400km^2 was designated out of bounds. Selective logging and mineral exploitation was thus permitted in more than 99% of the country. (The meagre area legally protected from logging was the small Ipassa Reserve and this core part of the Lopé National Park.)

The decision to create the national park network represents the successful culmination of years of hard work by environmental organisations and the Direction de la Faune et de la Chasse (Wildlife and Hunting Department; DFC), the government branch in charge of protected areas. In 1996, WCS biologist and *National Geographic* explorer Mike Fay flew over the forests of Congo and Gabon and realised there was a vast, intact forest corridor spanning the two countries, from the Oubangui River to the Atlantic Ocean. In a high-profile bid to raise awareness and funds for the precious habitats of Central Africa, he trekked through 3,000km of dense forest to the Atlantic coast, surveying trees, wildlife, and human impacts on 12 uninhabited forest blocks. This **Megatransect** took 15 months, during which Fay and his team tirelessly made notes and took photographs (for more details on the Megatransect see w nationalgeographic.com).

NATIONAL PARKS National park protection (and improved management of resources outside the national parks) is vital for the future of conservation in Central Africa. Gabon has undoubtedly made great strides in this regard, but it nonetheless ranked a lamentable 140th in Yale University's 2019 Environmental

Performance Index. The index ranks countries based on 22 indicators, measuring elements such as environmental management efforts, sustainability of natural resources and levels of pollution; Gabon ranked a considerably more encouraging 28th in the category of tree-cover loss.

Since the turn of the century, Gabon has committed much effort to supporting the sustainable development of its green heritage, and an exceptionally high percentage of Gabon's land is now protected. The late president, Omar Bongo Ondimba, set up 13 national parks in August 2002, covering 11% of the country's land mass or more than 30,000km² of vital wildlife habitats. The fact that Gabon's principal natural resource, oil, is running out may have played a role in this decision. In addition to the terrestrial national parks, there are plans to create other protected areas, and 2017 saw the declaration of nine new marine parks and 11 new aquatic reserves, bringing some 53,000km² of Gabon's territorial waters under protection. You can review the full list of new marine parks at w protectedplanet.net. The Ogooué Delta is also under consideration for eventual gazetting as a biosphere reserve.

ANPN To manage the country's protected areas, the government created the Agence Nationale des Parcs Nationaux (National Agency for National Parks; ANPN; page 88) in 2007. The agency's mandate revolves mainly around the protection and development of the national parks, but it is increasingly participating in the design of tourism products that can take advantage of the parks' natural heritage in a sustainable manner, with the purpose of encouraging new revenues from ecotourism.

When Ali Bongo succeeded his father as president in 2009, things changed for the better. He poured resources into the underfunded ANPN and appointed the British-born zoologist Lee White who, as the former head of WCS Gabon, had

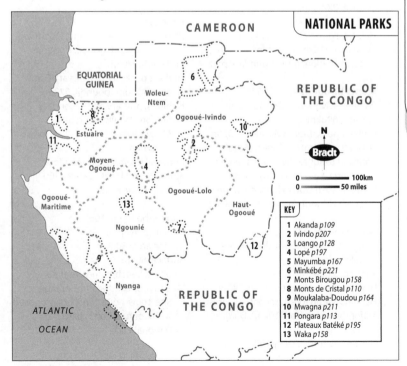

KEY

1 Akanda *p109*
2 Ivindo *p207*
3 Loango *p128*
4 Lopé *p197*
5 Mayumba *p167*
6 Minkébé *p221*
7 Monts Birougou *p158*
8 Monts de Cristal *p110*
9 Moukalaba-Doudou *p164*
10 Mwagna *p211*
11 Pongara *p113*
12 Plateaux Batéké *p195*
13 Waka *p158*

played an important role in the creation of the 13 parks. White led the ANPN until 2019, when he was named Minister of Forests, Oceans, Environment and Climate Change (w eaux-forets.gouv.ga) in a surprise government shakeup in the wake of the 'kevazingo-gate' lumber scandal (page 32). At the time this guide went to print, the ANPN's professionalisation and expansion was continuing apace; the agency has employed more than 700 staff, with a goal of bringing between 30,000 and 50,000 tourists per year to Gabon's national parks by 2025 and creating between 5,000 and 7,000 new jobs as a direct result.

Among the most notable new developments (from a visitor's perspective at least), is the opening of an ANPN-run network of upmarket eco-camps in several of Gabon's top national parks. Known as Gabon Wildlife Camps (page 88), there

NATIONAL PARKS

Akanda (page 109)
Province: Estuaire
Surface: 540km²
Highest peak: 60m
Habitats: mangroves, mudflats,
    coastal waters, coastal thickets,
    hyper-humid coastal forest
Status: RAMSAR site (2007)

Plateaux Batéké (page 195)
Province: Haut-Ogooué
Surface: 2,050km²
Highest peak: 860m
Habitats: grassland, gallery forest
Status: IUCN Critical Site for
    conservation; trans-boundary park

Monts Birougou (page 158)
Provinces: Ngounié, Ogooué-Lolo
Surface: 690km²
Highest peak: Mount Birougou, 975m
Habitats: tropical rainforest, cloudforest
Principal topography: watershed for
    Nyanga, Lolo and Onoy rivers
Status: least-disturbed section in the du
    Chaillu Mountains; IUCN Critical Site

Ivindo (page 207)
Provinces: Ogooué-Ivindo, Ogooué-
    Lolo
Surface: 3,000km²
Highest peak: Mount Kingué, 749m
Habitats: virgin forest, secondary forest
Major rivers: Ivindo (110km), Djidji
    (120km)
Highest waterfall: Djidji Falls (80m)

Loango (page 128)
Province: Ogooué-Maritime
Surface: 1,550km² with 86km of
    beach, 175km of lagoon shoreline
    and 50km of flooded rivers
Habitats: marine, beach, savannah,
    flooded and dry forests, lagoon,
    mangrove
Status: RAMSAR site (1986); IUCN
    Critical Site; proposed World
    Heritage Site

Lopé (page 197)
Provinces: Ogooué-Ivindo, Ogooué-
    Lolo, Moyen-Ogooué, Ngounié
Surface: 4,970km²
Highest peaks: two peaks at 960m
    each; Mount Iboundji, 972m
Habitats: primary and secondary
    rainforests, pioneer forest,
    Marantaceae forest, gallery forest,
    savannah
Principal rivers: Ogooué, Offoué
Status: World Heritage Site (2007);
    IUCN Critical Site

Mayumba (page 166)
Province: Nyanga
Marine area: 800km²
Surface: 60km²
Habitats: beach, dunes, marine
Status: proposed World Heritage
    Site; trans-boundary park proposed
    with Congo's Conkouati
    National Park

were three camps running at the time of publication, and there may well be a couple more within the lifetime of this edition.

CLIMATE CHANGE Gabon's forests, being a significant source of oxygen production and carbon sequestration, play a major role in the global fight against climate change and their preservation is crucial. Every minute, Gabon's trees and other vegetation absorb one tonne of CO_2 and stock this in wood, diminishing the negative effects of global warming. In turn, climate change also has a direct impact on the forest.

Research in Lopé has shown that low dry-season temperatures trigger flowering in about 20% of plant species whose fruits are eaten by gorillas and chimpanzees

Minkébé (page 221)
Provinces: Woleu-Ntem, Ogooué-Ivindo
Surface: 7,560km²
Highest peak: Mount Kokaméguèl, 938m
Habitats: primary and secondary forests
Status: IUCN Critical Site; proposed World Heritage Site

Monts de Cristal (page 110)
Province: Estuaire
Surface: 1,200km²
Highest peaks: Mount Mbilan, 925m and Mount Seni, 611m. Mount Seni has the highest rainfall in Gabon (350cm/year).
Habitats: elfin forest, cloudforest, primary and secondary forests
Status: IUCN Critical Site; one of two distinct Centres of Plant Diversity (CPDs) in the Atlantic Coastal Forest Ecoregion (CBFP, 2003)

Moukalaba-Doudou (page 164)
Provinces: Nyanga, Ogooué-Maritime
Surface: 5,000km²
Highest peak: Mount Doudou, 840m; the Doudou Mountains form the largest mountain range in southwestern Gabon
Habitats: mountain forest, rainforest, savannah, papyrus, raffia marshes

Status: IUCN Critical Site; crucial site for the protection of apes in Central Africa (WWF)

Mwagna (page 211)
Province: Ogooué-Ivindo
Surface: 1,160km²
Highest peak: 622m
Habitats: *Marantaceae* forest, Bai
Principal rivers: Lodié, Louayé
Status: Part of Trinational Landscape Dja-Odzala-Minkébé (TRIDOM) in the frame of the Congo Basin Forest Partnership

Pongara (page 113)
Province: Estuaire
Surface: 870km², with a beach length of 28km
Habitats: beach, lagoon, mangrove, marine, rainforest, savannah
Status: IUCN Critical Site; RAMSAR site (2007)

Waka (page 158)
Province: Ngounié
Surface: 1,070km²
Habitats: tropical forest, lower cloudforest
Principal rivers: Ikobé, Onoy, Oumba
Status: du Chaillu Mountains (as a Forest Refugium), a well-known conservation priority
Source: ANPN (page 29)

(and in some cases humans), suggesting that global warming expected in the remainder of the 21st century might have unexpected and sinister implications for tropical forests and their inhabitants – namely that a whole cohort of key plant species may stop flowering altogether.

One of the top priorities of the Gabonese government's Gabon Émergent (Emerging Gabon) development plan (see box, page 14) is to maintain the ecological equilibrium through sustainable forest management and developing ecotourism. Gabon is pursuing an ambitious policy to reduce CO_2 emissions linked to deforestation and forest degradation by 20 million tonnes a year; the country is in the process of setting up a market for carbon offsets.

The future of the Central African rainforest depends on the healthy interdependency between its plants and animals – one cannot survive without the other. Many forest trees depend on large mammals – notably elephant, gorilla and chimpanzee – to disperse their seeds. Where hunting is greatly reducing their numbers, the whole dynamics of the forest are threatened. Similarly, the loss of trees to logging (see below) represents a direct blow to the botanical composition of the forest on which the animals rely for their food. So the battle for conservation and the battle against logging and poaching are essentially one and the same.

President Ali Bongo views conservation as an essential part of economic development and has taken steps to unlock the potential of Gabon's exceptional landscapes and biodiversity, not least with the recent ministerial appointment of Lee White (page 29). The country had aimed to attract 100,000 tourists per year by 2020; this goal was missed, but the considerable political will to develop the ecotourism sector in Gabon is hopeful and, in many ways, unique.

LOGGING After oil, timber has traditionally been Gabon's most important export product. The logging industry is the country's main employer, providing approximately one third of the active population either directly or indirectly with their means of living. Okoumé and ozigo are the most heavily exploited woods, but other important trees are moabi, padouk, bilinga and sipo. Logging is one of the biggest threats to Gabon's extraordinary ecosystems, and the implications of forest destruction extend well beyond the country's borders.

As part of this drive the Gabonese government, in partnership with Olam Gabon, inaugurated the 1,126ha Nkok Special Economic Zone in 2014; it sits about 30km east of Libreville and is today a major centre for woodworking and lumber processing, with over 140 active investors from 18 different countries. The Gabon Wood Show (w gabonwoodshow.com) trade exhibition has also become an important annual event in the lumber industry.

Gabon's logging industry operates on a system of 'selective logging', which is supposed to ensure that only trees fitting certain criteria can be cut down. The criteria for okoumé, for example, stipulate that cut trees must be over a certain size – their trunks must have reached a diameter of 70cm at ground level – and no more than three to four trees per hectare can be felled. In reality, getting to a tree that fits the criteria can sometimes mean the loss of up to 200 trees in logging roads.

Despite the above, Gabon's logging industry still suffers from deep-seated corruption. This was spectacularly exposed in March 2019, when customs authorities discovered 392 containers of illegally felled kevazingo, with an estimated value of nearly US$250 million, awaiting export at Owendo's port. In a significant embarrassment to the state, after the containers were flagged as illegal, some 90% of them simply disappeared. The scandal quickly became known as 'kevazingo-gate', and was only intensified when President Ali Bongo stepped in to sack both

RAINFORESTS   *Derek Schuurman*

Rainforests are arguably the most important of the world's hotspots of biodiversity. Although they account for only 2% of the earth's surface, they hold the majority of the world's species. Almost half the world's rainforests are concentrated in just three countries – Brazil, Indonesia and the Democratic Republic of the Congo (DRC). Africa's rainforests belong either to the Guinean forests of West Africa, or to the Central African Congo Basin. The latter block includes the rainforests of Gabon.

Conservation International estimates that the DRC alone has 1.2 million square kilometres of rainforest. Add to that the rainforests of Gabon, Cameroon, Equatorial Guinea and the Central African Republic (CAR) and the figure shoots up to 1.9 million square kilometres.

Remarkably, today 80% of Gabon is still covered in rainforest. The so-called Gabonese Jungle Belt is not only the biggest intact forest area in all of Africa, but it is one of the largest worldwide, and it holds the highest tree and bird diversity for a given area anywhere in Africa. Of the 8,000+ plants, an estimated 20% are endemic, and there are also over 670 bird species. In such rainforests, a warm, even climate of around 25°C is maintained year-round and annual rainfall averages around the 2,000mm mark – significantly lower than, say, the rainforests in parts of Indonesia where rainfall can easily double that. So, the rainforests of Gabon and CAR experience a dry season and even feature some deciduous trees.

At every level of the forest – from canopy to the dark, damp forest floor – live a myriad life forms. These include many of Africa's most fascinating, enigmatic and poorly understood creatures. (Aside from the high bird species count, Gabon's 23 million hectares of rainforest also hold 190 species of mammal and an unknown number of reptiles and amphibians.)

the vice-president and Minister of Forests, Oceans, Environment and Climate Change. Encouragingly, he replaced the latter with former ANPN head and environmentalist Lee White. Some 200 of the containers were eventually recovered, but with kevazingo trees taking some 500 years to fully mature, the damage had already been done; it's hoped that White will oversee root-and-branch reforms of the sector to avoid a repeat of this tragic farce.

POACHING Hunting for subsistence living has traditionally been a way of life in Gabon, and is still permissible under certain criteria. All hunting is illegal between 15 September and 15 March, and at any time of year inside any of the national parks. Outside this period and areas, hunting the adult males of non-protected species is allowed (gorilla, chimpanzee, hippo, manatee, giant pangolin, sun-tailed monkey, mandrill and leopard are all protected). The limit is three mammals of the same species and up to four mammals of different species per day per hunter with a hunting permit. Any hunting that does not fit into these criteria is illegal poaching.

Poaching may be an informal sector of the economy, but it's a highly important one. Worryingly, it is not confined to subsistence levels. The threat of large-scale poaching is very real and growing urbanisation has increased the market for bushmeat. Furthermore, economic recession has meant unemployment for a lot of young men for whom commercial hunting is one way – sometimes the only way – to earn a bit of money. Poachers have usually grown up with the forest and know

ILLEGAL POACHING AND ORPHANED PRIMATES

Dr Anaïs Herbert

Despite the fact that hunting is restricted in Gabon by the law, many primates are victims of illegal poaching and the country's few sanctuaries are crowded with orphans.

Gorilla, chimpanzee, mandrill and sun-tailed monkey are entirely protected in Gabon, which means that they can never be hunted, captured, commercialised or detained. Other primates are not protected, which means that they can be hunted and commercialised, but only during capture season, from 15 March to 15 September of each year, and only in compliance with a number of rules (page 33).

For every primate species, it is strictly forbidden to detain a monkey at home. However, despite the legislation, primates are still kept as pets in many families, which raises serious concerns for human health and safety, as well as animal wellbeing. These animals saw their mothers being killed, and were captured to be sold or eaten by hunters or poachers. They are usually kept in small cages or with a cord around their abdomen, and are often malnourished and not looked after properly.

Some tourists may be tempted to buy a monkey on the road, thinking they are helping the animal, but they are actually encouraging poachers, who will kill other monkey mothers to sell more babies. So please don't ever buy a primate, even if it is in a bad shape. Refer it to the Ministère des Eaux et Forêts (Ministry of Water & Forests; ☏ 01 76 13 81; w eaux-forets.gouv.ga), which will confiscate the animal and place it in a sanctuary.

It's also forbidden for people to sell bushmeat during the non-hunting season – to buy it outside this period is also illegal, as well as supportive of poaching.

Thank you for respecting these rules. The future of primates in Gabon depends on it.

and understand its animals. A common hunting trick to attract prey is to imitate the animal's call, for example that of an injured monkey. Thus, the combination of persistent unemployment, ready availability of arms, and what's commonly seen as an inexhaustible resource in the forests can seem like an open invitation to potential 'large-scale' poachers.

Logging roads have facilitated the job of poachers by providing a means of reaching previously isolated tracts of forest and a route back to market. What's more, logging trucks are a readily available means of transport, and the logging camps themselves are an immediate market, requiring no transportation at all.

Bringing poaching down to sustainable levels is a conservation priority, and ecotourism may be part of the answer. Effective enforcement not only curtails the dactual operations by prosecuting illegal wildlife exploiters, but also introduces the idea that there are livings to be made from the forest beyond hunting, thus hopefully acting as a deterrent and reducing the overall level of illegal hunting and trade.

The present level of elephant poaching is a serious threat to the species. WWF, WCS and ANPN (page 29) began to ring alarm bells after studies showed that one of the most significant long-term massacres of forest elephants had taken place in Minkébé National Park. Between 2004 and 2014, as many as 25,000 of its forest elephant were slaughtered, corresponding to nearly 80% of the population. ANPN estimates that even now, as many as 12 individuals are killed per day by poachers with the help of illegal gold miners and the indigenous people of the forest.

Demand for ivory for use in jewellery and ornamental items seems insatiable in the Asian market, and Gabonese elephants have the 'extra-hard pinkish ivory' that is considered extremely valuable.

As a reaction to these staggering numbers, President Ali Bongo adopted a zero-tolerance policy for wildlife crime and shut Libreville's illegal ivory markets. To demonstrate the policy, in 2012 the president publicly burned Gabon's ivory stockpile – nearly five tons of tusks worth about US$10 million seized from poachers or retrieved from dead elephants. Poaching nonetheless remains a grave problem. In January 2014 Gabon, alongside four other African countries, became a founding member of the Elephant Protection Initiative (EPI; w elephantprotectioninitiative. org), a multi-national African coalition dedicated to eradicating the ivory trade and preserving the elephant. The EPI had grown to 19 members as of 2019.

Training with the US and UK militaries is also underway, with the aim of establishing a 'jungle brigade'; in Minkébé its members may be allowed to shoot armed poachers on sight. Critics contend that Bongo shows more concern for Gabon's wildlife than its impoverished citizens.

ENVIRONMENTAL ORGANISATIONS The foremost international environmental organisations are the **World Wide Fund for Nature** (WWF; w wwf-congobasin. org) and the **Wildlife Conservation Society** (WCS; w gabon.wcs.org). The former arrived in the country in 1992 and is heavily involved in conservation efforts in the Gamba Complex area, which encompasses two of Gabon's national parks, Loango and Moukalaba-Doudou, covering a combined area of some 6,500km².

The WCS has been working in the country since 1985, and today is still supporting conservation efforts in seven of the country's 13 national parks by training government conservation workers and partnering with communities to develop sustainable livelihoods, reduce human/elephant conflict, and promote ecotourism.

There are also a number of **local environmental organisations**:

Aventures Sans Frontières [78 B3] (ASF) near Feu rouge Gros Bouquet (Gros Bouquet traffic light), Libreville; ☏ 01 44 48 52; m 07 39 86 71/07 54 15 24; e asfgabon@gmail.com; ⨍ AventuresSansFrontieres. This local NGO was founded in 1991 by childhood friends Guy-Philippe Sounguet & Serge Akagah after they had completed a 1,200km tour of Gabon on foot. ASF confined itself to introducing children to the nature surrounding them, until a kayak trip from Libreville to Port-Gentil highlighted the plight of turtles. Now ASF has teams conducting surveys in a number of sites around Gabon, including Point Pongara, Mayumba, Iguela & Gamba. ASF also played a major role in the creation of Gabon's national marine parks.

Brainforest Camp de Gaulle, Quartier Ambowé, Libreville; ☏ 01 73 08 86; m 06 26 06 17/07 29 41 40; e info@brain-forest.org; w brainforest-gabon.org. Promotes & supports rational & sustainable exploitation of natural resources in the Congo Basin. Brainforest speaks out on corruption & abuse by big business & government, campaigns on human-rights issues like rainforest destruction & enables forest communities to increase their access to forest resources. Brainforest's president is Marc Ona Essangui, who was awarded the Goldman Prize in 2009 for his efforts to publicly expose the unlawful agreements behind a huge mining project threatening the sensitive ecosystems of Gabon's equatorial rainforests. As one of Gabon's most prominent environmental activists, he sometimes faces heavy governmental resistance.

Conservation Justice Libreville; e luc@ conservation-justice.org; w conservation-justice. org. Conservation Justice aims to protect elephants & other threatened species in Gabon from poaching & illegal wildlife trade by increasing the level of wildlife law enforcement nationwide & deterring potential elephant poachers & ivory traffickers from conducting these activities. Through its programme of investigation, operation, legal follow-up & media exposure,

Conservation Justice assists the Ministry of Water & Forests in wildlife law enforcement & tries to combat illegal hunting & trade at both a national & an international level.

Ibonga ACPE (Association Connaissance et Protection de l'Environnement; Association for Knowledge & Protection of the Environment) Quartier Bienvenue, Gamba; m 07 13 01 99; e ong.ibonga@yahoo.fr; w ibonga.org; f Ibonga ACPE. Founded in 1999 by Jean-Pierre Bayet, this Gabonese NGO sensitises local communities on nature conservation so that they can participate in sustainable natural resource management. Ibonga runs a research & monitoring programme for marine turtles nesting on the beaches of the Gamba Complex (page 137).

PROGRAM (L'association Protectrice des Grands Singes de la Moukalaba/ Association for the Protection of Moukalaba's Great Apes) Tchibanga [map, page 162]) & Quartier Louis, Libreville [95 B3]; m 07 12 68 04/06 62 25 72; e ong.program@ gmail.com/marieangele.program@gmail.com/ zangobamerina@yahoo.fr; w association-program. com; f ong.program. Gabonese NGO that aims to safeguard the region's natural & cultural heritages by encouraging ecotourism in Moukalaba-Doudou National Park. Its 4 goals are to protect the great apes residing in the park, preserve the park's biodiversity, improve conditions for local populations in 14 villages located in the area & establish ecotourism sites. In collaboration with WWF-Gabon, PROGRAM organises safaris to the park, where they work on the habituation of gorilla families near the village of Doussala. PROGRAM estimates that 40% of ecotourism revenue is passed on into local village economies.

WILDLIFE

MAMMALS The vast majority of Gabon's tourists to date have come to see the wildlife, specifically gorillas, of which there are an estimated 100,000 (according to a 2018 study). Gorillas have been identified as having mainstream appeal and gorilla trekking has therefore been the focus of the few tour operators and travel agencies who have shown any interest in the country. In actual fact, gorillas are just one of many reasons why a wildlife enthusiast should visit. Gabon has very important populations of large mammals, including an estimated 40,000–50,000 forest elephants and a similar number of chimpanzees. There is also a large number and variety of monkeys, including the black colobus monkey, the moustached monkey and the sun-tailed monkey (an endemic species). Other mammals include the Congo sitatunga, mongoose, forest buffalo, civet, hippopotamus, leopard, porcupine, and numerous different species of pangolin and squirrel, including flying squirrel.

Primates
Western lowland gorilla (*Gorilla gorilla gorilla*) Though a 2018 study put their Gabonese population at around 100,000, the western lowland gorilla is nonetheless categorised as critically endangered. (Indeed, three of the four gorilla subspecies share this unwelcome status.)

In comparison with the now-iconic **mountain gorilla** (*Gorilla beringei beringei*) found in the Virunga mountains of eastern Central Africa, the western lowland gorilla that inhabits Gabon's rainforests has wider, shorter body hair, longer arms and a wider, larger skull. This gorilla can be up to 1.8m tall when standing and can weigh over 200kg. It is a herbivore, feeding on leaves, fruit, shoots, bulbs and even tree bark. Gorilla groups are led by a silverback, who decides when the group plays, sleeps, eats and moves on. He is the only fully adult male among several females and can eat up to 3kg of vegetation a day.

The western lowland gorilla is a peaceful, non-aggressive animal, who never attacks unless provoked. However, if he fears for the safety of his family group, an adult male will attempt to intimidate his aggressor by standing on his legs, roaring and slapping his chest with cupped hands. As a last resort, he will charge towards the

MONKEY BUSINESS   *Derek Schuurman*

Gabon's marvellous assemblage of primates includes a large variety of monkeys. Among these conspicuous and animated characters are several of the guenons. Africa's 17 guenons are generally regarded as the most colourful group of monkeys in the world. Just as the tamarins of South America's rainforests often do, the African rainforest monkeys regularly travel through the forest in loosely knit multi-species troops. The various species then forage at the specific levels of the forest where each of their favourite foods are found. The advantage of the different species travelling together is that there are then many pairs of eyes to watch for predators at all different levels of the forest (visibility is generally not the best in the dark, densely foliaged, closed-canopy setting). It has been found that these monkeys have predator-specific alarm vocalisations, and that the different species understand each other's specific alarm calls. So, if for instance an arboreal colobus monkey spots a crowned eagle low overhead, it will sound the 'eagle' alarm and all the other monkeys, regardless of species and at which level in the forest they are, will react in the same way, ie: they will drop down and scramble for cover. In the same way, if one of the more terrestrial monkeys spots a leopard, it will give the 'leopard' alarm call and all the monkeys will hang around at a safe distance above the cat, creating a cacophonic din until the foiled predator has had enough and slinks away (they know the leopard is an ambush predator).

intruder, but his intention is not to crash into him. At the final second he will aim to veer slightly to the side. The western lowland gorilla's only known enemy is man.

Chimpanzee (*Pan troglodytes*) The common chimpanzee has a long, black coat covering all its body except the face, hands and feet. Chimpanzees have long digits, large ears and small beards in the adults of both sexes. (Unlike gorillas, their sexual organs protrude.) The chimpanzee is equally at home on the ground as in the trees, although invariably this animal will build its night nest above ground. Most of its diet is made up of fruits, but it will eat leaves, flowers, seeds, insects, birds' eggs and even monkeys. Chimpanzees live in groups of between 20 and 100 animals, within which there are smaller subgroups. The chimpanzee lives in ancient and post-agricultural rainforests in Gabon, up to altitudes of 3,000m.

Mandrill (*Mandrillus sphinx*) The mandrill is found in Cameroon, Equatorial Guinea and Gabon, where it is locally common. It is best known for the unmistakable, bright red and blue facial markings sported by males: the more dominant the male, the brighter his facial colours will be and the more offspring he will sire. Mandrills also boast strikingly coloured rumps which, besides being used for social and sexual signals, are thought to aid the navigation of troops through the dark rainforests. Weighing up to 50kg, male mandrills are the world's largest monkeys, and can often be double the size of females.

Mandrills are diurnal and omnivorous quadrupeds and they tend to forage widely by day. Though they prefer forested areas, they are known to occasionally enter the savannah as well. In the dry season (July–October), mandrills congregate in impressive numbers with such 'super groups' sometimes numbering hundreds of individuals.

Sun-tailed monkey (*Cercopithecus solatus*) Not surprisingly, the sun-tailed monkey takes its name from the bright orange colour at the tip of its tail. It is also characterised by its reddish back and blue scrotum. This monkey is known to inhabit a small area of about 12,000km², centring on the Forêt des Abeilles to the east of Lopé National Park. They normally live in groups, averaging fewer than 20 animals, but solitary males are also common. They are curious animals, and might be spotted either in the trees or on the ground.

Black colobus monkey (*Colobus satanas*) Of the five species in the colobus genus, three are found in Central Africa. Of these the one most likely to be seen in Gabon is the black colobus. As its name suggests, this monkey is entirely black. Other characteristics to note are its long, thin tail and its small, wide-set eyes. More often than not it will be spotted high up in the forest canopy in groups of 10–20 animals. Its food of choice are seeds and, failing that, young leaves.

Moustached monkey (*Cercopithecus cephus*) This monkey's preferred habitat is post-agricultural forests in Gabon, because of their dense, low vegetation. It is usually seen on branches lower than 15m or sometimes on the ground, in groups of 5–20 animals. Its identifying features are its white moustache, blue face, bluish-grey stomach and red tail. The largest part of its diet is made up of fleshy fruits. The females and young are much noisier than the males.

Putty-nosed monkey (*Cercopithecus nictitans*) This monkey lives in rainforest, relatively high up in the trees. It is entirely black apart from a white splodge at the end of its nose. On the male the tail may reach as much as 1m in length. It is a popular target with hunters (see box, page 34) as it is the largest and heaviest of the tree monkeys and the easiest to track down, mostly because of the distinctiveness and regularity of the male's call. Its diet is fruit-based.

Crowned monkey (*Cercopithecus pogonias*) The crowned monkey, also known as the crested mona monkey or golden-bellied guenon, takes its name from its white headband flanked by tufts of yellow fur protruding from the ears. These medium-sized monkeys tend to be found in groups of about 20, often of different species. Given the chance, it will eat mostly fruit, but when fruits are not available it makes do with seeds and young leaves. In Gabon, it is found high up in the canopy (never on the ground) of ancient forests on the left bank of the Ogooué River.

De Brazza's monkey (*Cercopithecus neglectus*) The young De Brazza's monkey is pale, but its coat darkens and it acquires a red crown as it gets older. It is one of the heavier monkeys, the male's weight of up to 8kg often being double that of the female. De Brazza's monkey is found from the Atlantic coast all the way to western Kenya. The enormity of its range can be explained by its ability to swim. For this reason it is often spotted in forests alongside rivers or on river islands, however small. This monkey lives in small groups of about five animals. Seeds, leaves, mushrooms and caterpillars are all part of its diet.

Red-capped mangabey (*Cercocebus torquatus*) This mangabey's coat has just a splash of identifying colour – its body is grey on top and white underneath, its black face is fringed with white and crowned by a red skullcap. It lives in mixed-sex groups of ten to 60 animals and eats fruits, leaves, roots and insects. It can be found in Gabon's coastal region, in swampy forests beside water and in mangroves.

Agile mangabey (*Cercocebus agilis*) This monkey is lighter and less distinctive in colour than the red-capped mangabey. It is grey with a white underbelly and a darker, blackish face with a single white spot on its crown. It lives in groups averaging 15 animals, led by a dominant male. The agile mangabey frequents the area inland north of the Ogooué River, and like its relative the red-capped mangabey, it inhabits swampy, flooded forests bordering water.

Grey-cheeked mangabey (*Lophocebus albigena*) This slim, agile monkey is noted for the long, grey hair on its large cheeks, which spreads over its shoulders. The rest of its body is black-flecked with dark-grey hairs. It lives in groups of about 15 animals – including several males – which sometimes divide into smaller groups that keep within sight or sound of one another as they climb in the treetops. This monkey, especially the female, spends a lot more time than most other monkeys searching for insects, though it also eats seeds and, to a lesser extent, fruit. It can be found all over Gabon in ancient forests, favouring the higher canopy and rarely being seen on the ground.

Antelopes Duiker (*Cephalophus*) are small forest-dwelling antelopes. They are the most widespread of all African forest antelopes and are separated into some 17 species. They have low-slung bodies on slender legs, and regularly run through areas of dense vegetation; when disturbed they tend to plunge into thick cover to hide – the name duiker means 'diver' in Dutch and Afrikaans. Gabon's duikers include the large, yellow-backed duiker, the attractive bay duiker and the Peter's duiker, as well as the much more widely distributed common (grey) duiker.

The **common duiker** (*Sylvicapra grimmia*) is small and greyish in colour, with a white underbelly and a short, black tail. Its identifying feature is the small tuft of black hair between its horns, which are v-shaped in males and very small, almost non-existent, in females.

Both the bay and yellow-backed duiker are heavily persecuted for bushmeat and also, regrettably, by certain European hunting tour operators (notably the largest,

NATURE HIGHLIGHTS	*Derek Schuurman*

Rainforests Gabon is one of the few countries where vast, pristine rainforests are not just a memory (see box, page 33). Botanists are in for a treat, with some 20% of the country's flora being endemic.

Beaches Where else can you see forest elephants on a deserted beach, while humpback whales cavort offshore? Lowland gorillas are also known to hit the beach and, strangest of all, hippos often frequent the surf in Loango (page 46).

Baïs At these meadow-like clearings in the forest with nutrient-rich sedges and salt licks you can take in wonderful sightings of forest elephant, forest buffalo, timid Congo sitatunga and, of course, western lowland gorilla, which can appear in large numbers.

Mandrill troops In the dry season, Lopé's mandrill troops (page 204) are enormous: 1,000+ may be seen together, one of the largest primate gatherings on earth (the other is Ethiopia's gelada baboon).

Smaller mammals Monkeys galore inhabit the forests, as do small forest-dependent antelope including various duikers. These are all important seed distributors. Other noteworthy species include Congo clawless otter, the tiny water chevrotain and the African golden cat.

the yellow-backed duiker). The attractive reddish-brown **bay duiker** (*Cephalophus dorsalis*) is strictly nocturnal and by day hides in hollow trees or in dense vegetation. Also known as the black-backed duiker, they tend to travel using tunnel-like paths through thick vegetation. While vegetable matter constitutes their main diet, they will stalk, kill and eat small animals and birds on rare occasions. Population densities are very low, with 12–20ha of habitat holding only two to three individuals. The **yellow-backed duiker** (*Cephalophus silvicultor*) is predominantly nocturnal, and can

Common duiker

be found resting alone during the day in 'forms', which are regularly used places under fallen tree trunks or in dense, tangled vegetation. They have been seen resting on termite mounds, possibly to survey their surroundings. They mark their territory with maxillary glands and communicate by means of shrill bleats and grunts. When alarmed, they erect their bright dorsal crests and emit a shrill whistle, before fleeing into the dense undergrowth.

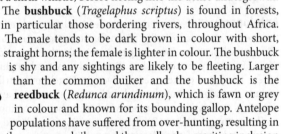

The **bushbuck** (*Tragelaphus scriptus*) is found in forests, in particular those bordering rivers, throughout Africa. The male tends to be dark brown in colour with short, straight horns; the female is lighter in colour. The bushbuck is shy and any sightings are likely to be fleeting. Larger than the common duiker and the bushbuck is the **reedbuck** (*Redunca arundinum*), which is fawn or grey in colour and known for its bounding gallop. Antelope populations have suffered from over-hunting, resulting in several – including both the common duiker and the reedbuck – meriting inclusion on Gabon's protected list.

Bushbuck

Less vulnerable to hunters is the **sitatunga** (*Tragelaphus spekei*), which inhabits swamp forests and marshes. Its skittishness means it is rarely seen by humans, but keep an eye out for it in boggy papyrus beds. Its excellent swimming ability means it can flee to safety through deep water, sometimes keeping only its nostrils above the water. Another antelope resident in Gabon is the **bongo** (*Tragelaphus eurycerus*), found in dense tropical forests below 4,000m. This is the largest forest antelope in the world. Its coat is a rich

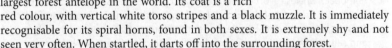
Sitatunga

red colour, with vertical white torso stripes and a black muzzle. It is immediately recognisable for its spiral horns, found in both sexes. It is extremely shy and not seen very often. When startled, it darts off into the surrounding forest.

The unusual **water chevrotain** (*Hyemoschus aquaticus*) superficially resembles a small duiker and is the most primitive of ruminants, sharing certain taxonomic features with pigs. Although the chevrotains are also called 'mouse deer', they are not closely related to true deer and are placed in their own family. The smallest of the hoofed mammals, they stand 20–35cm high at the shoulder. The body is rabbit-like, with an arched back; the slender legs end in small feet; the snout is tapered and somewhat pig-like. The reddish-brown coat is spotted with white in most species. Chevrotains lack antlers but have tusk-like upper canine teeth, used by the males for fighting. Solitary, nocturnal denizens of dense, humid forest, they browse on leaves and fruit. The water chevrotain of tropical Africa lives, as its name implies, near water. It has been seen feeding underwater and will readily take to water to escape predators such as snakes, eagles and cats. The three other chevrotains (*Tragulus* spp) are found in Asia, from India to Indonesia and the Philippines.

Other medium and large mammals

Hippopotamus (*Hippopotamus amphibious*) Hippos are most commonly found in still pools or slow-running water. Observers are more likely to see hippo tracks on the riverbank than a hippo itself, as they normally spend all day in the water, often totally submerged, or with just their eyes, ears and upper nose showing. Hippos are noisy and sociable, and are often found in groups of about ten. They are highly territorial, and are known for capsizing boats that drift too close or charging people that cross their path on land. When they defecate they rotate their stubby tails, thereby spraying their dung around in a good 2m radius. This habit probably functions as a territorial display for the benefit of hippos from other groups.

African forest elephant (*Loxodonta cyclotis*) With up to 50,000 individuals present, 60% of the remaining global forest elephant population is found in Gabon. Much less is known about the forest elephant than about its savannah relative, but forest elephants tend to be smaller and darker in colour, with smaller, rounder ears and a different skull shape. Another difference is in their tusks, which on forest elephants are straighter and aimed at the ground. The elephants use them to dig up saline soil and peel off tree bark for consumption.

Even though Gabon is known today as the forest elephant's main stronghold, studies carried out by WWF, WCS and ANPN show that a staggering 25,000 individuals were killed between 2004 and 2014 in Minkébé National Park alone (page 34). At its peak, 50 to 100 elephants were being killed daily; today that number is thought to be closer to 12. Though the poaching problem remains acute in Minkébé, many of Gabon's other parks have seen encouraging declines in poaching, thanks to improved monitoring and community outreach led by the ANPN.

Forest buffalo (*Syncerus caffer nanus*) Reddish-coloured, this buffalo is smaller than its savannah cousin, weighing no more than 320kg. The forest buffalo lives in lowland rainforest areas, where it tends to remain close to water and grassy glades, where it can graze. Social groups usually comprise no more than ten to 12 animals, with several females and their offspring accompanied by one or more males. Males often form bachelor groups. Forest buffalo can be seen in baïs in Gabon and Congo.

Leopard (*Panthera pardus*) This large, spotted cat is a solitary animal, a natural tree-climber and a nocturnal hunter. It eats antelope, birds, snake and fish. Its preferred habitats are wooded grassland and forest, and it tends to rest among large rocks or large trees alongside rivers. It is difficult to spot, being both easily camouflaged and wary of humans. It

Leopard

is territorial and will charge in defence of its home range. A charge is indicated by a series of short coughs followed by a chilling scream. Leopards in Gabon tend to have very dark fur. Melanistic examples are known to occur.

Side-striped jackal (*Canis adustus*) Found in Gabon's grassy savannah areas, such as the Batéké Plateau in the far southeast, the side-striped jackal grows to be around 15kg at most and can live either alone or in a small family group. The jackal is a scavenger, and its diet consists of insects, small reptiles, birds and vegetation. Its movements are very similar to those of domestic dogs. Jackals are generally most active at night or at dusk and dawn, and seek shade under shrubs or in long grass in the heat of the day.

Red river hog (*Potomochoerus porcus*) The red river hog is usually a striking reddish colour, with white markings on its large head and long black-and-white tassels hanging from its ears. It has a long, thin tail (up to 45cm) and short, pointy tusks, and weighs 65–100kg. Its preferred habitats are thickets, forests, savannahs and swamps throughout western and Central Africa. This pig is happy wallowing in water, hence its name. Until the 1990s, the red river hog and its eastern African counterpart the **bush pig** (*Potomochoerus larvatus*) were considered to be a single species, classified under *P. porcus*. Bush pigs live in noisy groups of six to 20 animals, led by a large male. They are nocturnal, staying hidden during the day, and will eat anything from reptiles to fruits. Their main predators are leopards and man. As a defence, the red river hog makes itself look much larger, by fluffing out its ear tassels and the erectile mane that runs along its spine.

African manatee (*Trichechus senegalensis*) The vulnerable African manatee is a large, grey, cylindrical mammal that lives in coastal areas, brackish lagoons and large rivers. It can be up to 4m long and weigh 500kg. It has a bristly upper lip, front flippers and a flattish, paddle-shaped rear end. A manatee may travel up to 40km a day through lagoons and rivers, but usually at speeds of between 5 and 8km/h. Actual sightings of manatees in Gabon are rare, but sometimes they are heard splashing. Though officially protected in Gabon, thanks to their slow movements, manatee remain particularly at risk from hunters and accidents with boat propellers or fishing nets.

Small mammals If you are lucky you might spot **genet** (*Genetta*), **mongoose** (*Herpestidae*) or **civet** (*Viverridae*) in the forest. With few exceptions these are small, nocturnal mammals with large eyes and long tails. They are deft and lively animals

Pangolin

with excellent speed and night vision. During the day they hide under bushes and in abandoned termite mounds. The **marsh mongoose** (*Atilax paludinosus*) is more diurnal. It is most likely to be glimpsed weaving through the bush, occasionally stopping to look around on its hind legs. Rare and rarely seen are **pangolin** (*Pholidota*), including the tree pangolin (*Phataginus tricuspis*) and the giant pangolin (*Smutsia gigantea*). They are distinctive because of their unique protective scales. Pangolin are insectivores, equipped with a long, thin tongue specially adapted for catching ants and termites. The tongue on a giant pangolin can be up to 70cm long, and it can eat up to 200,000 or 700g of ants a night. The **porcupine** (*Hystricidae*) is also nocturnal and is protected by spikes rather than scales. Also living in the forest, largely out of sight, are the nocturnal **bushbaby** (*Galagidae*) and **squirrel** (*Sciuridae*). The squirrel species include the flying squirrel, which is able to glide thanks to a membrane of skin joining its legs.

REPTILES There are several species of crocodile resident in Gabon, including **Nile crocodile** (*Crocodylus niloticus*), **African dwarf crocodile** (*Osteolaemus tetraspis*), and the newly described **Central African slender-snouted crocodile** (*Mecistops leptorhynchus*), which was only recognised as a separate species from its West African counterpart in 2018. Crocodiles can be found in many of Gabon's lagoons and rivers, though they are difficult to spot during the day – looking for them along riverbanks at night is easier as their eyes shine red. Gabon has also become famous for its 'orange' crocodiles, a small population of mutated, cave-dwelling African dwarf crocodile found in the Ogooué-Maritime province (see box, page 120).

Another commonly spotted reptile, particularly on branches overhanging rivers and lagoons, is the **monitor lizard** (*Varanus*). Gabon's most famous snake is the **gaboon viper** (*Bitis gabonica*), which is light brown in colour with detailed markings on its back. It eats rodent, hare, small monkeys, birds and toad. This venomous adder reaches up to 1.2m long and can weigh up to 8kg. It can be found in forests throughout the country. Owing to its nocturnal habits and docile nature, bites are thankfully rare.

MARINE LIFE
Sea turtles Gabon's beaches are world-renowned nesting grounds for turtles, in particular the vulnerable **leatherback turtle** (*Dermochelys coriacea*). It has a supple 'leathery' shell without plates or scales. It is also the largest turtle, measuring up to 2m and weighing more than 600kg. The beach south of Mayumba boasts the highest density of leatherback nests anywhere in Africa, while the beaches near Pointe Pongara are the second most important site in Gabon.

There are three other species of sea turtle known to nest in the country. The critically endangered **hawksbill turtle** (*Eretmochelys imbricata*), the endangered **green turtle** (*Chelonia mydas*), and the vulnerable **olive ridley turtle** (*Lepidochelys olivacea*).

Whale Gabon's coast is a very important breeding ground for **humpback whale** (*Megaptera novaeangliae*) – an estimated 800–1,500 of them can be seen from June to November each year. They work their way up the coast as far as Cap Lopez before heading towards São Tomé and Príncipe. These whales are spectacular to watch and easy to identify, both from the way they look and the way they behave. The females average about 15m and the males 12m. Both have knobbly heads and long flippers, black topsides and white or mottled undersides. The underside of their flukes is speckled black and white. Each animal's pigmentation is as unique as a human fingerprint, making identification of individual animals quite straightforward. Humpbacks sing long and complex songs, and enjoy breaching, lobtailing and flipper slapping.

In addition to humpbacks, the waters off the coast of Gabon are home to some 25 species of whale and dolphin. **Killer whale** (*Orcinus orca*), **sperm whale** (*Physeter macrocephalus*) and the critically endangered **Atlantic humpback dolphin** (*Sousa teuszii*) can all be found here.

BIRDING IN GABON   with Keith Barnes and Derek Schuurman
Rainforest birding in Central Africa can be slow and frustrating. Most species occur at low densities, others are frequently heard and rarely seen, and many of those that show up may do so only once. When species *do* show themselves, it is often fleetingly and generally in poor light. But for those who are patient, the rewards are endless – when a rockfowl finally leaps into view, the frustration vanishes and it becomes plainly obvious why you do it. The rainforest offers the most exotic and sought-after species in Africa, from blue cuckoo-shrikes to ant-thrushes and alethes. Birding the savannah is easier and more productive in short time spells;

the weather and conditions are also more conducive to seeing more birds. In the rainforest many of the larger and more spectacular species Africa is renowned for are absent or exceptionally rare. However, what Central Africa lacks in quantity it more than makes up for in quality; the region probably holds more desirable bird species than any other part of the continent. Ornithologically speaking, Gabon remains little known, despite holding some of the best forests in Africa for birds. Improvements in infrastructure, and adventures by the more intrepid travellers, combined with improvements in field guides, means that birding here is no longer the near-impossible task it once was.

Key birds Gabon's potential popularity as a birding destination is bolstered by it containing some of Africa's (and indeed the world's) most desirable bird species. The **grey-necked rockfowl** (*Picathartes*) is chief among these. The African river martin, black-headed bee-eater, Congo moor chat and Gosling's apalis are also more easily seen here than anywhere else in the world. But the forests of Gabon hold a full complement of the Congo Basin's avifauna, and well-represented members include hornbills, turacos, kingfishers, illadopsis and bee-eaters in the forests, and seedeaters, cisticolas, raptors and starlings in the southeastern woodlands.

Planning your visit Although occasionally frustrating, Gabon is moderately well connected with a **road and air network** that can (and usually does) get one from A to B. Regular flights connect the two main birding zones in the southeast (Franceville) and west (Libreville) (page 66). Roads in the southeast are good all year round. In the north, it is best to avoid the rainy season, when the roads become mud paths and places such as Ipassa are virtually inaccessible (though this too is improving).

July and August are the **optimal times** for birding in Gabon. This is before the heavy rains come and many birds are actively setting up territories.

Independent birders need to plan well and expect a few surprises en route. The best area for these travellers is Lopé National Park (page 197), where transport, accommodation, good guides and sound advice are all available. For those who wish to partake in a guided trip, a list of **specialist birding tour operators** can be found on page 50.

More **ornithological information** can be obtained from the African Bird Club C/O BirdLife International (The David Attenborough Bldg, Pembroke St, Cambridge CB2 3QZ; w africanbirdclub.org). This is the leading organisation concerning the conservation and study of African birds. For any additional information on birding in Gabon you can email **Keith Barnes** at e keith@tropicalbirding.com.

Birding site guide *by Keith Barnes and Derek Schuurman*
Akanda National Park (page 109) Just north of Libreville is Akanda National Park, established by president Omar Bongo in 2002. The best access is via boat from Libreville, and it can be done as a day trip, travelling to the mouth of the Moka River. The main habitat is sandflats, estuary and mangroves. Some birds found here with ease are more elusive elsewhere in Africa. The most local are **Loanga weaver** and **Damara tern**, but there are a variety of other good birds including carmelite, Reichenbach's and brown sunbirds, royal tern, rosy bee-eater, swamp boubou and a variety of more widespread shorebirds, terns and waterbirds.

Lopé National Park (page 197) Besides Akanda, this is the easiest site to reach, either via vehicle or train on the **Transgabonais** (Trans-Gabon Railwy) (page 66). There is a train stop nearby, and with notice your accommodation can arrange a pick-up. Try to spend three to five nights here. The habitat is a phenomenal mosaic of savannah and rainforest, with the bonus of the large Ogooué River forming the park's boundary. The river can be good for some **uncommon birds**, including Forbes' plover, grey and rock pratincoles, water thick-knee, African skimmer and white-crowned lapwing. The riverine fringes are home to the local violet-tailed sunbird, and Reichenbach's, green-headed and green-throated sunbird can sometimes be seen. The open grassy areas are home to black-chinned quailfinch, compact weaver, long-legged pipit and black-bellied seedcracker, but it is necessary to venture into the forest for a chance of spotting the best birds in this region. **Key species** include the Dja River warbler (discovered here by Patrice Christy in 1994), and the sought-after lyre-tailed honeyguide, the bizarre display flights of which are more often heard than seen. As night falls, search for the local Bates's nightjar, another of the region's scarce residents. The more general fare includes various hornbills (an indicator of a forest in good condition) such as black-casqued, white-crested and piping hornbills. Weavers include the enigmatic yellow-mantled weaver and several of the gorgeous malimbes (Cassin's, blue-billed and red-headed). The common flock constituents are greenbuls comprising some 15 species. Other delightful canopy dwellers are African grey and red-fronted parrot, while the strange great blue turacos betray their presence by their noisy mutterings. For those wanting a true adventure, try Mikongo Camp deep within the forests. Despite the basic camp facilities, a journey here is well worth it, as you are exposed to a great number of deep-forest species. Most interestingly, the **red-headed rockfowl** has a colony here, and with effort these amazing deep-forest specialists can be seen along with skulking ground birds like black guineafowl and Latham's forest francolin. The reversing-truck sound of the black-faced rufous-warbler often gives this species away, while the forest's edges may hold the rare olivaceous flycatcher and white-browed forest flycatcher. Lopé offers some of the best birding in Central Africa and is well worth an extended stay.

Ivindo National Park (Ipassa Reserve) (page 207) This place in the interior of

Gabon's great forests is a little tricky and expensive to get to, and once you are here, it makes sense to spend at least four nights; a week is even better. Ipassa, part of the larger 300,000ha Ivindo National Park, is a large 10,000ha reserve with a grid of paths and a species list of about 430. **Key species** include: blue-headed dove; bare-cheeked trogon; yellow-throated cuckoo; yellow-capped weaver; the tiny African piculet; Rachel's malimbe; the lovely blue cuckoo-shrike; yellow longbill; a huge selection of greenbuls numbering some 20 species; rufous-sided broadbill; a cluster of barbets, including bristle-nosed and hairy-breasted; tiny and little green sunbirds; Gosling's and black-capped apalises; and Maxwell's black and yellow-capped weavers. The canopy supports Africa's most impressive **kingfishers**: chocolate-backed and blue-breasted; and rosy and black bee-eaters. **Raptors** overhead may include the impressive long-tailed hawk, Congo serpent-eagle and Cassin's hawk-eagle. A bevy of rarer **hornbills** occur here, including the inconspicuous red-billed dwarf, black dwarf, white-thighed and white-crested hornbills. Other rarer gems include: African dwarf kingfisher; Cassin's honeybird; Gabon woodpecker; yellow-bellied and white-spotted wattle-eyes; Woodhouse's antpecker; olive and spot-breasted ibises; and Sjöstedt's owlet and plumed guineafowl. On the forest floor – especially at ant columns – look out for various ant-thrushes, illadopsis, alethes and the shy forest robin.

The 'Highlands' of southeast Gabon (page 195) Between Franceville and

the Congo border lies the small town of Léconi. Here the altitude rises and rainforest gives way to Brachystegia copses of the Batéké Plateau, open grassveld and heathland. Between Bongoville and Léconi birders have the best chance of finding the local red-throated cliff-swallow and scarce black-headed bee-eater. The habitat is quite distinct to that elsewhere in Gabon and holds a large number of unique birds. Birders come here to look for Finsch's francolin, Congo moor chat and black-chinned weaver, among others. Other 'megaticks' include the black-collared bulbul, Petit's cuckoo-shrike, Salvadori's eremomela, yellow-bellied hyliota, Joanna's sunbird, the sought-after black-headed bee-eater and Luhder's and Perrin's bush-shrikes. In addition there are some quite interesting local races of birds, including white-bellied 'Barrow's' bustard and rufous-naped 'Malbrant's' lark. In an African context, some local species that are reasonably easy to see include black-rumped buttonquail, short-tailed pipit, Angola batis and dambo cisticola. There is also a potentially undescribed bird remaining in this region, currently dubbed the 'téké cisticola'. Birders would do well to stay only two to three nights here, because the more open habitat means you can expect to catch up with the target birds a lot faster than in the rainforest, and also because much of this region's avifauna is more widespread and can be seen in other parts of Africa.

Loango National Park (page 128) This is a tricky region to visit. There are numerous issues with access and getting to the lodges here, although this seems to be improving. However, if you are both adventurous and patient, a visit to this national park is likely to be the single greatest highlight of your time in Gabon. Flying into Port-Gentil, visitors can arrange with the ecolodges or fishing camps to access the best reaches of Loango National Park. From a birder's perspective this region is fabulous and offers the best chance of encountering one of Gabon's star birds, the rare and enigmatic **African river-martin**. This bird breeds in large numbers and spends a lot of the year in the coastal areas surrounding the national park. There are a variety of habitats, but the narrow black-water channels (such as the Mpivié) offer perhaps the best birds in the form of the violet-tailed sunbird, both vermiculated and Pel's fishing-owls, white-crested tiger-bittern, African finfoot and Hartlaub's duck. Several of these are probably more easily seen here than any other locality in the world. The river edge supports white-bellied and shining-blue kingfisher, Cassin's and white-browed flycatchers, white-throated blue swallow, and a bevy of swifts and spinetails that use the rivers to traverse the forests. Another speciality is the Loango weaver, normally found closer to the coastal thickets. The regular fare of forest birding is fabulous, and any patch could support a huge diversity and variety of species, including many similar in Lopé. Species to watch for include purple-headed starling, red-billed helmet-shrike, Gabon coucal, blue cuckoo-shrike, and a plethora of smaller forest species. The mixed savannah-forest mosaic adjacent to the channels supports Bates's nightjar, which is local and difficult to see elsewhere in Africa.

3

Practical Information

WHEN TO VISIT

Gabon can be visited at any time of year. It is hot and humid all year round, but to a lesser degree during the long dry season (May–September). There's a short dry season from December to January. During the rainy season downpours may come at any time of day and can last for several hours.

Every season has different advantages, depending on which animals you wish to spot. It is worth noting from the start that getting around Gabon at any time of the year can be slow and frustrating, and in the wet season doubly so. Trains and planes – except for light aircraft – should not be affected by wet weather, but the roads pose more of a problem. Only too quickly the tarmac runs out, leaving you struggling in the mud.

FLORA AND FAUNA With the coming of the rains around mid-September, the country's forests burst into flower. By January, fruit is in abundance. The majority of Gabon's orchids flower in the savannah and open grasslands between October and January, while some marshy areas are covered in flower during December and January.

During the long dry season between mid-May and mid-September, fruit is scarce and primates and birds spend most of their time searching for food in the forest and are less likely to venture into the open savannah. Between November and April, birdwatchers can sight many migratory birds coming from Europe or northern Asia or Africa.

The season for **whale- and dolphin-watching** is between July and October, although the surest time to see them is between August and September. To see **turtles** laying their eggs on the beach at night you should come between mid-November and mid-January.

For more information on when to see Gabon's natural highlights, see the box on page 48.

HIGHLIGHTS

Gabon's main selling point is without a doubt its magnificent nature and wildlife. Over 80% of the country is covered in dense rainforest, and the remainder is savannah and coastline. The country boasts an exceptional biodiversity and is home to mammals ranging from whale to warthog, as well as a long list of endemic birds. This is a land where gorilla and elephant can be caught on camera on the same stretch of beach. Gabon is not yet a mainstream destination and therefore is one of Africa's best places to access the untouched rainforest. Go now and you're almost sure to have it all to yourself.

The table gives the most promising locations and times to see different species.

Animal	Time	National park
Hippos in the surf	Nov–Jan	Loango
Buffalo	Aug–Oct	Ivindo
	Sep–Dec	Lopé
	Dec–Apr	Loango
Mandrill	Jul–Aug	Lopé
	year-round	Lékédi
Elephant	Oct–Nov	Lopé, savannah
	Oct–Nov	Moukalaba-Doudou
	Jan–Apr	Loango, beach
Migratory birds	Nov–Apr	Akanda
Breeding weavers	Sep–Oct	Loango, Louri Lagoon
Gorilla and chimpanzee	Jul	Moukalaba-Doudou
	Apr–Jul	Ivindo, Langoué Baï
	Dec–Feb, May–Jul	Ivindo, Loango
	Aug–Sep, Nov	Lopé
Leatherback turtle	Nov–Jan	Pongara, Loango
Humpback whale	Jul–Oct	Pongara, Loango
Bottlenose and humpback dolphin	Jul–Oct	Pongara

LOANGO NATIONAL PARK Get up close and personal with a newly habituated troupe of lowland gorillas, then spend the afternoon watching buffalo and elephant prowl the seemingly endless beach in this most majestic of Gabonese national parks. Page 128.

LOPÉ NATIONAL PARK Head out into Lopé's dramatic patchwork of forest and savannah where, thanks to a new research and tracking programme, you can now reliably spot notoriously elusive mandrills in staggeringly large troupes of up to 1,000. Page 197.

MOUKALABA-DOUDOU NATIONAL PARK Join researchers tracking gorillas by day, then head to the village after dark and join a wild, all-night Bwiti ceremony in this mysterious, mountainous national park. Page 164.

POINTE DENIS AND CAP LOPEZ Leave the city behind and kick back with a cocktail on the powdery beaches of Pointe Denis or Cap Lopez, accessible in just minutes from Libreville and Port-Gentil. Pages 112 and 126.

LAKESHORE ISOLATION Explore the little-visited network of lakes west of Lambaréné and stay at the fabulous Tsam-Tsam ecolodge, a paradise for relaxation, built and run by the local community. Page 144.

IVINDO NATIONAL PARK Take your time in one of Gabon's wildest parks, where you can revel at the raw power of Koungou Falls, tick off some 350 species of bird, and visit the dreamlike Langoué Baï, a remarkable meeting point for hundreds of animals. Page 207.

AKANDA NATIONAL PARK Hop in a pirogue and get lost in Akanda National Park's impossibly green maze of mangrove creeks, located right on Libreville's doorstep. Page 109.

LÉCONI AND THE BATÉKÉ PLATEAUX Leave the forests behind to spot antelope, swim in rivers, and take in the bizarre, eroded landforms of the high, treeless plateaux near the Congolese border. Page 195.

MINVOUL Get about as far off the beaten track as possible in this remote forest settlement, surrounded by Baka 'Pygmy' villages that are known for their healing traditions. Page 219.

LIBREVILLE Drink, dance, shop and dine in this laid-back seaside capital – the beating heart of Gabon. Page 79.

SUGGESTED ITINERARIES

WEEKEND If, for whatever reason, you happen to be in Libreville (page 79) with a day or two to spare, the national parks of **Akanda** and **Pongara** are both accessible as rewarding day trips or fine overnight excursions from the city. Akanda (page 109) is best for mangroves and watery wilderness, while Pongara (page 113) is renowned for its windswept beaches and coastal savannah. Alternatively, it's unlikely you'll regret kicking back for a couple of days on the beaches of Pointe Denis (page 112), less than 30 minutes from central Libreville.

ONE WEEK With a full week, you can take in Libreville and the surrounding area and also visit one of Gabon's top national parks: **Lopé** or **Loango**. The trip to Lopé involves taking one of the daily Transgabonais trains (page 66), while getting to northern Loango requires a flight to Port-Gentil (there are numerous daily departures; page 120), then a vehicle transfer to the park. Either way, you can then spend several nights in your chosen park. The safari activities on offer in both are stunning, with mandrill tracking in Lopé and gorilla tracking in Loango among the highlights of any trip to Gabon. A few days allows you to get a good feel for either before heading back to Libreville.

TWO WEEKS Two weeks allows you to take in several of Gabon's national parks. Starting in Libreville, get on the Transgabonais to Lopé (page 200). After a couple of days here, you can continue by a combination of road and rail to Ivindo (page 207), where you will need several days to get the measure of the park, taking in the awesome power of the **Koungou Falls** and the serenity of **Langoué Baï**. From here, take the Okondja road to Franceville (page 177), and spend a day or two out in the startlingly open savannahs of the Haut-Ogooué region, near Léconi. Fly back to Libreville and connect directly to Port-Gentil for a last stop in northern Loango National Park (page 128) before heading back to the capital.

THREE WEEKS Three weeks will allow you to do everything covered in the itineraries above, plus another stop or two. If you're ready to relax, you can head from Loango back up to Port-Gentil and take a scenic boat ride along the Ogooué

3

to **Lambaréné** (page 121), where you can spend a couple of nights at the delightfully remote Tsam-Tsam ecolodge, set along the shores of **Lake Oguemoué**. Otherwise, if you're feeling active and are craving a continued wilderness adventure, the hike between northern and southern **Loango** is a safari in itself (see box, page 131), and can be followed by a day or two exploring the beaches, forests and lagoons found at the south end of the park. Real completists could perhaps squeeze in a gorilla trek at **Moukalaba-Doudou National Park** (page 164) from here, otherwise you can make your way back to the capital by road for your last couple of days and either enjoy day trips into Akanda or Pongara national parks or some well-earned time on Pointe Denis beach.

TOURIST INFORMATION

Given that tourism in Gabon is still in its infancy, it is hardly surprising that at the time of writing there were virtually no tourist boards outside the country. The closest thing to a tourist office in Gabon is the **Agence Gabonaise de Développement et de Promotion du Tourisme et de l'Hôtellerie**, better known as AGATOUR [83 D4] (Léon Mba International Airport; ☏ 01 73 30 10; e contacts@tourisme-gabon.org; w tourisme-gabon.org). This is the information arm of the Ministry of Tourism, who have a seemingly eternally closed office at Libreville airport. Fortunately, the **Agence Nationale des Parcs Nationaux du Gabon (ANPN)** and Gabon Wildlife Camps (page 88) are planning to open an office at the airport during the lifespan of this edition.

Alternatively, visit the sites of the travel agencies listed below. Gabon Untouched (which is English-speaking) and Eurafrique Voyages are both well-known operators with good reputations.

TOUR OPERATORS

The number of tour operators offering organised trips to Gabon is not extensive, but there are a few European-based options. Some of them combine trips to Gabon with São Tomé and Príncipe or the wildlife reserves of Odzala and Nouabalé-Ndoki in northern Congo.

Given the difficulties of getting around in Gabon, organised excursions can save a lot of time and energy (not to mention cash). There are some excellent local tour operators who can also help out with visa arrangements. For more flexibility, you can book excursions in Libreville. There is a list of reputable agencies on page 88. Check their websites and contact them for up-to-date details of the different trips on offer.

UK

Archipelago Choice ☏ 017 6872 1040; e info@archipelagochoice.com; w archipelagochoice.com. Runs a variety of 11–20-night trips to Gabon, some in combination with São Tomé & Príncipe. See ad, page 149.

Birdquest Ltd ☏ 01254 826317; e birders@birdquest-tours.com; w birdquest-tours.com. Specialist birdwatching trip to Gabon runs most years over Aug & Sep. It's about 20 days long & takes in Ivindo, Lopé & Loango, along with southeastern Haut-Ogooué around Léconi.

Encounter the Wild ☏ 020 8432 6484; e info@encounterthewild.co.uk; w encounterthewild.co.uk. Offers 12- or 16-day tours taking in Loango, Moukalaba-Doudou & Ivindo national parks.

Native Eye ☏ 01473 328546; e info@nativeeyetravel.com; w nativeeyetravel.com. Offers a unique 10-day itinerary taking in Bwiti ceremonies & aquatic safaris on the lakes near Lambaréné, as well as a longer trip that takes in Loango National Park & parts of neighbouring Cameroon.

Responsible Travel ☏ 01273 823700; e rosy@responsibletravel.com; w responsibletravel.com.

Gabon is well known as something of a holy grail destination in the sportfishing world, and while this guide has not been written with sport fishers specifically in mind, a number of the lodges listed cater primarily to those on fishing holidays. These include Gavilo (northern Loango; page 132), Setté Cama Aventure (southern Loango; page 135), and Likwale Lodge (Mayumba; page 167). Other good resources for fishing trips in Gabon include:

Fishing Gabon Club Libreville; m 02 44 04 10/07 38 59 08; e fishinggabonclub@gmail. com; f fishinggabonclub. Runs fishing & whale-watching excursions out of Libreville, & can put together customisable fishing trips as well.

Gabon Fishing Excursion Port-Gentil; m 07 61 70 86; e p.peysserre@gmail.com; f Gabon-Fishing-Excursion. Runs fishing & whale-watching excursions out of Port-Gentil, in the ocean & near the Embouchure d'Olendé (Olende Inlet) south of the city.

Pêche Gabon Iguéla/Mayumba; m 07 23 15 06; e jeanetienne.olembe@peche-gabon.com; w peche-gabon.com. Gabonese fishing outfitter specialising in the areas around northern Loango & Mayumba national parks.

Tourette Fishing South Africa; +27 33 342 2793; m +27 84 622 2272; e info@tourettefishing.com; w tourettefishing. com. South Africa-based outfitter arranging fishing trips all over Africa.

Offers a 10-day itinerary taking in Lopé, Loango & Lambaréné.

Steppes Travel 01285 880980; e inspire@steppestravel.com; w steppestravel.com. Offers a 13-day group tour taking in Loango & Ivindo national parks.

Zambezi Safari & Travel 01752 878858; e info@zambezi.com; w zambezi.com. Specialist safari planners with a focus on Central, eastern and southern Africa.

EUROPE
Gabon Untouched Spain; m 04 76 72 86/+34 660 337 503 (Spain); e info@gabonuntouched.com; w gabonuntouched.com; f gabonuntouched. Spanish tour operator & NGO offering customisable trips around Gabon, including to some of the country's remotest corners. See ad, 3rd colour section.

Middle Africa Spain; +34 657 569 738; e info@middle-africa.com; w middle-africa.com.

Renowned for their expertise in Central Africa. Arranges bespoke holidays in Gabon & the wider region.

Pac Voyages France; +33 047 8 33 48 70; e contact@pacvoyages.fr; w pacvoyages. fr. Fishing trips to northern & southern Loango National Park arranged on demand.

Rift Valley Expeditions Spain; +34 937 681 111; m +34 690 131 487; e info@rift-valley. com; w rift-valley.com. Runs a 2-week tour taking in Loango & Moukalaba-Doudou national parks, including a hike between the northern & southern sectors of Loango. See ad, 2nd colour section.

AFRICA
Birding Africa South Africa; +27 21 531 9148; e info@birdingafrica.com; w www.birdingafrica. com. Offers 2–3 week birding tours that take in Ivindo & Lopé national parks, along with Léconi in Haut-Ogooué & Gamba in Ogooué-Maritime.

RED TAPE

Needless to say, you must ensure you have a valid passport, and one that is not due to expire for at least six months. An **International Certificate of Vaccination** against yellow fever is also necessary for entry into Gabon and is the first thing to be checked upon arrival (page 55).

Visas are required for all travellers. If flying into Gabon, you will either need to apply for a visa at a Gabonese embassy before departure (see below) or take advantage of the new **e-visa system** (only available for travellers arriving by air to Libreville). Both one-to-three-month single-entry (€70 plus €15 processing) and six-month multiple-entry (€185 plus €15 processing) visas can now be applied for online at w evisa.dgdi.ga (e evisa@dgdi.ga). After filling out the form and uploading the required documentation (passport and colour photo), you will receive an application receipt (*reçu d'inscription*) which, assuming your paperwork is in order, should be followed by a travel authorisation (*autorisation d'entrée*) within 72 hours. Print this and bring it to the airport, where you will receive the visa sticker and pay in euros (cash only) on arrival.

Note that we've had reports of the system producing a variety of errors leading to rejected applications; make sure that your document uploads meet the specifications exactly and leave yourself time to get the visa at an embassy if necessary.

Though all have their own unique set of hoops to jump through, most Gabonese embassies in Europe require would-be travellers to come armed with at least a couple of passport-sized photos, photocopies of your airline ticket, proof of health insurance and confirmation of your accommodation, such as a hotel booking covering at least the first night(s) of a trip. An absolute minimum of five working days should be allowed for a visa application to be processed, but this varies between embassies. Applicants for a business visa will need a formal invitation letter from their company plus the above-mentioned documentation.

If you're in the area, it is usually easier and cheaper to obtain a visa from a Gabonese embassy in one of its neighbouring countries; Gabonese embassies or consulates can be found in Yaoundé (Cameroon), Brazzaville (Republic of the Congo), Malabo and Bata (Equatorial Guinea) and São Tomé (São Tomé and Príncipe). Visas were not available at land borders as of 2019, and Gabonese immigration at such borders was demanding a valid hotel reservation in order to enter (and phoning the hotel to check!). Rather perplexingly, the booking can be made with a hotel in Libreville and dated for when you expect to reach the capital.

Once in Gabon, visa extensions (usually up to three months) can be arranged at the Direction Générale de la Documentation et de l'Immigration (Directorate General of Documentation and Immigration; DGDI; often known by its former acronym CEDOC – after Centre de la documentation; Zone Industrielle d'Oloumi, Libreville; ✆ 01 76 24 24/01 76 00 24; w dgdi.ga), but in the first instance it might be advisable to talk to a travel agent.

Please note that after the UK leaves the European Union, documentation requirements for UK citizens may change. Check before travelling.

EMBASSIES

Comprehensive lists of embassies and consulates found in Gabon are available at w embassypages.com/gabon and w dgdi.ga/representations-du-gabon (in French). If you're travelling onwards from Gabon, you may need to visit one of the below-listed regional embassies or high commissions in Libreville for visa purposes.

❸ Angola [78 B3] av Houphouët Boigny, Trois Quartiers; ✆ 01 73 04 26/01 73 84 44; e ncosmefr@yahoo.fr

❸ Cameroon [78 C3] opposite Université Omar Bongo, bd Président Léon Mba; ✆ 01 73 28 00/01 73 82 70; e ambacamgabon@yahoo.fr

❸ Congo (Democratic Republic) [78 B3] rue André Minsta, Batterie IV; ✆ 01 73 11 61/01 73 64 70; e ambardcgabon@yahoo.fr

❸ Congo (Republic) [78 B3] rue Kringer, Batterie IV; ✆ 01 44 68 62/01 73 29 06; e ambacobrazzalibreville@yahoo.fr;

w ambacongogabon.wordpress.com. There is also a consulate in Franceville (opposite Hôtel Masuku; ☎ 01 67 17 39; e consulatcgfcv@gmail.com).
ⓔ Equatorial Guinea [78 B2] Centre de Tris Postaux, Charbonnages; ☎ 01 44 18 32; e embargega@yahoo.fr. There is also a consulate in Oyem [map, page 216] m 04 33 59 53.

ⓔ Nigeria [78 C3] opposite Université Omar Bongo, bd Président Léon Mba; ☎ 01 73 03 22/01 73 22 03; e nigembassygabon@yahoo.co.uk
ⓔ São Tomé & Príncipe [91 A2] next to Cour Constitutionnelle, bd de l'Indépendance; ☎ 01 72 15 27; f embaixadardstp. librevillegabao

GETTING THERE AND AWAY

BY AIR For all intents and purposes, Gabon has only one international airport, Léon Mba International Airport in Libreville (page 81). Port-Gentil's airport can technically handle international flights, but at the time of writing this was limited to a twice-weekly connection to Pointe-Noire in the Republic of the Congo with Equaflight (page 120). There are also international connections between Franceville and Brazzaville, also in the Republic of the Congo, on a similar schedule with Afrijet (page 180).

To fly direct to Libreville from Europe, your options are basically Air France from Paris, or Turkish Airlines from Istanbul. The direct flight time from Paris is about 7 hours. Other easy connections include flying with Ethiopian Airlines via Addis Ababa, Royal Air Maroc via Casablanca, or Rwandair via Kigali. Flights are not known for being especially cheap, but it's often possible to fly from Europe for under €700 return, depending on the city of departure.

There are no direct connections **from North America**, so you'll have to transfer in via one of the above-mentioned cities.

There are regular flights to Libreville **from other African countries**, including Benin, Cameroon, Congo (Republic and Democratic Republic), Ivory Coast, Equatorial Guinea, Ethiopia, Kenya, Nigeria, Rwanda, Togo, and São Tomé and Príncipe. For more information on airlines that serve Libreville, see page 82.

There are plans to replace Léon Mba International with a new airport near Nkok, about 30km east of central Libreville along the N1. The idea seemed to get a new lease of life in 2018, when GSEZ Airports (a subsidiary of Olam Gabon, the largest private sector employer in the country) was awarded a 50-year construction and management contract for the new airport, which will have capacity for five million passengers annually. Various opening dates have been proposed, but it seems unlikely it will be ready before 2022 at the earliest. For updates, see w bradtupdates.com/gabon.

BY LAND If you plan to enter Gabon overland you'll firstly need to acquire a visa in either a neighbouring country or your home country as, at the time of writing, visas weren't available at land borders (see opposite). The most popular route for overlanders involves entering Gabon from the north and crossing the Ntem River, which forms a natural border with **Cameroon.** There are two crossings in the northwest corner of Woleu-Ntem province, with the most popular being at the north end of the N2 between Eboro (Gabon) and Abang-Minko (Cameroon). Alternatively, there is a lesser-used but still reasonably busy crossing between Meyo-Kye (Gabon) and Kye-Ossi (Cameroon). Both crossings are 25–30km away from Bitam, which is reachable on surfaced roads. Your passport, visa and hotel booking will be examined at the border checkpoint, but you must formalise your stay with a passport stamp from immigration in Bitam. (If you're leaving Gabon via this route, don't forget to get your exit stamp from the same immigration office.) Border formalities in Cameroon are carried out in Ambam. There is also a remote and little-used crossing 20km north of Minvoul between Nsak (Gabon) and Aboulou (Cameroon).

3

Arriving from **Republic of the Congo**, there are a few options. The most popular route starts from the south in Dolisie (Congo) and heads north for 230 (mostly unsurfaced) kilometres before crossing into Gabon over the Ngounié River, where the two countries both have checkpoints. It's a further 50km from here to reach the immigration office and the resumption of tarmac road at Ndendé. There's also a remote crossing near Moulengui Binza to the south of Tchibanga, but we've had no reports as to its condition; immigration formalities for this route are conducted in Tchibanga. Remoter still, there's a crossing near Gabon's southernmost point at Ndindi (with formalities conducted in Mayumba).

To the east, near Franceville, there's a new tarmac road from Congo into Gabon. Opened in 2014, it's still not marked on most maps, but it begins at Congo's N2 trunk road at Obouya, near Oyo, and continues some 200km through Congo's Cuvette Department, entering Gabon around 30km east of Léconi. There's another remote crossing south of Franceville, between Mbinda (Congo) and Lekoko (Gabon), from where it's possible to connect to the Chemin de fer Congo-Océan (Congo-Ocean Railway) that connects Mbinda to Pointe-Noire and Brazzaville. It was supposedly running about once a week at the time of writing; be prepared for a rough ride. Immigration formalities are conducted in Bakoumba if using this route.

To the north, in Ogooué-Ivindo, the roads entering Gabon at Ékata or Mazingo (both near Mékambo) are in deplorable shape, with the Mazingo route reportedly completely impassable. Thus, this is not a practical route across the border unless you've got your own 4×4 and some considerable skills. (See the following trip report if you think we're being overdramatic: w bit.ly/gabon-ekata.) If you do attempt this route, immigration formalities are done in Mékambo.

Entering Gabon from **Equatorial Guinea**, there's a surfaced road from Ebebiyín to Bitam (25km) and a laterite route between Mongomo and Oyem (40km). There's public transport on both routes, but while foreigners may be able to exit Equatorial Guinea into Gabon at these crossings, they were not allowed to do the reverse at the time of writing. The same goes for the river border between Cogo (Equatorial Guinea) and Cocobeach (Gabon). For updates on this, check w bradtupdates.com/gabon.

BY SEA There are a few boats that regularly take passengers between Port Môle in Libreville and other regional ports. Société Hawa (m 06 19 50 09/04 83 21 44/06 75 43 09) runs large passenger boats to Douala (Cameroon), Calabar (Nigeria), Cotonou (Benin) and Lomé (Togo). Schedules change, so call or visit their bureau at Port Môle for upcoming departures.

Otherwise, freight boats bound for Libreville will sometimes take paying passengers. These usually leave from Bata (Equatorial Guinea), Abidjan (Ivory Coast), São Tomé and, most frequently of all, Douala (Cameroon). Crossings are irregular and you would need to make enquiries at the boats docked at the ports and negotiate with the captain. Prepare for a rough ride and take more food and drink than you think you will need.

Your only other option for getting to Gabon by water is with a pirogue (5,000CFA) from Cogo in Equatorial Guinea, which sits 15km up the Muni River from Cocobeach in Gabon.

HEALTH *with Dr Felicity Nicholson*

Gabon's medical facilities are relatively good. Most hospitals are public, but in the main cities (Libreville, Port-Gentil and Franceville) there are some good private clinics. The best known is without doubt Lambaréné's Albert Schweitzer Hospital (page 143), but better equipped to deal with emergencies are Port-Gentil's Clinique Mandji (page 125) or Libreville's Polyclinique El-Rapha Clinique (page 102). Be aware that few doctors speak English. If you are not confident of your language level, you might want to enlist the help of someone to act as your translator. Note that consultation fees and laboratory tests are comparable to those in most Western countries. The US Embassy maintains a list of doctors here w ga.usembassy.gov/u-s-citizen-services/doctors.

Pharmacies are omnipresent in larger cities and towns and commonly required medicines such as broad-spectrum antibiotics are widely available throughout the region, as are malaria cures and prophylactics. If you are on any medication prior to departure, or you have specific needs relating to a known medical condition (for instance if you are allergic to bee stings or prone to attacks of asthma), then you are strongly advised to bring any related drugs and devices with you. Sadly, there is a problem with counterfeiting drugs in Africa, Gabon included, so while pharmacists will be selling medicines in good faith, you would be wise to carry anything that you know you will need with you.

PREPARATIONS Sensible preparation will go a long way to ensuring your trip goes smoothly. Particularly for first-time visitors to Africa, this includes a visit to a **travel clinic** to discuss matters such as vaccinations and malaria prevention. A list of current travel clinic websites worldwide is available on w istm.org. For other journey preparation information, consult w travelhealthpro.org.uk (UK) or w wwwnc.cdc.gov/travel (USA). Information about various medications may be found on w netdoctor.co.uk/travel. All advice found online should be used in conjunction with expert advice received prior to or during travel. The Bradt website now carries a page to help travellers prepare for their African trip, elaborating on most points raised below (w bradtguides.com/africahealth), but the following summary points are worth emphasising:

- Don't travel without comprehensive medical **travel insurance** that will fly you home or to another country in an emergency.
- Make sure all your **immunisations** are up to date. Proof of vaccination against yellow fever is needed for entry into Gabon, and you may be asked to show this at police checkpoints as well. It is unwise to travel in the tropics without being up to date with immunisation against measles, mumps and rubella (MMR), tetanus, polio and diphtheria (now given as an all-in-one vaccine, Revaxis), hepatitis A and typhoid. Immunisation against rabies, hepatitis B, and possibly TB may also be recommended.
- The biggest health threat is **malaria**. There is no vaccine against this mosquito-borne disease, but a variety of preventative drugs is available, including mefloquine, atovaquone/proguanil (Malarone) and the antibiotic doxycycline. Malarone and doxycycline need only be started two days before entering Gabon, but mefloquine should be started two to three weeks before. Doxycycline and mefloquine need to be taken for four weeks after the trip and Malarone for seven days. It is as important to complete the course as it is to take it before and during the trip. The most suitable choice of drug varies depending on the individual (their health and age) and the country in which they are travelling, so visit your GP or a specialist travel clinic for medical advice. If you will be spending a long time in Africa, and expect to visit remote areas, be aware that no preventative drug is 100% effective, so carry a cure too. It is also worth noting that no homeopathic prophylactic for malaria exists, nor can any traveller acquire effective resistance to malaria. Those who don't make use of preventative drugs risk their life in a manner that is both foolish and unnecessary.

- Though advised for everyone, a **pre-exposure rabies vaccination**, involving three doses taken over 21–8 days, is particularly important if you intend to have contact with animals, or are likely to be 24 hours away from medical help. If time is short, a more rapid course of three injections can be done over a week, but this schedule requires an additional booster after a year to complete the primary course.
- Anybody travelling away from major centres should carry a **personal first-aid kit**. Contents might include a good drying antiseptic (eg: iodine or potassium permanganate), plasters, suncream, insect repellent, aspirin or paracetamol, antifungal cream (eg: Canesten), ciprofloxacin or norfloxacin (for severe diarrhoea), antibiotic eye drops, tweezers, condoms or femidoms, a digital thermometer and a needle-and-syringe kit with accompanying letter from a healthcare professional.
- Bring any **drugs or devices relating to known medical conditions** with you. That applies both to those who are on medication prior to departure, and those who are, for instance, allergic to bee stings or are prone to attacks of asthma. Carry a copy of your prescription and a letter from your GP explaining why you need the medication.
- Prolonged immobility on long-haul flights can result in **deep vein thrombosis (DVT)**, which can be dangerous if the clot travels to the lungs to cause pulmonary embolus. The risk increases with age, and is higher in obese or pregnant travellers, heavy smokers, those taller than 6ft/1.8m or shorter than 5ft/1.5m, and anybody with a history of clots, recent major operation or varicose veins surgery, cancer, a stroke or heart disease. If any of these criteria apply, consult a doctor before you travel.

COMMON MEDICAL PROBLEMS

Malaria This potentially fatal disease is widespread in low-lying tropical parts of Africa, a category that includes all of Gabon; the risk is heightened in remote areas including the national parks. While the risk of transmission is highest in the rainy season, it is present throughout the year. Since no malaria prophylactic is 100% effective, one should take all reasonable precautions against being bitten by the nocturnal *Anopheles* mosquitoes that transmit the disease (see box, opposite). Malaria usually manifests within two weeks of transmission, but it can be as little as seven days and anything up to a year. Any fever occurring after seven days should be considered as malaria until proven otherwise. Symptoms typically include a rapid rise in temperature (over 38°C), and any combination of a headache, flu-like aches and pains, a general sense of disorientation, and possibly even nausea and diarrhoea. The earlier malaria is detected, the better it usually responds to treatment. So if you display possible symptoms, get to a doctor or clinic immediately (in the UK, go to Accident and Emergency and say that you have been to Africa). A simple test, available at even the most rural clinic in Africa, is usually adequate to determine whether you have malaria. You need three negative tests on three consecutive days to be sure it is not the disease. And while experts differ on the question of self-diagnosis and self-treatment, the reality is that if you think you have malaria and are not within easy reach of a doctor, it would be wise to start treatment.

Travellers' diarrhoea Travelling in Gabon carries a fairly high risk of getting a dose of travellers' diarrhoea; perhaps half of all visitors will suffer and the newer you are to exotic travel, the more likely you will be to get it. Rule one in avoiding diarrhoea and other sanitation-related diseases is to wash your hands regularly, particularly before snacks and meals. As for what food you can safely eat, a useful

The *Anopheles* mosquitoes that spread malaria are active at dusk and after dark. Most bites can thus be avoided by covering up at night. This means donning a long-sleeved shirt, trousers and socks from around 30 minutes before dusk until you retire to bed, and applying a DEET-based insect repellent to any exposed flesh. It is best to sleep under a net, or in an air-conditioned room, though burning a mosquito coil and/or sleeping under a fan will also reduce (though not entirely eliminate) bites. Travel clinics usually sell a good range of nets and repellents, as well as Permethrin treatment kits, which will render even the tattiest net a lot more protective, and helps prevent mosquitoes from biting through a net when you roll against it. These measures will also do much to reduce exposure to other nocturnal biters. Bear in mind, too, that most flying insects are attracted to light: leaving a lamp standing near a tent opening or a light on in a poorly screened hotel room will greatly increase the insect presence in your sleeping quarters.

It is also advisable to think about avoiding bites when walking in the countryside by day, especially in wetland habitats, which often teem with diurnal mosquitoes. Wear a long, loose shirt and trousers, preferably 100% cotton, as well as proper walking or hiking shoes with heavy socks (the ankle is particularly vulnerable to bites), and apply a DEET-based insect repellent to any exposed skin.

maxim is: PEEL IT, BOIL IT, COOK IT OR FORGET IT. This means that fruit you have washed and peeled yourself, and hot foods, should be safe but raw foods, cold cooked foods, salads, fruit salads that have been prepared by others, ice cream and ice are all risky, and foods kept lukewarm in hotel buffets are often dangerous. That said, plenty of travellers and expatriates enjoy fruit and vegetables, so do keep a sense of perspective: food served in a fairly decent hotel in a large town or a place frequented by expatriates is likely to be safe.

Bilharzia Also known as schistosomiasis, bilharzia is an unpleasant parasitic disease transmitted by freshwater snails most often associated with reedy shores where there is lots of water weed. It cannot be caught in hotel swimming pools or the ocean, but should be assumed to be present in any freshwater river pond, lake or similar habitat, even those advertised as 'bilharzia free'. The most risky shores will be within 200m of villages or other places where infected people use water, wash clothes, etc. Ideally, however, you should avoid swimming in any fresh water other than an artificial pool. If you do swim, you'll reduce the risk by applying DEET insect repellent first, staying in the water for under 10 minutes, and drying off vigorously with a towel. Bilharzia is often asymptomatic in its early stages, but some people experience an intense immune reaction, including fever, cough, abdominal pain and an itchy rash, around four to six weeks after infection. Later symptoms vary but often include a general feeling of tiredness and lethargy. Bilharzia is difficult to diagnose, but it can be tested for at specialist travel clinics, ideally at least six weeks after likely exposure. Fortunately, it is easy to treat at present.

Rabies This deadly disease can be carried by any mammal and is usually transmitted to humans via a bite or a scratch that breaks the skin. In particular, beware the village dogs and small monkeys habituated to people, but assume that

Practical Information   HEALTH

3

any mammal that bites or scratches you, or even licks you, might be rabid even if it looks healthy. First, scrub the wound with soap under a running tap or while pouring water from a jug for a good 10–15 minutes, then pour on a strong iodine or alcohol solution, which will guard against infections and might reduce the risk of the rabies virus entering the body. Having a pre-exposure course of vaccine changes the treatment that you need after an exposure and makes it more likely that you can be treated in Gabon. If you have not had the rabies vaccine then post-exposure treatment involves four doses of vaccine and a preformed antibody called rabies immunoglobulin (RIG). RIG is unlikely to be found in Gabon so you will need to evacuate as soon as you can. Death from rabies is probably one of the worst ways to go, and once you show symptoms it is too late to do anything – the mortality rate is virtually 100%.

Tetanus Tetanus is caught through deep dirty wounds, including animal bites, so ensure that such wounds are thoroughly cleaned. Immunisation protects for ten years, provided that you don't have an overwhelming number of tetanus bacteria on board. If you haven't had a tetanus shot in ten years, or you are unsure, get a booster immediately.

HIV/AIDS Rates of HIV/AIDS infection are high in most parts of Africa (some 3% of Gabon's population aged between 15 and 49 is infected with the HIV virus), and other sexually transmitted diseases are rife. Condoms (or femidoms) greatly reduce the risk of transmission.

Tick bites African ticks are not the rampant disease transmitters they are in the Americas, but they may spread tick-bite fever and a few dangerous rarities in Gabon. Ticks should ideally be removed complete, and as soon as possible, to reduce the chance of infection. You can use special tick tweezers, which can be bought in good travel shops, or failing this with your fingernails, grasping the tick as close to your body as possible, and pulling it away steadily and firmly at right angles to your skin without jerking or twisting. Irritants (eg: Olbas oil) or lit cigarettes are to be discouraged since they can cause the ticks to regurgitate and therefore increase the risk of disease. Once the tick is removed, if possible douse the wound with alcohol (any spirit will do), soap and water, or iodine. If you are travelling with small children, remember to check their heads, and particularly behind the ears, for ticks. Spreading redness around the bite and/or fever and/or aching joints after a tick bite imply that you have an infection that requires antibiotic treatment. In this case seek medical advice.

Zika virus Zika virus is a flavivirus similar to dengue and is spread by the day-biting *Aedes* mosquito. All travellers to countries where Zika virus is reported, including Gabon, are at risk of infection. The longer you spend in these countries, the more at risk you will be. The infection is often asymptomatic but, in those with symptoms, the disease is usually mild, with an itchy rash, fever, joint pains and red, sore eyes. Severe disease is uncommon. Travellers are advised to use DEET-based repellents during the daytime on all exposed skin. In areas where mosquitoes are particularly prevalent, then covering up and using a permethrin spray on clothing is also advised.

Pregnant women need to discuss their travel plans with healthcare professionals and should, wherever possible, cancel the trip. Women wishing to become pregnant should use barrier methods of contraception while travelling, and for two months after. If travelling with their partners, barrier precautions need to be used during the trip and for three months after leaving.

Skin infections Any mosquito bite or small nick is an opportunity for a skin infection in warm, humid climates, so clean and cover even the slightest wound in a good drying antiseptic such as dilute iodine, potassium permanganate or crystal (or gentian) violet. One of these should be available in most towns.

Prickly heat, most likely to be contracted at the humid coast, is a fine pimply rash that can be alleviated by cool showers, dabbing (not rubbing) dry and talc, and sleeping naked under a fan or in an air-conditioned room. Fungal infections also get a hold easily in hot, moist climates, so wear 100% cotton socks and underwear and shower frequently.

Eye problems Bacterial conjunctivitis (pink eye) is a common infection in Africa, particularly for people who wear contact lenses. Symptoms are sore, gritty eyelids that often stick closed in the mornings. Sufferers will need treatment with antibiotic drops or ointment. Lesser eye irritations should settle with bathing in salt water and keeping the eyes shaded. If an insect flies into your eye, extract it with great care, ensuring you do not crush or damage it, otherwise you may get a nastily inflamed eye from toxins secreted by the creature.

Sunstroke and dehydration Overexposure to the sun can lead to short-term sunburn or sunstroke, and increases the long-term risk of skin cancer. Wear a T-shirt and waterproof suncream when swimming. On safari or walking in the direct sun, cover up with long, loose clothes, wear a hat and use sunscreen. The glare and the dust can be hard on the eyes, so bring UV-protecting sunglasses. A less direct effect of the tropical heat is dehydration, so drink more fluids than you would at home.

Other insect-borne diseases Although malaria is the insect-borne disease that attracts the most attention in Africa, and rightly so, there are also others, most of them too uncommon to be a significant concern to short-stay travellers. These include dengue fever and other arboviruses (spread by day-biting mosquitoes), sleeping sickness (tsetse flies) and river blindness (blackflies). Bearing this in mind, however, it is clearly sensible, and makes for a more pleasant trip, to avoid insect bites as far as possible (see box, page 57).

Two nasty (though relatively harmless) **flesh-eating insects** associated with tropical Africa are *tumbu* or *putsi* flies – which lay eggs, often on drying laundry, that hatch and bury themselves under the skin when they come into contact with humans – and jiggers, which latch on to bare feet and set up home, usually at the side of a toenail, where they cause a painful boil-like swelling. Drying laundry indoors and wearing shoes are the best way to deter this pair of flesh-eaters. Symptoms and treatment of all these afflictions are described in greater detail on Bradt's website (**w** bradtguides.com/africahealth).

Ebola The last outbreak of the virus in Gabon occurred in 2001. However, it is worth keeping up to date on regions that have outbreaks, and to avoid eating bushmeat or handling dead animals during your travels.

SAFETY

Although Gabon is, by and large, a safe country in which few travellers experience any problems, it doesn't hurt to remain cautious and be prepared for potential dangers.

Contrary to what you might expect, tropical disease, most notably malaria, poses the biggest safety threat at any time of year (page 56).

Serious **crime**, such as muggings and hold-ups, are comparatively rare, but travellers should guard against petty crime. As is the case anywhere in the world, pickpocketing and bag snatching can be a problem in busy areas like markets, buses and train stations. It's also worth being cautious in poorer areas and on isolated beaches, particularly around Libreville, and avoid walking on any beach at night. If you're headed to any of these places, it's best to take a few sensible precautions: keeping valuables safely stashed or – better yet – not bringing them at all. For the essentials you *are* carrying, simply work to make them less accessible – think money belt and front (buttoned) pockets.

Outside of Libreville and Port-Gentil, expect **attention** from men and women alike – many locals will simply be curious about who you are, where you come from, where you are going and, above all, why you are alone.

Taxis in Gabonese cities operate like public transport and are the easiest and most common way of getting around town, picking up passengers heading in the same direction until the car is full. Take taxis in the bigger towns and cities rather than walk and be sure to use authorised taxis only. The driver's ID should be hanging from the rear-view mirror. After dark it is better to avoid share taxis and pay for a private ride (*une course*). It's even safer to book a taxi through a restaurant or hotel.

Road travel in Gabon can be challenging and even dangerous. Owing to the lethal combination of hazardous road conditions and risky driving, accidents are common. You can lessen risks by avoiding reckless and/or drunken drivers, ill-maintained vehicles and travelling by road at night.

Carry your passport with you at all times, particularly when travelling. Random controls are a feature of life in Gabon and foreigners can be a lucrative target. You may even hear some unpleasant stories of nights spent in jails for those without papers. These may not be usual (or may not even be true), but it's simply not worth the risk.

As soon as you leave or enter a town by road, you will encounter several **checkpoints**. Firstly, passengers will often have their identification checked, and visitors will be asked to show their passport, visa and yellow fever certificate (or some combination of the three), so have these documents ready and in order. Secondly, the police will verify that all vehicles have a fire extinguisher and first-aid kit, and that all drivers have a licence, registration and proof of insurance. Often a quick look will suffice, but some officials tend to carry out a more detailed search, sometimes searching for a pretext in which to solicit a bribe. Traveller reports on this are mixed – some find the checkpoints chronically corrupt and an interminable hassle, while others seem to breeze through with a bit of better luck. Since 2011, police officers have been required to wear a badge with an identity number to aid citizens seeking to report extortion attempts. As anywhere, make sure you and your vehicle's paperwork are in order, stay calm, polite and smiling, and you'll be waved through – at some point.

Ecotourism is generally safe; however, be sure to use reputable guides who know the forest or rivers well, as fake guides posing as experts put their clients' (and their own) lives in danger. Do not venture away from your organised tour group.

In the unlucky event that something happens, don't expect miracles from the police: their response is often slow. They may do little or nothing to help, or may even request a payment to listen to you. For **police assistance**, call ❯ 01 76 55 85 in Libreville and ❯ 07 36 22 25 in Port-Gentil. If you need **emergency medical assistance** during your trip, dial ❯ 1300 or ❯ 1399, pray that somebody will pick up the phone, and ask for an ambulance.

It's essential to organise comprehensive **travel insurance** that covers medical complications, including an emergency flight home. The cost of travel insurance is based on a number of factors such as the type of cover requested, the age of the insured, the destination of travel, length of stay and any pre-existing medical conditions. A wide range of policies are available so shop around. Bear in mind that you may have to pay for medical treatment on the spot (and that this can be very expensive in Gabon) and claim later, so keep all documentation.

WOMEN TRAVELLERS Travelling alone in Gabon does not pose any particular security problems for women; although, as anywhere in the world, there are always *drageurs* (scoundrels) on the prowl.

Generally speaking, Gabonese men may try to flirt, but usually a (fictitious) boyfriend or husband does the trick in losing their attention. And the extra attention you may receive will tend to be more annoying than dangerous. It's worth noting that in Gabon, revealing dress will increase the amount of this type of attention you receive.

GAY TRAVELLERS In December 2008, Gabon co-sponsored and signed the non-binding UN declaration on sexual orientation and gender identity, calling for the global decriminalisation of homosexuality – one of only six African countries to do so. Homosexuality is not explicitly illegal (in contrast to most African countries) but is definitely frowned upon. Discrimination is a problem and many people turn away from gay individuals who are open about their sexual identity. Predictably, you won't find a vibrant gay scene here.

TRAVELLING WITH A DISABILITY Gabon has no infrastructure that suits visitors with disabilities. There are no laws for providing access to transportation, buildings or services, and few buildings in the main cities have disabled access. Only the more luxurious buildings have lifts. Staff at hotels are generally not used to taking care of visitors with specific needs, and disability awareness still has some way to go.

TRAVELLING WITH CHILDREN The Gabonese love children and will go out of their way to help you get by, but pushchairs are rare and you may have difficulty manoeuvring them in and out of buildings and along non-existent pavements and/or dirt roads. Baby milk is widely available, as are nappies, although for some mysterious reason the quality may be lower than that which the same brand offers at home. For older kids, Gabon's beaches and national parks offer countless exciting things to do. Check with tour operators where and when to go, as the less-visited parks may be a bit too rough and some excursions may have age limits.

INFORMATION ON TRAVELLING WITH A DISABILITY

The UK's **gov.uk** website (w gov.uk/guidance/foreign-travel-for-disabled-people) provides general advice and practical information for people with disabilities preparing for overseas travel. **Accessible Journeys** (w disabilitytravel.com) is a comprehensive US site written by wheelchair users who have been researching wheelchair-accessible travel full-time since 1985. There are many tips and useful contacts (including lists of travel agents on request) for slow walkers, wheelchair travellers and their families, plus informative articles, including pieces on disabled travelling worldwide. The company also organises group tours. **Global Access News** (w globalaccessnews.com/index.htm) provides general travel information, reviews and tips for travelling with a disability. The **Society for Accessible Travel and Hospitality** (w sath.org) also provides some general information.

Children can also be more vulnerable to some health risks, such as malaria, so ensure you are well prepared and that you take all medical precautions (page 55).

OTHER SAFETY CONCERNS

Wild animals Don't confuse habituation with domestication. Most wildlife in Africa is genuinely wild, and widespread species such as hippo might attack a person given the right set of circumstances. Such attacks are rare, however, and they almost always stem from a combination of poor judgement and poorer luck. A few rules of thumb: never approach potentially dangerous wildlife on foot except in the company of a trustworthy guide; never swim in lakes or rivers without first seeking local advice about the presence of crocodile or hippo; never get between a hippo and water; and never leave food (particularly meat or fruit) in the tent where you'll sleep.

Snake and other bites Snakes are very secretive and bites are a genuine rarity, but certain spiders and scorpions can also deliver nasty bites. In all cases, the risk is minimised by wearing closed shoes and trousers when walking in the bush, and watching where you put your hands and feet, especially in rocky areas or when gathering firewood. Only a small fraction of snakebites deliver enough venom to be life-threatening, but it is important to keep the victim calm and inactive, and to seek urgent medical attention.

WHAT TO TAKE

The inescapable conundrum of packing is not to over-pack and yet not to leave behind essential items that you won't be able to find on the road. The type of trip you are intending to take will obviously determine how you distinguish between what is essential and what is a luxury. If you are embarking on an organised trip, you probably needn't share the backpacker's overriding concern about having to walk long distances or struggle in and out of public transport laden with luggage. That said, you will still face a weight restriction if your trip involves a flight in a privately chartered plane at any point, usually of 15kg. Only those travelling in their own vehicle or who have a base where they can store items have the flexibility to bring the kitchen sink.

Getting the balance right requires careful planning. The classic 'novice traveller' trap is to fill a 75-litre rucksack and a daypack. Not only will you struggle in the heat, feel overburdened and look foolish, but to add insult to injury, you'll probably only use about a third of what you've packed. The trick is not to pack in a rush and not to think you have to take everything with you. Clothes can be washed, and everyday items replenished or substituted, not to mention that having room for impulse purchases is part of the travel experience. If in doubt, leave it out – travelling light is the most liberating. Of course, if you have camera equipment or require more in the way of a wardrobe, being this ruthless may not be possible.

Campers will need a large, sturdy rucksack, preferably with an internal frame. You'll be grateful for a second bag if there are any non-camping sections of the trip when heavy equipment can be temporarily offloaded somewhere that you are returning to. Non-campers on a tight budget may wish to pack a mosquito net and sheet sleeping bag, which can make a less-than-sparkling room more appealing.

Whatever luggage you decide on in the end, it's a good idea to use a padlock. Bags can of course be slashed or stolen, but a lock is at least some kind of deterrent.

CLOTHING Given the high temperatures and humidity throughout the year, cotton is the best fabric to wear. Lightweight, short-sleeved shirts and loose-fitting trousers or flowing skirts make the most comfortable outfits. Outside of the forest, people make an effort with their appearance, so it's worth taking at least one nice outfit. Most urban Gabonese are quite used to the presence of foreigners and easily overlook their differences when it comes to dress, but making an effort to keep skirts and shorts at knee length or below would certainly not be remiss.

For **trekking** in the forest, long-sleeved shirts and trousers are a must in order to avoid scratches and bites. So as not to scare off wildlife, browns and khakis should be worn on safari, and white should be avoided. Blue attracts tsetse flies so isn't recommended either. Gaiters will keep you dry-ish when crossing streams and are also excellent protection against biting ants and ticks. Some hikers wear gardening gloves for protection against thorny trees or vines.

Other clothing essentials, irrespective of the season, are a lightweight raincoat or poncho, a floppy hat, swimwear and sunglasses. It's also worth having at least one sweatshirt or fleece, as the air conditioning can be fierce on buses and trains, and in some tourist hotels and restaurants.

FOOTWEAR Boots are essential for forest trekking or any extended walk, but make sure they are lightweight. This is really important as the heat makes heavy footwear unbearable. Breathable canvas is therefore preferable to leather. Wear two thin pairs of socks and ensure your boots are well worn in if you want any reasonable hope of avoiding blisters. The forest floor is uneven and wet, so your boots must also give you sufficient ankle support and preferably be waterproof. Even waterproof boots, however, will not keep you dry when wading through streams or caught in a torrential tropical downpour. For everyday footwear, take trainers or sandals. Flip-flops can be easily bought.

CAMPING EQUIPMENT Although camping is not allowed in any protected areas, there's nothing to stop you pitching a tent elsewhere – though be sure to introduce yourself and get permission from the chief if you want to camp in or near a village. Some of the supplies you might need, such as mosquito nets, can be bought in Libreville, but you shouldn't bank on finding everything you need here. Some items to consider bringing include a GPS (page 64), Leatherman tool, roll mat, sleeping bag, tin plate, cutlery and mug, firelighters, and of course a lightweight mosquito-proof tent.

OTHER USEFUL ITEMS As far as documentation goes, it's worth having a few photocopies of all your important paperwork, especially of the relevant pages of your passport; this can make getting a replacement that much easier should you need to. Leave copies of everything with a couple of people back home and hide a couple more in the various pouches and pockets around your luggage.

Binoculars are essential for watching birds and monkeys, although if you have a long lens on your camera you could try making do with that instead. Compact 7×21 binoculars weigh very little and fit neatly into a pocket.

Other crucial items are a mobile phone, powerful torch (preferably a head torch), basic sewing kit, towel, water bottle, penknife, first-aid kit (page 56) and a handful of energy bars. For electrics, you may need a European-style 220v adapter. You may want to include a comprehensive wildlife guide in your reading material (page 227). Take several strong bin liners; these will keep your kit dry when the skies open.

If you are going to be hiring and driving, cycling or otherwise **going it alone**, you should add the following to your list of essentials: compass, whistle, electrical insulation tape for all-purpose repairs, biodegradable washing powder, shower gel, and a country or regional map, for example the 1:1,000,000 map of Gabon, complete with a 1:50,000 inset of Libreville, published by the Institut Geographique National (IGN). (The map was last revised and reprinted in 2009.) Given that no map of Gabon is entirely reliable, anyone intending to head anywhere really remote might want to invest in a **hand-held GPS** navigation system. This battery-powered device can tell you your latitude, longitude and elevation to within 100m anywhere in the world by corresponding with satellites. The downside is that in order to do so it needs open, unobstructed access to the sky, which cannot be relied upon if you are in the jungle. In the forest a GPS should be used in conjunction with, not instead of, a guide.

The mobile app **Maps.Me** (w maps.me) lets you download maps that are accessible offline, whether or not you have mobile signal; it has reasonably good coverage of Gabon, based on OpenStreetMap (w openstreetmap.org) data.

Your bare **health essentials** should include water-purifying tablets, insect repellent and antihistamine tablets in case of insect bites and stings. You may also consider a blister-treatment kit in this category. Suncream, lip balm and toilet roll are also key. Women should bear in mind that tampons and sanitary pads are not readily available outside the main towns. For more details of what to include in your medical kit, see page 56.

MONEY AND BUDGETING

The unit of currency in Gabon is the Central African **CFA franc**, which originally stood for Colonies Françaises d'Afrique but has long since been changed to Communauté Financière Africaine. The CFA franc is issued by the Banque des États de l'Afrique Centrale (Bank of Central African States) and is the currency in the following countries: Gabon, Cameroon, Chad, Equatorial Guinea, Congo (Republic) and the Central African Republic. One CFA divides into 100 centimes, and notes come in denominations of 10,000, 5,000, 2,000, 1,000 and 500CFA. The CFA was tied to the French franc at a guaranteed rate from the 1940s and has been fixed to the euro at a rate of €1 to 655.957CFA since 1999. The CFA was trading at 597CFA to US$1 and 730CFA to £1 as of October 2019. Note that the Central African CFA franc is equivalent in value to the West African CFA franc, but the two are not interchangeably accepted.

ORGANISING YOUR FINANCES Bringing a credit card is the most straightforward and the safest means of getting local currency, but bear in mind the **ATM network** in Gabon can be thin on the ground. Indeed, the vast majority of Gabon's ATMs are in Libreville, and this still only totals around 100 in the whole city. BICIG, BGFI, Ecobank and UGB are all represented, along with a couple of others. We strongly recommend that you draw out enough cash in Libreville before setting out on any excursions or further travels; the ATM network upcountry is sparse and unreliable. We have listed ATM locations in each province in boxes at the beginning of each chapter – check these well in advance as some provinces don't have any at all! Credit cards are also generally accepted in the more upmarket hotels in Libreville, but can't be relied upon in other places. As in much of Africa, Visa is much more widely accepted (at businesses as well as ATMs) than Mastercard.

Additionally, be very careful to check your **bank statements** after using ATMs in Gabon; we were erroneously debited for several attempted withdrawals that the machines simply reported as declined.

If you're in a bind and need money wired to you, there are branches of **Western Union** in most major towns. This isn't cheap, but it's quick and secure. Money sent is received immediately, as long as you have identification, and a password and ten-digit number given to you by the sender.

Given the challenges above, it's critical to carry some **cash** as a backup. Euros are by far the most widely accepted foreign currency, and **exchanging** them into CFA is easily done – most medium-sized shops or supermarkets will be happy to do this for you, or will be able to point you to someone who can. As the exchange rate with the euro is fixed, there's limited opportunity to rip you off, but be sure to know the rate and count your bills carefully.

BUDGETING As for advice on how much money to take, any budget will obviously depend on how, where and how long you travel. You get more for your money in terms of facilities outside Libreville, where top hotels charge some of the highest rates in the world and good restaurants cost no less than in Rome or Paris. But even outside the capital, budget travellers should bank on spending at least 20,000CFA a day – for a spartan lifestyle, that is. For couples this amount may be a little less, as hotels usually charge per room instead of per person.

The most basic **accommodation** outside the capital will set you back as little as 6,000CFA a night, but plan on spending around twice that for a somewhat higher comfort level. A standard hotel with a private bathroom, a restaurant of some sort, and sometimes a few additional facilities will cost about 40,000CFA per room (single or double) per night.

Food and drink in Gabon are not cheap because virtually everything is imported. A meal in a simple restaurant might set you back less than 4,000CFA, while a two-course meal in a typical tourist restaurant will cost about 15,000CFA, plus an additional 1,500CFA per beer or 15,000CFA per bottle of wine. Throughout the country, a soft drink in a local bar or shop costs 500CFA and a 65cl beer 600–800CFA. A bottle of drinking water goes for the same price as a bottle of beer and many Gabonese prefer to spend their money on the latter. A baguette typically costs 100CFA at a local bakery, while a croissant or pain au chocolat sets you back 600CFA.

If you intend to move around, you will need to take into account **transport costs**. Contrary to what you might expect, petrol isn't cheap in Gabon. Count on 700CFA a litre. Diesel is slightly cheaper at 670CFA a litre. See page 66 for an idea of prices on public transport.

Just as elsewhere in Africa, it's on **safari** that the money really goes. Allow in the region of 100,000–300,000CFA per day.

If you are spending all or most of your time on an **organised tour**, you will have had to pay in advance for everything except the occasional meal and tips. Make sure you know exactly what is and isn't covered.

GETTING AROUND

Getting from place to place in Gabon can be difficult, time-consuming and expensive; more often than not, it's all three. Despite this, it can also be a fantastic way to see the country and meet its people.

BY AIR Flight schedules change frequently and with little notice and airlines should be contacted directly for the most up-to-date information. They usually have offices in town as well as in the airports. Flying around Gabon isn't cheap. Depending on the distance and the airline, a one-way trip can cost 70,000–150,000CFA and a return flight will be double that.

At the time of writing, there were three airline companies serving the interior, of which Afrijet is by far the most reliable.

✈ **Afrijet** ☎ 02 00 90 01/02 29 93 93; w flyafrijet. online; **f** afrijet. The most reliable & often the cheapest operator, Afrijet offers online booking & flies between Libreville, Port-Gentil & Franceville, as well as Yaoundé & Douala (Cameroon), Brazzaville & Pointe-Noire (Republic of the Congo), & São Tomé. See ad, 3rd colour section.

✈ **La Nationale** Nationale Regionale Transport (NRT) ☎ 06 66 90 99/77/79; e infos@nrtgabon. org; **f** NationaleRegionaleTransport. Flies between Libreville, Franceville, Port-Gentil & Oyem.

✈ **Tropical Air Gabon** ☎ 02 28 28 67/8; w tropicalair.ga; **f** Tropicalairgabon. New operator with flights from Libreville to Franceville, Port-Gentil & Oyem.

If you have the funds, **hiring your own light aircraft** will give you even greater flexibility. It's expensive, but the views are amazing – that is, unless weather conditions force the pilot to fly above the clouds. Seeing the rainforest from 10 to 100m above is much more than a means of getting to your destination, it is an attraction in itself. Make enquiries with Afrijet (see above) or any of the tour operators listed on pages 50 and 88.

BY RAIL Gabon's only railway, the Transgabonais (Trans-Gabon Railway), bisects the country east–west, running from Libreville through over 20 stations to its terminus, Franceville. It plays a crucial role in the country's economy and in linking the capital to rural areas. The railroad is administered by the Société d'Exploitation du Transgabonais (SETRAG; m 06 99 82 44; **f** setrag.gabon.officiel).

SETRAG runs two types of train. The **Train Omnibus l'Equateur** links all 21 stations between Libreville and Franceville; the **Train Express Trans-Ogooué** stops only in Ndjolé, Lopé, Booué, Ivindo, Lastoursville and Moanda. The cheaper (and slower) Omnibus leaves Libreville on Tuesdays, Thursdays and Sundays, and the faster (and more expensive) Express departs on Mondays, Wednesdays and Fridays. According to the timetable, all trains depart at 18.50 and the fast train gets you to Franceville in 12½ hours, while the Omnibus needs 1 hour more. In reality, delays are chronic and a delayed departure followed by a 14–16-hour journey time on either train is more likely.

The Omnibus has a second and a first **class**, while the Express train has three classes of accommodation: VIP, first and second class. The Express train has been using comfortable new German-built rolling stock since 2017, while cars on the Omnibus are somewhat older.

Both first and VIP classes are air conditioned, but in VIP you may want to have a jumper or thermal sleeping bag handy – it's not nicknamed the refrigerator for nothing. As well as blankets, earplugs are indispensable: VIP has the dubious perk of some entertainment, namely very loud music alternating with Gabonese soaps. Although both trains currently run overnight, there are no sleeping berths, only seats.

Tickets between Libreville and Franceville cost between 33,100CFA to 64,300CFA, depending on the train and class. Children under the age of four travel free of charge; children between four and 12 pay half fare; children over 12 pay the full fare. As the station in Owendo (page 84) is rather out of the way, the easiest way to buy a train ticket in Libreville is at SETRAG's office in centre-ville or via a travel agency (the cost is the same). Tickets should be bought at least three days in advance. If you want to board at one of the smaller stations, there may be no ticket office operating, so you would then have to buy your ticket on the train. Though the departure **schedules** are theoretically fixed, delays mean that these are subject to change. SETRAG publishes the latest departure info on their Facebook page.

While there is usually a dining car on the train, in practice they may have little more than powdered coffee and tea to offer, so you should plan to bring your own **supplies**. Otherwise, you may be able to get a canned soda from the occasional ambulant salesmen, but that's about it.

It may be a good idea to ask the steward to wake you up once the train reaches your destination, because stations (and station announcements) are quite easy to miss, particularly at night.

Assuming it does eventually start running, it would be well worth taking the tourist **Train Forest Express** (see box, page 85) during the day. Almost as soon as it pulls out of Owendo you'll be rolling through the forest of the foothills of the Crystal Mountains. The rainforest is so dense in parts that it's not difficult to see why it took 14 years to build the railway. It's even less difficult to understand why it took Count Pierre Savorgnan de Brazza (page 5) three years to cut a path across the country with his *panga* a century earlier. Just past Ndjolé the tracks lead over the Ogooué River, which they then follow the course of for hours.

BY ROAD Despite remaining challenges, Gabon's infrastructure sector has seen large improvements since President Ali Bongo took over. When he came to power, only 10% of Gabon's 9,000km of roads were tarred and only 20% of the untarred roads were considered 'good'. Although the government missed their stated objective of tarring 3,600km of road by 2016, Ali Bongo's ten-year administration has seen more roads surfaced than the entirety of his father's 41-year tenure.

Major renovation of the road between Libreville and Ntoum, currently a main bottleneck for all incoming and outgoing traffic, was underway at the time this guide went to print, and the first stage of the road between Libreville and Port-Gentil (between Port-Gentil and Omboué) will be officially inaugurated at the end of 2019.

No matter how you get around on Gabon's roads, **checkpoints and roadblocks** are a fact of life here and will inevitably slow you down. It's not uncommon for officials to try and catch you on a mistake (or simply invent one) in order to attempt to solicit a bribe, so make sure your paperwork is in order and always carry your passport. To avoid unnecessary hassle, also carry your international immunisation record (yellow booklet).

Minibuses and clandos Apart from the railway and some larger Sogatra buses around Libreville and Franceville, Gabon has no public (ie: government-administered) transport. It does, however, have upwards of 9,000km of road, and plenty of people coming and going around the country despite the often-difficult conditions. During the rainy season, travel on certain roads is challenging, but the absence of surfaced roads does not mean an absence of transport. Broadly speaking, minibuses are the backbone of the Gabonese transport system, and some combination of minibuses or *clandos* reach all but the remotest corners of the country. Clandos (also sometimes referred to as *taxis-brousses* – bush taxis) are the – usually unregistered – cars and pick-ups that ferry people and their packages between towns, beeping for passengers as they pass through villages. They are easily recognisable as always being in poor condition and crowded. They offer the cheapest form of transport, and a little money will take you quite far. Minibuses and clandos are found at the *gare routière* (bus station) for any given town. They generally only depart when full, though there are thankfully now some minibus companies (listed in the relevant chapters) offering fixed departures, too. Choose a seat behind the driver, near the window, and on the side with the most shade.

Taxis Taxis are the lifeblood of the transport system within towns. They differ in colour depending on where you are – red and white for Libreville, blue and white for Port-Gentil and so on – but they almost always look as if they are falling apart. *Une course* is when you hire an empty taxi and the driver takes you directly to your destination. Each town has a set of recognised points beyond which the fare increases, but they will often start at around 1,000CFA for *une course*. For example, going from the city centre to the airport or Owendo in Libreville, or to Cap Lopez from Port-Gentil, will cost you 2,000CFA. All fares double after 21.00.

Paying for just *une place* (one seat) in a shared taxi is cheaper, slower and usually involves walking the final part of your journey. The system works as follows: hail a taxi and as it slows alongside you, shout out '*une place*' and then the recognised landmark nearest your destination. The driver will hoot if he's going your way. Costs for *une place* start at around 200CFA. *Une demi-course*, or *une demi*, is where separate passengers in the taxi are dropped directly at their destination in turn, not unlike an UberPool. If you are on a main road and happen to hail an empty taxi, the driver will assume you want a *course* unless you specify otherwise. Try to pay in exact money, as taxi drivers have neither the time nor the inclination to give change.

If you have lots of errands to run, you can ask the taxi to wait rather than find a new ride each time. In this instance you should pay 4,000CFA an hour, or 30,000CFA for the whole day (you can bargain for less if you will be hiring the taxi for more than one day). For anything other than a straightforward *course*, the golden rule for happy taxi relations is to give an estimate of time and distance, and then agree the rate before you set off.

Taxi drivers are generally very friendly and willing to chat. They are rarely Gabonese, usually coming from Mali, Cameroon, Benin or Nigeria.

Hiring and driving Driving in Gabon is certainly adventurous by European standards, but as far as African traffic goes, city driving here is just about manageable (though be ready for Libreville's legendarily snarled rush hours). Rural roads are another story, however, and unsurfaced road conditions are notoriously bad and not to be underestimated or approached lightly; travel can become very remote very quickly, and mobile phone reception cannot be relied upon beyond towns and the largest main roads. You should be skilled and comfortable with driving a 4×4 in off-road conditions if you want to explore the Gabonese countryside under your own steam.

Should you feel up to the challenge, it's possible to hire an ordinary car or 4×4 from a number of agencies in Libreville, Port-Gentil, and Franceville (pages 87, 121 and 180). Prices for a saloon car generally start at around US$75 per day. To hire the same car with a driver costs an additional 15,000–30,000CFA per day. The same agencies also hire 4×4s, with prices between 60,000CFA and 100,000CFA per day.

Depending on the type of car you hire, the **insurance** may only cover you within cities, so be sure to clear your itinerary with the agency before making a deal. (That being said, you'll almost certainly need a 4×4 if you plan on heading out of the city.) Your International Driving Licence is valid for the first three months, after which point you are supposed to get a Gabonese licence. Beware that driving is on the right side of the road and try to travel during daylight hours only.

If you encounter one of the ubiquitous barriers in the road, slow down and stop completely, and remember that patience and courtesy are key when it comes to successfully navigating checkpoints. If you are driving overland with your own vehicle, you will need a Carnet de Passages en Douane (CPD).

Cycling Assuming you can take humidity (even during the dry season), then cycling in Gabon can be equal parts challenging and rewarding. Road conditions range from smooth tarmac to seemingly never-ending mud, and distances between settlements can be quite long, depending on where in the country you are, so it's imperative to plan your route carefully and be self-sufficient on the basics.

On tarmac roads, the main hazard is other traffic, particularly minibuses and timber trucks which are often driven by maniacs. Accidents aren't uncommon and bikers in particular are very vulnerable. It's also not uncommon to encounter wild animals en route, so an understanding of how to handle yourself in such a situation is key. Bring your own bike, a comprehensive repair kit and an inexhaustible sense of humour. For cycling enthusiasts, Gabon is home to Africa's biggest road cycling event, the La Tropicale Amissa Bongo (page 72).

Hitching Getting a lift in the interior with a timber truck is possible, but not necessarily advisable. Truck drivers are renowned for heavy drinking and dangerous driving. A safer and quicker form of hitching is to get a lift in a private car. In fact, it's quite common for a private driver with spare seats to pass by the gare routière and offer the remaining places in their car for sale. As such, hitchhiking is not really a concept in Gabon and you should expect to pay for lifts offered by Gabonese. Finding such a lift is easiest if you are heading towards Libreville on a Sunday, when weekenders are returning for the working week.

BY BOAT Pirogues, or dugout canoes, are the traditional method of transport wherever there is water. Increasingly, pirogues are now motorised. A man who directs a pirogue is called a *piroguier*, or a *pagayeur*, after the *pagaye* or pole used in traditional pirogues. Ferries run between Libreville and Port-Gentil and between Port-Gentil and Lambaréné. See pages 82 and 121 for more details.

ACCOMMODATION

There's no shortage of **hotels** in Libreville, a handful of which conform to an international standard of luxury, with the price tags to match. In fact, the problem lies at the opposite end of the scale: finding a cheap hotel. Most hotel rooms, in whatever price category, have en-suite facilities, a double bed, and a choice of fan or air conditioning. Budget travellers are hard pushed to find a hotel bed for less than 15,000CFA a night.

ACCOMMODATION PRICE CODES		
Based on the cost of a standard double room per night (usually without breakfast).		
Luxury	$$$$$	> 120,000CFA
Upmarket	$$$$	80,000–120,000CFA
Mid-range	$$$	40,000–80,000CFA
Budget	$$	15,000–40,000CFA
Shoestring	$	< 15,000CFA

Outside the capital, the urban norm in Franceville, Port-Gentil and Lambaréné is for there to be one or two would-be luxury hotels (with a swimming pool, nightclub, restaurant and room service) and many more middle-range ones (usually with a bar-restaurant). Port-Gentil is also unique in the sheer number of its **self-catering apartments**. These are essentially hotels made up of self-contained, furnished flats – one or more bedrooms, bathroom, sitting room, kitchenette – that are charged on a nightly or monthly basis.

Safari accommodation tends to be of a good standard, with attractive wooden cabins or fully furnished, semi-permanent safari tents, with mosquito nets and running water (though this is not always hot). Electricity is generally provided by solar panels, or a generator is used at certain hours of the day. The expanding network of national park lodging run by Gabon Wildlife Camps in partnership with the ANPN (page 29) is worth noting as a recommended option.

At the cheapest end of the scale are *cases de passage*, which are simple establishments with a handful of rooms at around 5,000CFA a night. These are used by truck drivers, sometimes double as brothels, and can be very rowdy. The best have clean sheets, a fan and either a shared shower room or a bucket of water in each room. Toilets – often outside and often long-drops – are always shared. Every town has at least one case de passage, often in the market – just ask. Cases de passage and some hotels have a rate for rest (*repos*), which is use of the room during the day.

Although not always centrally located, **mission houses** with rooms for visitors are a good bet for just a little bit more than a case de passage. Rooms are invariably clean and good value, and sometimes there are facilities for cooking. Often there are gardens in which you can pitch a tent. It's possible to cross Gabon hopping from mission to mission.

If you find yourself in a **village** in need of a place to sleep, ask for the village chief, who will help set you up with a place for the night. Chances are he will be very welcoming, inviting you to eat, putting a hut at your disposal or finding you a place to pitch your tent, if you have one. If you are able to contribute to the meal with food or wine, or even better, whisky, the gesture will be much appreciated.

Having your own **tent** is invaluable for anyone intending to spend prolonged periods in out-of-the-way places, such as the forest, but note that unauthorised camping is not allowed in protected areas. In (or near) populated areas, it's important to ask for permission from the village chief before setting up camp.

See the inside front cover for an at-a-glance breakdown of the price codes and categories used throughout this guide.

EATING AND DRINKING

It is possible to eat very well in Libreville and Port-Gentil if you can afford the international prices. Some of the world's most popular cuisines are readily available, notably Italian, Chinese and, of course, French. There are French-style *boulangeries* selling all manner of croissants and pastries, and the supermarkets are stocked with cheeses, wines and even meat and vegetables imported from France. The choice is supplemented by goods imported from Cameroon, Equatorial Guinea and South Africa. In Libreville, Port-Gentil and other places where there are tourist restaurants and hotels, it is usual to find both European and African dishes on menus, and often tasty *grillades* (barbecued fish or meat) as well. In smaller towns and out-of-the-way places there may be a handful of small African restaurants or *maquis*. These tend to be Senegalese or Cameroonian, and the best serve generous portions of good food for not very much money. No meal is complete without *piment*, a very hot sauce made of

Based on the average price of a main course.

Expensive	$$$$$	> 20,000CFA
Above average	$$$$	15,000–20,000CFA
Mid-range	$$$	10,000–15,000CFA
Cheap and cheerful	$$	5,000–10,000CFA
Rock bottom	$	< 5,000CFA

peppers and herbs. Fish-lovers will be in heaven in Gabon as fresh fish is available all over the country, from upmarket restaurants to local *maquis*. Gabonese-style *crabes farcis* (stuffed crabs; made from shredded crab meat cooked with onion, garlic, chilli, lemon juice, parsley and other spices then baked in the shell) are a must-try.

The quickest and cheapest sources of prepared food, however, are **les bédoumeuses**. These are the women selling doughnuts, small brochettes of meat and filled baguettes on the street. Amazingly, fresh baguettes are sold every morning in just about every market in the country, no matter how remote. French baguettes are one of the Gabonese staples, alongside smoked or salted fish, manioc, plantain and rice.

Typical **sauces** are prepared with *arachides* (peanuts), *nyembwe* (the pulp of palm nuts) or *odika* (an oil-producing seed also known as *chocolat*). Chocolat in fact consists of crushed, fermented odika seeds. This paste of crushed seeds is stuffed into plastic bottles used as moulds, and dried until the chocolat is solid. Ready-made chocolat can be found in the big supermarkets in Libreville.

Bushmeat – antelope, porcupine, monkey, snake and so on – has traditionally been an important part of the Gabonese diet. However, attitudes are slowly changing, largely because of the bad publicity of ebola fever and growing awareness about endangered animals.

Vegetarians will probably end up relying on omelettes, hard-boiled eggs and avocados (if they are in season) for protein if they are travelling outside of Libreville. In the capital they will be able to vary their diet with pizzas and the occasional pasta dish. There is also, of course, no shortage of fresh fruit; locally loved *atanga* fruits make a good savoury option – their buttery flesh is generally boiled or roasted and eaten with salt.

DRINKING To be on the safe side, it is better not to drink the tap water in Gabon unless you have water-purifying tablets. Bottled water is widely available, as are beers, wines and spirits, and soft drinks (often simply – and somewhat confusingly – referred to as *jus*) like Coca-Cola, Sprite, Fanta, and local brand D'jino.

Drinking is an extremely popular pastime and, particularly in rural areas, it's quite often easier to find a bar than something to eat. The local **beer** Régab, a light lager sold in 65cl bottles, is good value. Its brewery, the Société de Brasseries du Gabon (Sobraga, owned by the French Groupe Castel), is one of the country's biggest employers. Sobraga also brews Guinness, 33 Export, Castel and Beaufort under licence. Count on paying 600CFA for a Régab in the local wooden shack, rising to 1,000CFA in a mid-range bar or restaurant, and over 1,500CFA in an upmarket hotel or restaurant.

In rural areas, the ubiquitous **palm wine** is the usual tipple. It's extremely cheap and easy to produce by extracting the sap from a wine palm and leaving it to ferment over the course of a day. The wine produced is sweet in the morning, but starts to pack a punch by nightfall.

Everything closes on public holidays – banks, shops and government offices – so it is worth being aware of them. Muslim holidays, which vary from year to year, are also public holidays. Bear in mind that during the lunar month of Ramadan business hours may not always run as normal.

FIXED HOLIDAYS

1 January	New Year's Day
17 April	Gabonese Women's Day
1 May	Labour Day
17 August	Independence Day
1 November	All Saints' Day
25 December	Christmas Day

ROTATING HOLIDAYS Note that Islamic holidays are based on the lunar *Hijri* calendar, and the dates below marked with a * are predictions. Islamic holidays usually shift by about 11 days annually when compared with the Gregorian calendar, but this can move around by a day or two depending on when the moon officially kicking off the holiday is sighted.

	2020	2021	2022	2023
Easter Monday (Pâques)	13 Apr	5 Apr	18 Apr	10 Apr
Ascension	21 May	13 May	26 May	18 May
Eid al-Fitr*	23 May	12 May	3 May	21 Apr
Pentecost/Whit Monday	31 May	23 May	5 Jun	28 May
Eid al-Adha*	30 Jul	19 Jul	9 Jul	28 Jun
Mawlid*	28 Oct	18 Oct	7 Oct	26 Sep

SPORTING EVENTS Gabonese love sports (particularly football) and in the last decade the country has been the stage for some major international sporting events, including the prestigious Africa Cup of Nations in both 2012 and 2017.

La Tropicale Amissa Bongo (organised by Fonds National pour le Développement du Sport; w tropicaleamissabongo.com). Since 2006, Africa's best cyclists have competed in this annual international cycle event that marks the start of the world calendar of the International Cycling Union (UCI) in January. La Tropicale contains seven daily stages (which are explained on the event's website), following a series of routes in Estuaire, Woleu-Ntem, and Haut-Ogooué, and the 2019 event passed through Mongomo in Equatorial Guinea as well. Italian Niccolò Bonifazio took home the prize in the 2019 race.

Marathon du Gabon (w marathondugabon.com; f marathondugabon) The inaugural race of the Gabon Marathon took place in Libreville on 1 December 2013, and it has now become an annual event, held at the same time each year. Over 5,000 runners participate in either a full or half marathon, with others opting for a 10km or 5km course. Kids can do one of the special junior courses.

Run in Masuku (w runinmasuku.com) Gabon's newest running event, this 10km race takes athletes up and down the hills of Franceville every September. Nearly 6,000 participants joined the 2019 race.

FESTIVALS AND CULTURAL EVENTS The centre of Gabon's cultural life is Libreville, and the major part of the city's cultural events, such as concerts, the yearly Fête de la Musique and several film festivals, is organised by the **Institut Français du Gabon** (IFG or CCF; w institutfrancais-gabon.com; page 104). Check their website for their monthly programme. Below is a list of Gabon's annual cultural events.

Note that a number of previously long-running events, such as the Akini-a-Loubou dance festival, Dire en Fête slam poetry festival, and Gabao Hip Hop Festival were on seemingly indefinite hiatus at the time this guide went to print. It's possible they'll be resurrected in future, but it's impossible to say with any certainty.

Gabon 9 Provinces Launched by the Ministère de la Culture et des Arts (Ministry of Culture and Arts) in 2016, this is a festival of song, dance, art and traditional culture that aims to expose, valorise, and preserve the many forms of expression unique to Gabon's nine provinces. It's held in Libreville every August, during which time you'll find a series of concerts and exhibitions around the city.

Gabon Music Expo (f gabonmusicexpo) Launched in May 2019, this is a pan-African concert series held in restaurants and bars around Libreville, drawing talent from Gabon, Cameroon, Equatorial Guinea, Congo and beyond. In addition to the evening concerts, they also put on a series of daytime workshops and discussions.

Guardians of Africa (f guardiansofafrica) This pan-African tourism festival was held for the first time in July 2019 in Port-Gentil. It aims to promote sustainable and experiential tourism, with a focus on community collaboration and authentic interaction. It plays host to a number of tourism exhibitors from across the continent, and puts on concerts with Gabonese and international musicians to open and close the festival.

Escales documentaires de Libreville (w escalesdoclibreville.com; f FestivalEDL) Organised by l'Institut Gabonais de l'Image et du Son (Gabonese Institute of Image and Sound) and IFG, this documentary festival takes place annually at the end of November. More than 20 African films are shown in different locations in Libreville.

Rencontre International des Peuples et des Arts de Mighoma (Mighoma International Meeting of People and the Arts) The RIPAM, previously known as Les Nuits Atypiques de Mighoma, is one of the few events to take place outside Libreville. Gabonese singer Annie Flore Batchiellilys started Les Nuits Atypiques de Mighoma in her birth town Mighoma, close to Tchibanga (Nyanga), in August 2006. Inspired by two international festivals – **Les Nuits Atypiques de Langon** (France) and **Les Nuits Atypiques de Koudougou** (Burkina Faso), Batchiellilys aims to empower rural people through this cultural and musical event. As the festival doesn't take place every year, you should confirm that it's on before heading to Mighoma – the Institut Français (page 104) would be a good place to ask.

SHOPPING

Unlike some other countries in the region where you can't take two paces without tripping over a craftsman, in Gabon you have to make a bit more effort to find souvenirs (and a lot of what you do find has been imported from Mali, Cameroon, Benin or even East Africa). You can expect to hear expats lamenting that Gabon is not a nation of craftsmen (or indeed producers of anything at all), and invariably any kind of tourist project involves an attempt to stimulate a local craft industry.

The best place to shop is in Libreville, where there is far and away the greatest choice. As to what there is to buy, it's mostly masks, wooden items, tie-dye clothes, batik tablecloths and stone sculptures. If you are after something genuinely Gabonese, a *mbigou* stone sculpture is what you should look for. **Mbigou stone**, a steatite (magnesium silicate), is quarried around Mbigou in the south of the country. Extracting the soft stone is a time-consuming operation, as the rocks are scattered about and buried in the earth. Mbigou exists in different colours varying from brown and grey to green. The Libreville-based Coopérative des Produits Artisanaux de Mbigou (page 100) is the best place to buy.

The quality of the carving of larger objects, such as chairs and boxes, varies, as do the prices. Bargaining is not always welcome, although it is grudgingly accepted in Libreville's artisans' markets, where shoppers may end up paying just two-thirds of the original quoted price.

All basic necessities and more are available in Libreville and Port-Gentil. Most towns have at least one reasonably stocked supermarket, usually the nearly omnipresent **Cecado**. As a general rule, most shops open at 08.00 or 09.00 and close for the day by 19.00. The majority shut between 12.30 and 15.30, although some have even longer lunch breaks. The poor – who include many migrant workers from other African countries – are generally priced out of Gabon's expensive supermarkets and buy their basic goods at street markets.

MEDIA AND COMMUNICATIONS

While the constitution and law provide for freedom of speech and press, the government takes a keen interest in the country's media and what is not government-controlled is subject to close scrutiny. It is not uncommon for too-critical newspapers or TV channels to be suspended for disrupting public order.

NEWSPAPERS AND MAGAZINES Gabon's newspapers, all published in French, are readily available at kiosks throughout the country. The two daily newspapers, *L'Union* (w union.sonapresse.com) and *Gabon Matin*, are government-affiliated and sold at major traffic junctions in the early morning. The *Gabon Matin* is a publication of the Agence Gabonaise de Presse (Gabonese Press Agency; w agpgabon.ga).

Approximately 15 privately owned weekly or monthly newspapers represent independent views and those of political parties, but some appear irregularly, owing to financial constraints or, in some cases, government suspension of their publication licences. *Le Temps*, *Le Temoin*, *La Lowe* and *La Relance* are private weekly publications. *Echos du Nord*, *l'Aube*, and *Le Journal* are independent, fortnightly publications. The opposition papers include the weekly satirical *La Griffe*, *Le Nganga* and the bi-monthly *Misamu*. Gabonese newspapers are regularly suspended for 'non-compliance with the communications code', but it's widely acknowledged that these suspensions are often political in nature; *Echos du Nord* and *l'Aube* were both suspended as this book went to print in 2019.

Two interesting French-language Africa-centric **magazines** are the monthly *Am Afrique Magazine* (w afriquemagazine.com) and the weekly political and economic *Jeune Afrique* (w jeuneafrique.com).

It is possible to get hold of a good selection of **foreign publications**, including *Time*, *Newsweek*, *The Economist*, the *Herald Tribune* and *Le Monde*, in the big hotels and bookshops in Libreville, normally for at least twice the price they are sold back home.

TELEVISION AND RADIO Gabon Télévision, formerly known as Radio-Television Gabonaise (RTG), is the government-controlled national broadcaster operating two French-language television channels. It also operates two national radio channels and several provincial stations.

There are over 20 private **television channels**, the majority affiliated to political movements. Like the newspapers, Gabonese TV channels are also frequently subject to politically motivated suspensions.

On the **radio**, Urban FM (104.5 FM; w urbanfm.fm) is one of Libreville's most popular stations. Founded in 1981, the Gabonese radio station Africa No 1 (94.5 FM; w africa1.com) was long one of the most important sources of music in Francophone Africa, broadcasting from Haut-Ogooué, but recent years have seen the station's international broadcasts become irregular.

INTERNET Gabon is connected to the Africa Coast–Europe fibre-optic cable, and most regional towns have a decent 3G (or increasingly 4G) data connection. Thanks to the ready availability of Wi-Fi (in hotels and restaurants) and mobile data, many of the internet cafés that had opened in recent decades have already closed their doors.

TELEPHONE Today, almost all Gabonese have access to a mobile phone and landlines are used less and less. Top mobile phone operators are Airtel (formerly Zain; numbers start with 07 or 04) and Gabon Telecom (trading as Libertis and Moov; numbers start with 02, 05 or 06). Both offer a comparable service, but Airtel has perhaps a slightly larger network. All larger Gabonese towns have decent 3G or 4G connection at this point, but this can quickly drop off in the countryside. There is usually some signal along the larger roads, but don't expect to be within range when leaving major routes. You may even find specific points along roads where vehicles will regularly stop, because they are able to connect to the network there.

Visitors from overseas may find their network is unavailable in Gabon. Thus, many travellers opt to get a local SIM card for their unlocked mobile. These cost 1,000–2,000CFA at most and are available from any service provider. All offer voice, SMS and mobile-data services on a prepaid basis, with a variety of packages available to suit your needs. Gabonese people are also prolific users of WhatsApp; if you're trying to reach someone this is often a good way to do it. Just add their number to your phonebook to see if they have the app installed. This can also be a good way to get in touch with businesses (ie: tour agents, service providers, etc).

Gabon's **country code** from anywhere in the world is +241; when dialling a Gabonese number from abroad, drop the leading 0 from the telephone number.

Note that ARCEP was in the process of changing the national phone numbering scheme at the time of writing. This will impact all phone numbers in the country (and therefore in this guide); see the box on page v for details.

POST There used to be a post office in every town, but today many are closed. In theory, airmail to the UK takes one to two weeks. However, sending post to Gabon can take forever. Even within Gabon the post is not very reliable, which is why minibuses often double up as parcel-delivery services. It's about 600CFA to send a postcard to Europe.

CULTURAL ETIQUETTE

As in most African countries, politeness and respect, particularly for the elderly, are the main virtues in Gabonese society. Displeasure at your rudeness may not be expressed – the same tradition of respect requires that displeasure is not shown – but you can rest assured that your behaviour has been noted. Questions may not be asked or answered directly. Criticism is given in a diplomatic way, or not at all.

The **dress code** is rather conservative throughout the country and people tend to dress well, no matter what temperature it is outside. Shorts are OK if you have a bike, are hiking, or are engaged in another sport. In general, the more conservatively you dress, the better you will be received.

Traditional **greetings** are lengthy affairs, including long handshakes and enquiries about your health and family. Today these conventions are weakening, but asking how somebody's doing will always be appreciated. A simple '*Bonjour, ça va?*' goes a long way. Friends greet each other with a series of two or four kisses. Men often walk holding hands, a sign of brotherly affection.

Be careful about the way you comment on Gabon or Africa. Derogatory statements will sometimes be seen as neo-colonial arrogance, although people usually get friendlier if they find out that you're not French. Proclamations of atheism and smoking (particularly for women) are usually not appreciated.

If you come from a Western country, people often automatically assume that you have some money to spend, as most Western foreigners in Gabon are well-paid expats. If you are unwilling or unable to spend, you risk being perceived as 'greedy'.

Conversely, you will notice that people often avoid eye contact during conversation. While this may be considered rude in Western cultures, it is indeed a sign of respect. Looking somebody in the eye can be regarded as a provocation.

Tipping isn't common, though in upmarket restaurants it's polite to add up to 10% to your bill. Taxis don't require any gratuity, but if you're travelling with drivers or guides it's appropriate to tip them at the end of your trip. Between 6,500 and 13,000CFA per day would be satisfactory, assuming you're happy with their service.

TRAVELLING POSITIVELY

Tourism can be very beneficial for Gabon, as tourists not only bring economic benefits, but also make a significant contribution to biodiversity protection. Additionally, travellers have a direct impact on the places they visit. To optimise the positive impact and minimise any negative effects, try to favour locally owned businesses, buy locally produced goods and food, support durable tourism initiatives, and use energy, water and other resources efficiently and in keeping with local practices. Avoid places that use limited resources like water and electricity to the detriment of local people. Observe but do not disturb natural systems. Minimise your waste and don't leave any litter. Use only biodegradable soaps and detergents, and never order bushmeat (*viande de brousse*), including elephant, gorilla, chimp and monkey, forest antelope (duiker), crocodile, porcupine, bush pig, cane rat and pangolin. Commercial hunting for bushmeat is the primary threat to wildlife populations (page 33), not to speak of the considerable threat to human health.

There are a number of local and international **NGOs** that are doing excellent work in partnering with local communities to preserve Gabon's unique natural heritage, and a contribution to any of these would go a long way. This list includes organisations such as Aventures Sans Frontières (page 35), PROGRAM (page 36), WCS (page 35), Ibonga ACPE (page 36), Mandrillus Project (page 191), WWF (page 35), or any of those listed on page 89.

Part Two

THE GUIDE

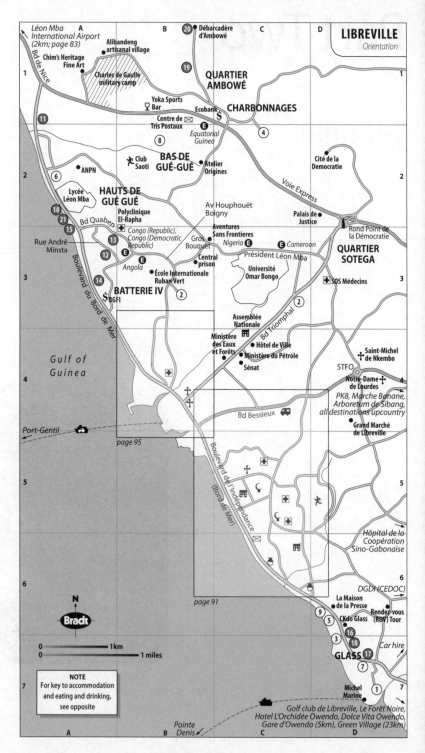

LIBREVILLE
Orientation

Léon Mba
International Airport
(2km; page 83)

20 Débarcadère
d'Ambowé

**QUARTIER
AMBOWÉ**

CHARBONNAGES

Alibandeng
artisanal village

Chim's Heritage
Fine Art

Charles de Gaulle
military camp

Yoka Sports
Bar

Ecobank

Centre de
Tris Postaux

*Equatorial
Guinea*

**BAS DE
GUÉ-GUÉ**

Club
Saoti

Atelier
Origines

Cité de la
Democratie

Voie Express

**HAUTS DE
GUÉ GUÉ**

ANPN

Lycée
Léon Mba

Polyclinique
El-Rapha

Av Houphouët
Boigny

*Congo (Republic),
Congo (Democratic
Republic)*

Gros
Bouquet

Aventures
Sans Frontieres

Nigeria

Angola

École Internationale
Ruban Vert

Central
prison

Palais de
Justice

Rond Point de
la Démocratie

**QUARTIER
SOTEGA**

Cameroon

Président Léon Mba

Université
Omar Bongo

SOS Médecins

BATTERIE IV

BGFI

*Gulf of
Guinea*

Rue André
Minsta

Bd Quaben

Assemblée
Nationale

Bd Triomphal

Ministère
des Eaux
et Forêts

Hôtel de Ville

Ministère du Pétrole

Sénat

Saint-Michel
de Nkembo

STFO

Notre-Dame
de Lourdes

*PK8, Marche Banane,
Arboretum de Sibang,
all destinations upcountry*

Bd Bessieux

Grand Marché
de Libreville

Port-Gentil

page 95

Boulevard du Bord de Mer

Boulevard de l'Indépendance
(Bord de Mer)

page 91

*Hôpital de la
Coopération
Sino-Gabonaise*

DGDI (CEDOC)

La Maison
de la Presse

9

5 CKdo Glass

3

16

18

GLASS **17**

Rendez-vous
(RDV) Tour

Car hire

7

N

Bradt

0 ———— 1km
0 ———— 1 miles

NOTE
For key to accommodation
and eating and drinking,
see opposite

Michel
Marine

1

Pointe
Denis

*Golf club de Libreville, Le Forêt Noire,
Hotel L'Orchidée Owendo, Dolce Vita Owendo,
Gare d'Owendo (5km), Green Village (23km)*

Bd de Nice

4

Libreville and Estuaire

Gabon's capital lies in the far northwest of the country, splayed haphazardly along the shores of the Atlantic Ocean for close to 30km. Libreville – or Elbévé, as the locals call their home town (just pronounce L-B-V in French) – is a beguiling hodgepodge of a city: a grab-bag mix of gleaming, vainglorious government buildings, modern tower blocks turned black with tropical mould, and single-storey shops and tin-roofed shacks of the style found across the African continent. While the architecture may seem incoherent, the welcome is well established – Libreville is a laid-back capital city and the Librevilleois who call it home are warm, genuine, and inevitably intrigued to hear that you've come to their town as a tourist.

Arriving by air in the daytime offers a fantastic view over the riotous greenery and labyrinthine creeks of Akanda National Park to the north, and by night you see the city's isolated glow – surrounded by the Atlantic's inky blackness to the west and Gabon's famous forests to the east. You can sometimes even spot the eerie fires of oil platforms burning off excess natural gas offshore. The runway is no more than 500m from the palm-studded shore, and the tropical humidity will have you in its pillowy grasp before you're down the boarding stairs. From here, the city is your oyster, and Libreville has a little something for everyone, whether you're after glittering nightclubs and fine gastronomy or traditional art and secretive ceremony.

One of the city's major downsides, and a constant gripe of visitor and resident alike, is the high cost of living (or visiting). Ranked as the world's 18th most expensive city, it costs more to live in Libreville than in London, Paris or New York. Les Librevilleois, whether native-born or recently arrived, can all agree: the city is *très, très cher*.

Most visitors spend much of their time in the neighbourhoods more or less along the oceanfront, but there is another, less visible side of the city behind the slick office blocks and whirring construction cranes. Les Mapanes, as the informal settlements ringing the city on the hilly outskirts of town are known, often lack reliable water, power and sewage, or some combination of all three. Worse still, these slums are often located on hillsides and in valleys prone to flooding – all this in one of the world's wettest capitals, clocking over 2.85m of precipitation annually. Here, Libreville's dirty laundry – overpopulation, insecurity and unemployment – is on full display. Many residents of les Mapanes, if they are employed at all, work as waiters, cooks, drivers or labourers, and the conditions of their employment are often precarious indeed, particularly for immigrants. A significant number of Libreville's slum-dwellers hail from Senegal, Cameroon, Benin, Togo and elsewhere in West Africa.

Much like the rest of Gabon, Libreville has seen a general slowdown in business activity over the past few years thanks to depressed global oil prices – known locally as *la crise* (the crisis) – and the city's considerable reliance on the industry, but it nonetheless continues to be a magnet for immigrants and young people seeking a better life. The city elected its first female mayor, Rose Christiane Ossouka Raponda, in 2014; her successor, Léandre Nzué, was elected in 2019, and promised a thorough clean-up of this often-disorderly city – we wish him luck.

HISTORY

French for 'free town' and inspired by the example of Freetown in Sierra Leone, the city's name was chosen by colonial lieutenant Bouët-Willaumez (page 4) when Africans freed from the captured Brazilian slave ship *L'Elizia* settled here in 1849. The shore on which they first set foot, just opposite the current Presidential Palace, is marked by an impressive monument by the Gabonese sculptor and painter Marcellin Minzé Minkoe (page 21).

The day on which the freed slaves arrived in Gabon is generally regarded as the founding date of the city, although people, mostly the Mpongwé, had been living in this area long before. In fact, in preceding years the French had been making great efforts to increase their power on this part of the coast. In 1839 the local Mpongwé chief Rapontchombo put his mark to a treaty placing his territory under the French flag, the first of many such treaties signed with local chiefs.

By 1860, Libreville is said to have consisted of little more than the village of the freed slaves, a trading post and a handful of missionaries. The city started to grow a bit after World War II, but the real expansion wouldn't come until the years following Gabon's independence in 1960 and the 1970s petrol boom, which turned the city into a magnet for immigrants from neighbouring countries and caused a rural exodus in Gabon itself.

From the 1970s onwards the city's **population** increased in great leaps: 31,000 in 1960, 77,000 in 1970, 185,000 in 1980, 337,700 in 1990 and 450,000 in 2003. Today, Libreville (including its suburbs of Akanda and Owendo) has an official population of 818,000, which accounts for 40% of the country's inhabitants. With the rest of Estuaire province (the country's second-smallest by area), nearly half of all Gabonese are Estuariens.

Former president Omar Bongo had big ideas for his capital back in the days when the coffers were overflowing with petrol money, and for most of the 1970s the city resembled a massive building site. Bongo built a new waterfront Presidential Palace, the first skyscrapers, wide roads, new ministries, luxury hotels, and a succession of futuristic buildings that line boulevard Triomphal Omar Bongo Ondimba, the boulevard he – unsurprisingly – named after himself.

Since he came to power in 2009, Ali Bongo has also been heavily investing in public works, but on the whole is probably a touch less megalomaniacal than his father. To meet the city's increasing demand, the government pledged to build 5,000 social housing units per year in 2009, though, thanks in part to *la crise* and declining oil revenues, has yet to meet this target. Nonetheless, more kilometres of road have been surfaced since Ali came to power than during his father's entire 41-year reign.

The **Coupe d'Afrique des Nations** (Africa Cup of Nations; CAN) tournaments that Gabon co-hosted in 2012 and hosted in 2017 accelerated large-scale construction activities such as the Chinese-funded 40,000-seat Stade de l'Amitié sino-gabonaise (China-Gabon Friendship Stadium) [78 D5]. During the months leading up to these high-profile football events, workers were brought in to work both day and night shifts in a frantic attempt to complete the works on time. It is thanks to the 28th and 31st CANs that (most of) the city's roads are in good shape today.

Libreville's current flagship is the **transformation of old Port Môle** and the coastal area around boulevard Triomphal Omar Bongo Ondimba into a prestigious new centre, adding to the city's international allure. The project, known as Baie de la Rois (Bay of Kings) [95 B3], involves 34ha of land reclamation (corresponding to a volume of 2.1 million cubic metres) and the new site will, it is said, host a shopping centre with restaurants, a yacht basin, a waterfront hotel, offices and cultural centres, a residential marina and a monument. Underground parking facilities will guarantee a car-free and pedestrian-friendly area, a novelty in Libreville.

GETTING THERE AND AWAY

Libreville is the hub of Gabon's transport system. It's the home of the country's primary international airport and has reasonable links by air, rail and road to the rest of the country. A detailed breakdown of getting to and from other parts of the country can be found in the relevant sections of this guide, but there is a brief overview below.

BY AIR Léon Mba International Airport [83 D1] (w libreville-airport.com) is, for all intents and purposes, Gabon's only international airport. As of 2018, it's managed by GSEZ Airports, and compared with other African airports it makes a straightforward, clean and orderly impression. Officials are not unfriendly, and travellers usually don't feel too overwhelmed by over-enthusiastic porters, taxi drivers and other people asking for their attention. If you do wish to use the services of a porter, count on paying 1,000CFA. There's a newsstand outside that acts as a semi-official exchange bureau and offers reasonable rates.

Note that there are long-standing plans to replace Léon Mba International with a new airport near Nkok, about 30km east of central Libreville along the N1. For more information, see page 53.

For details of both international connections and national flights, see pages 53 and 65.

International airline offices The following airlines all fly to Libreville.

✈ **Air Côte d'Ivoire** [95 D3] Galeries les Jardins d'Ambre, bd Triomphal Omar Bongo Ondimba; ✎ 01 77 05 60/1; e aircotedivoirelbv@ aircotedivoire.com; w aircotedivoire.com. Serves Abidjan (Ivory Coast) & Cotonou (Benin).

✈ **Air France** [91 A3] bd de l'Indépendance & Léon Mba Int Airport; ✎ 01 79 64 64; m 04 02 14 34 (airport); w airfrance.ga. Serves Paris (France).

✈ **ASKY** Immeuble les arcades, rue Coniquet, centre-ville; ✎ 01 72 22 30; m 02 22 85 00; e lbvkpcto@flyasky.com; w flyasky.com. Serves Lomé (Togo), Lagos (Nigeria) & Johannesburg (South Africa).

✈ **Camair-Co** rue Ange Mba, centre-ville; ✎ 01 76 17 22; w camair-co.cm. Serves Douala & Yaoundé (Cameroon).

✈ **Ceiba Intercontinental** [91 B4] rue Colonel Parant, centre-ville; ✎ 01 77 35 76/7 & 01 74 05 11/2; w fly-ceiba.com. Serves Malabo (Equatorial Guinea) & São Tomé.

✈ **Ethiopian Airlines** [91 D6] Immeuble Pyramide, Glass; ✎ 05 93 16 60/01 74 13 15; e LBVAgent@ethiopianairlines.com;

w ethiopianairlines.com. Serves Addis Ababa (Ethiopia).

✈ **Kenya Airways** Opposite Chambre de Commerce, av Colonel Parant, centre-ville; m 05 12 78 78/07 41 95 04; e customer.relations@ kenya-airways.com; w kenya-airways.com. Serves Nairobi (Kenya).

✈ **Royal Air Maroc** [91 B5] bd de l'Indépendance; ✎ 01 73 10 25/01 73 44 51; m 06 60 16 60; w royalairmaroc.com. Serves Casablanca (Morocco).

✈ **RwandAir** [91 B4] rue Colonel Parant, centre-ville; ✎ 01 76 48 82; m 05 99 13 99/05 99 13 98; e sales.libreville@rwandair.com; w rwandair.com. Serves Kigali (Rwanda).

✈ **Trans Air Congo** [83 D4] Léon Mba Int Airport; m 07 39 03 90/07 93 60 79; w flytransaircongo.com. Serves Pointe-Noire, Brazzaville (Republic of the Congo), & Bamako (Mali).

✈ **Turkish Airlines** [91 C5] ✎ 01 76 35 35/01 44 28 28; e lbvsales@thy.com; w turkishairlines.com. Serves Istanbul (Turkey).

Airport transfer The Léon Mba International Airport is 12km north of central Libreville. Radio taxis and ride-hailing services like Uber have yet to reach Gabon, so unless you've arranged a pick-up with your hotel (easily done with most upmarket options), you'll probably end up taking a **taxi** from the airport. They will charge 2,000CFA to take you into town or 4,000CFA after 21.00. Aside from attempting to overcharge you, we haven't had many reports of problems with taxi driver in Libreville. Though airport taxis are reasonably priced, if you don't have many bags and want to save some CFA, it's only about 150m to the main road in front of the airport, where you can flag down a passing taxi for *une place* rather than hiring the whole cab for *une course* from the terminal (page 68).

BY BOAT There are currently three companies sailing between Libreville's Port Môle and Vieux Port in Port-Gentil, but this situation is subject to regular change so it's always best to check the schedule a couple of days before you wish to travel.

The **Compagnie Nationale de Navigation Interieure et Internationale (CNNII)** [95 C4] (Port Môle; ✆ 01 72 39 28; m 02 52 01 46 (Libreville)/02 51 06 07 (Port-Gentil); e c.navigation@cnnii-gabon.com; f CNNIIGABON) runs two types of ferry: the rapid *Ntchengue Express* (4hrs; 24,000/28,000/35,000CFA economy/business/VIP) on Wednesdays, Fridays and Sundays, and the slower overnight boat, somewhat confusingly named (after a village in southern Gabon that the ferry doesn't serve) *Sette Cama* (8hrs; 17,000CFA), on Tuesdays, Thursdays and Saturdays. It's 120,000CFA to ship your car in either direction.

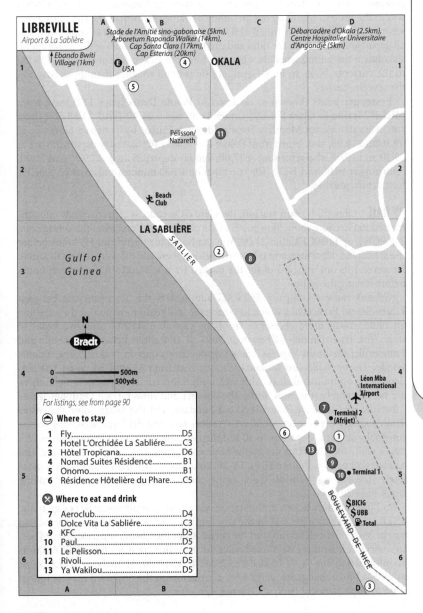

LIBREVILLE
Airport & La Sablière

Stade de l'Amitié sino-gabonaise (5km),
Arboretum Raponda Walker (14km),
Cap Santa Clara (17km),
Cap Esterias (20km)

Débarcadère d'Okala (2.5km),
Centre Hospitalier Universitaire
d'Angondjé (5km)

Ebando Bwiti
Village (1km)

USA

OKALA

Pélisson/
Nazareth

Beach
Club

LA SABLIÈRE

Gulf of
Guinea

SABLIER

N

Bradt

0   500m
0   500yds

Léon Mba
International
Airport

Terminal 2
(Afrijet)

Terminal 1

BOULEVARD DE NKÉ

$ BICIG
$ UBB
P Total

For listings, see from page 90

🛏 **Where to stay**

1	Fly	D5
2	Hotel L'Orchidée La Sabliére	C3
3	Hôtel Tropicana	D6
4	Nomad Suites Résidence	B1
5	Onomo	B1
6	Résidence Hôtelière du Phare	C5

✖ **Where to eat and drink**

7	Aeroclub	D4
8	Dolce Vita La Sablière	C3
9	KFC	D5
10	Paul	D5
11	Le Pelisson	C2
12	Rivoli	D5
13	Ya Wakilou	D5

Sonaga [95 C4] (Port Môle; ☎ 01 56 43 34; m 07 51 56 66 (Libreville)/07 16 29 06 (Port-Gentil); e sonagagab@yahoo.fr) operates an equally slow daily ferry (8hrs; 26,000CFA), generally departing between midnight and noon. As of late 2018, **Logistique Maritime 241** (m 05 95 90 11/8 (Port-Gentil); 05 95 90 15/6 (Libreville); f) was running fast boats (3–4hrs; 25,000/35,000CFA economy/VIP) between the two cities five times weekly; see their Facebook page in advance of travelling for current schedules.

Whichever company you travel with, it's best to reserve your tickets as early as possible – days in advance if you can – as they are frequently sold out. CNNII was in the process of rolling out an online booking platform at the time this guide went to print; check if it's functional at w reservation.cnnii-gabon.com. Note that all departures depend on the tides and can take place at all hours of the day or night, so confirm the sailing schedule when you buy your tickets and arrive early. Owing to the currents, boats to Port-Gentil are slower and rougher than those covering the reverse journey.

Passenger boats (known as *navettes*) to **Pointe Denis** (page 112) leave from **Michel Marine** in Glass [78 D7] (m 05 31 80 80/06 26 40 77/07 14 68 56); these run every day except Monday. Tuesday through Friday, boats depart Libreville at 09.30 and 16.00, and return from Pointe Denis at 17.00; Saturday departures are at 09.30 and 15.00, also returning at 17.00; Sunday departures are at 09.00 and 11.00, returning at 16.00 and 17.30. The trip takes under 30 minutes and costs 12,000CFA for a return journey.

BY RAIL Libreville's **train station**, the Gare d'Owendo, is (appropriately enough) located in Owendo, about 9km south of the city centre. A taxi from the centre costs 2,000CFA, or 4,000CFA after 21.00. You can board the train from 1½ hours before the scheduled departure, and it is worth getting there early if you are heavily laden. However, it is not unheard of for the packed train to stand still for several hours before leaving the station.

Gabon's railway company SETRAG administers the Transgabonais between Libreville and Franceville, which has made the southeastern region, and everything en route, much more accessible from the capital. SETRAG runs two types of train. The Train Omnibus l'Equateur links all 21 stations between Libreville and Franceville; the Train Express Trans-Ogooué stops only in Ndjolé, Lopé, Booué, Ivindo, Lastoursville and Moanda. Tickets cost from 33,100CFA to 64,300CFA, depending on train and class. Although both trains currently run overnight, there are no sleeping berths, only seats. The cheaper and slower Train Omnibus leaves Libreville on Tuesdays, Thursdays and Sundays, and the faster, more expensive Train Express departs on Mondays, Wednesdays and Fridays. According to the timetable, all trains depart at 18.50 and the fast train gets you to Franceville in 12½ hours while the Omnibus needs one hour more. In reality, delays are chronic, and a delayed departure followed by a 14–16-hour journey time on either train is more likely. The express train has been using comfortable new German-built rolling stock since 2017.

In Libreville, buy tickets at the station, via a tour operator (page 88) or go to the SETRAG sales office [91 B5] in the city centre (⊕ 08.00–17.30 Mon–Sat), located on rue Victor Schoelcher, around the corner from the Casino supermarket. It's best to reserve at least three days in advance, as the trains are often full. SETRAG runs an information line (☎ 01 70 80 04/35 39/82 42; ⊕ 07.30–21.30 daily), which is just as well as times change regularly. For information on the proposed express tourist train to Lopé National Park, see the box opposite.

BY ROAD Libreville's location on a peninsula can make entering or leaving the city a time-consuming and frustrating undertaking. There's only one route out of town, the N1, which was in inexplicably bad condition at the time of writing, with long stretches of ruined tarmac running a few dozen kilometres east of Nkok. Consequently, there are eternal, unavoidable traffic jams, no matter what time you hit the road. In a bit of good news, however, the N1 from the city centre to PK8 (point kilometre 8) to the east of the city centre, and on to Nkok will soon be a dual carriageway all the way through, largely to serve the Gabon Special Economic Zone in Nkok.

Most of the unscheduled **minibus services** operating between Libreville and other towns such as Cocobeach (120km; 3hrs; 5,000CFA), Lambaréné (235km; 5hrs; 6,000–7,000CFA), Mouila (430km; 7hrs; 13,000CFA), Tchibanga (590km; 9–10hrs; 18,000CFA), Makokou (630km; 10–12hrs; 17,000CFA), and Franceville (770km; 2 days; 25,000CFA) leave from the multi-storey **Marché Banane** at PK8. Transport to closer destinations such as Lambaréné can usually be found until at least the early afternoon, while vehicles to further-flung destinations tend to leave in the early morning. Most of the ticket offices are found at the edges of the market, including **Sergio Transports** (m 04 81 01 07), which is recommended for Tchibanga and destinations along the N1.

For **destinations in Woleu-Ntem**, your best bet is probably **Le Transporteur Voyages** (m 06 40 15 30/07 13 08 08/05 94 33 33/06 34 33 33; e transporteurvoyages@ yahoo.com), which runs daily vehicles from their offices near Maison Liebermann [91 C1] to Oyem (520km; 8–9hrs; 12,000CFA) and Bitam (595km; 9–10hrs; 14,000CFA), as well as to Minvoul (635km; 11–13hrs; 20,000CFA) and Ambam (Cameroon; 630km; 10–11hrs; 15,000CFA) a couple of times weekly. Head to PK5 to pick up transport to Ntoum (30km; 1hr; 1,500CFA) and Kango (90km; 2½ hours; 2,500CFA).

ORIENTATION

So, what's where? Libreville is divided into six *arrondissements* or districts and over 40 *quartiers* or neighbourhoods, which each have their own centre.

Most of the city's main points of interest sit inside the oblong, roughly D-shaped area bordered to the west by the Atlantic Ocean and to the east by the dual carriageway Voie Express, a bypass route connecting the airport in the north with suburban Owendo in the south.

Indeed, one of the city's most significant landmarks is the **Léon Mba International Airport** [83 D4], located 11km to the north of the centre and 200m from the coast. North of the airport lies the **La Sablière** neighbourhood, home to the presidential family, ministers and other VIPs. La Sablière is unusually calm for Libreville, with little street life and most residents gliding past in slick limousines and 4×4s. All the luxurious mansions and villas are hidden from sight by high walls (but you can still count the swimming pools online by using satellite view).

Across the road lies the growing residential suburb of **Angondjé**, intended to relieve some of the city's notorious housing pressure. Designed to host 30,000 homes and 120,000 people, the neighbourhood is also home to administrative and social infrastructure including schools, parks, offices and a university hospital. Based on international urban development models, Angondjé aims to attract a social mix of inhabitants and offers housing for a variety of budgets.

When you take a left from the airport, **boulevard de Nice** takes you south, changing into **boulevard du Bord de Mer** – typically shortened to Bord de Mer – as you get closer to the city. The road changes names again (to **boulevard de l'Indépendance**) south of Port Môle, but it's generally referred to as Bord de Mer regardless of where in the city you are. It continues south along the coast and on to the port of Owendo, south of the city along the Gabon Estuary. Roads lead away from the waterfront into the different quartiers, such as **Bas de Gué-Gué** and **Batterie IV**, grand areas full of embassies and large houses. **Quartier Louis** [map, page 95] is primarily an entertainment district and one of the city's most visited neighbourhoods; there are plenty of restaurants, bars and nightclubs to choose from here.

The first arrondissement is bordered by **boulevard Bessieux** or the N1, which is the only route out of town and therefore perpetually crammed with traffic. All distances in Gabon are measured from *le point kilométrique zéro du Gabon* – the Bessieux roundabout opposite Port Môle is marked by an obelisk showing distances to different points around the country. When people refer to quartiers PK5, PK8 and PK12 they mean the areas 5km, 8km or 12km from this point. Boulevard Bessieux leads inland from here up to **Mont-Bouët**, the busiest part of the city, where Libreville's central market is located.

The second main west–east axis is the illustrious **boulevard Triomphal Omar Bongo Ondimba** (often shortened to boulevard Triomphal), lined with former president Bongo's fancy and futuristic governmental buildings that were constructed during the 70s oil boom, including the Assemblée Nationale (National Assembly) [78 C4], which was famously set alight during the 2016 election protests and, at the time of writing, is yet to be repaired. The boulevard sits atop what was once the marshland of the Sainte Marie Valley and leads to **Cité de la Democratie**, a former convention centre that's of little interest today. Just after boulevard Triomphal, the third arrondissement begins, home to many of Libreville's slums, including Petit Paris, Venez-Voir and Kinguele.

The fourth arrondissement stretches from the waterfront Palais Présidentiel (Presidential Palace) as far inland as avenue Félix Éboué. Here you'll find the **centre-ville**, Libreville's central business district [map, page 91]. It's home to a number of airline and other transport offices, banks, and a handful of good restaurants. The city's oldest quartiers, the colonial neighbourhoods of **London** and **Glass**, are directly to the south. Many colonial-era trading companies once had their headquarters here (page 5), but today the area is largely modern and offers little in the way of sightseeing opportunities.

Continuing south into the fifth arrondissement brings you to a lively residential area, melodically known as **Lalala** (where you'll also find Michel Marine, the port for Pointe Denis), and finally the train station and industrial port of **Owendo** at the southernmost edge of town. A local tradition has it that Lalala got its name from a real estate agent: when asked where he had constructed buildings, he responded with a short and sweet: *là, là, là* (there, there, there).

GETTING AROUND

Doing something about the daily traffic jams that obstruct all movement will certainly be one of Libreville's new mayor's major challenges. Traffic in Libreville can be chaotic, to say the least, and the current infrastructure dates from a time of fewer inhabitants and cars and has not been updated to the demands of today. Cars are ubiquitous and driving habits don't help: overtaking on the wrong side of the road and driving the wrong way are commonplace. An infamous bottleneck is the boulevard Bord du Mer, which comes to a complete standstill during rush hours. Furthermore, there's only one route out of town: via the N1 to the east which, though it is being expanded, is in woeful shape and doesn't have anywhere near the capacity to deal with the city's incoming and outgoing traffic.

Gabon's transport authority (Sogatra) runs a **public bus service** in the capital, but mismanagement and repeated strikes in 2017 and 2018 over unpaid salaries mean there are too few buses to meet demand. A new parastatal bus company, Trans-Urb, was launched in 2019 with the promise of 300 new buses for Libreville, but these had yet to materialise when this guide went to print. Thus, the most common way to get around town is by using **minibuses** or **share taxis**. The minibuses generally follow fixed routes, connecting the city centre to the furthest reaches of town, for no more than a few hundred CFA, while share taxis are more flexible in terms of deviations from their intended route.

Unfortunately, the minibus routes can be quite opaque to a casual visitor, meaning **taxis** are often a simpler option. To that end, you can hire the whole taxi (*une course*; prices start at 1,000CFA) and be taken direct to your destination or, alternatively, you can ask for just '*une place*' (one seat; 200CFA, longer distances cost slightly more), and others will be picked up along the way (not unlike an UberPool). It can be a bit hit-and-miss using collective taxis at first, but as a basic formula, when flagging down a taxi, be ready with the following information: whether you want *une course* or *une place,* your destination (or a nearby landmark), and how much you'd like to pay. Some rapid-fire roadside negotiations will likely follow, and you'll either be waved into the cab or left in the dust to try your luck again. Unsurprisingly, during rush hour, when there are crowds of people at the main road junctions desperately signalling their required direction of travel in the hope that a taxi will pick them up, it's much harder to get a ride.

Although they exist, street names are not used much in Libreville; people orientate themselves in relation to key junctions (such as carrefour Etranger near Mbolo) and prominent buildings (CK2, *la poste*, hôpital Jeanne Ebori).

The core city centre – where you'll find banks, travel agencies, clothes shops, souvenir shops and a Casino supermarket – can be easily tackled **on foot**. Once again, expect directions from locals to be given not in relation to street names but in relation to landmarks – opposite, around the corner from, behind, and so on.

CAR HIRE For information on how to **hire a car** for use within the city, see page 68. Generally speaking, count on spending at least 60,000–100,000CFA per day for a 4×4, and under 60,000CFA for a saloon car to be used in the city.

The below-listed agencies can arrange self-drive car hire, although many have restrictions on where you're allowed to drive, so be sure to confirm this before settling on a deal. They can also arrange vehicles with drivers. Several have branches at the airport, while others are represented in hotels or the Zone Industrielle d'Oloumi (Oloumi Industrial Zone) on the south side of the city, near Glass and Lalala.

🚗 **Africar** [91 C4] av de Cointet, centre-ville; 📞 01 76 12 78/9; m 04 46 94 58/02 04 39 80; e contact@africar-services.com; f AfricarGabon

🚗 **Avis (Loxea)** Léon Mba Int Airport [83 D4] & Oloumi Industrial Zone [78 D7]; 📞 01 74 58 45/6; m 05 93 86 21; w avis-gabon.com; f loxea. avisfleet.gabon

🚗 **EGCA-SATRAM** [83 D4] Léon Mba Int Airport; m 02 49 04 00/02 49 04 07/02 49 04 08; e info@satram.ga/location.lbv@satram.ga; w satram.ga

🚗 **Equateur Autos** [83 D4] Léon Mba Int Airport; 📞 01 44 32 50; m 07 14 23 82/04 05 46 74; e commercial@

equateurautos.com; w equateurautos.com; f equateurautoslocations

🚗 **Gabon Autosur** [78 D7] Oloumi Industrial Zone; 📞 01 76 98 22; e gabonautosur@yahoo.fr

🚗 **Gesparc** [78 D7] Oloumi Industrial Zone; m 07 08 28 05/07 77 84 75/07 24 96 00; e gesparc@groupesogafric.com; w gesparc.com; f

🚗 **Les Transports Citadins (LTC)** Hôtel Re-Ndama [78 D6] & Hôtel Le Cristal [91 B4]; 📞 01 79 32 54; m 04 13 83 74/05 50 73 36/07 63 25 24; e w.asseko@transports-citadins.com; w transports-citadins.com; f

TOURIST INFORMATION AND LOCAL TOUR OPERATORS

The **Agence Nationale des Parcs Nationaux du Gabon** [78 A2] (ANPN; behind Radisson Blu Okoume Palace Hotel; 📞 04 52 14 63; f parcsgabon), though not strictly a tourist office, is certainly the best source of information for visits to the national parks, particularly now that they are offering transport and accommodation services through their **Gabon Wildlife Camps by Parcs Gabon** initiative (m 04 41 65 69; e info@gabonwildlifecamps.com; w gabonwildlifecamps.com; see ad, 3rd colour section). By the time you read this, they will have three camps in Loango National Park, one in Lopé, and one in Ivindo; their English-speaking staff can arrange all accommodation and transport between them and they also plan to offer fixed-date group safaris in the future. Better still, they will soon have an information booth at Léon Mba International Airport.

Otherwise, the closest thing Gabon has to a tourist office is the **Agence Gabonaise de Développement et de Promotion du Tourisme et de l'Hôtellerie**, better known as AGATOUR [83 D4] (Léon Mba International Airport; 📞 01 73 30 10; e contacts@tourisme-gabon.org; w tourisme-gabon.org). This is supposedly the information and marketing arm of the Ministry of Tourism, but unfortunately they're a bit short on information and their office at the airport seems to be perpetually closed. They may be able to give you a map (don't count on it) or supply you with the odd leaflet, but that's about it. Nor do they run any trips to the country's interior. For this sort of service you'd be better off getting in touch with the ANPN or Gabon Wildlife Camps, or consult one of the tour operators listed below. Don't be misled by the signs for 'Agence de Voyages' around town, as most travel agencies just do flights.

LOCAL TOUR OPERATORS
241 Tour [91 A2] Opposite Prix Import en Ville, bd de l'Indépendance; 📞 01 72 51 51;

e demande@241tour.com; w 241tour.com. Offers tours to Lopé, Loango, Ivindo, Pongara, Lambaréné & more. See ad, 3rd colour section.

Chica Voyages [95 D3] Galeries les Jardins d'Ambre, bd Triomphal Omar Bongo Ondimba; 01 76 99 22; m 02 88 35 04/05 98 60 26; e chicavoyages@yahoo. fr; w chicavoyages.com. This company has been operating trips to Loango, Nyonié, Lopé, Franceville & Plateau Batéké since 2006.

Eurafrique Voyages [91 B5] centre-ville; 01 76 27 87; m 03 19 26 88; e eurafrique_voyages@ yahoo.fr; w eurafriquevoyages.com; Eurafrique Voyages. Another long-established & reliable agency offering trips to Pongara, Lopé, Loango Plateaux, Batéké & Lékédi, Cap Esterias or Arboretum Raponda Walker. They also cover the usual air & train tickets.

Gabon Untouched m 04 76 72 86/+34 660 337 503 (Spain); e info@ gabonuntouched.com; w gabonuntouched. com; . Based between Spain & Gabon, this is a commendable tour operator & NGO, with a focus on sustainable, community-based ecotourism. They run customisable trips around the country, including to some of the remotest corners, & are currently working to develop community-based conservation & ecotourism initiatives in Setté Cama (Loango National Park). See ad, 3rd colour section.

Gabon Vert Tour m 04 15 58 11; e contact@ gabonverttour.com; w gabonverttour.com; . Professional & well-connected new agency that comes recommended for trips around Estuaire (Akanda, Pongara, Crystal Mountains, Nyonié), as well as excursions further afield.

Gabon's Eden m 04 36 00 43; e info@ voyagegabon.fr; w voyagegabon.fr; gabon. is.eden. Well-regarded local agency offering trips throughout Gabon, from Estuaire to Haut-Ogooué. They also arrange airport pick-ups & other transport & receptive services.

Les Guides de l'Ogooué m 06 68 23 26/07 29 23 19; e lesguidesdelogooue@gmail.com; guidesdugabon241. This is a well-known collective of local guides with experience in all parts of Gabon. Many have also worked as park guides with ANPN.

Lopé Hôtel [91 B4] rue Ange Mba, next to Le Palmier Doré, centre-ville; 01 72 05 96/02 01 78 33; m 07 44 68 11; e hotellope@yahoo. fr; LHGabon. Satellite office of the Lopé Hôtel (page 202), where you can book your stay & safari in Lopé National Park directly.

Nkombe Remy Tour m 02 26 03 83/07 05 49 26; e nkomberemy.tour@yahoo. fr; w nkomberemytour.simplesite.com; nkomberemy.tourgabon. The English-speaking Remy cut his teeth as a guide at Lopé National Park & knows it like the back of his hand. He's worked in many of Gabon's parks, however, & today guides visitors to all parts of the country.

Nyoni Voyages & Samba Tour [91 C1] Maison Liebermann; m 07 99 70 58/06 03 97 93/05 28 75 50; e nyoni.voyages@yahoo.fr/samba.tour@ yahoo.fr; . Smaller agency based at Maison Liebermann, mostly does air tickets & such but can also arrange trips around Gabon.

Rendez-vous (RDV) Tour [78 D6] carrefour Hassan; m 05 13 72 79/07 89 07 09; rendezvoustour. Newer operator affiliated with several major hotels & offering trips to all parts of the country, from Libreville city tours & Akanda National Park day trips to multi-day excursions to the interior.

ECOTOURISM BY LOCAL NGOS

Aventures Sans Frontières [78 B3] near Feu rouge Gros Bouquet (Gros Bouquet traffic light); 01 44 48 52; m 07 39 86 71/07 54 15 24; e asfgabon@gmail.com; AventuresSansFrontieres. ASF is working to protect the turtles & whales of Gabon's coast & takes tourists on wonderful excursions to visit nesting sites in Pongara National Park (page 113). They may also be able to arrange visits to Gamba & Mayumba with enough advance notice.

PROGRAM [95 B3] L'Association Protectrice des Grands Singes de la Moukalaba/Association for the Protection of Moukalaba's Great Apes; in the WWF-Gabon Country Office, Montée Louis, Quartier Louis; m 07 12 68 04/06 62 25 72; e ong.program@gmail.com/marieangele. program@gmail.com/zangobamerina@yahoo. fr; w association-program.com; ong. program. PROGRAM is a local NGO that promotes conservation & community-based ecotourism in Moukalaba-Doudou National Park in association with WWF-Gabon. It organises trips to this magnificent park, departing from Tchibanga (page 161). They also have an office in Tchibanga (page 162), but all arrangements can be made at the WWF office in Libreville.

4

There's no lack of good hotels in Libreville but the price/quality ratio tends to be rather dire and it can be difficult to find a decent room under 40,000CFA. If you fancy international standards, prices quickly increase (count on at least 130,000CFA) and the sky seems to be the limit. Note that calling is often the most practical way to make reservations, as emails seem rarely responded to. It's also worth adding a hotel to your phone directory and checking if they're on WhatsApp, as this is increasingly popular.

As is the case in much of the world, **Airbnb** (w airbnb.com) is now present in Gabon; while it's not very popular upcountry, there are a number of good listings now available in Libreville, which may be of particular interest if you plan on staying a while.

All luxury, upmarket and mid-range hotels offer **Wi-Fi**. Most (but not all) budget options have it now as well, although it may be provided at an extra cost.

LUXURY

⌂ **Fly Hotel** [83 D5] (40 rooms) Léon Mba Int Airport; ☎ 01 44 21 70/1; e info@flyhotelgabon. com; w flyhotelgabon.com. Mostly of note for its location inside the airport grounds, this is nonetheless a trim & modern option with swimming pool & resto-bar attached. *Rooms from 150,000CFA, but deals can be had when booking online.* $$$$$

⌂ **Hôtel Le Cristal** [91 B4] (46 rooms) pl de l'Indépendance, centre-ville; ☎ 01 72 27 78; e reservations@lecristal-hotel.com; w legacyhotels.co.za/en/hotels/lecristal. Managed by the South African Legacy group, the rooms at this 4-star hotel offer great sea views & are well equipped with modern amenities including a Lavazza coffee machine, minibar & flat-screen TV. Fitness & swimming pools are available. L'Orchidée de Mer (page 94), within the hotel, is one of Libreville's best restaurants. Not cheap, but at least b/fast is included. *Rooms start at 140,000CFA.* $$$$$

⌂ **Hôtel Re-Ndama** [78 D6] (256 rooms) Bord de Mer, Glass; ☎ 01 79 32 00; e reservations@hotelrendama.com; w hotelrendama.com. Under new management since Dec 2018, this was formerly part of the Méridien chain & is still often known by that name. Though the gardens & pool facing the Atlantic are undeniably idyllic, the rooms are unforgivably dated for the price. There are 2 ATMs in the lobby. *Starting at 165,000CFA for a standard room without b/fast.* $$$$$

✳ ⌂ **Nomad Suites Résidence** [83 B1] (40 suites) bd Georges Rawiri, Okala; ☎ 01 45 45 45; m 05 40 77 20; e info@nomadlibreville. com; w nomad-residence-hoteliere.com. Offering 4-star luxury 1-bedroom apartments with kitchen area & terrace, this is a likeable & deservedly popular option north of the airport. There is also a swimming pool, fitness centre & spa. The restaurant keeps long hours & puts on a Gabonese buffet every Sun for 25,000CFA ($$$$), including live music & use of the pool. Discounts are available with direct booking or for long stays. *From 160,000CFA.* $$$$$

✳ ⌂ **Radisson Blu Okoume Palace Hotel** [78 A2] (306 rooms) Bord de Mer; ☎ 01 44 80 00; e info.libreville@radissonblu.com; w radissonblu. com/hotel-libreville. Fully refurbished & reopened under the Radisson brand in Dec 2016, the rooms & suites here are as smart, modern & stylish as you would expect, & many offer phenomenal ocean views to boot. The amenities are equally impressive, with a fitness centre, business lounge, 3 swimming pools & a popular poolside bar with music at w/ends. The restaurants serve everything from sushi to burgers & they do it well. There are 2 ATMs in the lobby. *From 160,000CFA.* $$$$$

⌂ **Résidence Hôtelière du Phare** [83 C5] (16 rooms) rond point de l'aéroport, La Sablière; m 04 12 13 14/00 00; e residenceduphare@ yahoo.fr; w residencehoteliereduphare.com. This 4-star hotel on the beach at the entrance to Quartier La Sablière area is a good choice for a splurge, with a lovely location, pool with bar, & clean, comfortable rooms with sea views. The oysters in the restaurant are delicious & they can organise whale-watching tours in season. *From 130,000CFA.* $$$$$

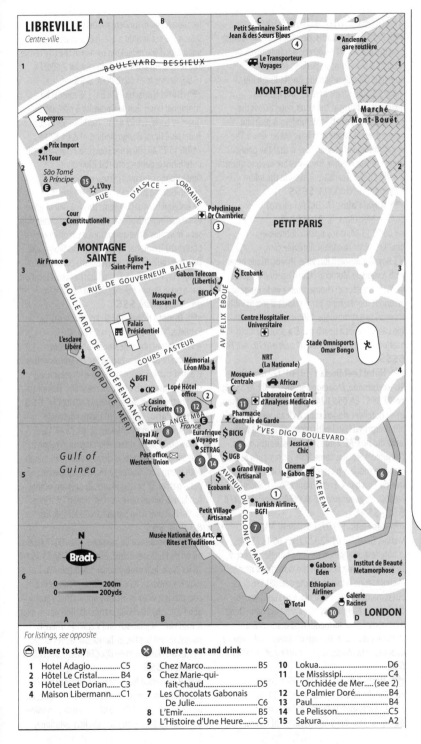

LIBREVILLE
Centre-ville

BOULEVARD BESSIEUX

MONT-BOUËT

Petit Séminaire Saint Jean & des Sœurs Bleus

4

Ancienne gare routière

Le Transporteur Voyages

Marché Mont-Bouët

Supergros

Prix Import

241 Tour

São Tomé & Príncipe

15 L'Oxy

RUE D'ALSACE - LORRAINE

Polyclinique Dr Chambrier

3

PETIT PARIS

Cour Constitutionelle

MONTAGNE SAINTE

Église Saint-Pierre

Air France

RUE DE GOUVERNEUR BALLEY

BOULEVARD DE L'INDÉPENDANCE (BORD DE MER)

Gabon Telecom (Libertis)

Ecobank

BICIG

Mosquée Hassan II

Centre Hospitalier Universitaire

Palais Présidentiel

COURS PASTEUR

L'esclave Libéré

Mémorial Léon Mba

Stade Omnisports Omar Bongo

BGFI

CK2

Lopé Hôtel office 2

NRT (La Nationale)

Mosquée Centrale

Africar

AV FÉLIX ÉBOUÉ

Casino Croisette 13 12

Laboratoire Central d'Analyses Medicales

11

RUE ANGE MBA

France

Royal Air Maroc 8

Pharmacie Centrale de Garde

Eurafrique Voyages

BICIG

YVES DIGO BOULEVARD

Gulf of Guinea

Post office, Western Union

SETRAG

9

Jessica Chic

5 14

UGB

Grand Village Artisanal

Cinema le Gabon

6

Ecobank

Petit Village Artisanal

AVENUE DU COLONEL PARANT

Turkish Airlines, BGFI

1

7

J A K E R E M Y

Musée National des Arts, Rites et Traditions

N

Bradt

0 ——— 200m
0 ——— 200yds

Gabon's Eden

Institut de Beauté Metamorphose

Ethiopian Airlines

Total

Galerie Racines

10

LONDON

For listings, see opposite

⊖ **Where to stay**

1 Hotel Adagio C5
2 Hôtel Le Cristal B4
3 Hôtel Leet Dorian C3
4 Maison Libermann C1

✴ **Where to eat and drink**

5 Chez Marco B5
6 Chez Marie-qui-
   fait-chaud D5
7 Les Chocolats Gabonais
   De Julie C6
8 L'Emir B5
9 L'Histoire d'Une Heure ... C5

10 Lokua D6
11 Le Mississipi C4
   L'Orchidée de Mer ..... (see 2)
12 Le Palmier Doré B4
13 Paul B4
14 Le Pelisson C5
15 Sakura A2

UPMARKET AND MID-RANGE

🏠 **Park Inn by Radisson** [78 A2] (140 rooms) 5 bd de Nice; ☎ 01 44 80 80; e info.libreville@ rezidorparkinn.com; w parkinn.com/hotel-libreville. Directly adjoining the Radisson Blu (page 90), the rooms here are not quite as luxurious as those at the sister hotel across the lobby, but they are bright, modern & pleasant nonetheless, & many also have ocean views. The big advantage of staying here is that the pools, fitness centre & other amenities are open to guests of either hotel. There are 2 ATMs in the lobby. *Rooms from 100,000CFA.* **$$$$**

🏠 **Royal Palm** [78 D6] (21 rooms) Bord de Mer, Glass; ☎ 01 77 03 17; m 06 00 15 14; e royalpalm.libreville@ gmail.com; w royalpalmlibreville.com; 📘 RoyalPalmHotelLibreville. This boutique hotel with a vaguely Moroccan touch opened its doors in 2013. Guests can choose from a wide range of luxurious rooms: from 21m² standard rooms with showers to a sumptuous 450m² apartment with spa bath. There's a beach bar & a pool bar, both overlooking the ocean. *Rooms start at 110,000CFA.* **$$$$**

🏠 **Hôtel Leet Dorian** [91 C3] (22 rooms) rue Alsace-Lorraine, Montagne Sainte; ☎ 01 72 55 46; m 07 38 51 84/05 73 24 24; e leet-dorian@yahoo. fr; w hotelleet-dorian.com. A clean, welcoming but overpriced hotel with rooms kitted out with large dbl bed, AC, cable TV & a small sitting area. The junior suite has some little extras, such as a carpet, a fridge & pictures on the wall. There is free Wi-Fi, a bar & a restaurant (**$$$**). *Rooms 70,000CFA, junior suite 85,000CFA. B/fast 4,500CFA.* **$$$–$$$$**

🏠 **Les Flots** [78 D7] (20 rooms) Michel Marine, Glass; ☎ 01 72 92 22; m 06 18 75 73; e hotellesflots@yahoo.com; w hotellesflots.com. This long-serving hotel on the waterfront next to Michel Marine is looking quite dated these days, but remains a convenient place to stay if you're catching an early-morning *navette* to Pointe Denis. It has a nice pool surrounded by gardens & a children's play area, though it's overpriced, even by Gabonese standards. *Rooms starting at 60,000CFA.* **$$$**

🏠 **Hotel Adagio** [91 C5] (28 rooms) rue Mapako James, centre-ville; ☎ 01 76 31 13; e infoshoteladagio@gmail.com; 📘 hoteladagiolbv. With an excellent central

location & clean, modern rooms (with AC & flat-screen TV) set around a green courtyard, this is a good pick if you're looking to stay in the city centre. The restaurant does a plat du jour for 7,500CFA (**$$**). *Rooms from 50,000CFA.* **$$$**

🏠 **Hôtel Hibiscus** [78 B3] (38 rooms) bd Triomphal Omar Bongo Ondimba & bd Quaben, Quartier Louis; m 07 87 10 70/06 83 55 18 (bd Triomphal Omar Bongo Ondimba) & 04 62 14 74/06 13 75 45 (Quartier Louis); e reservationHB@ hotelhibiscusgabon.com (bd Triomphal Omar Bongo Ondimba) & reservationHL@ hotelhibiscusgabon.com (Quartier Louis); w hotelhibiscusgabon.com. This is a pair of good-value mid-range hotels under the same ownership, set a few mins' drive away from each other on boulevard Triomphal Omar Bongo Ondimba & in Quartier Louis, respectively. Rooms come with fridge, TV, AC & Wi-Fi, & the Quartier Louis location has a pool. *Rooms from 42,000 to 65,000CFA, depending on size.* **$$$**

🏠 **Onomo Hôtel** [83 B1] (118 rooms) La Sablière; ☎ 01 45 91 00; m 05 60 90 35; e reservation.libreville@onomohotel.com; w onomohotel.com. Facing the US Embassy, this is a mid-market business hotel with reasonably smart rooms & lots of art on the walls. There's an ATM in the lobby. *Rooms around 80,000CFA.* **$$$**

🏠 **Le Patio** [95 C2] (20 rooms) descente Jeanne Ebori, Quartier Louis; ☎ 01 73 47 16; m 06 60 37 86; e reservation.lepatio@yahoo.fr. This simple little hotel is clean & well maintained, with rooms surrounding a small but pleasant patio garden of potted plants. Rooms are simply furnished, but all have AC, flat-screen TV, fridge & Wi-Fi. *Rooms from around 55,000CFA. B/fast 8,000CFA.* **$$$**

☀️🏠 **Résidence Le Havane** [78 D7] (8 rooms) off bd de l'Indépendance, Glass; m 06 44 83 15/04 16 93 27; e lehavanegabon@gmail.com. Still mostly known by its earlier name of Résidence Léa, this is a small & friendly option that's pretty good value by Libreville standards. Rooms are neat & trim with AC, flat-screen TV & Wi-Fi. There is no restaurant but the in-house bar serves drinks, snacks & b/fast. *From 46,000CFA (add 5,000CFA pp for b/fast).* **$$$**

🏠 **Résidence Hôtelière Le Jomonia** [78 B2] (14 rooms) descente du Bas de Gué-Gué, Bas de Gué-Gué; m 07 06 40 00; e info.lejomonia@ gmail.com; 📘 Lejomonia. Slightly overdone, but nonetheless modern & well-kept rooms with AC & flat-screen TV in a quiet (& somewhat out-of-the-way) residential neighbourhood. Studios with kitchenette also available. *Rooms from 45,000CFA.* **$$$**

BUDGET

L'Etoile d'Or [95 B2] (15 rooms) Quartier Louis; 01 73 53 13. Formerly known as the **Bilbouqet**, this is a simple, small hotel with reasonable rooms & free Wi-Fi. The terrace resto-bar serves pizzas & grills. *Rooms 30,000–40,000CFA.* **$$–$$$**

Green Village [78 D7] (14 rooms) commune Igoumié, east of Owendo; ✪ 0.3376, 9.5579; m 06 46 33 88; e office@greenvillagegabon.org; w greenvillagegabon.org; f Greenvillagegabon. Set in a remote rural location along a branch of the Komo River on the furthest southeastern outskirts of Libreville, this fetching ecotourism outpost makes for an easy escape from the city. Hiking, fishing, canoeing & other excursions into the surrounding forests & mangroves can be arranged, along with archery, trampolining & lawn games at the lodge. Rooms come with AC & hot showers, & are set in standalone or duplex bungalows scattered throughout the grassy grounds. The restaurant serves a menu of European & African dishes (**$$$**). Morning & afternoon transfers (to be arranged in advance) are done by boat (7,000CFA pp) from the Centre d'appui à la pêche artisanale de Libreville (CAPAL; Libreville Artisanal Fishing Support Centre; ✪ 0.3670, 9.4609) near Michel Marine, or by 4x4 (3,000CFA pp) from Le Forêt Noire restaurant/bakery (page 97) at carrefour SNI in Owendo. To get here on your own, it's 12km past the Lycée Technique National Omar Bongo Ondimba (✪ 0.3260, 9.5039) in Owendo by road, of which 10km or so is unsurfaced. *35,000/50,000CFA standard/superior dbl.* **$$–$$$**

Hotel L'Orchidée Glass [78 D7] (45 rooms) bd de l'Indépendance, Glass; 01 74 85 92; m 07 15 16 55; e s.e.h.g.hotellerie@yahoo.fr; w hotel-orchidee-gabon.com. With well-kept AC rooms (with fridge, TV & Wi-Fi) & a well-regarded pizza restaurant, this is a solid budget pick at the south end of town, not far from Michel Marine. They have 2 other (more expensive) locations in La Sablière [83 C3] & Owendo [78 D7]. *From 30,000CFA.* **$$–$$$**

✳ **La Pirogue** [95 C1] (6 rooms) Anguene, Quartier Louis; m 07 39 81 80; f littlebodega. Known for its popular terrace resto-bar serving grills & continental dishes, the handful of upstairs rooms here are cheerily done up in colourful African art & all come with AC, hot water & Wi-Fi. There's a billiard table & *pétanque* pitch as well. *Good value at 35,000–45,000CFA.* **$$–$$$**

Hôtel Louis [95 C1] rue Pierre Barro, Quartier Louis; m 05 40 56 70/04 44 96 26. This identikit-feeling guesthouse is a bit cheaper, but not nearly as nice as La Pirogue just up the road. *En-suite rooms start at 25,000/28,000CFA with fan/AC.* **$$**

Hôtel Tropicana [83 D6] (around 40 rooms) bd de Nice; 01 73 15 31/2; e tropicana.resa@gmail.com. Long-term favourite because of its magnificent location on the beach combined with its relatively inexpensive rooms. The cheapest rooms show their age & are very much in need of renovation: they are shabby & spartan, with basic en-suite facilities (no hot water) & noisy AC. The newer rooms cost more, & although they could still hardly be called modern, they are nonetheless much better value. The restaurant opens directly on to the beach, offering a splendid view & good (though not exactly cheap; **$$$**) seafood meals. It's a perennial favourite among expats, so make advance reservations & be prepared to meet some characters at the bar. It gets reliably crowded with Librevilleois enjoying a beachside lunch at w/ends. Paid Wi-Fi. *Older rooms 25,000CFA (sgl), newer rooms 35,000CFA.* **$$**

Hotel Padonou Charbonnages [78 C2] (20 rooms) off Voie Express, Charbonnages; 01 44 55 48; m 06 25 48 93; w hotel-padonou-charbonnages.business.site. Though rather out of the way in the Charbonnages neighbourhood, this is a good budget pick & potentially convenient for trips to Akanda NP from the Débarcadère d'Ambowé. Rooms come with AC, hot water & Wi-Fi. *Rooms start at 15,000CFA.* **$–$$**

Maison Libermann [91 C1] (20 units) bd Bessieux ('avant l'ancien gare routière, en face du Petit Séminaire Saint Jean & des Sœurs Bleus'); ✪ 0.4039, 9.4492; m 06 34 68 98/05 20 98 86; e accueil.libermanngabon@gmail.com. It's worth having the directions down pat in French (as above), as this is not a place that taxi drivers tend to know. Once exclusively a *maison d'accueil* (welcome house) for new Roman Catholic missionaries arriving in West Africa, the Maison Libermann has long been the saving grace for budget travellers in Libreville. There are dbls in the yellow building with fridge, AC & TV, while upstairs you'll find the cheapest decent rooms in town (with fans). Additionally, there are about 10 rather spartan studios. There is no restaurant, &

not much in the immediate vicinity either, but it's a short ride to Géant CKDO (page 99) or Galerie Mbolo (page 101). Be extra vigilant if you are wandering around the neighbourhood at night, as you're just around the corner from Marché Mont-Bouët where muggings are not unheard of. *11,500/18,000CFA dbl with fan/AC; 25,000CFA studio with AC & TV*. **$–$$**

✗ WHERE TO EAT AND DRINK

There are so many restaurants in Libreville that it's not possible to list them all, or indeed to keep track of them all. This is a city that's growing and changing all the time, and inevitably places disappear and are replaced. Quartier Louis has long been the city's most happening district in the evenings, so you could just wander around until somewhere takes your fancy. It's not very well lit, but it's a safe area. Below you'll find a number of reliable places in different price categories, but if you want to dig into the very latest in Libreville dining, ⬜ @lbvfoodies is a tasty place to start.

UPPER RANGE

✗ **Le Bateau Ivre** [95 A1] Bord de Mer, Batterie IV; ☏ 01 44 34 87; ❚ BateaulvreLbv; ⏰ noon–15.00 & 19.00–23.00, until 02.00 Fri & Sat. The place to see & be seen in Libreville, with a beautiful view out on to the ocean thanks to an exceptionally huge window. Haute cuisine with prices like those in the best Parisian restaurants. **$$$$$**

✗ **Le Confidentiel** [95 B3] Bord de Mer, Quartier Louis; m 05 79 00 00; ❚ LeConfidentielLibreville; ⏰ noon–16.00 & 18.30–23.00 Mon–Sat. Serving fine French cuisine on the waterfront, this is another contender for Libreville's top restaurant. Mains start around 20,000CFA & the atmosphere is equally rarefied. **$$$$$**

✳ ✗ **Lokua** [91 D6] bd de l'Indépendance, London; m 06 83 51 83; ⏰ noon–15.00 & 17.00–01.00 Mon–Fri, 17.00–01.00 Sat. This popular restaurant opened in 2004 & offers fine cuisine in a sophisticated ambience. Original dishes such as *caviar d'Atanga* (fruit from Central Africa) & a choice of more than 130 different wines, whiskies & liqueurs. Not cheap but worth it. **$$$$$**

✗ **L'Orchidée de Mer** [91 B4] Hôtel Le Cristal; ☏ 01 72 27 77; ⏰ lunch & dinner daily. Fine cuisine with fresh local seafood, grills & pasta in classy surroundings. **$$$$$**

✗ **Palais d'Amine** [78 A3] rue André Minsta, Batterie IV; m 05 26 88 88; ❚ Restaurant Gastronomique Le Palais d'Amine; ⏰ 09.30–18.30

daily (*salon de thé*), 19.30–23.30 (restaurant), 09.00–18.00 Sun (reservation-only brunch). Excellent Moroccan cuisine including couscous & tajines in a wonderful garden. Indoors the restaurant looks like a grand Moroccan mansion. During the day it functions as a *salon de thé* (tea room), & there's a reservation-only Sun brunch. **$$$$$**

✗ **Le Phare du Large** [78 A3] Bord de Mer, Batterie IV; ☏ 01 73 02 73; ❚ PhareDuLarge; ⏰ noon–15.00 & 20.00–23.00 Mon–Fri, 20.00–23.00 Sat, closed Sun. Pricey, gastronomic French haute cuisine in a stiff & formal environment. There is an extensive wine list with bottles ranging from 13,000CFA to 1 million CFA. **$$$$$**

✗ **Le Wapety** [95 B2] Montée Louis, Quartier Louis; m 07 52 61 74; ❚ Wapety; ⏰ 18.30–late daily. A long-time Libreville hotspot, Le Wapety is an inviting restaurant with original décor. It has the look & feel of an après-ski bar, with several giant flat-screen TVs & illuminated aquariums. After an excellent dinner the place turns into a trendy club where you can dance until deep into the night. The menu is European & covers tapas, pasta & grilled steak. For a 3-course meal not including drinks, expect to spend at least 25,000CFA. **$$$$$**

ABOVE AVERAGE AND MID-RANGE

✗ **The Pearl** [95 B3] Montée Louis, Quartier Louis; m 02 77 05 05; ❚ pearllibreville; ⏰ 18.00–late Tue–Sat. Trendy restaurant

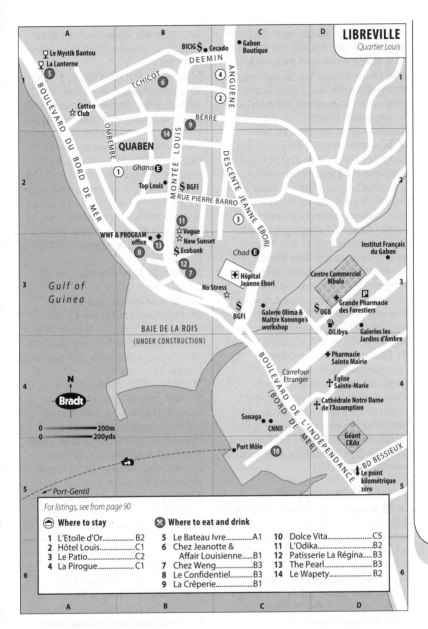

For listings, see from page 90

LIBREVILLE
Quartier Louis

Where to stay

1 L'Etoile d'Or.................. B2
2 Hôtel Louis.................... C1
3 Le Patio......................... C2
4 La Pirogue.................... C1

Where to eat and drink

5 Le Bateau Ivre.............. A1
6 Chez Jeanotte &
    Affair Louisienne...... B1
7 Chez Weng................... B3
8 Le Confidentiel............ B3
9 La Crêperie.................. B1
10 Dolce Vita................... C5
11 L'Odika....................... B2
12 Patisserie La Régina.... B3
13 The Pearl.................... B3
14 Le Wapety................... B2

decorated in purple, black & white that turns into a lively club after midnight (page 98). European cuisine. **$$$$**

Le Sud [78 D6] bd de l'Indépendance, Glass; **m** 07 53 28 28; ☉ noon–23.00 Mon–Fri, 19.00–01.00 Sat. Set along the main drag in Glass, this French-run restaurant is legendary in Libreville for its fresh seafood. The owner prepares the catch of the day himself, & the interior is suitably nautical-feeling, with wood-panelled walls & a large aquarium. Recommended. **$$$$**

Chez Marco [91 B5] rue Victor Schoelcher, centre-ville; ☎ 01 77 83 24; ☉ lunch Mon–Sat. Across from Le Pelisson & formerly known as the Marquisat, this place is popular for business lunches, with a limited & expensive menu. **$$$**

✳ ✕ **Chez Marie-qui-fait-chaud** [91 D5] off av Akandé, Likouala; ✆ 0.3865, 9.4530;✆ 01 32 13 59. Marie is very warm & friendly, which can make a welcome change from the stuffy reception at some of Libreville's fancier establishments. She cooks excellent langoustines & local dishes from her home country Cameroon & sometimes even sings for her clients. Recommended. **$$$**

✳ ✕ **L'Odika** [95 B2] Montée Louis, Quartier Louis;✆ 01 73 69 20; m 06 25 34 34; ⏱ closed Tue. Don't miss out on this old favourite that serves a mixture of European & Gabonese/African dishes. Not only is the food good, but so is the refreshingly breezy open-sided design, with interesting wooden statues, soft lighting & greenery. **$$$**

✕ **Life by Mayena** [78 A1] Bord de Mer; w lifebymayena.com; ⏱ 09.00–midnight daily. This new multi-storey oceanfront entertainment complex is home to 4 different high-end restaurants covering Asian, Italian, Gabonese & even Tex-Mex cuisines, with mains at any of them going for 10,000CFA & up. There's an ice-cream parlour & rooftop lounge-bar (page 99), too. **$$$**

✕ **Sakura** [91 A2] rue d'Alsace Lorraine, Montagne Sainte; m 06 52 25 74/07 75 29 58; ☐ sakuralbv; ⏱ noon–23.00 Tue–Fri, 19.00–midnight Sat & Sun. Widely regarded as Libreville's best Japanese, this popular place offers a menu of sushi, *sashimi* & *maki* (starting at around 5,000CFA/roll), along with a number of Thai dishes (from 7,000CFA). It's cool & refined, but refreshingly unfussy. **$$$**

CHEAP AND CHEERFUL

✳ ✕ **Aeroclub** [83 D4] Directly left of the airport's Afrijet terminal;✆ 01 73 57 77; ⏱ noon–22.00 daily. This time-warped pilot's hangout is well hidden in the airport grounds, but open to the public. The back windows overlook the runway & it makes an exciting place to watch planes take off & land. The menu is chalked up on a board near the entrance, & there's a tasty variety of African & continental dishes on offer from around 7,000CFA. **$$**

✳ ✕ **Chez Jeanotte & Affair Louisienne** [95 B1] rue Tchicot, Quartier Louis; m 07 68 52 50/05 33 50 86; ⏱ lunch & dinner daily. Hugely popular local place for beer & brochettes served with rice or fried plantains & a fiery pepper sauce, all for just a couple of thousand CFA. **$$**

✕ **Chez Weng** [95 B3] Montée Louis, Quartier Louis;✆ 01 73 00 22; ⏱ noon–15.30 &

18.00–23.30 daily. Famous Chinese restaurant with a popular all-you-can-eat buffet on Fri & Sat nights. **$$**

✕ **Dolce Vita** [95 C5] Port Môle;✆ 01 72 42 38; w ladolcevitagabon.com; ⏱ noon–15.00 & 19.00–22.30 Mon–Sat, dinner only Sun. Don't let the grey surroundings of Port Môle mislead you, as Dolce Vita is a lovely Italian restaurant that has served fresh pizza, pasta & risotto since 1996. Pizzas start at 7,000CFA; meat & seafood dishes are slightly more expensive. If you sit at one of the window tables, it feels a bit like being in the cabin of a large boat – the décor is all wood & you have a great view over the water towards the city centre. They have a 2nd location in La Sablière [83 C3] (m 07 84 61 00) & a 3rd in Owendo [78 D7] (m 07 51 13 72). **$$**

✕ **L'Emir** [91 B5] rue Ange Mba, centre-ville; ✆ 01 77 41 87; m 06 68 68 17; ⏱ 09.00–23.00 Mon–Sat. Serves good Lebanese dishes in a modern setting, with shawarma & falafel sandwiches for 3,000CFA & kofta brochettes for 7,000CFA. Keeps some of the longest hours in the city centre & has a pretty terrace if you're sick of the AC inside. **$$**

✕ **L'Histoire d'Une Heure** [91 C5] av de Cointet, centre-ville; m 02 70 22 49; ⏱ lunch until 21.00 Mon–Sat. This is a relaxed & affordable option in the city centre, with comfortable indoor & outdoor seating & a daily menu (listed on the chalkboards out front) covering snacks, sandwiches, & West African dishes from 2,000CFA. **$$**

✕ **KFC** [91 D5] rond-point de l'Aéroport; ✆ 02 23 73 28; ⏱ 10.00–23.00 daily. This American fast-food chain landed in Gabon in 2019 & serves exactly what you'd expect in a shiny new building just outside the airport. **$$**

✳ ✕ **Le Mississipi** [91 C4] bd Yves Digo, centre-ville; m 06 10 00 55/06 24 47 23; ⏱ 09.00–15.00 & 19.00–midnight Mon–Sat, dinner only Sun. Casual, well priced, & as central as can be, this unassuming restaurant has long been the best address in Libreville for grilled fish. The short menu covers sea creatures large & small, including Gabonese-style *crabes farcis* (stuffed crabs), but meat lovers are taken care of as well – vegetarians less so. Portions are large & start at around 6,000CFA. **$$**

✕ **Tivoli** [78 D7] bd de l'Indépendance, Glass; m 06 26 58 03; ☐ restauletivoli; ⏱ noon–23.00

daily. Very popular with foreigners & Gabonese alike. Extensive menu with dishes from all over the world including Senegalese *thiéboudiène*, Moroccan couscous & of course Italian pizza. There's another branch, Rivoli [83 D5] (rond-point de l'Aéroport; **m** 06 26 58 03; ⏲ noon–23.00 daily), which serves good pizza. **$$**

✖ Vert Jaune Bleu (Le Débarcadère) [78 B1] Débarcadère d'Ambowé; **✆** 01 76 21 63. Set right at the Débarcadère d'Ambowé, this is a good spot for grilled fish & a popular bar at w/ends. It's also one of the jumping-off points for trips into Akanda National Park. **$$**

✳ ✖ La Voile Rouge [78 A2] Opposite Lycée Léon Mba, Bord de Mer; **m** 06 62 62 66; ⏲ noon– midnight Sun–Wed, until 02.00 Thu, until 03.00 Fri & Sat. Best known of the trio of restaurants on the **beach opposite Lycée Léon Mba**, La Voile Rouge is probably also the nicest of the bunch. (Though neighbouring **Family Beach** [78 A2] or **Samo Beach** [78 A3] also have their loyalists.) All serve a variety of seafood plates & smaller meals like burgers & shawarma. At w/ends a line of grills pops up along the beach here selling freshly caught & barbecued fish. It's a popular spot for a cold Régab as well (& they're open late at w/ends to accommodate). *Sandwiches from 3,000CFA & plates from 7,000CFA.* **$$**

✖ Ya Wakilou [83 D5] Across the street & just north of the airport entrance; **m** 06 25 11 15. This no-frills Senegalese hangout does the cheapest plat du jour for miles (1,500CFA) & makes a great last stop to get in some African cuisine if you're on your way out of town. **$$**

SNACK BARS AND BAKERIES

🍽 Les Chocolats Gabonais De Julie [91 C6] av du Colonel Parant, centre-ville; **m** 07 52 19 64; **f**; ⏲ 08.30–19.00 Mon–Sat. Step into this unsuspecting hole in the wall in the city centre to meet Julie, Gabon's premier chocolatier, making a variety of award-winning chocolates – spiced with everything from ginger to chilli pepper – from purely Gabonese ingredients. **$**

🍽 La Crêperie [95 B1] Montée Louis, Quartier Louis; **m** 02 43 70 14; **f** lacreperiebar; ⏲ noon–22.00 daily. Good crêpes in a cute café setting on Montée Louis, with prices starting around 2,000CFA. **$**

🍽 Le Forêt Noire [78 D7] carrefour SNI, Owendo; **m** 06 77 97 47; **f** Lfn241; ⏲ 06.00–

21.30 Mon–Sat & 06.00–13.00 Sun. Just opposite Owendo's Super CKdo, this is a well-loved address on the south side of town for pastries, cakes, coffee, sandwiches, salads, burgers & freshly baked bread. There's also a plat du jour for 6,000CFA. **$**

🍽 Le Palmier Doré [91 B4] rue Ange Mba; **m** 01 72 64 77; **f**; ⏲ 06.00–19.00. Here since 1996, this is a landmark bakery & coffee shop in the city centre (right next to the office for Lopé Hôtel) selling freshly baked pastries, quiches, sandwiches & ice creams, along with a selection of teas & coffees. **$**

🍽 Patisserie La Régina [95 B3] Montée Louis, Quartier Louis; **m** 04 44 12 12; **w** patisserielaregina.com; **f** PatisserieLaRegina; ⏲ 07.00–22.00. At the entrance to Quartier Louis, this is a perennially popular patisserie serving croissants, sandwiches, crepes, pizzas & juices, & a rotating plat du jour for 6,500CFA. They also do custom cakes, tarts, & other sweets. **$**

🍽 Paul rue Ange Mba, centre-ville [91 B4], bd Quaben, Trois Quartiers [78 A3] & Léon Mba Int Airport [83 D5]; **✆** 01 44 29 02; **w** paul-gabon.com; ⏲ 07.00–22.00 daily. The first franchise of this famous French chain of patisseries opened in Libreville in 2018 & they have since expanded to 3 locations around town, serving freshly baked breads, pastries, coffees & other light meals. **$**

✳ 🍽 Le Pelisson [91 C5] rue Coniquet, centre-ville; **✆** 01 76 52 58; ⏲ 06.00–20.00 Mon–Sat. This popular *salon de thé* is a Libreville institution, having been around since 1936. The salon with terrace is on the 1st floor of a charming colonial building. There is a mouthwatering adjoining boulangerie-patisserie. They have a 2nd location in Okala [83 C2] (rond-point Pélisson; **m** 07 66 13 24), just north of the airport. **$**

🍽 Touti Frouti [78 D7] bd de l'Indépendance, Glass; **m** 04 16 78 78/05 16 78 78. This is a colourful & unpretentious patisserie serving waffles, crepes & light meals, along with fresh fruit shakes & milkshakes, all starting from around 3,000CFA. They also do some Middle Eastern sweets like *kanafeh* & *baklava*. **$**

🍽 Village Coffee [78 B1] 700m before Débarcadère d'Ambowé, Charbonnages; **m** 06 89 68 68; **w** villagecoffeegabon.com; ⏲ 13.00–midnight Tue–Sun. This is a trendy but unpretentious resto-bar with coffee, cocktails & karaoke. **$**

Orchestre Stukas had it right when, in their 1983 hit 'Ballade a Libreville', they said 'Les Librevilleois aiment bien danser' ('the Librevilleois love to dance'). Indeed, in the capital, it's party time all the time. The city's buzzing nightlife attracts a mixed crowd of middle- and upper-class Gabonese, expats and *tuées* (prostitutes). Quartier Louis is Libreville's most concentrated entertainment district, with venues staying open from early evening until early morning, or until the punters can no longer stand.

Libreville is home to a whole lot of flashy nightclubs where people go to see and *be* seen, but is unfortunately a little short on more characterful hangouts. **Le Mystic Bantu** [95 A1] (✳; Bord de Mer; m 04 73 73 09; f MysticBantu), hidden away next to the Archives Nationales (National Archives), is a notable exception, with seating in an art-filled garden under palm palapa huts and a bar mixing up tropical cocktails. They do simple meals and grills as well, so it's a great place to kick off the night. A few steps to the south along Bord de Mer, you'll find the brand-new **La Lanterne** [95 A1] (next to Le Bateau Ivre; m 06 45 74 46; lanterne.bar). Opened in late 2019, this is a chic rooftop bar done up in a vaguely Moroccan style, serving a full cocktail menu and Spanish tapas to soak up the booze. There's room to dance, and every Thursday night they have an open bar (including cocktails; ⊕ 19.00–midnight; 55,000CFA).

From here, just inside Quartier Louis and along rue Tchicot is Libreville's evergreen nightspot, **Cotton Club** [95 A1] (rue Tchicot, Quartier Louis; m 04 13 00 00). The crowd here is usually a bit older than some of the other spots in Louis listed in this section, but it's nonetheless a reliable address for a party. Depending on the night, they put on salsa, karaoke, and other themed events.

From here, you've got a host of options inside Quartier Louis, most of which sit along the main drag of Montée de Louis. To start, there's the glitzy **Vogue** [95 B2] (Montée Louis; m 06 56 30 63; ⊕ 22.00–03.00 Wed–Thu, 21.00–04.00 Fri–Sat), one of the city's most exclusive and fashionable clubs (with prices to match). Dress to impress and arrive late, preferably after midnight. Equally glamorous and just a few wobbly steps down the road, **New Sunset** [95 B3] (Montée Louis; m 07 62 86 76; f newsunsetloungebar; ⊕ 18.00–02.00 daily, until 04.00 Thu–Sat) is cool and glittering, with staff decked out in crisp black and white, and a long menu of premium cocktails for between 7,000 and 10,000CFA. Just across the road is **The Pearl** [95 B3], a restaurant (page 94) that turns into a lively nightspot as the evening wears on. As with Vogue and New Sunset, it's not cheap: champagne cocktails cost 18,000CFA and a beer at the bar will set you back 3,000CFA.

For a somewhat more inclusive vibe and a broader mix of tunes and clientele, head towards the bottom of Montée Louis to the aptly named **No Stress** [95 C3] (m 06 26 66 94; ⊕ 18.00–05.00 Tue–Sun), where you'll find regular theme nights and the occasional live performance as well; early evenings here are for lounging, but things really start to get moving after midnight. On the other side of Quartier Louis, **Luxor Lounge** [78 B3] (bd Quaben; m 04 00 74 04; f luxorloungeclub; ⊕ 16.00–01.00 Tue–Thu, 16.00–04.00 Fri–Sat) is a newly popular lounge-bar inside the Louis branch of Hotel Hibiscus (page 92), where you can catch the football, sing karaoke or dance kizomba, depending on the night of the week.

Closer to the city centre in Montagne Sainte (and very close to the excellent Japanese food at Sakura; page 96), **L'Oxy** [91 A1] (rue d'Alsace Lorraine, Montagne Sainte; m 06 20 44 02; f L'Oxy Night Club) isn't as high end as any of the above, but is nonetheless a relaxed place to drink and dance under the disco lights with a somewhat older crowd. Not far from here in centre-ville, gamblers can try their luck at **Casino Croisette** [91 B4] (Bord de Mer; m 06 35 89 17; f Le Casino Croisette; ⊕ 11.00–04.00 daily). Leaving the centre, **Yoka Sports Bar** [78 B1] (Voie Express, Bas de Gué-Gué; f YokaSportBar; ⊕ 17.00–02.00 daily) is a fabulous spot to catch a football match (despite being rather out of the way in Bas de Gué-Gué), and there's usually a DJ or live music on after the final whistle blows.

If you really want to splash out for the night, there's only one place to go: the newly opened **Sky Life by Mayena** [78 A1] (inside Life by Mayena; m 07 04 89 89; f skylifebymayena; ⊕ from 17.00 Tue–Sun). Perched on the sixth-floor rooftop above the restaurants of Life by Mayena (page 96), this has quickly become a favourite among Libreville's sophisticated set. The terrace lounge out front offers ocean breezes and views, while the sparkling dance floor inside is host to a rotating schedule of fashion shows, parties, concerts, DJs and more. Cocktails normally start at 10,000CFA, but if you'd like to drink in a bit of the atmosphere without sinking your budget, happy hour runs from 17.00 until 20.00 every Tuesday to Friday.

SHOPPING

Bear in mind when contemplating a shopping trip that Libreville virtually comes to a standstill over lunchtime and nothing is open.

SHOPPING CENTRES AND SUPERMARKETS Libreville is well catered for by supermarkets. Owing to negligible local production almost everything is imported and, as a result, astronomically expensive. Not only luxury products, but also daily ones are usually more than twice the price of those back home. Nonetheless, if you're willing to pay for them, Libreville's supermarkets stock a wide range of wines, yoghurts and cheeses.

Centre Commercial Mbolo [95 D3] on boulevard Triomphal Omar Bongo Ondimba is the city's primary shopping centre, though it's rather dull and feels outdated. The centrepiece is an enormous Casino supermarket, accompanied by a newsagent/bookshop, cyber café, travel agency, a couple of souvenir boutiques and a decent coffee shop, all under one roof. The Grand Pharmacie des Forestiers, also inside the centre, is well stocked with insect repellents, vitamins, baby foods and every recognised brand of face cream.

Besides Mbolo, there's the ubiquitous **Cecado** (known as CKdo at the larger stores) supermarket chain. From the enormous Géant CKdo at the end of boulevard Bessieux [95 D5] (⊕ 08.30–12.30 & 15.00–20.00 Mon–Thu, 08.30–20.00 Fri–Sat) to more modest branches in Libreville's slums, Cecado is unavoidable. There's another Géant CKdo down the road in Glass.

Casino is another popular supermarket chain, with its main location on rue Lafond in centre-ville. **Top Louis** [95 B2] is the largest supermarket in Quartier Louis. **CK2** [91 B4] (bd de l'Indépendance) sells everything, from tools to furniture.

MARKETS Prices in the formal supermarkets are beyond the reach of a large proportion of Librevilleois, who usually do their shopping in street markets. Therefore, nearly every quartier in the city has its own market, which sell everything you might need – shoes, spices, household goods – and more besides, including plenty of bushmeat, vegetables (looking well past their prime), and occasionally even ivory. Haggling is the name of the game here, and is generally good-natured.

The largest of these local markets is Marché Mont-Bouët [91 D1/2] (next to the *ancienne gare routière*), which takes its name from the hill commemorating Commandant Bouët-Willaumez, who named the city back in 1849. You can find just about anything here, and there are plenty of snack stands to choose from, but leave your valuables elsewhere. Unregulated expansion has led to dangerous operating conditions and the market catches fire almost once a year.

Plans for a **new central market** to replace Mont-Bouët were announced in 2013, but the Grand Marché de Libreville [78 D4] was nowhere near complete in 2019 and the project, initially planned to accommodate more than 3,000 merchants in the Peyrie neighbourhood, seems to be indefinitely stalled.

Though you'll likely only end up out here to pick up transport upcountry, **Marché Banane** [78 D4] at PK8 sells a whole lot more than just bananas, with several floors of stalls selling everything from mangoes to mobile phones.

GALLERIES: ARTS, CRAFTS AND CURIOS There are two covered artisans' markets in the city centre, the Grand Village Artisanal [91 C5] and the Petit Village Artisanal [91 C5], within a couple of streets of each other. They sell crafts from all over Africa, including carved masks, statues and jewellery, as well as bowls, boxes, chairs, beads and more. Before you enter, make sure you feel ready for eager salesmen. If you're on the hunt for something genuinely Gabonese, look for carvings made of *mbigou* stone (page 158). All mbigou carvings you'll find at the markets here likely originate from the Coopérative des Produits Artisanaux de Mbigou [78 A1] (COOPAM; Alibandeng artisanal village, behind the Charles de Gaulle military camp not far from the airport; m 07 72 06 40/07 89 58 89). COOPAM was created in 1980 by the French–Gabonese sculptor Basile Allainmat. More than 60 sculptors, specialised in carving the mbigou stone, sell their pieces – mostly female figures – through the co-operative. There are other interesting arts and crafts shops around here, including Chim's Heritage Fine Art [78 A1] (near the entrance to the Charles de Gaulle military camp; m 06 24 63 53; w chimsheritagefineart.com; f). Chim specialises in paintings of nature scenes, but he also does portraits. More excitingly, you can even have one commissioned.

Libreville's most famous sculptor is **Maître Konongo**, and you can find his workshop [95 C3] on Descente Jeanne Ebori in Quartier Louis. Practically next door is the lovely **Galerie Olima** [95 C3] (☏ 01 73 02 90), where sculptor Bambi Tigoé and her team produce beautiful wooden statues carved from the different coloured woods found in Gabon's forests. Each piece is unique and hand-signed.

At the top of Quartier Louis, **Gabon Boutique** [95 C1] (bd Quaben; m 07 41 00 06/07 53 57 94; w gabonboutique.com; ⊕ 10.00–18.00 Mon–Sat) sells a fine variety of traditional masks and musical instruments, alongside more contemporary pieces. It works closely with the artists and artisans of the Coopérative Les Arts Originaires du Gabon (COOPAROG).

In centre-ville near Le Palmier Doré, you'll find the **Galerie d'Arts Efaro** (m 04 56 21 46; f Efaro0), home to **Georges Mbourou**, one of Gabon's most celebrated contemporary painters. **Galerie Racines** [91 D6] (☏ 01 74 11 48; m 05 37 66 58; f GalerieArtRacine) on rue Anchouey (Montée London) offers a surprisingly large collection behind a small door: household decorations, sculptures, jewellery, haute couture – all made in Gabon.

Galeries les Jardins d'Ambre [95 D3] (opposite Centre Commercial Mbolo, bd Triomphal Omar Bongo Ondimba; m 06 21 19 56/05 10 47 38; ⊕ Mon–Sat) houses **Images du Gabon**, a photo gallery specialising in large-format prints by British-born David Harwood. To the north in Batterie IV, **La Galerie Éphémère** (near St André; **m** 07 64 01 49; **f** galeriephemere) is a stylish boutique selling very fashionable jewellery and homewares made in Gabon. Up the road in Bas de Gué-Gué, **Atelier Origines** [78 B2] (next to Prix Import; **m** 04 14 38 35; **f**) opened in June 2019 and sells chic jewellery, clothing, purses, and other accessories designed and manufactured in Gabon.

Upmarket hotels also often function as galleries. **Hôtel Le Cristal** (page 90), for example, is decorated with works by Marcellin Minzé Minkoe and Marc Obiang Nguenia.

For an excellent selection of colourful wax-print cloth, head for **Jessica Chic** [91 D5] (cnr bd Yves Digo & rue Jacques Akeremy), just west of the city centre in the Nombakélé neighbourhood – they can also refer you to a tailor to have outfits made.

BOOKS, MAPS AND NEWSPAPERS Kiosks selling national papers are commonplace in Libreville. Most of the big hotels in the capital also have a few week-old issues of foreign papers and magazines available for about twice the price that they cost back home.

For books, head to **La Maison de la Presse** [78 D6] (📞 01 72 21 31; **w** maisondelapressegabon.com) opposite the **Hôtel Re-Ndama** in Glass, the **Galeries les Jardins d'Ambre** [95 D3] opposite Mbolo, or the bookshop inside **Galerie Mbolo**. La Maison de la Presse has the largest selection, with French/African novels, coffee-table books about Gabon and children's books, but (as is also the case in the other shops) next to nothing in English.

OTHER PRACTICALITIES

BANKS, ATMS AND FOREIGN EXCHANGE Cash rules in Gabon, and Libreville is the place to get it. There is now a decent network of **ATMs** around the city: BGFI, BICIG and Ecobank accept Visa, and UBA accepts Mastercard. Most upmarket hotels accept major credit cards and/or payment in euros, and several even have ATMs in their lobby, such as Hôtel Le Cristal, Radisson Blu, Onomo, and the Re-Ndama. There's a newsstand at the airport [83 D4] that acts as a **semi-official exchange bureau** and offers reasonable rates. If you're in a pinch, most banks and some post offices also offer Western Union services. Keep in mind that banks always close on the dot.

MEDICAL SERVICES Gabon's public hospitals are usually under-resourced and overburdened. Most of the doctors work at them on the side and make the bulk of their money running private clinics. Better public hospitals in Libreville include the Centre Hospitalier Universitaire d'Angondjé [83 C1] (📞 01 45 90 00) in Angondjé and the Hôpital de la Coopération Sino-Gabonaise [78 D5] (📞 01 72 01 28) in Belle-Vue. The US Embassy also maintains a list of doctors in Gabon at **w** ga.usembassy. gov/u-s-citizen-services/doctors.

Private clinics
The following clinics are known to offer better quality of care than the public hospitals.

⊞ **Hôpital Jeanne Ebori** [95 C3] Bord de Mer, Quartier Louis; 📞 01 73 20 30

⊞ **Laboratoire Central d'Analyses Medicales** [91 C4] behind the Commissariat Central, av de Cointet; 📞 01 72 50 50

⊞ **Polyclinique Dr Chambrier** [91 B2] Montagne Sainte; 📞 01 76 14 68; **w** polycliniquedrchambrier.com

✚ **Polyclinique El-Rapha** [78 B3] bd Quaben, Trois Quartiers; ☎ 01 44 70 00/73 38 50; 📋 la. polyclinique.el.rapha. Generally regarded as the best care in town.

✚ **SOS Médecins** [78 D3] off bd Triomphal Omar Bongo Ondimba, Sotega; ☎ 01 74 08 80/8; w sosmedecins-gabon.com. Operating since 1993, this is another well-regarded clinic. They have several ambulances.

Pharmacies

✚ **Grande Pharmacie des Forestiers** [95 D3] Centre Commercial Mbolo; ☎ 01 72 23 52/43

67; ⊕ 08.15–19.45 Mon–Sat; 📋. Probably Libreville's most luxurious & best-stocked pharmacy.

✚ **Pharmacie Centrale de Garde** [91 C4] Opposite Commissariat Central, centre-ville; m 07 07 01 99; ⊕ 19.00–08.00 daily. Should you need any medication during the night, head to this pharmacy that is open 365 nights a year.

✚ **Pharmacie de Glass** bd de l'Indépendance, London; ⊕ Mon–Sat. A landmark for taxi drivers.

✚ **Pharmacie Sainte Mairie** bd Triomphal Omar Bongo Ondimba; ☎ 01 74 00 52; ⊕ 08.00–20:00 daily

SPA AND BEAUTY For massages, manicures, haircuts, hammam baths, and all manner of other beauty treatments, Institut de Beauté Metamorphose [91 D6] (rue Jacques Akeremy, Glass; m 06 24 67 17; w institutmetamorphose.com; 📋 institutmetamorphose; ⊕ 08.00–20.00 daily) is the place to go for pampering.

COMMUNICATIONS

Internet With the advent of affordable mobile data, the internet cafés that sprung up here several years ago have now for the most part closed, with most people getting online using their mobile phones. Most hotels in Libreville, including some of the cheaper options, now offer free Wi-Fi, but whether or not it's working can often be another story. A number of cafés and restaurants offer the same.

Post The main post office lies in the city centre [91 B5] (bd de l'Indépendance, centre-ville). Being one of Libreville's landmarks, la poste is known by all taxi drivers.

Telephone The two major mobile providers, Airtel and Gabon Telecom (which administers Libertis & Moov), are both represented at the airport and can set you up with a SIM card and data (assuming your phone is unlocked, of course). Otherwise, both providers have a number of offices scattered throughout the city that can also sign up new users. Be sure to bring your passport, as the SIM card must be registered to your name.

Note that Gabon was in the process of changing its phone numbering scheme at the time this guide went to print; see the box on page v for details.

SPORTING FACILITIES The capital's best fitness club is **Club Saoti** [78 B2] (☎ 01 73 03 95; m 04 17 83 03; 📋 ClubSaotiLbv), which is located in the Hauts de Gué Gué quartier and offers tennis, squash, handball, football, basketball, martial arts, dance, yoga, swimming and bowling. The Hôtel Re-Ndama and the Radisson Blu also have gyms and tennis courts that can be used by non-residents.

Swimming For a dip in the ocean without crossing the estuary to Pointe Denis, your best bet is probably the beach in front of the Hôtel Tropicana (page 93), which the hotel keeps tidy. Otherwise, if your hotel doesn't have a swimming pool and you fancy a dip, one of the best places to head to is the **Beach Club** [83 B2] (La Sablière; m 05 08 88 88/07 17 17 77; 📋 beachclublbv), which has a sparkling blue pool and charges an entry fee of 5,000CFA – it's not too expensive by Libreville standards.

The restaurant ($$$–$$$$) is on the pricey side, though, with mains starting around 13,000CFA. For alternative activities and watersports around Pointe Denis, see page 112.

Golf The **Golf Club de Libreville** [78 D7] (✪ 0.3651, 9.4782; ✆ 01 76 03 78; w golfclubdelibreville.com/fggolf.org); has an 18-hole, 38ha course on the south side of Libreville, across the Voie Express from the Lalala neighbourhood. The course is private but welcomes visitors and has rental golf clubs available. Green fees start at 20,000CFA for 18 holes. The clubhouse has a friendly, good-value restaurant ($$$).

SAFETY For the most part, Libreville is a calm, friendly place. As in any city there are places where extra care should be taken, and which should preferably be avoided altogether after dark, such as along the beach, around the gare routière, Marché Mont-Bouët and Petit Paris. Avoid being a target by not wearing jewellery, even a watch, and carrying the bare minimum in the way of money and bags in crowded places. Police are generally not too much of a bother in the city, but note that you are obligated to produce your passport if asked, so keep it on you.

EDUCATION Libreville has lots of private institutions of varying quality.

École Internationale Ruban Vert [78 B3] av Félix Houphouët Boigny, Batterie IV; m 04 84 33 80/01 44 26 70; e reception@ecolerubanvert. com; w ecolerubanvert.com. Founded in 2013, today this is Gabon's premier international school, offering primary & secondary education according to the International Baccalaureate curriculum for learners aged between 3 & 18.

Université Omar Bongo (UOB) [78 C3] av Président Léon Mba; ✆ 01 73 29 56; e contact@ uob.ga; ⚑. Gabon's biggest public university opened in 1971 & has over 17,000 students today. Its faculties of arts, law, humanities, economics & management studies are underfunded, standards of maintenance are poor & the library is in desperate need of an overhaul. Strikes that last for months are commonplace.

WHAT TO SEE AND DO

Congolese band Orchestre Stukas had it right again when they said 'Libreville mérite d'être visité' ('Libreville deserves to be visited'). Though it's not exactly long on conventional sightseeing opportunities, there's enough to keep you busy for a couple of days. However, if busy is the last thing you want to be, you could spend the day at a hotel with a pool or beach for the price of your lunch. Alternatively, there are also several rewarding day trips possible from the city (page 106).

ARBORETUM DE SIBANG [78 D4] (Sibang Arboretum; just north of the PK8, take the road to here and look for the signposted left-hand turn-off; ✪ 0.4176, 9.4903; ⊕ 08.00–noon & 14.00–17.00 Mon–Fri; admission 3,000CFA, including a guided tour) In 1931, 16ha of the trees to be found in Gabon's forests were planted just beyond PK8 for the purpose of scientific research. Today the arboretum makes a great introduction to the different species of the forest such as okoumé, mahogany, ebony, ozigo and padouk. There are daily guided tours and it's a fine way to escape the city for an hour or two.

MUSEUMS, CULTURAL CENTRES AND INTERESTING SITES For a long time a somewhat underwhelming introduction to Gabon's undeniable cultural richness, the **Musée National des Arts, Rites et Traditions** [91 C6] (National Museum of Arts, Rites and Traditions; ✆ 01 76 14 56; f museedugabon) may soon do a much better job of living up to its vast potential. Set to open as this book went to print in late 2019, the museum has moved from its long-time home at the bottom of the Total building on the waterfront to a newer, larger location some 250m down boulevard de l'Indépendance in the former US Embassy.

The fully modern new facility will take visitors through Gabon's natural history (including an entire section designed as if you were underground in a cave), ceremonial rites (including a room dedicated to Bwiti), and artistic output (with a collection of sculpture and masks representing Gabon's many ethnic groups). The outdoor gardens are full of indigenous Gabonese plants, including the odika tree (*Irvingia gabonensis*; from where Gabonese *chocolat* sauce is produced) and the iboga shrub (*Tabernanthe iboga*), used in Bwiti rituals. The gardens are also home to a replica *pont des lianes* (vine bridge), like the one found in Poubara (page 183), and a traditional domed Pygmy dwelling. The museum should be open by the time you read this, and all signs point to the happy transformation from a once-underachieving museum into one of Libreville's absolute must-sees.

Libreville also has a number of buildings of architectural interest. To start, the building on boulevard Triomphal Omar Bongo Ondimba with the wavy roof is both an architectural gem and the epicentre of cultural Libreville: **Institut Français du Gabon** (French Institute of Gabon) [95 D3] (✆ 01 76 11 20; w institutfrancais-gabon.com; f ifgab), which hosts regular exhibitions, talks, live music, dance and film screenings, and also has a library and internet facilities; check their Facebook page for upcoming events. Continuing east along boulevard Triomphal Omar Bongo Ondimba, there are a number of other impressive Modernist structures to be found, starting with the glass-and-tile **Ministère des Eaux et Forêts** (Ministry of Water and Forests) [78 C4], decorated with incongruously colourful palm trees and birds. East again, keep your eyes out for the cylindrical **Ministère du Pétrole** (Ministry of Petrol) [78 C4] and the **Flamme de la Paix** (Flame of Peace) statue out front, the broad-roofed **Sénat** (Senate) [78 C4], the fire-damaged **Assemblée Nationale** (National Assembly; page 86) [78 C4], and the time-warped **Hôtel de Ville** (City Hall) [78 C4].

Nearing the end of boulevard Triomphal Omar Bongo Ondimba, head south along boulevard du Président Léon Mba and you'll reach what many claim to be the capital's most beautiful church: **Saint-Michel de Nkembo** [78 D4] (on the left at the STFO roundabout). The intricately carved wooden pillars here were made by the Gabonese artist Zéphirin Lendogno, and depict a combination of Christian and African legends, including Saint Michel felling the dragon in a blaze of colour over the main entrance. The church dates from 1949 and can seat up to 1,000 people. Just a few blocks from here is another intriguing church, **Notre-Dame de Lourdes** [78 D4], which was consecrated in 2008 and is covered in fine Portuguese-style *azulejo* tiles.

Returning towards the centre along boulevard Bessieux and rue Mont-Bouët (through the market; page 100), you'll eventually reach the modern **Église Saint-Pierre** [91 B3] (rue de Gouverneur Bailey), worth a look for its unusual soaring rooftop (which, to this author at least, looks strikingly like a manta ray from behind). A few blocks south of here is the grand green-white-and-gold **Mosquée Hassan II** (Hassan II Mosque) [91 B3], Gabon's largest mosque, which was built with Moroccan funding and inaugurated here in 1983. It boasts space for up to 5,000 worshippers and an elegant square minaret more than 40m high. Continuing south into the city centre along avenue Félix Éboué, the **Mémorial Léon Mba**

[91 C4] pays homage to the father of the nation. The **Mosquée Centrale** (Central Mosque) [91 C4] sits just south of here, and though it's technically Gabon's oldest mosque, it's been so thoroughly modernised and rebuilt in recent decades that little of this history remains visible.

Several blocks west on the waterfront, you'll find **L'esclave Libéré** (The Freed Slave) [91 A4], a remarkable statue representing a half-male, half-female figure breaking free from the chains of the past. Unveiled in 2007, it is dedicated to the freed slaves that settled in Libreville, beginning with the captives on the Brazilian slave ship *L'Elizia* in 1849. Be careful taking pictures as its location opposite the **Palais Présidentiel** (Presidential Palace) [91 B4] is heavily protected by suspicious guards – it's better to keep your camera pointed towards the ocean. The palace itself, clad in enormous panes of golden reflective glass, dates to 1977 and measures nearly double the size of the Élysée Palace in France.

Finally, head north from the palace and L'esclave libéré for 1.5km, passing the grand (some might say overwrought) **Cour Constitutionnelle** (Constitutional Court) [91 A3] after 500m, until you reach the **Cathédrale Notre Dame de l'Assomption** (Cathedral of Our Lady of the Assumption) [95 D4] atop a hill looking down on Port Môle; this is the seat of Libreville's archbishop. It was built in 1958, and carefully positioned to preserve the 1864 **Église Sainte-Marie** [95 D4] that sits directly behind it on the former site of the 1843 Fort-d'Aumale; this fetching red-steepled church is among Gabon's oldest structures.

Cultural villages There are two cultural villages in Libreville, which aim to give visitors a greater understanding of Gabonese religion and tradition. Ceremonies for anyone wishing to be initiated into Bwiti can be arranged at both (see box, page 18). A word of warning: ingestion of iboga can be dangerous and particularly people suffering from heart conditions should think twice.

The **Association Kool d'Ayele** and its group of performers Mbeng-N'tam is run by Christophe and his wife Marie-Claire (PK12; m 06 27 09 90/07 13 53 17/06 27 51 95; e etincelledi@gmail.com; w bwitietincelle.net). Mbeng-N'tam, meaning beauty and prosperity in Fang, have been quite successful since their start in 1998 and perform regularly at international festivals outside of Gabon. They are committed believers in the spiritual and physical benefits of Bwiti, and are keen to bring the intense music and dancing that accompanies it to a wider audience. They organise 90-minute shows followed by a traditional Gabonese meal served on manioc leaves for groups of around 30 people. Smaller groups are welcome to visit for less formal evenings. The village is very much a family affair. The dance troupe is made up of the couple's children and Marie-Claire's sisters. Marie-Claire makes all the dance costumes, as well as the jewellery and clothes on sale. The village is located at PK12. To get there, take a bus from Sainte Marie or the gare routière. At PK12, take a left turn off the surfaced road and walk for 300m along the old Lambaréné road as far as the black wooden gate.

Ebando Bwiti Village [83 A1] (rte des Pêcheurs, La Sablière; ✪ 0.4943, 9.3838; m 06 25 09 17; e ibogabon@ebando.org; w ebando.org; f hugues.o.poitevin) is beyond the airport in La Sablière, following the waterfront road north, 2km beyond the new US Embassy. Ebando is a quite unconventional NGO providing initiations, therapies, trainings, art and entertainment. It also arranges forest tours that allow visitors to discover the authentic Pygmy lifestyle.

Residents at the village include the *nganga*, Tatayo (the healer who leads the traditional ceremonies), as well as several young Gabonese being instructed in traditional skills, including dance, music, cooking, basketry and jewellery-making.

Being the first European who was initiated into Bwiti, the unusual *nganga* is well known in Libreville and beyond. Every year he receives about 25 foreign guests who want to participate in the Bwiti initiation rites. Contact Tatayo, alias Hugues Poitevin, for further information. They've got a few basic guest rooms as well, though these are typically used by initiates.

AROUND LIBREVILLE AND ESTUAIRE

Within Estuaire (Estuary) province are a number of places where it's shockingly easy to forget the proximity of the big smoke. Just minutes out of Libreville on the airport road the forest begins. Both along this coast and on the other side of the estuary, there are dreamy beaches where it's possible to walk for miles along the shore at low tide.

Two national parks are within easy reach. On the southern side of the estuary is Pongara National Park and the picturesque tourist resort of Pointe Denis, and just north of town lies Akanda National Park. Neither side of the estuary is short on birdlife – kingfisher, little egret, reef heron, sanderling and other fast-moving waders abound. From June to September whales pass the coast and from November to February the leatherback turtle crawls ashore.

NORTH OF LIBREVILLE

Cap Santa Clara About a 15-minute drive from Libreville's airport is the left turn-off to Cap Santa Clara. The turning (✪ 0.5477, 9.3568) is difficult to miss for two reasons: there is a large sign and invariably a crowd of small vendors selling palm wine. From here, the road is unsurfaced and can be rough in places. Santa Clara is a popular hangout for French expats. There are occasional clando share taxis running here from the Pélisson/Nazareth roundabout north of the airport near Nomad Suites Résidence.

 Where to stay, eat and drink Map, page 108

⌂ Akouango Village (18 rooms) m 07 40 80 18/04 89 25 00; e akouangovillage@ gmail.com; w akouangovillage.com; ∎ akouangovillage; ⊕ closed Tue. From the turning, follow the piste to Cap Santa Clara for 5km until a sign indicates a 2nd turn-off. Take the left turn & continue for another km or so. Lovely Akouango Village lies right on the beach with well-kept bungalows, a good restaurant ($$$) & an invitingly blue pool. It's a good deal at 26,000CFA/night for the most basic dbl room, so reservations are recommended. $$

✕ Nerina Beach m 04 89 40 29; ∎; ⊕ 09.00–23.00 Fri–Sun. This relaxed beachfront address opened in 2018 & offers garden seating in a clutch of colourful wooden gazebos, set under swaying palms. The menu covers seafood favourites including *crevettes & crabes farcis* along with desserts such as crêpes & crème caramel. $$$
✕ Le Paradis Chez Jacky m 06 25 15 14/07 57 16 00. Good buffet lunch on the beach. Reserve in advance as this is not a fixed restaurant; Jacky brings out his tables & dishes only during the w/ends & just for lunch. The buffet will set you back 22,000CFA; kids eat half price. $$$$

Arboretum Raponda Walker Just a 20-minute drive from Libreville, beautiful Arboretum Raponda Walker (formerly known as the Mondah Forest; ✪ 0.5788, 9.3352; ☏ 01 44 67 46) is a fantastic escape from the big city, accessible from the Cap Esterias road 5km past the turn-off to Cap Santa Clara. Minibuses to Cap Esterias can drop you at the entrance. Thanks to its high humidity, the forest boasts some rare palms and unique orchids (28 species are found nowhere else in Gabon or even in the whole of Africa), including the *Phyllobotryon spathulatum*, whose flowers

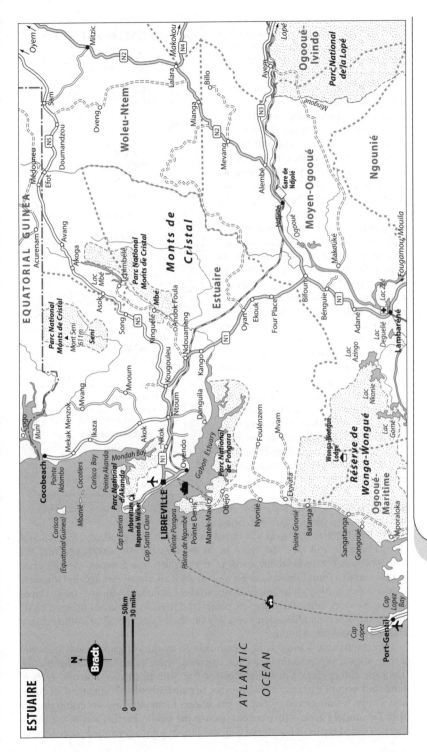

ESTUAIRE

appear on the central nerve of the leaf. The area has long been sacred for Myènè peoples, who have many myths and legends related to the forest here.

The arboretum is also the most accessible indigenous forest in the region. Continue past the turn-off to Cap Santa Clara until you see the colourful board on the left. The board outlines five walks, ranging from 800m to 4.6km. The longest circuit takes about 1½ hours, not including any stops. There are a couple of places with rustic benches for those who want to have picnics. The Ministry of Water and Forests has compiled a tree list identifying the trees you pass according to their number, although it's quite difficult to get hold of. The most frequent number is 123, for the okoumé. Many trees have now been more helpfully labelled with informational plaques as well. There are plans to develop new trails here beyond the original five.

It's not obligatory to have a guide, but a guided walk provides unique insights into the trees and their different uses. You should generally be able to arrange one on the spot, but don't expect them to speak English. Some travel agencies will arrange a half-day trip to the forest for you, including a guide and transport and a pirogue trip in the mangroves of nearby Mondah Bay.

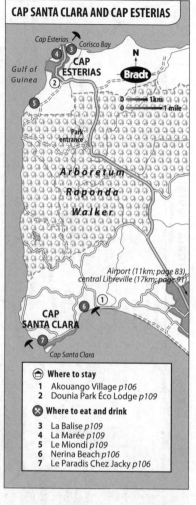

CAP SANTA CLARA AND CAP ESTERIAS

Where to stay
1 Akouango Village p106
2 Dounia Park Éco Lodge p109

Where to eat and drink
3 La Balise p109
4 La Marée p109
5 Le Miondi p109
6 Nerina Beach p106
7 Le Paradis Chez Jacky p106

Cap Esterias Continuing past the turn-off to Cap Santa Clara will bring you to Cap Esterias. The road was tarred in 2013 and is in good shape. A minibus from Libreville will take you there in 30 minutes for 500–1,000CFA from the Pélisson/Nazareth roundabout north of the airport. Cap Esterias was the place people came to from Libreville to get away from it all some years ago, but the same clientele now mostly go to Pointe Denis, so the restaurants here are largely closed during the week when there are few potential diners. At weekends things pick up a little bit, when families come for a day on the beach, though accommodation choices are somewhat limited.

Cap Esterias has a long, sandy beach fringed by the obligatory palm trees and strewn with tree trunks that have run aground. There's a rather squat lighthouse. The cape also overlooks beautiful Corisco Bay, with its picture-postcard islets of sand and coconut palms, including the disputed islands of Mbanié, Cocotiers, and Conga, administered by Gabon but subject to an ongoing ownership dispute with Equatorial Guinea. They are not open to the public. Further north, the 15km² Corisco Island is part of Equatorial Guinea (although not a permitted port of entry).

Where to stay, eat and drink *Map, opposite*

The following restaurants lie on the Cap Esterias beach, while the lodge sits about 1.5km back towards the entrance of the village.

Dounia Park Éco Lodge (26 rooms) m 06 83 86 86; e douniaparkresa@gmail.com; ⓕ douniaparkgabon. The nicest accommodation at Cap Esterias, this resort opened in 2015 & sits in 13ha of grassy grounds that are planted with fruit trees, towards the entrance of the village. Rooms are clean & colourful, & all come with AC & mini-fridge. There's a swimming pool, spa, lawn games & a large terrace restaurant ($$$), & they also offer bike rental & horseriding. They maintain their own stretch of beach, though it's about 1km from the resort. Rooms start at around 80,000CFA. **$$$$**

Le Miondi Rte Cap des Pères; ⓕ; ⏲ 11.00–22.00 Sat & 11.00–17.00 Sun. Set on its own stretch of beach about 2km from Dounia Park, this is a chic w/end getaway for in-the-know Librevilleois. It serves a short menu of fine seafood & grills on a breezy shaded terrace overlooking the water. **$$$**

La Balise End of the Cap Esterias rd; m 06 63 66 34; ⓕ Restaurant sous les cocotiers cap esterias a la balise. This relaxed joint is cheaper than others in the area & the portions are generous & good, but there is only an obscured view of the water. The speciality is *palourdes*, a triangular shellfish usually cooked in garlic butter. Service can be slow. **$$**

La Marée End of the Cap Esterias rd; m 06 27 35 36. Have your grilled fish on this popular covered terrace overlooking the water. *Main courses start at 8,000CFA.* **$$**

Parc National d'Akanda The area bordering the Mondah and Corisco bays has been protected as the 54,000ha Akanda National Park (entry 10,000/5,000CFA tourist/foreign resident) since 2002. The park has two main biological areas: coastal forest in the north, dominated by okoumé and ozouga trees; and mangroves extending around the bay towards the city to the south. Akanda harbours one of the largest populations of wintering birds in Africa and is an ornithologist's dream; it was recognised as an Important Bird Area back in 2001. At low tide, the mud flats provide food for around 30,000 shorebirds migrating from Europe. The biggest flocks can be seen between September and December and from February to March. African skimmers are in the park year-round except during their nesting periods.

Akanda is also a vital feeding zone for turtle. Tangles of mangrove roots (one of the few kinds of trees that are able to grow in salt water) serve as a protective nursery for juvenile barracuda, skipper and most of the marine fish found here. You might also see mudskippers: highly refined fish that hop out of the water like frogs to hunt for insects on land.

Visiting the park You can visit the park on a **day trip** from the capital; most Libreville-based tour agencies, such as Gabon Vert Tour (page 89), can arrange this. Alternatively, and assuming you trust your negotiating (and French) skills, it's also possible to charter your own pirogue directly with the boatmen at either **Débarcadère d'Okala** (⊕ 0.4913, 9.4207) northeast of the airport, or **Débarcadère d'Ambowé** (⊕ 0.4499, 9.4372) in Charbonnages, just after the restaurant Vert Jaune Bleu [78 B1] (better known by its previous name of Le Débarcadère; page 97).

If you've got the time to spend the night, the best way to see Akanda is with the **Hôtel Le Beau Retrait** (❊; 16 rooms; ⊕ 0.5807, 9.4529; ☏ 06 26 53 88/04 21 19 02; e mondahecotour@yahoo.fr; ⓕ LeBeauRetrait; **$$$**), a lovely ecolodge managed by a local family with a superb location on the shore of the Tsini River. It organises guided forest walks and excursions by pirogue. A night in the lodge including dinner, transport and an excursion will set you back 50,000CFA per person (groups of one to four) or 30,000CFA (groups of four plus) – a steal in Gabon. Alternatively,

6km upriver towards Libreville, **Cap Caravane** (✵ 0.5356, 9.4368; m 02 00 00 34; ▯ capcaravaneofficiel) is more of a recreation centre for weekending Gabonese families than a natural getaway, but it does have a fetching location along the Tsini at the fringes of Akanda National Park. They have bungalow rooms for 45,000CFA a night (**$$$**), and it's 20,000CFA per person for the Sunday buffet (**$$$$**). It's reachable by road, 9.5km from the Nazareth/Pélisson roundabout in Libreville.

Approaching Akanda from the south, **La Mangrovia Beach** (✵ 0.4224, 9.5818; m 07 57 12 43; e mavbayonne50@gmail.com; ▯ La Mangrovia Beach-Bikélé; **$**) sits outside of the park but near its southern border. This is a new accommodation option about 2km north of the N1 at Bikélé. They have several wood-built overwater bungalows facing a mangrove-lined creek (good for swimming) that connects northwards towards Mondah Bay. It's a popular weekend destination for families.

Cocobeach

Cocobeach A good 3 hours' drive north of Libreville is the small coastal town of Cocobeach (population 2,600), set at the mouth of the Muni River. There's very little to see or do here, but it's a nice enough place to spend a couple of days. It's so small there are no taxis, just a market, the beach and a couple of picturesque fishing villages nearby. The catch of the day arrives directly at the beach behind the market. The other main sights in town are a lighthouse dating to 1950 and a 2008 memorial to the 1914 battle of Ukoko, which saw French and German troops clash here.

You can also approach the fishermen if you want to hire a pirogue for a spin. But even though Cogo (Equatorial Guinea) is only about 15km away, along the Muni River, and local boats regularly make the trip, as best we know this crossing was closed to foreigners at the time of writing. The best beach for swimming is a 20-minute walk along the road left of the market – keep an eye out for fossilised fish on rocks at low tide.

Getting there and away There are minibuses (5,000CFA) running between Libreville (PK8) and the main roundabout in Cocobeach a few times daily. The journey takes about 3 hours, but can sometimes end up a lot longer if the gendarmes manning the checkpoints are feeling prickly. The road is surfaced until Ntoum, after which it is mostly good dirt road, though drivers tend to travel way faster than is safe.

Where to stay, eat and drink The largest hotel in town is the **Hôtel Esperance** (m 02 32 23 90; **$**), which is next to the market on the waterfront. There are seven rooms with air conditioning at 15,000CFA and two rooms with fan at 12,000CFA. All rooms have en-suite facilities and small balconies that open out into a garden. The hotel has seen better days, but is nonetheless good value. Breakfast – and possibly other meals – can be served (for an additional cost) if enough advance warning is given. Your other eating options aren't exactly extensive, but the Gabonese dishes at **Chez Tante Mado** (**$$**) are probably the best in town.

Parc National Monts de Cristal

Parc National Monts de Cristal Northeast of Libreville, the Crystal Mountains National Park consists of two halves, separated by the N5 and a series of predominantly Fang villages along the road. The western side of the park is named after its highest peak, Mount Seni (611m), while the eastern side owes its name to the impressive Lac Mbé (occasionally spelled Mbèi). The forests of Mbé are among the oldest in Gabon and boast an exceptional plant biodiversity. Almost constantly engulfed in clouds and mist, Crystal Mountains served as a botanical refuge for plants, birds, insects and snakes during the last Ice Age. The high mountains trapped humid air, creating enough rain to support forest growth, even in the driest climatic periods. Owing to its altitude, it's relatively cool. Large numbers of plant species that became extinct in other regions managed to survive in these humid refuges.

Crystal Montains boasts the highest diversity of trees in Africa, with an average 97 tree species per hectare. The humidity nourishes moisture-loving epiphytic plants growing on trees. Orchids and begonias are particularly prolific, and you should expect to see many mosses and lichens. Specific research still needs to be done on the park's high concentration of endemic plants. Research is also needed into the unique flora that grows on the bizarre inselbergs found around the village of Médouneu along the border with Equatorial Guinea.

The forest is also home to an extraordinary diversity of butterflies. When the clouds lift, thousands emerge to feed and mate. Other inhabitants of these misty forests include giant pangolin (the heaviest and largest of living pangolins), mandrill and elephant. Unfortunately, this is historically an area of concentrated poaching, which is hardly surprising given its proximity to the markets of Libreville.

The Société d'Energie et d'Eau du Gabon (the electricity and water board; SEEG) operates two hydroelectric dams at Kinguélé and Tchimbélé in Mbé that provide about 50% of Libreville's electricity. The latter site is the more interesting, with access to Lac Mbè, an orchid garden of more than 200 different species, and a *sentier botanique* (botanical path) in the surrounding forest. The lake is also a key water resource for Libreville.

The best time to see flowers in bloom is between September and January. At any time of year, take plenty of insect repellent and be sure to wear long sleeves, long trousers and socks.

In 2014, ANPN and SEEG signed an agreement on the management and upgrading of tourist and educational sites in the park. To that end, the former SEEG **accommodation** at Tchimbélé has been opened for use by tourists and researchers at a cost of roughly 60,000CFA a night. Planned upgrades had yet to take place at the time this guide went to print; the multi-room brick chalets are basic but sufficient as things stand, but you must come prepared with all supplies including food and water. Advance arrangements with ANPN (page 88) are required in order to stay here; this can be done directly, or through a Libreville-based tour operator such as Gabon Vert Tours (page 89).

Activities within the park are currently limited to ANPN guided hikes, but these take in some stunningly beautiful terrain, weaving through the well-watered forests to find a series of waterfalls, gorges and boulder-strewn riverbeds.

Getting there and away Until a basic tourist infrastructure is in place, there is no prescribed way of visiting the Crystal Mountains (entry 10,000/5,000CFA tourist/foreign resident), although that is not to say it is impossible. The western park (Seni), is currently best approached from the sea via Cocobeach, while a round trip in a 4×4 from Libreville to Tchimbélé is just about possible in a (very long) day (150km; 4hrs each way), though it would be preferable to spend the night. Follow the N1 until the signposted intersection at ⊕ 0.2989, 10.0400, where you take the piste on your left. The turn-off is 35km past Ntoum, and 22km past the N5 turn-off. From here, it's a further 43km to Kinguélé (⊕ 0.4489, 10.2802) and 80km to Tchimbélé (⊕ 0.6233, 10.4049). Despite its rough condition, the route is nonetheless very pretty, with views over the mountainous terrain, cut through by a series of small roadside waterfalls.

The N5 passes between the two halves of the park, though there's no park access along the route. This unsurfaced road departs the N1 some 13km east of Ntoum and

4

continues for 315km until joining the N2 near Bibassé, passing through Médouneu (population 2,500) after 165km. If you go this way, look out for the dramatic (and unmissable) pair of forested granite inselbergs that seemingly rise out of nowhere, 10–15km east of Médouneu.

The N5 is actually a shortcut between Libreville and Woleu-Ntem, but thanks to the poor condition of the road, almost all traffic goes via Ndjolé instead.

SOUTH OF LIBREVILLE

Pointe Denis The village of Pointe Denis, situated at the northeastern corner of the peninsula of the same name, has become Gabon's most established seaside resort and an ideal getaway for a weekend. It was here that the local Mpongwé chief Rapontchombo of the Assiga clan, who put his mark to a treaty placing his territory under the French flag, ruled over the left bank of the Gabon from 1811–76. Rapontchombo was called King Denis by the French and the peninsula was named after him.

The village itself sits on a narrow spit of land, separated from the main peninsula by a large mangrove-lined creek. Many French expats have built holiday homes here, taking advantage of the narrow peninsula to overlook the beach from their front windows and mangroves to the rear. If you're among the cohort not fortunate enough to have a holiday home here, fret not as there's still plenty of good hotel accommodation to be had. Librevilleois who can (and there are more than a few) make a beeline here at the weekends, but it remains pretty quiet during the week. (Some places even close down on weekdays, so it may be wise to call in advance.)

The north end of the peninsula is fringed by silky sand beaches on all sides; Pointe Denis village and most hotels are set along the east coast of the peninsula, where the beach runs for about 6.5km from a mangrove swamp in the south to Pointe Pongara in the north. Rounding Pointe Pongara and continuing west, you'll reach Pointe Ouingombé and La Baie des Tortues Luth (page 114) after about 5km. Most of the rest of the peninsula is officially protected as Pongara National Park (see opposite).

Getting there and away It's a 25-minute journey from Michel Marine to Pointe Denis. Most hotels on Pointe Denis have their own *navettes* and happily arrange your transport, but it's usually also possible to take an independent boat. A round trip costs 12,000CFA and tickets are sold at the small ticket booth on the pier (Navette Andza; m 05 31 80 80/06 26 40 77/07 14 68 56). *Navettes* leave Libreville Tue–Sun between 09.00 and 10.00 and 15.00 and 16.00, returning between 16.00 and 18.00. There are no boats on Mondays and no afternoon departure to Pointe Denis on Sundays.

All the establishments at Pointe Denis are close together along the same stretch of beach, so if you're not sure yet where you want to go, just get off the boat anywhere and make up your mind on foot.

⌂ *Where to stay, eat and drink* Map, opposite

⌂ **River Lodge** (18 rooms) Near the boat launch, Pointe Denis; m 02 62 15 24/02 30 23 02; e riverlodgegabon@yahoo.com; **f**. The most recent establishment on Pointe Denis. Accommodation here is in stylish 2-storey wooden bungalows overlooking the estuary. There's a sizeable swimming pool & a resto-bar (**$$$**) that overlooks a sandy beach, where volleyball, ping pong & other beach games are available & you can rent jet skis, pedal boats, canoes & more. A 2-day, 1-night package (including transport, meals & accommodation) goes for 165,000/250,000CFA for 1/2 guests. **$$$$**

⌂ **Assiga Village** (18 rooms) 400m south of River Lodge, Pointe Denis; ✆ 01 76 33 47; m 06 18 38 38/03 04 48 08; e contact@ assiga-village.com; w assiga-village.com; **f** assigavillageofficiel. Set on the estuary rather

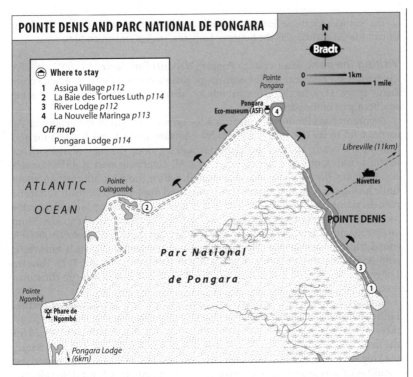

POINTE DENIS AND PARC NATIONAL DE PONGARA

Where to stay

1 Assiga Village *p112*
2 La Baie des Tortues Luth *p114*
3 River Lodge *p112*
4 La Nouvelle Maringa *p113*

Off map
Pongara Lodge *p114*

Pointe Pongara

Pongara Eco-museum (ASF)

Pointe Ouingombé

ATLANTIC

OCEAN

Pointe Ngombé

Phare de Ngombé

Parc National de Pongara

Libreville (11km)

Navettes

POINTE DENIS

Pongara Lodge (6km)

---

than the beach, this is a popular option with a terrace restaurant offering views over the water. Rooms are clean, comfortable & well equipped & there's a small pool, jacuzzi & sauna. Quad bikes, jet skis & forest hikes can all be arranged. Buffet or 3-course menu à la carte 25,000CFA (**$$$$$**). *Room rate depends on the day: 70,000CFA Mon–Fri, 100,000CFA including b/fast Sat & Sun.* **$$$–$$$$**

La Nouvelle Maringa (15 rooms) 500m south of Pointe Pongara; m 05 35 53 55/05 93 89 38; ☐ lanouvellemaringa. Under new management since late 2017, La Nouvelle Maringa's restaurant serves a tasty buffet on Sat & Sun for 17,500CFA (**$$$$**). The whitewashed rooms are simple, but comfortable & well kept. *Rooms with dbl bed & en-suite shower around 50,000CFA/night, plus 5,000CFA for b/fast.* **$$$**

Parc National de Pongara One of Gabon's most accessible parks, Pongara National Park is astonishingly beautiful. Extending for 870km² over much of the Pointe Denis peninsula and the riverine landscapes of the southern Gabon Estuary, it was granted protected status because of its diverse scenery – vast mangrove flats, forest, savannah, and of course the beach itself. It harbours a rich and varied birdlife, including the vulnerable Damara terns. The beach at Pointe Pongara, where the estuary meets the ocean, is famous for the large number of vulnerable leatherback turtles that crawl ashore to lay their eggs. As in Akanda, Pongara's mangroves are full of shrimp and young saltwater fish. Its forests have remnant populations of monkey, buffalo, duiker and even a few chimpanzee and elephant.

From November to February, the local environmental organisation Aventures Sans Frontières (ASF; page 35) monitors Pongara's beaches to protect the turtles' eggs and reduce human-generated threats. ASF tags and tracks the turtles, conducting research and running a turtle hatchery, which plays a big role in their local education programmes.

The leatherback turtle features in traditional Gabonese stories where, thanks to its cunning, the turtle gets the better of leopards, snakes and crocodiles.

Visiting the park Most visits to Pongara National Park (entry 10,000/5,000CFA tourist/foreign resident) take in only the peninsula portion that surrounds Pointe Denis (page 112), as there is currently no tourist development in the riverine southern part of the park.

Aventures Sans Frontières organises wonderful excursions to the peninsula. As turtles tend to lay their eggs at night, the company offers to pitch a tent for you right on the beach. You can spend the day walking along the coast on the lookout for turtle traces, or join a guided forest tour. All excursions start at ASF's Pongara Eco-museum (located near Pointe Pongara), which provides information about turtle biology, threats and conservation issues, and displays several shells and turtle models, giving you an idea of these creatures' grand scale. The trip is excellent value for money and not expensive: count on 10,000–50,000CFA for the guide(s) and 10,000CFA for a tent. ASF can arrange a boat from Michel Marine (10,000CFA round trip). It's equally possible, or perhaps even preferable, to join a turtle tour with ASF while staying at any of the hotels in Pointe Denis (page 112). Pongara Lodge (see below) and La Baie des Tortues Luth (see below) both run their own excursions for guests, too.

Walking down the endless beach, you pass the idyllic resort **La Baie des Tortues Luth** (see below), a perfect place for a break. From here, a short hike in the forest takes you to the place where chief Rapontchombo, alias King Denis, was buried for the first time. Rising sea levels forced the villagers to dig the body up and rebury the king somewhere deeper in the forest. If you want to visit his current grave, you should ask the village's chief – who is one of Rapontchombo's direct descendants – for permission and directions.

Continuing south brings you to **Pointe de Ngombé** and its lighthouse, which dates to the end of the 19th century. There used to be a nice restaurant here, but it closed its doors in 2012 after the death of its proprietor, Monsieur Moustache, and has since fallen into disrepair. It may be possible to climb to the top of the lighthouse for spectacular views of the ocean, but do use your judgement. From June to September, it's possible to spot passing humpback whales from up here.

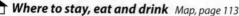

Where to stay, eat and drink *Map, page 113*

La Baie des Tortues Luth (10 bungalows) Pointe Ouingombé, Pongara; ✆ 0.3290, 9.3249; m 07 51 05 46/02 22 22 04/06 22 60 00; e info@labaiedestortues.com; labaiedestortues.com. Surrounded by blue seas, white beaches & green forest, La Baie des Tortues is the perfect place to relax & enjoy nature. The nicely decorated bungalows are each equipped with 2 dbl beds, AC, TV & en-suite facilities; the round bungalows have impressive tree trunks in the middle. There is a far-side bungalow for those who really want to get away from it all. The restaurant on the beach is excellent & uses local ingredients whenever possible – a rarity in Gabon – including fresh herbs & vegetables from their on-site gardens. They can organise kayaking, fishing & quad biking as well as turtle- & whale-watching tours in season. Day trips including transport, a welcome cocktail & 3-course lunch cost 50,000CFA pp. They have their own info desk at the airport. *2-day package including transport, a night in a bungalow, lunch, dinner & b/fast costs 200,000CFA pp.* **$$$$**

Pongara Lodge (6 bungalows) ✆ 0.2420, 9.3142; m 05 99 00 99/02 90 00 90; e pongaralodge@gmail.com; f pongara. lodge.7. On the Atlantic, about 7km south of Pointe de Ngombé, this comfortable & charming ecolodge actively tries to minimise its impact on the environment & to promote responsible tourism. However, remoteness & sustainable tourism – & an excellent restaurant – have their price: a 2-day package costs around 200,000CFA. They run *navettes* from Michel Marine twice daily.

At the time this guide went to print, Gabon Wildlife Camps (page 88) was in talks to take over the property, so contact details may change during the lifespan of this edition. **$$$$**

Réserve de Wonga-Wongué and Nyonié

Wonga-Wongué Reserve has been a *réserve présidentielle* (presidential reserve) since 1972. It covers 500,000ha of sandy beaches, dense forest, startlingly open savannah, hills, valleys, and several eroded *cirque* canyons reminiscent of those found in Haut-Ogooué (page 194). There are plenty of animals, including elephant, buffalo, chimpanzee, bongo, sitatunga – even leopard – and an extensive network of roads. Unfortunately, the reserve itself is closed to the public, but you can skirt its edges from the well-loved **Nyonié Camp (Chez Beti)** (20 bungalows; m 07 57 14 23/07 05 00 28; e castorene7@live. fr; f sitetouristiquedenyonie; **$$$**), from where it's more than possible to catch a glimpse of the wildlife. Run by Monsieur Beti, Nyonié is a welcoming and relaxing camp on the beach in the village of the same name (⊕ -0.0389, 9.3402).

An **all-inclusive weekend** costs 120,000CFA, with supplementary nights at 35,000CFA. Unless you have your own means of transport, day trips from Libreville are not possible. Weekends start at 09.00 on Saturday, when the boat leaves Libreville's Michel Marine for the dock at Matek-Mavi village (⊕ 0.0703, 9.4283), about 2 hours away. Here a 4×4 awaits to transport visitors the last 19km to the camp. The price includes transfers, food, drinks (including liqueurs, for those who are interested), simple accommodation in air-conditioned rooms, plus a game drive and guided early morning walk. Very popular with Libreville's expat families, the camp gets a bit crowded during the vacations. Bookings are essential, either through a travel agent or via Monsieur Beti direct. Those arriving under their own steam (ie: by boat or even light aircraft) pay 10,000CFA less, and children are half price.

Mission Saint Paul de Donguila

Some 70km southeast of Libreville and 30km south of Ntoum, the village of Donguila is set on the north bank of the Komo River. Its main attraction is the St Paul Catholic Mission (⊕ 0.1992, 9.7323), which was founded in 1878 and remains one of Gabon's oldest and best-preserved missions, particularly after it underwent a careful restoration in 2004. The mission and school are still active, and visitors will be given a tour of the grounds and the church, which is still home to many impressive original wooden carvings. There is no overnight accommodation available, however.

4

FOLLOW US

Tag us in your posts to share your adventures using this guide with us – we'd love to hear from you.

f BradtGuides
🐦 @BradtGuides & @shanboqol
📷 @bradtguides & @shanboqol
𝓟 bradtguides
▶ bradtguides

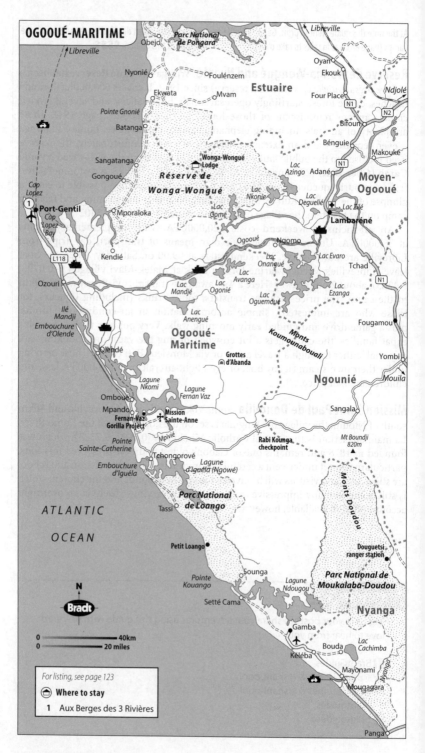

For listing, see page 123

Where to stay
1 Aux Berges des 3 Rivières

5

Ogooué-Maritime

The Ogooué-Maritime (Coastal Ogooué) province holds in its 23,000km² a delicate balance of immense natural resources and exceptional natural beauty. With its capital at Port-Gentil, the region is also Gabon's third most populous, with 158,000 resident Marigovéens. From the late 15th century, Europeans descended on the coastal communities to trade in ivory and timber. Later, in the 17th century, their commercial interest turned to slaves, while by the 19th century the missionaries were arriving to battle for souls. In the 20th century the attraction was oil, and that of the 21st century could hopefully be tourism, thanks to the region's spectacular scenery and plentiful wildlife.

Intensely beautiful and blessed with nearly untold natural riches, Ogooué-Maritime takes in a wide variety of ecosystems – forests, lagoons, lakes, floodplains, savannahs, and over 200km of coastline – and has enormous biodiversity to match. Research has shown it to boast one of the highest densities of elephant and ape anywhere in Central Africa.

Home to Gabon's flagship Loango National Park, dubbed 'Africa's last Eden' by biologist Mike Fay during his epic Megatransect (page 28), Ogooué-Maritime is probably the only place on the African continent where western lowland gorilla, forest elephant, leopard, buffalo and hippopotami can all, with luck, be seen on the same beach. There is also a chance to see manatee and crocodile and, at the right times of year, nesting sea turtles and passing whales and dolphins.

Loango National Park is part of the larger Gamba Complex of Protected Areas, which, ironically, is also the beating heart of Gabon's oil production. Since oil giant Shell sold off their Gabonese investments in 2017, Assala Energy manages the complex of oilfields sandwiched between Loango and Moukalaba-Doudou national parks. The fields of French oil company Total are mainly found offshore, with Port-Gentil as its base of operation. In addition to the other associated environmental risks, the presence of oil and logging companies in Ogooué-Maritime has unfortunately both improved access routes for poachers and increased the demand for illegally hunted meat.

PORT-GENTIL

Port-Gentil (often abbreviated to POG) is located on the northeastern edge of Île Mandji (Mandji Island), some 30km by 5km, surrounded by ocean and swamps. At the end of the 15th century it was named Lopez Island by a Portuguese sailor, Lopez Gonzalvez. The name didn't stick, although the westernmost point is still known as Cap Lopez. Instead, the island kept its traditional Myènè name, so given because of the concentration of mandji trees (*Milicia excelsa*) growing here.

The city itself takes its name after a certain Frenchman, Emile Gentil, an administrator for Afrique Equatoriale Française (AEF) who was sent to perform a mission here between 1890 and 1892. Port-Gentil at this time was little more than a handful of villages and a mission, and was to remain so until at least the end of World War I. Some 100 years later, Port-Gentil is Gabon's second largest city and the nation's *capitale économique* (economic capital). The city is home to 136,000 people, comprising over 85% of Ogooué-Maritime's total population. It got rich quick, and in the process acquired a disproportionate number of hotels, restaurants and expats (mostly French and Lebanese). The city's meteoric financial growth is based on *l'or noir* (black gold; oil) and, to a lesser extent, on timber.

To that end, the 2014 drop in global oil prices hit Port-Gentil hard. Previously trading at around US$100, the price for a barrel of crude has hovered close to US$50 ever since, with drastic consequences for the town. Several ambitious plans have been shelved or indefinitely delayed, including the proposed Port-Gentil University, Mandji Island Free Zone and a new oil refinery, meant to replace the current one which dates to 1967. You may have heard about *la crise* (the crisis) over oil prices from Gabonese elsewhere in the country, but there's nowhere where its effects are so clearly visible as here in Port-Gentil, where *les pétroliers* have long run the show.

Although Port-Gentil itself does not boast any major tourist attractions, it's the gateway to some of the one-of-a-kind sites in its direct surroundings, including Fernan Vaz Lagoon and Loango National Park. The city itself, stretching for around 15km along the coast of Cap Lopez Bay, is pleasant enough for a visitor, and shares the low-key vibe of most Gabonese towns. The banks, post office, hospital, police station and most other major services all sit along the main commercial thoroughfare, avenue Savorgnan de Brazza.

Owing to its isolated location, Port-Gentil is arguably even more expensive than Libreville. It's a highly segregated society and residents claim there are three

PORT-GENTIL
For listings, see from page 122

🛏️ **Where to stay**

1	Chez Jimmy	B2
2	Hôtel Le Bougainvillier	B3
3	Hotel Gamba	C6
4	Hôtel L'Hirondelle	B3
5	Hotel Mandji	C4
6	Hotel Tara-Me	A3
7	Hôtel Les Terrasses de la Médina	B3
8	Lagon Bleu	A2
9	Ophelia Lodge	C4
10	Parthénon Résidence Hôtelière	C6

Off map

Aux Berges des 3 Rivières	A1
Hôtel du Parc	A2
Hôtel Le Ranch	A2
Résidence Yassmani	A2

❌ **Where to eat and drink**

11	Le Bistrot	C3
12	Boulangerie Patisserie Sogabi	B3
13	Byblos	C4
14	Café du Wharf	B2
15	Cakes & Gourmandises	D5
16	Copacabana	B4
17	Léon Mba Park	A3
18	Le Lido	B2
19	Marina Social Beach	B1
20	Le Massena	C2
21	Memorial du Cinquantenaire	B3
22	Mole Pêche	C2
23	Pizza House	C3
24	Le Retro	B4
25	Taverne Lisboa	B3

Off map

La Case	A1
Le Pétrolier	A2
Mami Wata	A1
Sogara Club	A2

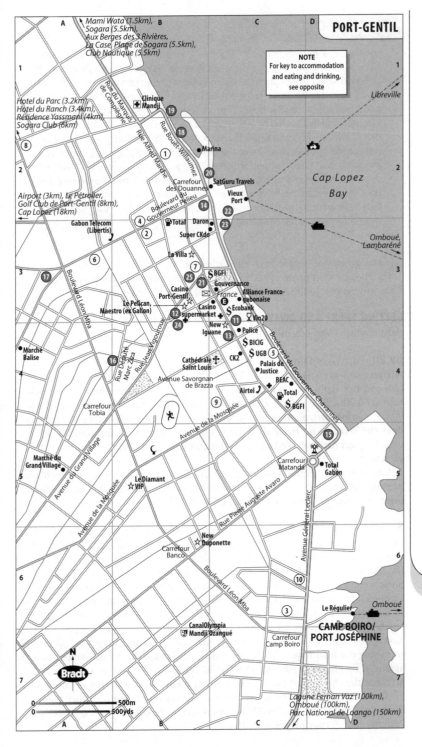

PORT-GENTIL

NOTE
For key to accommodation
and eating and drinking,
see opposite

Mami Wata (1.5km),
Sogara (5.5km),
Aux Berges des 3 Rivières,
La Case, Plage de Sogara (5.5km),
Club Nautique (5.5km)

Hotel du Parc (3.2km),
Hotel du Ranch (3.4km),
Résidence Yassmani (4km),
Sogara Club (6km)

Clinique
Mandji

Marina

Airport (3km), Le Pétrolier,
Golf Club de Port-Gentil (8km),
Cap Lopez (18km)

Carrefour
des Douannes

SatGuru Travels

Vieux
Port

Cap Lopez
Bay

Libreville

Omboué,
Lambaréné

Gabon Telecom
(Libertis)

Total

Daron

Super CKdo

La Villa

BGFI

Casino
Port-Gentil

Gouvernance

Alliance Franco-
gabonaise

France

Casino
supermarket

Ecobank

Le Pelican,
Maestro (ex Galion)

New
Iguane

Vin20

Police

BICIG

UGB

Cathédrale
Saint Louis

CK2

Palais de
Justice

BEAC

Avenue Savorgnan
de Brazza

Airtel

Total

BGFI

Marché
Balise

Carrefour
Tobia

Avenue de la Mosquée

Marché du
Grand Village

Carrefour
Matanda

Total
Gabon

Le Diamant
VIP

New
Duponette

Carrefour
Banco

Boulevard Léon Mba

CanalOlympia
Mandji Ozangué

Carrefour
Camp Boiro

Le Régulier

Omboué

CAMP BOIRO/
PORT JOSÉPHINE

N

Bradt

0   500m
0   500yds

Lagune Fernan Vaz (100km),
Omboué (100km),
Parc National de Loango (150km)

Located in a remote corner of Ogooué-Maritime province east of Lagune Nkomi (Nkomi Lagoon), the Grottes d'Abanda (Abanda Caves) hold one of Gabon's many ecological mysteries: an isolated population of some 20 African dwarf crocodile (*Osteolaemus tetraspis*) living in total darkness deep inside a cave, itself only accessible down a 7m pit. The crocodiles, measuring up to 1.7m in length and discovered by archaeologist Richard Oslisly in 2008, survive on a diet of bats, crickets and algae. Thanks to their longstanding genetic isolation, possibly for thousands of years, the crocs exhibit several unusual mutations, including near blindness and strikingly orange skin, which may be 'bleached' over time by the mix of bat guano and water, in which they spend much of their lives. Researchers have theorised that they are in the process of mutating into a separate species altogether. The last expedition here was in 2015; for more information, see w abanda-expedition.org.

separate groups of people here: the Gabonese, the expats and those working for Total. The question on everybody's mind – particularly now, thanks to *la crise* – is, what will happen to the city when the petrol actually runs out?

GETTING THERE AND AWAY Port-Gentil is all but inaccessible by road, and the most common way of getting there is by plane (30mins from Libreville).

By air Port-Gentil's modern airport sits just over 3km west of the city centre. **Afrijet** (✆ 02 00 90 01 (LBV)/02 03 32 01 (POG); w flyafrijet.online) runs between two and five daily 30-minute flights between Libreville and Port-Gentil; tickets start at 60,000CFA each way and can be booked online. **La Nationale** (NRT; ✆ 06 66 90 95; e infos@nrtgabon.org; w nrtgabon.org; NationaleRegionaleTransport) does the same route twice daily (morning and afternoon) for 100,000CFA one way. **Tropical Air** (page 66) also flies this route four days weekly from 75,000CFA each way.

Internationally, **Equaflight** (m 07 07 26 78; e reservationpog@equaflight.com; w equaflight.com) flies between Port-Gentil and Pointe-Noire in Congo (90mins) three times weekly (on variable days) for 220,000CFA one way.

By road It's now technically possible to drive between Port-Gentil and Libreville, but it's not a simple journey. First, the **new 100km road** from Port-Gentil to Omboué was partly operational at the time of writing, but remained closed to the public and special permission was required to drive on it (page 127). As this book went to print, the road (and its impressive pair of 4.5km bridges over the Ogooué and the Nkomi Lagoon) was scheduled to be inaugurated for public use in September 2019. From Omboué, it's some 250km on laterite roads until you reach the N1 at Yombi (◈ -1.4081, 10.6257). This remote road crosses the Rabi Kounga oil field, which is privately administered by Assala Energy and all vehicles transiting the field require an escort vehicle. Officially, escorts are supposed to be arranged by phone in advance (✆ 01 55 87 54/01 55 87 07); it may be possible to arrive at the checkpoint (◈ -1.8996, 9.8704) unannounced during opening hours (🕑 06.30–18.30) and be assigned one, but this can't be relied on. Once you reach the N1 at Yombi, it's a further 340km to Libreville, making for an impressively long 700km road journey between the two cities.

Public transport options are also sure to improve with the official opening of the new road in late 2019, but at the time of writing the only public road transport was run by Hotel Georges Faustin Aurat in Omboué (page 127), who put on early morning vehicles five times weekly (⊕ around 07.30 Mon, Wed, Fri to Port-Gentil, 07.30 Tue & Sat to Omboué). Vehicles leave from Carrefour Camp Boiro in Port-Gentil and cost 10,000CFA per person.

By boat Sonaga and CNNII both connect **Libreville** and Port-Gentil by boat. For further details of these companies and the ferries they operate, see page 82. In Port-Gentil, both companies sail from Vieux Port [119 C2], where you'll also find their ticket offices. It's best to reserve your tickets as early as possible – days in advance if you can – as boats are frequently sold out. As of late 2018, Logistique Maritime 241 (m 05 95 90 11/8 (POG)/05 95 90 15/6 (LBV); ◼ Logistique Maritime 241) was also running fast boats (3–4hrs) between the two cities five times weekly; see their Facebook page for current schedules.

Hôtel Olako (page 127) organises transport between Port-Gentil and **Omboué** by private boat. The boats sail several times a week, departing from Port-Gentil on Mondays, Wednesdays and Saturdays and returning on Sundays, Wednesdays and Saturdays. The trip takes 3 to 4 hours and costs 25,000CFA per person, with children half price. Boats depart at 09.30 from Mole Pêche [119 C2], behind Pizza House. A cheaper option, although somewhat slower and considerably less comfortable, is to take a pirogue with Le Régulier (Popoye Express; m 06 58 84 45) from Port Joséphine in Camp Boiro [119 D7]. These go roughly twice weekly in both directions (best to ask at the port for the next departure) and cost 8,000CFA. Bring suncream.

It's quite simple to travel by boat between **Lambaréné** and Port-Gentil, and it makes for a scenic journey up the Ogooué to boot. Several companies including CCB (m 06 66 47 66/05 99 87 72) and Mabiayi Express (m 07 00 91 39/07 50 22 26) run boats, and there's a departure every morning at 06.00 from Mole Pêche. The journey takes about 5 hours upriver; a bit less going with the current. The day before departure, agents hang around Mole Pêche selling tickets (15,000/22,000CFA standard/VIP). Just ask around if you can't find one. The boats are covered and often intensely air conditioned (particularly in VIP class), so have a sweater handy and potentially some snacks (there are always vendors at the port before departure). Minibuses to Libreville and Mouila wait to meet the arriving boats in Lambaréné.

Please note that, at the time of writing, there were no longer any ferries serving **Gamba**.

GETTING AROUND Generally speaking, central Port-Gentil is small and safe enough to explore **on foot**, but for longer trips there is no shortage of **taxis**, and a seat going somewhere in the city centre should be around 100–300CFA. If you stumble across a taxi that doesn't feel as if it's about to fall apart and you want to hang on to it, the going rate is 3,000CFA per hour or 25,000CFA per day. There are **car hire agencies** renting vehicles at the usual rates including Gesparc (☏ 01 55 02 40), but the condition is town-use only which, owing to the town's small size, makes them rather pointless. Hertz and Avis both have offices on avenue Savorgnan de Brazza.

Recently, Port-Gentil offered public transport in the form of bright yellow-and-blue Transpog **buses** (300CFA/ride), but many of these had fallen into disrepair at the time of writing. Even if you spot a bus driving past, it's harder still to find a bus stop and discover the different routes through town – one of the reasons most visitors stick to taxis.

TOUR OPERATORS SatGuru Travels [119 C2] (**m** 06 64 65 65/05 05 65 65) has an office opposite Marché Balise. For agencies specialising in tours to Loango, see page 130.

WHERE TO STAY Port-Gentil has a good range of (expensive) hotels catering primarily for business people working in the oil industry. The number of hotels with self-catering apartments also hints at the high concentration of foreigners here on long-term business. Deals can be negotiated for stays of more than a month at all of them.

Luxury–upmarket

❋ ⌂ Chez Jimmy [119 B2] (23 rooms) rue Alfred Marche; **☏**01 53 12 37; **m** 07 47 54 89/06 30 26 06; **e** hotelchezjimmy@begoubitia.com. This exclusive upmarket hotel is said to be Port-Gentil's best. Clean, comfortable rooms come with safe, fridge & Wi-Fi. There's a lovely, recommended restaurant, a swimming pool & a business centre. **$$$$$**

⌂ Hotel Mandji [119 C4] (88 rooms) bd du Gouverneur Chavannes; **☏**01 55 21 03; **e** reservation@cityhotelmandji.com; **w** cityhotelmandji.com. Centrally located, this long-serving hotel reopened in 2019 after a top-to-bottom renovation. Formerly part of the Méridien chain, it boasts all the facilities you would expect, including restaurants, a swimming pool, business & conference facilities & rooms with balconies & sea views. It's not cheap, but the facilities are undoubtedly among the smartest in town. **$$$$$**

⌂ Hôtel du Parc [119 A2] (120 units) rte Sogara; **m** 07 48 21 21/07 07 52 94; **e** info@ hotelduparcpog.com; **w** hotelduparcpog.com. Close to the port & industrial area, Hôtel du Parc is frequented by business travellers, but the spa, swimming pool & fitness centre would suit leisure travellers just as well. There are 6 categories of comfortable rooms, ranging from standard to 2-bedroom villas, spread over 17ha of green gardens. The Eden Restaurant (**$$$$**) serves seafood & continental dishes either inside or on their terrace. **$$$$**

⌂ Hôtel Le Ranch [119 A2] (47 rooms) rte Sogara; **☏**01 55 10 05; **w** hotel-leranch-pog.com; **f** hotelleranchportgentil. Le Ranch not only has a popular restaurant (**⊕** 05.00–midnight daily; **$$$$**), but also boasts a gym, a swimming pool & tennis courts. **$$$$**

⌂ Hotel Tara-Me [119 A3] (30 rooms) bd du Gouverneur Pelieu; **☏**01 56 85 06; **m** 04 17 09 00;

e info@tara-me.com; **w** tara-me.com. The newest upmarket option in Port-Gentil, this well-managed place sits in a large compound near Carrefour Léon Mba. Rooms come in a variety of configurations, but all are comfortably equipped with AC & terraces. There's a restaurant (**$$$**), pool & fitness centre on site & they can help arrange regional excursions. **$$$$**

Mid-range–budget

❋ ⌂ Hôtel Le Bougainvillier [119 B3] (20 rooms) bd du Gouverneur Pelieu; **m** 07 72 14 14; **e** hotel_le_bougainvillier@yahoo.fr; **w** tourisme-aventure-gabon.com. Rooms here are comfortable & classic-feeling & some come with a kitchenette. The well-regarded l'Hacienda Restaurant (**$$**) does pizzas, grills & more. Free Wi-Fi. It's under the same management as the new Campement Liambissi down the coast (page 132). **$$$**

⌂ Hôtel L'Hirondelle [119 B3] (24 self-contained studios) bd du Gouverneur Pelieu; **☏**01 55 17 82; **e** vcombalot@yahoo.fr. This long-serving hotel is trim & elegant, offering clean & inviting studios with a kitchenette, bedroom area, lounge area & bathroom. All rooms have AC, flat-screen TV & fridge. *Good value at 52,000CFA for a dbl.* **$$$**

⌂ Hôtel Les Terrasses de la Médina [119 B3] (25 rooms) opposite the post office, rue Jean Vigouroux; **m** 04 39 54 50; **e** lesterrassesdelamedina@yahoo.fr; **f** LesTerrassesDeLaMedina. Unpretentious hotel with spotless rooms. *From 40,000CFA.* **$$$**

⌂ Ophelia Lodge [119 C4] (25 rooms) rue Dr Ballay; **☏**01 56 87 89; **m** 03 31 31 91/05 99 97 97; **e** contact@ophelialodge.com. Done up in reds & whites, this is a stylish & centrally located hotel with modern rooms. All come with fridge & Wi-Fi. *Starting at 56,000CFA for a dbl.* **$$$**

⌂ Parthénon Résidence Hôtelière [119 C6] av Général Leclerc (15 rooms, 20 apts); **m** 05 05 56 06/05 98 90 21; **e** marembeyo@

parthenongabon.com; w parthenongabon.com. The attractive apartments – bright & modern – have nice bathrooms with bathrobes & toiletries. The kitchenette includes a fridge & a microwave & meals can be arranged on request. The Parthénon is a 10min walk from Total Gabon, heading out of town. It is easy to catch a taxi into town from here. **$$$**

🏠 **Résidence Yassmani** [119 A2] (44 units) rte Sogara; m 07 37 27 42/05 40 93 93; e sci-yassmani@hotmail.fr; w sci-yassmani.com. Secure compound next to the port with choice of self-contained studios, 2- or 4-bedroom villas, & 1 villa with private pool. **$$$**

🏠 **Hotel Gamba** [119 C6] (19 rooms) m 04 11 40 69; av Général Leclerc. Also known as the Hotel Matanda, this place south of the city centre is run by the Ndougou Departmental Council & is one of the best deals in town. *23,000CFA for en-suite room with fridge, AC, hot water & flat-screen TV.* **$$**

🏠 **Lagon Bleu** [119 A2] (28 studios) bd Léon Mba; m 07 50 32 10; e lagon_b@yahoo.fr; f HotelLeLagonBleu. Simple studios with kitchenette & sitting area. **$$**

Out of town *Map, page 116*

✱ 🏠 **Aux Berges des 3 Rivières** (7 rooms) ⊕ -0.6508, 8.7234; m 02 45 01 19/04 60 37 60/07 39 14 04/05 98 17 55; e auxbergesdes3rivieres@gmail.com/redondo.virginie@gmail.com; f Aux berges des 3 rivières. Set on a stunning white-sand beach at the mouth of a small river system between Cap Lopez & Port-Gentil, this idyllic getaway is only about 5km from town as the crow flies, but feels a whole lot further. Accommodation is in comfortably equipped wooden bungalows sleeping 3–4, & the restaurant (**$$$**) is known for its seafood & cocktails. There are kayaks & hammocks for you to use, depending on your mood. Call ahead to arrange a boat transfer from Sogara in Port-Gentil. **$$$**

✕ **WHERE TO EAT AND DRINK** There are masses of places to eat in Port-Gentil, although many serve a rather identikit, continentally inspired menu. Old places change hands and names frequently, and new places are always springing up. For details of hotel restaurants, see opposite. Expect to pay an average of 15,000CFA for a main course in the best restaurants in town, but most places do special menus, at least at midday, which are much better value. Some of the more upmarket places have an English menu – just ask. Most are open seven days a week.

✕ **Le Bistrot** [119 C3] av Savorgnan de Brazza; m 07 15 01 11; f lebistrotpog; ⊕ 09.00–05.00 Mon–Sat. Serves b/fast, cocktails & everything in between. The salads come particularly recommended & the colourful décor is pure Instagram fodder. It's a popular hangout in the evenings. **$$$**

✕ **Café du Wharf** [119 B2] bd du Gouverneur Chavannes; m 05 92 82 05/07 39 31 64; f Café du wharf; ⊕ 07.00–23.00. Big, airy & attractively old school, this place first opened its doors for custom more than 50 years ago & has been a POG landmark since. Here you can combine wining, dining & dancing, or come for the buffet every Sun from 12.30. **$$$**

✱✕ **La Case** [119 A1] m 07 33 33 41/06 23 76 56/05 45 58 78; f RestaurantBarAlaPlage; ⊕ 18.00–02.00 Fri, 09.00–02.00 Sat, 09.00–21.00 Sun) Set on a beautiful stretch of white-sand beach 1km across the estuary facing the Petit Village/Sogara neighbourhood at the north end

of town, this weekend-only stilted restaurant-bar is an easy & satisfying retreat from the city & is well known for its seafood & parties. Call ahead to arrange a pick-up. **$$$**

✕ **Le Lido** [119 B2] rue Bouët-Willaumez; m 07 26 89 80; f Le Lido Marina. Perched on top of stilts over the sea, Le Lido is another popular expat hangout, particularly for its Thirsty Thursday deals or during football matches. Good cocktails & good pastas. **$$$**

✱✕ **Marina Social Beach** [119 B1] rue Bouët-Willaumez; m 02 35 99 99; f Marina Social Beach; ⊕ 07.30–late (kitchen until 22.00) Mon–Sat, 07.30–21.30 Sun. This delightful new open-air spot on the waterfront near the marina does fab tapas, paninis & cocktails, along with what some say is the best burger in Central Africa – quite the claim, but we'd be hard pressed to argue. **$$$**

✕ **Le Massena** [119 C2] rue Bouët-Willaumez; m 05 92 82 05; ⊕ Mon–Sat. This is a longstanding & well-loved eatery serving up good continental & African dishes on a small beach overlooking the sea. $$$

✗ **Le Pétrolier** [119 A2] rte du Cap Lopez; ☏ 01 36 48 89. This popular w/end haunt is a recommended open restaurant above the beach at Cap Lopez. The food is delicious – particularly the *grillades*. To get there follow the Cap Lopez road & turn left down the road at Total Gabon. It's about a 20min drive from the centre of Port-Gentil. $$$

✗ **Sogara Club** [119 A2] At the end of rte Sogara; ☏ 02 56 31 79; m 07 60 57 65. Very popular with Port-Gentil's expats, particularly at w/ends when the weather is good & eating on the terrace by the beach is a real pleasure. There's a large menu with pizzas, crêpes, pastas, ice creams, fish & meat dishes. $$$

✗ **Taverne Lisboa** [119 B3] rue Jean Vigouroux; ☏ 02 76 19 31. Opened in 2018, this restaurant & wine bar has quickly gained a reputation for its Portuguese-style *petiscos* (small plates). $$$

✗ **Byblos** [119 C4] av Savorgnan de Brazza; ☏ 01 56 12 53. A change from the norm, & less pricey than any of the above. Here you can enjoy excellent Lebanese food in a relaxed atmosphere. The extensive menu has a good range for vegetarians & falafel or shawarma sandwiches for just 2,000CFA. $$

✗ **Copacabana** [119 B4] rue Député Marc Ziza; m 07 19 19 04; ⊕ closed Sun. Don't miss out on this local restaurant, one of the best in town. Service may be a bit slow but the food – mostly fish, brochettes & other grills – is inexpensive and very tasty. $$

✗ **Mami Wata** [119 A1] rte de Sogara. Unpretentious local eatery on a small beach serving meat & chips & cheap beer. $$

✗ **Pizza House** [119 C3] bd du Gouverneur Chavannes; m 07 77 44 44; ⊕ 10.30–23.00 Mon–Sat, 17.30–23.00 Sun. Serving good pizzas from 4,500CFA on their terrace at the edge of a green & tidy park. They host occasional *pétanque* competitions as well. $$

✗ **Le Retro** [119 B4] rue du Gouverneur Bernard; ☏ 01 55 27 67. French restaurant serving European dishes, pizzas & crêpes, with a lunch deal for 10,000CFA. Downstairs is a small café selling ice cream. $$

✗ **Memorial du Cinquantenaire** [119 B3] av Savorgnan de Brazza; m 06 33 24 83. Popular garden hangout & kids' park with burgers & grills starting at 4,000CFA. **Léon Mba Park** [119 A3] (m 07 57 02 15; $–$$) across town is very similar. $–$$

✗ **Mole Pêche** [119 C2] Behind Pizza House (see above). This warren of shipping-container restaurants & bars next to the port is a bit chaotic, but nonetheless a lively & likeable address for heaping plates of Gabonese & other African dishes from 1,500CFA. $

☕ **Cakes & Gourmandises** [119 D5] Near Carrefour Matanda; m 07 96 37 36; ⊕ 07.00–19.00 Tue–Sun. Hidden away on the 1st floor, this pretty café opened in 2018 & serves excellent juices, smoothies, tea & coffee, along with pastries, light meals & sandwiches. Free Wi-Fi. $$

☕ **Boulangerie Patisserie Sogabi** [119 B3] rue du Gouverneur Bernard; ☏ 01 55 24 60; ⨍ Sogabi Boulangerie Patisserie. Popular & long-serving bakery with all manner of sweet & savoury pastries on offer. $

ENTERTAINMENT AND NIGHTLIFE

Expats in Port-Gentil (and locals alike) work hard and play hard. There are enough watering holes in Port-Gentil to constitute an extensive pub crawl, though you'll find the hotspots are in constant flux. Check out **Port-Gentil Groove** (⨍ POGROOV) for the latest parties and events. **Clubs** usually open at 22.00 but things only get lively after midnight. Count on 10,000CFA a drink in the fancier places. **Marina Social Beach** [119 B1] and **Le Bistrot** [119 C3] (page 123) are reliably popular and friendly hangouts, and both stay open late. Otherwise, **Vin20** [119 C4] (bd du Gouverneur Chavannes; m 07 63 36 32; ⨍ vinsur20; ⊕ until 01.00 Mon–Sat) is a safe bet to start the evening with a glass of wine and a charcuterie board, and they often have live music at weekends.

More upbeat is the equally hip and crowded **New Iguane** [119 C4] (av Savorgnan de Brazza; m 06 59 28 53). **New Duponette** [119 B6] (Carrefour Banco; m 07 01 34 92; ⨍ New Duponette Club Port-Gentil) is another long-time favourite with POG punters. The newer **Maestro (ex Galion)** [119 B3] (rue du Gouverneur Bernard; m 04 40 15 15; MaestroGalion) is a good option as well, with areas for billiards, dancing and a snack bar.

If the night goes long enough, you might also find yourself at the sleek and centrally located **La Villa** [119 B3] (av Savorgnan de Brazza; m 05 82 69 59; lavillaportgentil), but come dressed to impress or you'll be sent on your way. Other slightly less flashy options for drinking and dancing include **Le Diamant VIP** [119 B5] (bd du Président Léon Mba; m 04 77 55 95/07 10 53 53; Diamant VIP POG) and **Le Pelican** [119 B3] (rue du Gouverneur Bernard; ☏01 53 02 97; PelicanBarPrivePog; ⊕ 19.00–late).

The first **cinema** in Port-Gentil for many years, CanalOlympia Mandji'Ozangué [119 B7] (rue Jean-Marie Rousselot; w canalolympia.com/mandjiozangue) opened its doors in December 2018, so it's now possible to see Hollywood and French films here for a very reasonable price. The **Alliance Franco-gabonaise** [119 C3] (bd du Gouverneur Chavannes; ☏01 56 59 41; e alliance.fg.pog@gmail.com; w alliancefgpog.wixsite.com/afgpog; Alliance Franco-Gabonaise POG) also occasionally screens films.

Finally, there's the rather pokey **Casino Port-Gentil** [119 B3] (rue du Gouverneur Bernard; ⊕ 22.00–late daily), which is (somewhat confusingly) just around the corner from the Casino supermarket and has blackjack, roulette, poker and the usual machines.

SHOPPING Unless otherwise specified, the shops and markets mentioned here all operate under standard opening times with long lunch breaks (page 74).

As well as the Daron [119 C3] (bd du Gouverneur Chavannes), Casino [119 C3] (av Savorgnan de Brazza) and Super CKdo [119 C3] (bd du Gouverneur Chavannes; ⊕ 08.30–12.30 & 15.00–19.30 Mon–Fri, all day Sat) supermarkets, there are a handful of open-air markets in Port-Gentil. The largest and loudest is the **Marché du Grand Village** [119 A5] (✪ -0.7287, 8.7775), which lies north of Carrefour Tobia in the animated quartier of the same name. It sells everything under the sun, and then some. **Marché Balise** [119 A4] (✪ -0.7221, 8.7752), just north of the Léon Mba roundabout, is smaller and sells a selection of agricultural products, ranging from fruit and veg to wood and building materials.

Otherwise, avenue Savorgnan de Brazza is the main commercial street where you'll find a number of shops selling everyday goods, including **CK2** [119 C4], which carries everything you might need for your house, from furniture to jacuzzis. For stylish African-inspired designer clothes, head for **Enami Shop** (rte des Hydrocarbures; ☏07 42 42 05; w enami-shop.com;), whose name means 'elegance' in Myènè.

OTHER PRACTICALITIES
Banks There are branches of all the major banks with ATMs that accept Visa and/ or Mastercard (BICIG, Ecobank, UGB, BGFI) on avenue Savorgnan de Brazza.

Communications Port-Gentil's central post office is in the city centre on avenue Savorgnan de Brazza [119 B3]. Both Airtel and Gabon Telecom (Libertis) have offices in town.

Medical services Clinique Mandji [119 B3] (rue du Marquis de Compiègne; ☏ 01 55 35 56; w clinique-mandji.com) is the most reputable hospital in town. **Pharmacie Centrale** (rue du Gouverneur Bernard), **Pharmacie Von**

Okuwa [119 C4] (av Savorgnan de Brazza) and **Pharmacie du Cap** [119 C3] (av Savorgnan de Brazza, next to Casino supermarket) are well stocked.

Petrol There are two Total petrol stations.

Red tape The **French consulate** [119 C3] (av Savorgnan de Brazza; \01 55 20 86/01 55 18 93; e cad.port-gentil-consulat@diplomatie.gouv.fr) reopened here in 2019.

WHAT TO SEE AND DO One building in the city centre of historical and architectural interest is the **Cathédrale Saint Louis** [119 C4], which dates back to 1927. It's a pretty building, with striking windows, a clock tower and covered arcades down each side. There's a statue of Saint Louis by the French sculptor Maxime Real Del Sarte (1888–1954) under the porch. If the church is closed, ask around for the father, who will be happy to open up for you. Services are held Monday to Thursday at 06.10, Fridays and Saturdays at 06.30, and Sundays at 08.30 and 10.00.

Part of the Hôtel du Parc complex is the small **Zoo Au Ranch** (free admission, but not recommended for the humane-minded), founded by the hotel owner. He has landscaped a large area with cages and pens around a pond traversed by a liana bridge. The unlucky residents include palm vulture, mandrill, moose, chimpanzee and even a gorilla housed in a small cage. Understandably, the zoo has caused some controversy since its creation in 1994, with charges of poor animal care.

One of the best beaches around town is the idyllic **Plage de Sogara** (Sogara Beach) [119 A1], where the sand is white and the water is calm, warm and a postcard-perfect shade of turquoise. Sogara Club (see below) itself is a great place to hang out with tennis courts and a lovely restaurant, but doesn't charge for the use of the beach. Between June and September, it's possible to see whale and dolphin swimming right off the coast on the way to their breeding grounds.

The beach at **Cap Lopez** [map, page 116] – reached by a decent road leading 15km north of the airport – is another popular spot with picnickers at the weekend, who make use of the open beach shelters here (or come to eat at Le Pétrolier; page 124). The water is colder and the currents are stronger than at Sogara. Although there are no physical signs left, Cap Lopez was an important slave port during the 18th and 19th centuries.

Walking down the beach, you'll come across the abandoned **lighthouse** that was built in 1911. Just like St Anne's Mission (page 128), the lighthouse's structure was designed by Eiffel and constructed with materials shipped from Paris. In its current state of neglect it looks a bit creepy. Leave behind any valuables, as we've had occasional reports of beach theft. There's another inactive lighthouse back in town at the south end of the city centre, a tower of metal lattice believed to date to the 1920s.

The area around Port-Gentil is also known for its **avian life**, with an incomplete checklist already covering more than 320 species, including a resident population of the vulnerable Loango weaver (*Ploceus subpersonatus*). As such, BirdLife International recognised the whole of Mandji Island as an Important Bird Area in 2001.

Sports Club Nautique [119 A1] (rte de Sogara; e clubnautpog@gmail.com; ⓕ ClubnautiquePOG) is an excellent place to practise watersports and organises the yearly sailing championship in May. The **Golf Club de Port-Gentil** [119 A2] (w fggolf.org) is not far out of town, 4.5km past the airport towards Cap Lopez. Surrounded by greens, there is a good clubhouse restaurant-bar with a regularly changing menu. There are tennis courts at **Sogara Club** [119 A2] (\01 56 31 79) for roughly 5,000CFA per hour; if you'll be sticking around there are monthly deals to be had here.

OMBOUÉ AND LAGUNE FERNAN VAZ

A trip to the **Fernan Vaz Lagoon** is one of the highlights of any exploration of the Ogooué-Maritime region and, with the opening of the new road from Port-Gentil, it is more accessible than ever. The setting is delightfully dramatic, with the lagoon's dark waters ringed by an impossibly green and vegetated shore. The lagoon takes its name from the Portuguese sailor Fernão Vaz, who discovered it at the end of the 15th century, but its most famous landmark, the Mission Sainte-Anne and its rust-red *église*, dates from four centuries later. Today, the lagoon is also home to the commendable Fernan-Vaz Gorilla Project, which has been caring for orphaned gorillas since 2001.

Omboué is the jumping-off point for the area's main attractions. While it's a sleepy town of just 2,000 people, the facilities here are surprisingly good and it's got a fetching location on the west coast of the lagoon, where boat trips, jet skis and other watersports are available.

GETTING THERE AND AROUND Omboué is the rather unlikely terminus for the new 100km tarmac road from Port-Gentil (page 120), from where works will one day continue towards the N1 at Yombi, currently a further 270km of laterite road. (We'd advise you not to hold your breath.)

To get around the **Fernan Vaz Lagoon**, take a pirogue from Omboué. Hôtel Olako (see below) and Hotel Georges Faustin Aurat (see below) both run boats that bring you to the village of Sainte-Anne (page 128), Gorilla Island (page 128), or the Mpivié River; a full day-trip costs around 150,000CFA.

WHERE TO STAY, EAT AND DRINK

🏠 **Hôtel Olako** (7 rooms) Facing the Fernan Vaz Lagoon, Omboué; m 04 41 20 23/06 19 01 84; e hotelolako@hotelolako.com/hotelolako18@gmail.com; w hotelolako.com. A rightly popular base for exploring the region, this is a friendly & well-decorated hotel with rooms on the shore & a stilted dining room above the lagoon. The trim rooms are en suite with AC. They organise 4×4 safaris, boat trips on the lagoon (around 25,000CFA pp or 150,000CFA/boat for a full day) & regular ferry services to Port-Gentil (page 121). **$$$**

🏠 **Hotel Georges Faustin Aurat** (20 rooms) Facing the Fernan Vaz Lagoon, Omboué; m 04 77 57 77/06 28 08 92. Opened in 2015, this is a modern & colourful hotel on the lagoon offering en-suite rooms with TV, fridge & hot water. It's less characterful than the Olako, but also cheaper. The restaurant does pizzas & grills, & there are some beachfront hammocks too. They can arrange 4×4 safaris & boat trips (around 25,000CFA pp or 150,000CFA/boat for a full day), along with regular vehicles to Port-Gentil (page 121). **$$**

🏠 **Evengué Lodge** (5 bungalows) m 07 79 22 07; e info@loango-safari.com. Although closed to visitors at the time of writing, it's possible this lodge overlooking the lagoon next to the gorilla sanctuary may reopen during the lifetime of this edition. Contact ANPN (page 88) for the current status.

WHAT TO SEE AND DO Though the Fernan-Vaz Gorilla Project and Mission Sainte-Anne are the biggest draws, the lagoon itself offers plenty of recreational opportunity and both hotels in Omboué (see above) can arrange jet skis and paddleboats to take you out on the waters near town.

Further afield, the black-water Mpivié River slices through dense jungle at the south end of the lagoon and trips here offer good wildlife-spotting opportunities, including monkeys and crocodiles. With an early start, a trip to the Mpivié can be combined with visits to Mission Sainte-Anne and/or the Fernan-Vaz Gorilla Project. Either hotel can arrange a motorised pirogue to take you here, starting at around 30,000CFA per person.

Fernan-Vaz Gorilla Project (PGFA; ✆ -1.6575, 9.3256; m 07 72 54 26/07 73 86 92; e fvgp@scd-conservation.com; w gorillasgabon.org; f gorillasgabon; admission 10,000CFA foreigners, 5,000CFA children, free for nationals) About 12km from Omboué as the crow flies, Île Evengué-Ezango (Evengué-Ezango Island), popularly known as Île aux Gorilles (Gorilla Island), is the location of the Fernan-Vaz Gorilla Project, initiated in 2001 when a family of orphaned gorillas was transferred from the Centre International de Recherches Médicales de Franceville (Franceville International Centre for Medical Research; CIRMF) to the island. The project runs a sanctuary and reintroduction centre. The four gorillas in the sanctuary, a forested enclosure on the island, act as conservation ambassadors to help educate national and international visitors to Evengué-Ezango on the plight of great apes. The rehabilitation centre is located on nearby Île Oriquet (Oriquet Island), away from human exposure, where eight orphaned gorillas currently reside. The aim is to reintroduce them back into the wild. The PGFA base camp is located at Mpando (on the mainland) just 600m across from Oriquet Island. Visits generally last about 90 minutes, including a short introduction to the centre.

Mission Sainte-Anne (✆ -1.6453, 9.4032; 5,000CFA) Set at the tip of a headland where the Fernan Vaz Lagoon slowly begins to narrow into the Mpivié River, the Mission Sainte-Anne is only about 18km from Omboué as the crow flies, but the lost-in-time ambiance here feels much, much further. The church was built in 1889, the same year as the Eiffel Tower, and, unlikely as it may seem, there's actually a connection. Look no further than Gustav Eiffel himself, who shipped the plans and materials all the way from Paris at the behest of Mrs Bichet, the mother of Sainte-Anne's founding priest and a wealthy woman with Paris connections. The church stands tall and elegant, the metal worn to a deep, rusty red over the years.

In addition to touring the mission, you can take guided walks in the surrounding forest or along the beach (where you can also go for a dip) and visit some of the surrounding villages. Most visitors arrive by boat on a day tour with one of the hotels in Omboué (page 127), but it's also theoretically accessible on some 50km of unsurfaced roads and sandy tracks (4×4 only) connecting the mission to Omboué. Ask locally for advice on the route if you're planning on going this way. If you'd like to spend the night, the mission offers basic **accommodation** (m 07 32 75 79/07 11 40 22; e sainteanne.tv@gmail.com; $) in rather austere first-floor rooms built of wood.

PARC NATIONAL DE LOANGO

Loango National Park (15,000/10,000CFA tourist/foreign resident) is the jewel in the crown of Gabon's 13 parks and offers one of the world's most exhilarating safari experiences, thanks to its irresistible combination of scenery and wildlife. With more than 175km of uninhabited shoreline, it is widely regarded as one of Africa's last great coastal wildernesses. Lagoons, forests, savannahs and wetlands all come together within the park's 1,500km². Loango's endless beach is one of the few places in the world where buffalo and forest elephant still have access to the sea, and even gorilla families are occasionally seen foraging in beachside trees. The park is also home to the legendary 'surfing hippos', memorably captured on film by *National Geographic* photographer Michael Nichols in 2004. In season, humpbacks and dolphins may be seen frolicking in the warm equatorial waters of the Atlantic Ocean just offshore. Many rare bird species have been spotted here, including Forbes's plover, Loango weaver, quail finch, rosy bee-eaters and Congo

River martins. The park is a paradise for lovers of sport fishing and record catches of tarpon, as well as barracuda, rouge, and big sharks are possible here.

The current park incorporates the former Iguéla and Petit Loango reserves. To the north, the former Iguéla Reserve covered an area of 230,000ha surrounding the Iguéla (Ngowé) Lagoon, and neighbouring it to the south was the smaller coastal reserve of Petit Loango. Though today the reserves have been merged into a unified national park, each side still has its own separate access route (pages 130 and 135). As such, most visitors will visit either the northern or southern ends of the park, but not both. It *is* possible to connect between the two while staying within the park if you're willing to hike (see box, page 131), but this requires advance planning.

Loango's attractions change depending on the time of year but, regardless of season, the park is worth at least two or three days of your time, should your budget allow. The **whale season** begins around mid-July and continues through to mid-September, the **tarpon fishing season** lasts from October to mid-November, and the **turtle season** is October to mid-January. For the best chance of seeing elephant wandering the

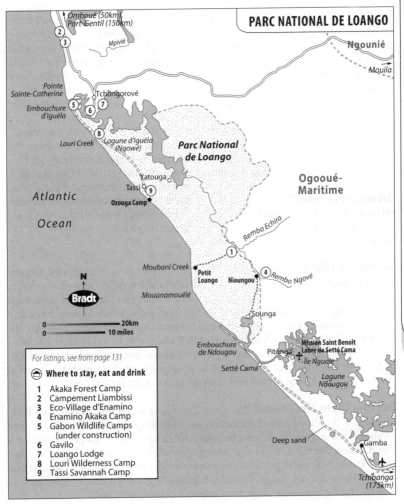

PARC NATIONAL DE LOANGO

Omboué (50km),
Port-Gentil (150km)

Mpivié

Ngounié

Mouila

Pointe
Sainte-Catherine

Tchongorové

Embouchure
d'Iguéla

Louri Creek

Lagune d'Iguéla
(Ngowé)

**Parc National
de Loango**

Yatouga

Tassi

Ozouga Camp

Atlantic

Ocean

Ogooué-
Maritime

Rembo Echira

Moubani Creek

Petit
Loango

Nioungou

Rembo Ngové

Mouanamouélé

Sounga

N

Bradt

0 ——— 20km
0 ——— 10 miles

Embouchure
de Ndougou

Pitanga

Mission Saint Benoit
Labré de Setté Cama

Ile Nguale

Setté Cama

Lagune
Ndougou

For listings, see from page 131

🛏 **Where to stay, eat and drink**

1 Akaka Forest Camp
2 Campement Liambissi
3 Eco-Village d'Enamino
4 Enamino Akaka Camp
5 Gabon Wildlife Camps
    (under construction)
6 Gavilo
7 Loango Lodge
8 Louri Wilderness Camp
9 Tassi Savannah Camp

Deep sand

Gamba

Tchibanga
(175km)

white-sand beaches, visit during the **rainy season** from October to April. At all times, you're likely to see at least some of the following: buffalo, hippo, crocodile, manatee, elephant, chimpanzee and gorilla. Moreover, with the 2018 introduction of treks to visit a troop of habituated **lowland gorilla** at Yatouga in the north of the park, Loango's offerings grow richer still. **Sport fishing** and **boat or walking safaris** that provide for excellent animal spotting can be done on either side, but 4x4 safaris and habituated gorilla trekking are only available in the north.

Historically, the park has a reputation for exclusiveness and, while visiting it still can't be done on a shoestring, there are a few possibilities for those on a tight-ish budget who might be willing to splurge a little. There are currently a couple of lodges north of the Iguéla (Ngowé) Lagoon that offer great trips for less exorbitant prices and, in the south, Setté Cama is home to decent accommodation and ecotourism community projects, though still nothing that could be honestly called budget-friendly. As many of the activities here involve boat or 4x4 journeys, visiting in a group is probably the best way to defray costs.

TOUR OPERATORS All trips into Loango must be arranged in advance and all hotels at the north and south ends of the park (see opposite) offer package tours including excursions. They will arrange transport from your place of departure (Port-Gentil, Omboué or Gamba respectively) to their accommodation and also trips into the park itself. Eco-Village d'Enamino (page 132) also operates its own satellite camp along the Rembo Ngové River in the Akaka Forest area, and can arrange excursions to all corners of the park. The companies listed here will also be able to assist you:

Gabon Untouched For contact details, see page 89. This Spanish operator can arrange bespoke itineraries, including coordinating guided hikes between the 2 sides of the park. See ad, 3rd colour section.
Gabon Wildlife Camps/ANPN For contact details, see page 88. ANPN now administers 3 camps within the park – Akaka Forest Camp, Tassi Savannah Camp & Louri Wilderness Camp – which

are all best accessed in partnership with Loango Lodge (page 132). See ad, 3rd colour section.
GIC Tourisme (Cooperative Abiétu) Setté Cama; m 07 33 99 51/06 89 95 99/06 84 62 46; e cooperativeabietu@yahoo.com; f Cooperative Abietu. An independent community initiative that promotes ecotourism in Setté Cama. They have a pleasant lodge & arrange excursions.

NORTHERN LOANGO The northern sector of the park is centred around **Lagune d'Iguéla (Ngowé)** (Iguéla (Ngowé) Lagoon); large and irregularly shaped, the riotous greenery of the shoreline here is nearly uninterrupted, save for a handful of vanishingly small fishing villages dotted along it. To the west, a patchwork of deep forest and grassy savannah covers the long peninsula between lagoon and ocean, ending at the windswept Embouchure d'Iguéla (Iguéla Inlet) and the wide, sandy beach of Pointe Sainte-Catherine. To the south, the forests seem to somehow grow even more intense, and this wall of greenery is cut through by the equally impenetrable black waters of the Rembo Ngové River, which feeds into the lagoon from the southeast.

Getting there and around Northern Loango is accessible by 4x4 from Port-Gentil, via Omboué (for information on travelling between Port-Gentil and Omboué, see page 120). From **Omboué**, there's no public transport (save for a more-or-less daily *taxi-brousse* to Tchongorové, the village next to Loango Lodge; ask in Omboué about departures), so a 4x4 transfer to one of the lodges is your best option. There are two lodges facing the Iguéla (Ngowé) Lagoon at Tchongorové and two facing the ocean along the Omboué–Tchongorové road.

Put simply, there's no easy way to travel between the two halves of the park. There used to be flights from Port-Gentil to Gamba which made it much easier but, at the time this book went to print, no-one was serving this route. Moreover, it's theoretically some 680km by **car** between the northern access point at Tchongorové and the southern access point at Setté Cama (via Yombi, Ndendé and Tchibanga), but you can hardly say this route is efficient (the distance is less than 85km as the crow flies, and you'd need your own 4×4).

Thus, an 18km **hike** through the centre of the park is currently the only way to visit both sides of the park in a single trip, without returning to Libreville or the N1. If you're up for it, the path runs between the abandoned village of Nioungou (⊕ -2.2820, 9.7220; about a 3hr boat ride from Tchongorové or Loango Lodge in northern Loango) on the Rembo Ngové River and the one-family settlement of Sounga (⊕ -2.4074, 9.7320; just over 30mins by boat from Setté Cama in southern Loango) on the Ndogo (Ndougou) Lagoon. Whichever direction you're headed, the route must be walked with the accompaniment of a guide, and requires advance coordination with your accommodation (see below and page 137) and/or a tour operator (see opposite), who will ensure the boat and guide are waiting to meet you at the start of the trail.

The path itself is relatively undemanding and can be walked in around 4 or 5 hours; en route you'll note a couple of long-abandoned vehicles, attesting to the fact it was once-upon-a-time possible to drive this route – definitely not the case today.

Guides from GIC Tourisme (Cooperative Abiétu) in Setté Cama (see opposite) know the trail well. Eco-Village d'Enamino's Akaka camp (page 132) is very near Nioungou; they are also well equipped to arrange this connection in collaboration with Cooperative Abiétu. Tour operator Gabon Untouched (see opposite) is also well recommended for arranging trips along this route.

Arrange transfers with the lodge of your choice in advance (see below) – they will be able to give you pricing and timing details – but, as an example, at the time of writing Loango Lodge offered 4×4 transfers (around 5hrs total) on the new Port-Gentil–Omboué road in partnership with Hôtel Le Bougainvillier (page 122) and Campement Liambissi (page 132), where passengers change vehicles. The first leg to Liambissi (3½hrs) costs 150,000CFA for one to three passengers and 50,000CFA for each additional person, up to a maximum of eight. A Loango Lodge vehicle covered the remaining 75 minutes of the transfer, charging 100,000CFA per vehicle, with a maximum of nine passengers. (Prices are one way.)

If you wish to **self-drive**, the 50km road from Omboué to Tchongorové and the Iguéla (Ngowé) Lagoon is fairly arduous and suitable for 4x4s only.

Where to stay, eat and drink *Map, page 129*

Generally speaking, facilities are more comprehensive in the north of the park than in the south, and visitors can base themselves at one of several lodges on or near the Iguéla (Ngowé) Lagoon. All accommodation sits along the fringes of the park, with the exception of Loango Lodge's satellite camps run by Gabon Wildlife Camps (see opposite), which are within the park itself. Though it's a touch far away (50km), it is also possible to stay in Omboué and explore this half of the park from there; the hotels in Omboué know how to arrange this.

🏠 **Loango Lodge** (11 bungalows) Tchongorové; **m** 04 92 00 54; **w** loango@gabonwildlifecamps.com/ gabonwildlifecamps.com. Formerly known as Africa's Eden, Loango Lodge is probably Gabon's most famous safari lodge: exclusive (& exclusively expensive) accommodation in the midst of stunning nature. There is a beautiful restaurant on stilts overlooking the river that separates the lodge from the national park, a nice swimming pool & a bookshop. The bungalows made of bamboo are equipped with AC & hot water. See page 131 for details on transfers to the lodge.

Along with Loango Lodge, the ANPN-affiliated Gabon Wildlife Camps operates 3 satellite camps spread over the Iguéla (Ngowé) Lagoon: Akaka Forest Camp, Tassi Savannah Camp & Louri Wilderness Camp, enabling visitors to make a comprehensive tour of the northern half of the park & enjoy its variety of magnificent landscapes. The lodge & all 3 satellite camps charge the same price, which includes transport between the camps & standard land & water safaris, but not whale watching or gorilla trekking.

The satellite camps are luxurious tent camps in East African-safari style, sleeping a max of 10 persons in 5 comfortable tents on platforms, equipped with beds, en-suite bathrooms with shower & toilet. After spending the night in Loango Lodge, it is possible to continue by boat to **Akaka Forest Camp** (⊕ -2.2254, 9.6801), 66km or a 3hr journey southeast by motorised pirogue. Throughout the year, Akaka is the ideal place for birdwatchers. Elephant & buffalo often cross the river & visit the camp in the dry season (May–Oct). Akaka's mirror-like black waters are excellent for expeditions. Beware: there is an infernal number of tsetse flies on the river, so avoid black or blue clothing & wear insect repellent.

Tassi Savannah Camp (⊕ -2.0433, 9.4148) lies on the other side of the lagoon, in the savannah 800m from the beach. It's 25km or a 2hr drive from Loango Lodge & ideal for turtle observations or early morning walks in search of wildlife.

The newest camp, **Louri Wilderness Camp** (⊕ -1.9812, 9.3554), opened in 2018 and is the closest to Loango Lodge, just a few mins across the Iguéla (Ngowé) Lagoon on the shores of Louri Lagoon. From here you can often spot elephant or buffalo on the beach. To the north, Pointe Sainte-Catherine, where the lagoon empties into

the ocean, is a heaven for fishermen, containing some of the largest game fish in the world; fishing excursions can be arranged. It's also an ideal location for turtle watching from Nov–Feb. A yet-to-be-named 4th camp (⊕ -1.8795, 9.2809) is also in development, and may open during the life of this edition. *Around 240,000/400,000CFA for a standard sgl/dbl or 270,000/450,000CFA for a suite sgl/dbl, including meals but exc drinks.* **$$$$$**

✳ 🏠 **Eco-Village d'Enamino** (4 bungalows, 2 safari tents) Between Omboué & Tchongorové; ⊕ -1.7279, 9.2535; **m** 07 98 88 34/02 26 27 97; **e** enamino@gmail.com; **w** enamino.com. Halfway from Omboué to Loango, this small camp has a stunning location on a rocky cliffside lining a long & deserted beach. The lovingly decorated & carefully kept bungalows are made of local materials & the meals are exquisite. The camp tries to minimise its impact on the environment by using fertilising toilets, collecting rainwater & sending out regular beach-cleaning crews. Fishing trips, safaris, trekking & excursions to Fernan Vaz & Loango are easily arranged with master guide & camp manager Philippe Robin, including to their own bush camp, **Enamino Akaka Camp**, near Nioungou, where rustic but comfortable camping tents sit overlooking a floodplain, frequented by all manner of wildlife (from 205,000CFA for 2 nights, based on 4 guests; **$$$**). 4x4 transfers from Port-Gentil/ Iguéla/Omboué cost 150,000/70,000/50,000CFA. See the eco-village's informative website for further details. *60,000CFA FB.* **$$$$**

🏠 **Gavilo** (8 bungalows) Tchongorové; ⊕ -1.8919, 9.3145; **m** 06 25 08 88/06 25 08 88; **e** gavilo2001@yahoo.fr/tourismlguéla@yahoo. fr; **w** gavilo-iguela.com. This is predominantly a fishing lodge, with small green & white bungalows with hot showers & private bathrooms & a restaurant on a platform over the lagoon. The chef's speciality is *carpaccio* and grilled fish *à la Gavilo*. There's electricity from 06.30 to 08.00 & 18.00 to midnight. *Count on 90,000CFA pp/night, including all meals & transport.* **$$$$**

🏠 **Campement Liambissi** (5 rooms) Between Omboué & Tchongorové; ⊕ -1.7549, 9.2653; **m** 06 50 60 70; **e** liambissi.resa@yahoo.com. About 3km south of Eco-Village d'Enamino as the crow flies & under the same ownership as Le Bougainvillier in Port-Gentil (page 122), this colourful & newly renovated campement enjoys a prime location between the beach & lagoon. The cool &

comfortable en-suite bungalow rooms sleep up to 5 & are filled with African art; there's also a family suite sleeping 7 with kitchen & AC. Hikes, fishing, safaris, surfing & canoe trips on the lagoon can all be arranged here. Alternatively, the pool, *petanque* & a *paillote* hut in the sand are equally tempting options. *50,000CFA dbl bungalow (plus 5,000CFA/additional guest), 140,000CFA family suite. W/end deals inc all meals, activities & transport from Port-Gentil 290,000CFA pp.* **$$$**

What to see and do All accommodation operators (page 131) in northern Loango arrange excursions into the park. Activities on offer include vehicle, walking and boat safaris, as well as whale watching, gorilla tracking and even kayaking through some of the area's many mangrove-lined creeks. As the northern sector of the park centres around the Iguéla (Ngowé) Lagoon, activities – including the walking or 4×4 safaris – generally involve a short boat trip to begin with.

The belt of grassy savannah that runs some 35km along the coast between Pointe Saint-Catherine in the north and Ozouga Camp (see below) in the south is perhaps Gabon's top animal-spotting destination. Elephant, buffalo, hippo, red river hog, sitatunga (and more) are all represented on this stunning stretch of land. There are no proper roads in the park, but the area is crisscrossed by a small network of tracks, along which open-sided 4×4 safari vehicles wind their way through the patchwork terrain of forest, savannah and beach. This area is also home to the Tassi Savannah and Louri Wilderness camps (see opposite); while either make an ideal jumping-off point for **walking and 4×4 safaris** in the area, the same can be arranged every morning or afternoon from Loango Lodge or another accommodation provider. Guests at Tassi Savannah Camp can also take a guided **kayak excursion** in the nearby creeks, from where it is possible to spot crocodile and hippo. Between October and February, **sea turtles** come to nest on the beaches here, and any of the lodges can arrange night-time excursions to visit their nesting sites.

Also in this area, at the southern end of the Iguéla (Ngowé) Lagoon, you'll find Loango's newest attraction: treks to visit a habituated group of **western lowland gorilla** (300,000CFA pp). Based at Yatouga (⊕ -2.0698, 9.5399), researchers from the Department of Primatology at the Max Planck Institute for Evolutionary Anthropology in Leipzig have been working with gorillas here as part of the Loango Gorilla Project (w bit.ly/loango-gorillas) since 2005. They've been habituating the 16-member Atananga Group since 2014, and tourists have been able to visit the gorillas since 2016. The treks follow similar rules and procedures to mountain gorilla treks in East Africa. You begin in the early morning with a 45–60-minute boat ride from Tchongorové to the Yatouga research camp, where you will be given a safety briefing before setting out. Trackers will already be out in the forest following the gorilla group's movements, and will radio in to the camp when they have been located. At this point it's likely you'll get back on the boat with the Yatouga researchers and guides, so as to get nearer to the gorillas before you start hiking. The hike to reach them can range from a couple of minutes to a couple of hours, depending on luck; while it's generally hot and humid in the forest, the terrain is (for the most part) relatively flat (very much unlike mountain gorilla tracking in East Africa). Once with the gorillas, you'll be given a surgical mask to wear to prevent the spread of communicable diseases. Visits last for an hour and are as enchanting, thrilling and unique as those on offer anywhere in the world, but unlike almost anywhere else, here you're more than likely to have the place to yourself.

To the far south of the savannah area, **Ozouga Camp** (⊕ -2.1180, 9.4820) is another research outpost associated with the Max Planck Institute. It is set in a forest clearing 11km southeast of Tassi Camp, just before the savannah fully transitions into deep forest as you continue south towards Petit Loango. The **Loango Chimpanzee Project** (w bit.ly/loango-chimps) has been based here

If you are lucky enough to have the opportunity to observe gorillas, here are some common-sense reminders to help ensure it is a positive and safe experience for both parties.

- Don't point – it's rude! Plus, raised arms can be perceived as threatening.
- Don't stare – this is also rude, and direct eye contact can be mistaken for a challenge.
- Don't use camera flashes. If you have an automatic flash, cover it with opaque tape.
- Don't run! If you are charged, fight the urge to flee and instead crouch down in a submissive pose.
- Don't make noise – talking or crashing through the undergrowth will alert wildlife to your presence and greatly reduce your chances of seeing anything.

since 2005, working with the roughly two dozen-strong Rekambo community of habituated chimpanzees. Excitingly, the research team reported never-before-seen chimpanzee behaviour here in 2019: they observed chimps picking up tortoises and cracking them open against tree trunks in order to eat the meat inside. Though vehicle safaris from Louri or Tassi may pass by, there were no official chimpanzee treks open to the public at the time of writing.

During the season (page 47), **whale-watching** trips can be made from Tchongorové (300,000CFA/boat, max 4 passengers). The inlet here is notorious for a particularly tricky wave that hits as you leave the lagoon, so it takes a strong boat and a knowledgeable captain to cross from the lagoon to the ocean – fortunately, Loango Lodge has both. Be sure to bring a plastic bag for your electronics and a poncho, unless you're prepared to get drenched.

The whole of Loango is something of a holy grail for **sport fishing**, and the waters off the coast here are well known for tarpon, African red snapper, barracuda, crevalle jack, giant African threadfin, and more. You can take a boat out of the lagoon on to the open ocean (again, note the challenging wave), or simply cast from the shore during a night-fishing excursion on the beach, departing in the evening and returning late in the night.

Dedicated **boat safaris** on the lagoon itself are known for turning up a prodigious number of birds, along with crocodile and occasionally manatee. A trip across the lagoon from Tchongorové into the Rembo Ngové River to either the Akaka Forest Camp (page 132) or Enamino Akaka Camp (page 132) would rightly rank as a highlight of any trip to Loango, or even Gabon on the whole. From a motorised pirogue on the river, you can get closer to the wildlife than almost anywhere in the park, and it's not uncommon to find elephant foraging just metres away on the riverbanks. The area is often flooded between November and April, so this excursion may not be possible during these months. From Akaka Forest Camp, it's also possible to **hike** the 12 or so kilometres between the Rembo Ngové and the Atlantic Ocean, emerging from the forest at the abandoned settlement of Petit Loango, today a profoundly isolated and wave-beaten spot where any of Loango's many beach-going animals can be seen.

SOUTHERN LOANGO AND SETTÉ CAMA
The pinprick village of **Setté Cama** (fewer than 100 inhabitants) is just one of a number of tiny fishing villages that grace the shores of the expansive Lagune Ndougou (Ndogo (Ndougou) Lagoon) at the southern end of Loango National Park. The village sits in a picturesque spot

between ocean and lagoon, and is the jumping-off point for all visits into the southern section of the park. Visitors come here to go on walking safaris as well as boat trips, and to fish. Wildlife enthusiasts are unlikely to leave unsatisfied.

A typical day might start with an exploration of the Ndogo (Ndougou) Lagoon by motorised pirogue, keeping an eye out for crocodile and manatee. Then, in the afternoon, you can go deeper into the park for a hike through the forest, emerging at sunset to the sound of waves crashing on the wide, windswept beach. It's hard work walking along the beach, but absolutely worth it, as it's possible to see gorilla, buffalo and elephant.

Getting there and around To reach southern Loango, you'll first have to aim for Gamba (for information on how to reach here, see page 137), from where you can travel on to the village of Setté Cama, where all activities in this half of the park originate. There is no public transportation to Setté Cama, so transfers from Gamba are generally arranged with your accommodation provider (page 137) and included in the cost of your stay. Most transfers are done by boat across the Ndogo (Ndougou) Lagoon, as the deep-sand conditions along the 40km track between the two villages mean it's quite easy to get stuck, even in a 4×4.

Where to stay, eat and drink *Map, page 129*
At present, there are two places to stay in Setté Cama. The more luxurious accommodation is at **Setté Cama Aventure**, formerly known as CH2O (m 04 60 92 33/05 32 06 06; e settecama.aventure@gmail.com; w settecama-aventure-gabon. com; $$$$), consisting of five beautiful and spacious chalets. Each chalet has a large double bed, en-suite bathroom, mosquito nets and a small veranda. This is primarily a fishing camp but also welcomes other guests and boat or walking safaris can be arranged here. The restaurant-bar is equally breezy and pretty. The daily rate starts at 80,000CFA. There is a plaque under the trees commemorating Maurice Patry (1924–98), a legendary guide hunter whose ashes were scattered over the area.

GIC Tourisme (Cooperative Abiétu) (page 130) is a locally based initiative that works towards community development and employment generation through the promotion of ecotourism in Setté Cama. To that end, they've constructed the attractive **Case Abiétu** (✳; 6 rooms; $$$), which was renovated in 2018. This option – occasionally also referred to as Le Case de Passage – is the best Loango National Park has to offer for those on a budget, but it still can't be called cheap. A night's stay goes for 45,000CFA, without any activities or meals. The all-inclusive pricing system (including boat transfer from Gamba, accommodation, full board and excursions) is a touch opaque, but rates vary based on the size of your group and the length of your stay. For example, an individual traveller staying one night pays 296,000CFA, while a pair spending three nights pays 96,000CFA per person per night. Activities include treks in the park and boat safaris by day and by night. The traditional meals prepared by local women and served on the terrace overlooking the lagoon are a treat.

Other practicalities Aside from the two accommodation options (see above), there are no other services on offer in Setté Cama, save for a couple of tiny shops selling the absolute basics. At the time this guide went to print, the village had mobile reception with Airtel, but not Gabon Telecom (Libertis).

What to see and do All excursions in the park can be arranged through your accommodation provider (see above). The broad, windswept **beach** that outlines the western edge of Loango National Park is easily accessed from Setté Cama –

indeed, it's only about 500m on foot between the shores of the Ndogo (Ndougou) Lagoon (where all the accommodation is located) and the crashing waves of the Atlantic. It's a stunning location and it's easy to lose yourself watching the ocean here, although it's not unheard of for elephants to wander through the village, so try and remain aware of your surroundings.

Walking safaris generally start with a short boat trip towards the lagoon's inlet, a wide embouchure where water and sand meet in a thoroughly dramatic fashion. On foot from here, you'll be guided into the forest and eventually out on to the beach where, depending on season, you may see elephant, buffalo, sitatunga, duiker, red river hog, or even chimpanzee or gorilla in the trees nearby.

Boat trips on the lagoon are also a treat, and can be done by day or (with a powerful torch) by night, scanning for the glinting eyes and hulking shapes of crocodile and hippo. Though they're considerably more elusive, manatee have been spotted here and at nearby Lac Sounga by keen-eyed visitors in the past. **Fisherfolk** have a choice of taking a boat out of the lagoon on to the open ocean, or simply casting from the shore, where night-time beach-fishing trips (departing in the evening and returning late) are standard. The area is known for its world-beating catches (page 129).

It is difficult to believe that in the 16th century Setté Cama was an important port on the African coast for traders of padouk timber and ivory. The **ruins** behind the village are those of the house of the last French governor, and there is a small **cemetery** on the beach near the Brigade des Eaux et Forêts, which visitors are welcome to drop in to. Here, you'll also find a small **museum** filled with skulls, bones, teeth and trap cables found in the forest. The exhibition and materials were initially developed by Ibonga ACPE, a local NGO that runs a research and monitoring programme for marine turtles nesting on the beaches of the Gamba Complex (see opposite). The museum was mostly derelict at the time of writing but it's unlocked, so you can still poke around the remains.

On the boat trip between Gamba and Setté Cama (page 135), it's possible to make a quick stop to see the remains of the late 19th-century **Mission Saint Benoît Labre de Setté Cama** on Île Nguale (Nguale Island; ✥ -2.5030, 9.8548), set just a short walk inland through the forest. To be honest, there's not a whole lot to see here anymore, save for a statue of Saint Benoît himself, the old bell and a few sections of rotting balustrade. There are, however, eventual plans to cut walking trails on the densely forested island.

GAMBA

Much like Port-Gentil to the north, Gamba is a town inextricably linked with the oil industry, and most of the 10,000 residents are in some way or another reliant on it. In 1963 oil giant Shell discovered the Gamba oilfield, and the town grew quickly after that. The company located its Gabonese headquarters here for more than 50 years until they sold everything to Assala Energy for US$628 million in 2017. Though the oil is still flowing, the departure of Shell is hugely significant to Gamba – they were once practically synonymous, and the town's fortunes were long seen as inseparable from the company's. Gamba's original residents are concerned that the departure may spell socio-economic disaster and turn Gamba into a ghost town; it's probably too early to tell, but the combination of this and chronically low global oil prices means the town feels a long way indeed from the boom times of years past.

Most visitors pass through town on their way to Setté Cama; there is very little to detain you, save for perhaps the scenic lagoon-side location. It's a small but structured place divided into six *plaines* or districts, aptly called Plaine 1, Plaine 2, Plaine 3, Plaine 4, Plaine 5 and Bienvenue (welcome).

Outside the town proper is Yenzi, a vast and typical compound for les Shellois (Shell's – now Assala's – expat employees), boasting everything from a gym and a hockey pitch to a swimming pool and an 18-hole golf course. It's accessible for residents only.

The Gabonese NGO **Ibonga ACPE** (Association Connaissance et Protection de l'Environnement; Quartier Bienvenue; m 07 13 01 99; e ong.ibonga@yahoo.fr; w ibonga.org; f Ibonga ACPE), founded in 1999 by Jean-Pierre Bayet, works to sensitise local communities to nature conservation so that they can participate in sustainable natural resource management. Ibonga runs a research and monitoring programme for marine turtles nesting on the beaches of the Gamba Complex, and visitors can now join them on their night-time patrols between November and April. The walks last 2 to 3 hours and cost 10,000CFA per person; they've also got plans to buy a few tents for visitors who want to overnight on the beach. They share an office in Gamba with ANPN and the WWF.

GETTING THERE AND AWAY The airport is located 10km out of town towards Tchibanga, but there were no public flights to Gamba at the time of writing. (You still may find yourself visiting the airport as there's a supermarket and BICIG ATM – the only one for hundreds of kilometres – just next door to the terminal.)

Thus, most visitors now arrive to Gamba **via Tchibanga**, 175km away. The 125km road from Tchibanga to the ferry crossing at Mougagara/Mayonami is now entirely surfaced, and the remaining 50km between the ferry and Gamba are well-maintained laterite. Note that the ferry crossing itself takes you 2.5km (5mins) up the Nyanga River from Mougagara to Mayonami; vehicles (10,000CFA) ride on a motorised ferry and passengers (1,000CFA) ride separately on a motorised pirogue. If you're waiting for the boat, Mayonami is the larger of the two settlements and has a handful of little shops and kiosks selling food and drink, including some tasty grilled fish. Public minibuses make the trip between Tchibanga and Gamba a few times daily for 11,000CFA.

There were no direct vehicles between Gamba and **Mayumba** at the time of writing, but with the increase in traffic thanks to the new road, you might have some luck trying to find a lift at the N6 junction village of Loubomo, 35km from Mayumba, rather than backtracking all the way to Tchibanga.

There are also direct buses covering the 765km between Gamba and **Libreville** (25,000CFA; ⊕ every other day); ask in town about the next departure.

WHERE TO STAY, EAT AND DRINK La crise and Shell's departure have seen accommodation options here shrink alongside Gamba's economy, but there are still a few good options to spend the night in or grab a meal at. The **Laguna Guest House** (m 04 20 91 94; e lagunaguesth@gmail.com; $$) is probably the preferred option for its enviable location on the water in Plaine 1, but the colourful rooms & resto-bar are also quite pleasant. At the entrance to town in Bienvenue, the **Motel du Conseil Départemental de Ndougou** (m 07 14 37 58; $$) offers simple rooms with AC from 16,000CFA. **Motel Herman** (☏ 01 50 06 14; m 07 16 36 81/06 69 30 56; $$) in Plaine 2 comes recommended by readers for budget-friendly self-contained rooms.

To eat, **Le Perroquet** (Plaine 2; $$) and **Mississippi** (Plaine 5; $$) both come recommended for their grilled fish, and **Restaurant Baobab** (Plaine 2; $) does filling plates for those on a budget. There's also no shortage of casual drinking dens scattered around Gamba serving cold Régab and not much else. **Self-caterers** should head for the well-stocked Economat supermarket at the airport, or Cecado in the centre.

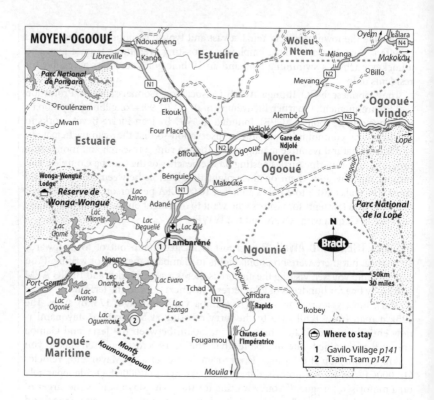

6

Moyen-Ogooué

Sandwiched between five other provinces in the west of the country, Moyen-Ogooué (Middle Ogooué) is Gabon's smallest region by area, with a population of about 70,000 Migovéens. The Ogooué River bisects the region quite neatly, splitting into two channels at Lambaréné for nearly 100km and rejoining in a large alluvial plain with a series of picturesque lakes fringed by papyrus marshes, reedbeds and dense forests. This is one of the largest deltas in Africa, extending from Lambaréné to Port-Gentil, and it is hoped it will be granted protective status as Gabon's 14th national park. In 2009 the area was designated a RAMSAR Wetland of International Importance; it's a paradise for ornithologists, with waterbirds appearing just about everywhere along the river. During the dry season thousands of terns, plovers, swallows, grey pratincoles and African skimmers breed on the exposed sandbanks, while colonies of pelicans, herons and darters nest in the riverside trees. Additionally, the lakes are home to hippo, and crocodile, and even manatee can be seen here throughout the year with a bit of luck. Lambaréné is easily accessible from Libreville and makes the best jumping-off point for excursions to the province's lakes.

Aside from the lakes, this region is known for two things: the hospital founded by '*le grand blanc de Lambaréné*' ('the great white man from Lambaréné'), Albert Schweitzer, and the peculiar fierceness of its mosquitoes.

LAMBARÉNÉ

Split into three unequal parts by the bifurcation of the Ogooué, Lambaréné is a river-island city with around 39,000 inhabitants. The three parts of the city – the Rive Gauche (Left Bank), Île Lambaréné (Lambaréné Island) and the Rive Droite (Right Bank) – are divided by the river and united by bridges and pirogues. Each part feels different from the others.

Quartier Isaac on the Left Bank has the highest concentration of small eateries and bars, but also the most rubbish and hustlers. As soon as you cross over the Pont d'Isaac (Isaac Bridge) on to Lambaréné Island, the city feels cleaner and greener. Continuing over the Pont d'Adouma (Adouma Bridge) brings you to the Right Bank and the site of Albert Schweitzer's hospital, which put Lambaréné on the map for Europeans and remains the town's most significant institution and premier tourist attraction to this day. Quartier Isaac's mild freneticism aside, there is a relaxed, friendly atmosphere here, making it the sort of place you feel like strolling around

$ ATMS

The only ATMs in Moyen-Ogooué are in Lambaréné, where BGFI is represented. Otherwise, the nearest alternatives are in Mouila or Libreville.

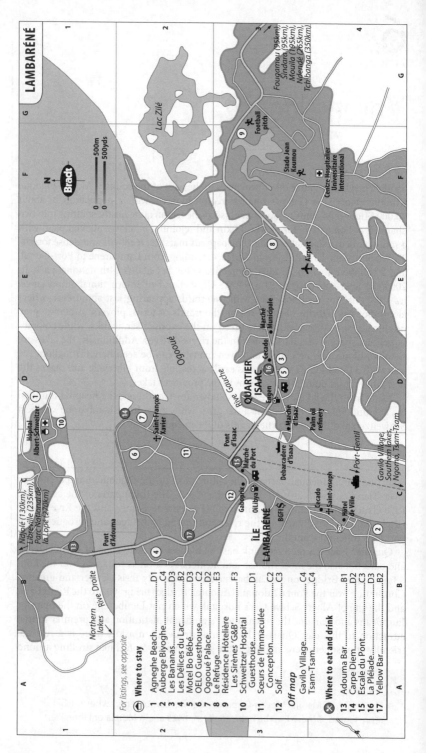

LAMBARÉNÉ

For listings, see opposite

🛏 **Where to stay**
1 Agneghe Beach.............D1
2 Auberge Biyoghe..........C4
3 Les Bananas................D3
4 Les Délices du Lac........B2
5 Motel Bo Bébé.............D3
6 OELO Guesthouse.........C2
7 Ogooué Palace.............D2
8 Le Refuge....................E3
9 Résidence Hôtelière
   Les Sirènes 'G&B'.......F3
10 Schweitzer Hospital
   Guesthouse................D1
11 Soeurs de l'Immaculée
   Conception................C2
12 Solf..........................C3

   Off map
   Gavilo Village.............C4
   Tsam-Tsam................C4

✗ **Where to eat and drink**
13 Adouma Bar...............B1
14 Carpe Diem...............D2
15 Escale du Pont...........C3
16 La Pléiade................D3
17 Yellow Bar................B2

Nabélé (130km),
Libreville (235km),
Parc National de
la Lopé (220km)

Fougamou (95km),
Sindara (195km),
Mouila (195km),
Ndendé (265km),
Tchibanga (350km)

Lac Zilé

Ogooué

Northern
lakes

Rive Droite

Pont
d'Adouma

Hôpital
Albert-Schweitzer

Saint-François
Xavier

Pont
d'Isaac

Gabopipi

OiLibya

BGFIS

Lecado

Saint-Joseph

Hôtel
de Ville

ÎLE
LAMBARÉNÉ

Marché
du Port

Débarcadère
d'Isaac

Rive Gauche

QUARTIER
ISAAC

Engen

Marché
d'Isaac

Palm oil
refinery

Lecado

Marché
Municipale

Airport

Stade Jean
Koumou

Football
pitch

Centre Hospitalier
Universitaire
International

Gavilo Village,
Southern lakes,
Ngomo, Tsam-Tsam

Port-Gentil

0   500m
0   500yds

N

Bradt

140

purposelessly. It is well worth a stay of a couple of days or more, particularly if you want to make excursions on to the surrounding lakes.

GETTING THERE AND AWAY The **airport** sits right on the edge of Quartier Isaac, but no-one was flying here at the time of writing.

By road The road approach to Lambaréné – both from Libreville and from the south – is a lovely one, with forests on either side of the road and small roadside villages selling chillies, pineapples and taro (although the quantity of fresh bushmeat dangling in the sun can be startling). An assortment of **clandos** and **minibuses** ply the 235km route along the N1 between Lambaréné and Libreville (5hrs; 6,000–7,000CFA) multiple times daily. Continuing south, minibuses connect all the way down the N1 to Mouila (195km; 3hrs; 7,000CFA) and Ndendé (265km; 5hrs; 9,000CFA), where you'll likely have to change for Tchibanga and Mayumba. This road is surfaced and in good condition in both directions.

Transport to Libreville departs from opposite OiLibya on the waterfront of Lambaréné Island. Southbound vehicles leave near the central roundabout in Quartier Isaac, but you'll sometimes find Libreville-bound cars here as well.

By boat It's quite simple to travel by boat between Lambaréné and **Port-Gentil** (page 121). If you're departing from Lambaréné, agents sell tickets (15,000/22,000CFA standard/VIP one way) the day before departure at the port near the Isaac Bridge [140 C3]. If you're travelling from Port-Gentil, minibuses to Libreville or Mouila and points south wait to meet the arriving boats in Lambaréné. The cost of transfer is not included in the cost of your boat ticket.

GETTING AROUND Lambaréné Island is small and green enough to make getting about **on foot** a real pleasure. To move between the different parts of the city, there are plenty of blue-and-white **taxis** picking up and dropping off customers. A shared taxi all the way across town from Quartier Isaac to the Schweitzer Hospital will be about 300CFA. Pirogues ferry passengers between the market on Lambaréné Island and the Débarcadère d'Isaac near the market on the Left Bank for around 100CFA.

TOUR OPERATORS At the time of writing, there were four organisations offering tourist trips on to the lakes surrounding Lambaréné. **Organisation Écotouristique Lac Oguemoué (OELO)** specialises in trips to their delightful ecolodge on Lake Oguemoué (Tsam-Tsam; page 147), while the **Schweitzer Hospital** (page 143), **Ogooué Tours** (page 145) and **Ogooué Palace Hôtel** (page 142) can all arrange a variety of fixed-price pirogue excursions.

WHERE TO STAY, EAT AND DRINK Lambaréné boasts excellent accommodation options, most of which also serve food. Alternatively, Quartier Isaac is home to a number of hole-in-the-wall restaurants serving budget-friendly Gabonese food and other African dishes. Out of town, 4km downstream on the north bank of the Ogooué, **Gavilo Village** [map, page 138] (6 rooms; ✪ -0.7380, 10.2103; m 04 72 75 18/05 30 52 72; e gavilovillagelambarene@gmail.com; w gavilovillage. net; ◆ gavilovillagelambarene; from 40,000CFA dbl B&B; w/end packages from 165,000CFA; **$$$**) has trim rooms on stilts with air conditioning and hot water, and can arrange pirogue trips, hikes, and village excursions.

Lambaréné Island

🏠 **Ogooué Palace Hôtel** [140 D2]
(54 rooms) ☎01 58 18 65; m 07 16 28 02;
e hotelogoouepalace@gmail.com. Renovated a
few years back, this colonial-style hotel directly
overlooking the Ogooué remains one of the
smartest options in town. There is a nice pool &
tennis court plus a bar & a restaurant surrounded
by lush gardens (**$$$**). Non-guests may use the
pool for a charge of 4,000CFA. The hotel organises
boat trips on the lake (page 145). **$$$**

🏠 **Auberge Biyoghe** [140 C4] (12 rooms)
☎01 58 24 50; m 05 35 32 17/03 19 28 69.
Opened in 2018, this is the newest kid on the block
& the trim, tidy rooms with AC & TV show it. It's in
an unmissable orange building & has a good resto-
bar attached (**$$**). **$$**

🏠 **Les Délices du Lac** [140 B2] (6 rooms)
m 07 91 88 87. In one of the higher areas of town,
this homey place offers a handful of rooms & a
nice view of the Ogooué. The restaurant serves
traditional Gabonese dishes (**$$**), but it's essential
to call in your order well in advance, even if you are
staying here, as service can be slow. **$$**

🏠 **Solf Hôtel** [140 C3] (18 rooms) ☎01 58
23 03. Also known as the Paul Djonguinyo, this
relatively new hotel offers spacious rooms with
modern furniture & a good restaurant serving fresh
food (**$$**). Wi-Fi is available. **$$**

✴🏠 **OELO Guesthouse** [140 C2] (3 rooms)
m 07 01 49 01/07 28 73 07; e tsam.tsam@
rocketmail.com; w oelogabon.org. Sharing premises
at the north end of Lambaréné Island with the offices
of the Organisation Écotouristique du Lac Oguemoué
(OELO; page 141), who also manage Tsam-Tsam
(page 147), this homey guesthouse offers a clutch of
breezy, top-floor en-suite rooms with fan, hot water
& kitchen access, plus a terrace overlooking the river.
Excellent value at 15,000CFA dbl. **$**

✴🏠 **Sœurs de l'Immaculée Conception**
[140 C2] (6 rooms) ☎01 58 10 73. Not far from the
Ogooué Palace Hôtel & separated from the river by
the road is this magnificent complex of cloistered,
red-brick buildings surrounding a courtyard garden
alive with birdsong. The adjoining church, Saint-
François Xavier, was constructed in 1898. The mission
is a wonderfully relaxing place to stay & might be
the best value for money in the whole of Gabon.
There are 6 rooms with fan & between 2 & 5 sgl beds
in each. The mission is often full so it is advisable
to call in advance. There are kitchen facilities for

guests to cook for themselves, or it's a short walk to
Escale du Pont (see below) or over the bridge to the
eateries in Quartier Isaac. *Flat rate of 8,000CFA pp.* **$**

✕ **Escale du Pont** [140 C3] m 04 20 53 35.
Overlooking the river at the base of the Isaac
Bridge, this is a popular resto-bar that had just
been renovated at the time of writing. **$**

🍷 **Yellow Bar** [140 B2] Painted bright yellow,
this nameless spot on the main road rolls out the
grills in the evenings & keeps the Régab cold. **$**

🍷 **Carpe Diem** [140 D2] Perched on the north
end of Lambaréné Island, this bar built on a
wooden terrace has one of the prettiest locations
in town. It was under renovation when we checked
in, but ought to be slaking thirsts once again by
the time you read this.

Right Bank

🏠 **Agneghe Beach Hotel** [140 D1]
(8 rooms) Quartier Abongo; m 05 23 76
22; e agneghebeach-infos@gmail.com;
f agneghebeach.officiel. Set behind the
Schweitzer Hospital in Quartier Abongo, this new
riverfront hotel has green gardens, a sandy beach
& a wide terrace overlooking the water. Neat rooms
& occasional events at the resto-bar. **$$**

✴🏠 **Schweitzer Hospital Guesthouse** [140
D1] (20 rooms) Schweitzer Hospital premises;
m 07 14 16 62; e museelambarene.schweitzer@
yahoo.fr; w schweitzer.org. This is undoubtedly
the most characterful place to spend the night. The
historical buildings Maison C & Case Bouka have
been renovated & adapted to suit travellers & are
run by the Fondation Internationale Schweitzer
Lambaréné. Some of the historical rooms have
been adapted with AC, but thanks to the superb
construction taking advantage of the natural air
flow, even the fan rooms are amazingly cool. There's
a good restaurant that is used by guests & staff alike,
serving b/fast (3,000CFA), lunch (5,000CFA) & dinner
(5,000CFA; **$$**). The Schweitzer Foundation is also
able to arrange excursions on the lake (page 145).
15,000/20,000CFA fan/AC dbl. **$$**

🍷 **Adouma Bar** [140 B1] Enjoyable local bar with
cold drinks, a bit of garden seating out the back &
great murals on the walls.

Left Bank

🏠 **Le Refuge** [140 E3] (45 rooms) Quartier
Isaac; m 04 75 48 40. Opened in 2017, this
business hotel opposite the airport aims to be the

sharpest in town & makes a credible case for the title. Rooms are tasteful & well equipped, plus there's a large swimming pool & resto-bar. *From 35,000CFA.* **$$–$$$**

🏠 **Résidence Hôtelière Les Sirènes 'G&B'** [140 F3] (20 rooms) Quartier Mbole; m 06 05 07 41/07 53 05 56/07 77 23 87; e infosirenes2@ yahoo.fr; ⨍ ResidenceHoteliereLesSirenesGB. About 3km towards Fougamou from central Quartier Isaac, this standby hotel lies in an amazing setting overlooking the lake & offers comfortable rooms & 2 pools. **$$–$$$**

🏠 **Les Bananas** [140 D3] (22 rooms) Quartier Isaac; ☏ 01 58 12 28; m 05 22 26 57; e sajoux25@

gmail.com. This used to be your best bet in Quartier Isaac, but today it's looking pretty dingy & claustrophobic. **$**

🏠 **Motel Bo Bébé** [140 D3] (20 rooms) Quartier Isaac; m 06 24 12 95/07 01 39 30. Probably the smartest option in central Quartier Isaac, but rooms are still small & stuffy (albeit with AC & en-suite facilities). **$**

✕ **La Pléiade** [140 D3] Quartier Isaac; m 07 38 16 36; ⊕ 09.00–23.00 Tue–Sun. This restaurant & nightclub is a good address for a sit-down meal, with Gabonese dishes from 5,000CFA & fish from 7,000CFA. **$$**

SHOPPING For a town of its size, Lambaréné has more than its fair share of **markets**. The most animated is the **Marché d'Isaac** (Isaac Market) [140 D3], the place where fishermen come ashore and is therefore the best place to buy fresh or smoked fish, along with just about everything else, for low prices. Directly across the river on the other side of town, the **Marché du Port** (Port Market) [140 C3] gets busy with the coming and going of the boats to Port-Gentil, selling fish, foodstuffs, and other odds and ends. Back in Isaac, the covered **Marché Municipale** (Municipal Market) [140 D3] was built by the city a few years back to replace the disorganised Marché d'Isaac, but it was an unpopular move and consequently has never really taken off.

As in most Gabonese towns, Cecado and Gaboprix supermarkets are both represented, selling a decent selection of packaged food.

OTHER PRACTICALITIES Lambaréné is home to a decent array of services, including a BGFI branch with an ATM. There is a hospital (Centre Hospitalier Universitaire International; Albert Schweitzer University Hospital), a post office, a couple of petrol stations and a police post.

WHAT TO SEE AND DO

Hôpital Albert-Schweitzer [140 D1] (Albert Schweitzer Hospital; m 07 14 16 62; w schweitzer.org) Founded in 1924 by Albert Schweitzer, today the hospital treats about 30,000 patients a year. It is well known, and people come from all over Gabon to get treated. Additionally, the premises house the country's only geriatric and psychiatric units.

The Schweitzer Hospital is a private, non-profit medical centre run by the Fondation Internationale de l'Hôpital du Dr Albert Schweitzer à Lambaréné. The Gabonese government contributes approximately 50% of the hospital budget, while the Schweitzer Foundation and private donations cover the rest. Most of the doctors and nurses are volunteers from abroad, working here for between three months and two years. (Most Gabonese medics work for the state hospitals, which pay better for fewer hours.) The hospital's research arm, known as the Centre de Recherches Médicales de Lambaréné (w cermel.org), is particularly active in the fields of tuberculosis and bacterial ailments.

The atmosphere is as lively and relaxed as a small village, with women selling fruit near the entrance, patients' kids playing in the dust and a small shop stocking basic provisions. As well as being a place of healing it has also become a place of pilgrimage. Admirers of *le grand docteur* (see box, page 144) come to see the

On the basis of an article published in the Paris Missionary Society's monthly journal, Albert Schweitzer decided to become a doctor and dedicate himself to working in Gabon. The year was 1904, and Schweitzer was 29 years old. He was very religious, and the article extolling the need for proper health care near the Andendé Mission had struck a chord with his belief that true Christianity meant helping one's fellow man and woman. It was 1913 before he had completed his medical training and raised the necessary funds to cover passage for himself and his wife, Hélène Bresslau, from Alsace in Germany to Lambaréné.

The doctor's – and Gabon's – first clinic was located in a converted hen house at the Andendé Mission, but it wasn't long before war broke out and Schweitzer was arrested in 1917 for being a German on French soil. He did not return to Gabon until April 1924. The new Schweitzer Hospital was built on the site of Trader Horn's (page 143) old Hatton and Cookson factory, on the Right Bank of the Ogooué River. The factory had been moved some 40 years previously and the land left to grow wild. Funnily enough, at the same time that Schweitzer was clearing the old factory site, Trader Horn was having his tales recorded in South Africa, and the book *Trader Horn* was published in 1927, the same year that the new hospital opened. The Trader Horn connection tickled Schweitzer, who was a big fan of this 'enterprising but self-willed agent', and he dedicated a whole chapter to him in *From My African Notebook* (1938).

Unlike the Europeans who had descended on Africa before him, Schweitzer was motivated by a desire to help 'the black peoples'. His motto was 'reverence for life' and he was determined that Africans should have access to medical treatment. That is not to say that he considered the local people as equals, and his views – uncomfortably racist and paternalistic by modern standards – remain

museum (⏰ 08.30–17.30 daily; entry 2,500CFA) that since 1987 has occupied his former lodgings. His room is simplicity and order itself: his white doctor's apron, his pharmaceutical cabinet, his narrow bed, his parrot's cage. Visitors can also visit his study, his wife's room and the conference room that before his death served as a dormitory for nurses. There is a small **souvenir shop** selling books, T-shirts, teddy bears (elephants, actually), and items made at the leprosy village (see below). Behind the house is a cemetery with the tombs of hundreds of care-givers and patients, as well as the doctor's grave.

It's easy to get to the hospital in a shared taxi for 300CFA, or you can hire a pirogue at the Débarcadère d'Isaac for a more scenic journey. There is always a stream of taxis dropping people off at the hospital so it's very easy to get a ride back to town.

A road leading off to the right as you approach the hospital leads to the leprosy village, named **Village de Lumière** (Village of Light). At its peak there were about 600 inhabitants living here.

The lakes An excursion into the lakes by motorised pirogue is a wonderful way of passing the time. The northern lakes (Deguelié, Azingo, Nkonie, Gomé) tend to be less visited than the southern ones (Avanga, Evaro, Ezanga, Onangué, Ogonié, Oguemoué), perhaps because access is trickier, with sandbanks, rapids and whirlpools in places.

Lac Zilé [140 G2] (⊕ -0.6820, 10.2682) is the closest lake to the city. It's small but very pretty, and its handy location, just adjacent to Lambaréné, makes it the most popular introduction to the region for those pressed for time.

a stain on his otherwise impressive legacy. As a young man he had excelled at philosophy, theology and music, and after a day's work at the hospital he would write on these disciplines. From these works we have a clear picture of how he viewed the African people and their world. To Schweitzer, Africans were no different than children, to be directed with a firm and kind authority. It was said that he had scarcely ever talked with an adult African on adult terms. Schweitzer was incredulous and pitying in the face of 'primitive' African taboos and fetishes, announcing 'it is our duty to endeavour to liberate them from these superstitions'.

Schweitzer was awarded the Nobel Peace Prize in 1952 and used the money to found the hospital's leprosy village, at a time when sufferers were driven from their villages. He died in Lambaréné in 1965, 90 years old, and was buried next to an urn containing the ashes of his wife. His legacy lives on in the hospital and in his prolific writings. There are now state hospitals in Gabon, but the Schweitzer Hospital is still one of the country's best and most popular. It's not free, but patients are only asked to pay what they can afford, and after they have been treated, become an important continuation of Schweitzer's founding ethos.

In 2013 there were grand celebrations for the 100th anniversary of Doctor Albert Schweitzer's arrival in Lambaréné, and more than 350 VIPs, including President Ali Bongo, came from all over the world to meet here and celebrate the legacy of the late Nobel Prize winner. On this festive occasion, the state-of-the-art Centre Hospitalier Universitaire International (Albert Schweitzer University Hospital) was inaugurated. Today it serves as a hospital and medical research and training centre, providing technical, human and financial resources for research on malaria and tuberculosis. It also hosts a yearly Albert Schweitzer International Symposium on African Healthcare, convening medical doctors from Africa and beyond.

It's possible to visit **Lake Azingo** (✪ -0.5775, 10.0429) in a day's round trip, but to explore the northern lakes properly visitors will need camping gear and to be prepared to spend the night at a fishing village.

Visiting the lakes Trips out of Lambaréné can be booked through the Schweitzer Foundation (page 143), the Ogooué Palace Hôtel (page 142), or the locally based **Ogooué Tours** (m 07 58 23 23; e ogoouetours@gmail.com; [f]). The hotel offers rather pricey set excursions in a pirogue for up to six passengers, including tours of Lac Deguelié (120,000CFA), Lac Azingo (260,000CFA), Ngomo and Lac Onangué (220,000CFA); and a trip taking in the Schweitzer Hospital, several river islands, and the town's bridges, famous for the enormous number of *chauves-souris* (bats) nesting underneath them (120,000CFA).

The Schweitzer Foundation can also take you on more affordable visits to Lac Zilé (60,000CFA), Lac Evaro (100,000CFA), and Ngomo (120,000CFA). Prices are for groups of one to four, with extra passengers 20,000CFA each. Ogooué Tours is better value than either of the above, with prices roughly 25% lower than those offered by the foundation.

Cheaper still, you can always deal directly with a piroguier at the Marché du Port, but you still have to count on at least 50,000CFA for an afternoon. This is probably advisable anyway if you are hoping to make a deal for several days or have specific plans not covered by the hotel tours. (OELO Guesthouse may also be able to recommend a piroguier with advance notice; page 142.) Do ensure that

At the end of the 19th century, West Africa was a surprising, even alarming, choice of destination for an English lady from Cambridge to travel around alone. Mary Kingsley (1842–1900), of course, was not altogether ordinary. Her father, a doctor, spent virtually Mary's entire childhood travelling the world. Mary was left at home without any formal education and with no companions except for her depressive mother and sickly younger brother. When her father finally retired and came home, it was to spend nearly all his time in his study researching sacrificial rites. Later, Mary was to nurse both parents for almost two years, until they died within weeks of one another in 1892. Grief-stricken but free, Mary was, as she herself put it, 'for the first time in my life… in possession of five or six months that were not heavily forestalled, and feeling like a boy with a new half-crown, I lay about in my mind… as to what to do with them'.

What she did with them was to go to West and Central Africa. Little is known about that first trip in 1893, but her second trip – made the following year – took her from the Canary Islands to Sierra Leone and on to Gabon, where she travelled up the Ogooué River, first by steamboat and then by canoe. We know she was looking for fish for the British Museum of Natural History and a greater understanding of African 'fetish'. Plus, of course, the sort of adventure that couldn't be found in upper-middle-class England (like Brazza, she too had read du Chaillu).

She found plenty of all three and wrote an entertaining account of it all on her return. When *Travels in West Africa* was published in 1897, it was a runaway success. Immediately pounced upon as an authority on all things African, Mary Kingsley was plunged into a whirlwind of speeches and social events and urged to write more. The results were *West African Studies* (1899), *The Story of West Africa* (1899) and, finally, an overwhelming desire to escape. She had not wanted the fame – right from the start she had requested to be published anonymously – and it did not agree with her. In 1900 she once more set out for Africa; she was never to return. She fell ill and died while nursing typhoid patients in a military hospital in South Africa.

QUINTESSENTIAL ENGLISHNESS The tone of Mary Kingsley's writing is often ironic, funny and blasé. She is a formidable woman of her time, taking whatever is thrown at her without compromising her quintessential Englishness. She made huge

you trust the piroguier's competence to undertake your chosen route(s). The cost will vary according to the distance, the time and the number of passengers, and both parties should be absolutely clear on the itinerary before setting off. This is the time to establish the desired pace, and to make it clear if you would like the motor to be cut for quiet periods so you can observe the birds. For short journeys requiring little petrol, such as the Schweitzer Hospital or even Lake Zilé, you could open negotiations by asking the piroguier how much he usually makes in an hour of ferrying passengers, and then add 1,000–2,000CFA to make an hourly rate.

With the possible exception of very localised trips, all excursions will need to be arranged, and partially paid for, at least a day in advance so that petrol can be bought. Passengers should come prepared with suncream, sunglasses, insect repellent, a windbreaker and appropriate provisions.

If you're looking to spend longer at the lakes, your best bet is to book a stay at Tsam-Tsam, who will transfer you from Lambaréné to their site by boat, and also offer several excursions (see opposite).

efforts to learn to row and to get to grips with the languages and customs she encountered, but steadfastly refused to wear anything other than the clothes befitting an English lady, whether she was crossing mountains or valleys, forests or swamps. Mary had occasion to defend this seemingly ridiculous get-up when she fell into a game pit. 'It is at these times you realise the blessing of a good thick skirt... here I was with the fullness of my skirt tucked under me, sitting on nine ebony spikes some twelve inches long, in comparative comfort, howling lustily to be hauled out.' Despite her efforts to maintain this feminine wardrobe, she was continually called 'Sir' by the people she met while travelling. She felt sure the reason for this was not due to any wish to show disrespect on the part of the African people (quite the contrary), but from the absence of gender in their languages.

IMPARTIAL OBSERVER For her time, Kingsley's approach was surprisingly non-judgemental (elsewhere she identifies drinking unboiled water as her own taboo). In this her reactions are quite different to those expressed by the eminent Dr Albert Schweitzer years later (see box, page 144). Unlike Schweitzer, she tried not to judge or interfere. She saw her role as that of an impartial observer, and as such her responsibility was to try to understand and record African rites and customs, not change or undo them.

Unless you can be pliant enough to follow the African idea step by step, however much care you may take, you will not bag your game. I heard an account the other day of a representative of Her Majesty in Africa who went out for a day's antelope shooting. There were plenty of antelope about, and he stalked them with great care; but always, just before he got within shot of the game, they saw something and bolted. Knowing he and the boy behind him had been making no sound and could not have been seen, he stalked on, but always with the same result; until happening to look round, he saw the boy behind him was supporting the dignity of the Empire at large, and this representative of it in particular, by steadfastly holding aloft the consular flag. Well, if you go hunting the African idea with the flag of your own religion or opinions floating ostentatiously over you, you will similarly get a very poor bag.

All quotes are taken from *Travels in West Africa* (London, 1897).

Where to stay, eat and drink   *Map, page 138*

Despite their striking natural beauty, the lakes remain almost entirely undeveloped for tourism. At the time of writing, there was only one lodge offering tourist accommodation, so unless you're self-sufficient in terms of camping gear or prepared to ask a village chief to put you up for the night, this is your only option. Fortunately, it's a fantastic one.

✳ 🏠 **Tsam-Tsam** (6 rooms) Sahoty, Lambaréné; m 07 01 49 01/07 28 73 07; e tsam. tsam@rocketmail.com; f TsamTsamGabon. Located on southern Lac Oguemoué, this admirable ecotourism project rightly ranks among the highlights of any trip to Gabon. It was founded in 2011 by OELO (page 141), a local NGO working with lakeshore villages to develop ecotourism & conservation strategies that protect both wildlife & local livelihood. Tsam-Tsam has 6 secluded platforms with tents & mattresses in idyllic locations along an island/peninsula (depending on the season) overlooking the lake & the forest. Guests are hosted on an FB basis (excluding soft drinks & alcohol, including boat transfers from Lambaréné & activities). The 1st night costs 80,000CFA pp, & each subsequent night is 60,000CFA. Meals are inspired by traditional Gabonese cuisine, but no bushmeat is served, & the camp runs exclusively on solar power & kerosene lamps. Activities on offer, available for those staying at Tsam-Tsam only, include guided forest hikes, village visits, birding excursions, canoe trips & day or night lake tours. Mammals to be spotted include the rare water chevrotain, & birders can tick off both Pel's fishing owl & the vermiculated fishing owl here. **$$$**

What to see and do The appearance of the lakes differs depending on the time of year, as there can be a three-to-four-metre difference in water level depending on the season. February is a good month to visit, as the piercing light seems to make the greens greener and the blues bluer. During the dry season (July–September) the colours are duller and the water level is lower, but birds are easily spotted using the exposed sandbanks as breeding colonies. At all times, keep an eye out for hippo in areas of low water, and a (hopeful) ear cocked for the tell-tale splash of a manatee. **Birds** to look out for include the black-headed bee-eater and African river martin (which breeds here in November), along with herons, skimmers, egrets, pelicans, cormorants and pratincoles, including the grey pratincole.

Those with an interest in **architecture** should allow time to stop at the village of **Ngomo** (✪ -0.8304, 9.9841; see page 145 for information on getting here), 1¼ hours from Lambaréné on the Ambila River, site of a Protestant mission that was founded in 1898 by the Alsacian pastor Ernest Haugh, who is buried behind the church. Today the church, school and dispensary are still in use.

NDJOLÉ

After Lambaréné, the only settlement of any size in Moyen-Ogooué is Ndjolé, home to 7,000 inhabitants on the banks of the Ogooué River. In itself this is not a reason to visit. In fact, it's the sort of place where you might find yourself killing a bit of time on your way somewhere else. Being the largest town for a good stretch in either direction, however, it does have the advantage of certain amenities, including a petrol station, pharmacy, police station, church, mosque and supermarkets, as well as a handful of places to eat and sleep. Ndjolé is also on the railway line; the station is 12km north of town along the N2 towards Alembé. Trains to Franceville (47,000/41,000/31,000CFA VIP/1st/2nd class Express & 34,000/24,000CFA 1st/2nd class Omnibus) depart around 23.00; the reverse journey passes through en route to Libreville (17,900/15,800/11,800CFA VIP/1st/2nd class Express & 13,200/9,200CFA 1st/2nd class Omnibus) at around 01.00. Traditionally, Ndjolé was the place where logging companies emptied their cargo into the Ogooué for transportation to the coast. This system is still practised today, but the good state of the road means logging trucks are increasingly common. For those travelling west between Lastoursville and Libreville, it's also the first major settlement after getting back on the tarmac road at Alembé. Given all this, it's hardly surprising that it's a popular stopping point. Coming from Lambaréné, it's 130km northeast on surfaced roads, but you may wind up having to change vehicles at the N1/N2 junction in Bifoun (where you could sleep at the **Hotel Bif Bambou**; **$**) if you're on public transport.

The main road junction is where it all happens. This is the location of the market, petrol station, food stalls, and the pick-up and drop-off point for minibuses and clandos to Franceville, Libreville or Lambaréné (would-be passengers should ask about likely times and be prepared to wait, particularly if you're heading to Franceville, where the train would be a better option). There's usually music and a lot of people milling around; try **Le Moyen Ogooué Pâtisserie** (m 07 12 14 14) for road snacks, should you need them.

If you need to spend the night here, the newest and nicest option is the **Hotel Kedyann** (near the Total petrol station; m 04 74 61 69/07 04 13 24/07 56 15 15; e motel.kedyann.ndjole@gmail.com; **$$**), which offers modern en-suite rooms from 35,000CFA as well as espresso coffee at their reliable resto-bar (**$$**). Not far away is the long-serving **Hôtel Papaya** (☏ 01 59 33 15; m 07 88 53 42; **$**), which is certainly a step down, but has cheaper rooms with fan (11,000CFA) or AC (17,000CFA). Also near the Total station, **Hotel Le Kevazingo** (m 06 68 59 46/07 24 19 73; **$**) is another long-serving budget option. If you head past the market and over the bridge, you'll see the church on a hill. This is the town's most attractive building, a simple design with pleasing lattice brickwork. If, on the other hand, you turn right immediately past the petrol station you'll reach the **Auberge Saint Jean** (m 05 31 72 10; **$**), where you'll find reasonable rooms which get good feedback from readers and the best food in town (**$$**). It's also set on a good birdwatching spot overlooking the small island of Samory Touré, so named for the Guinean anti-colonialist fighter exiled and imprisoned here for two years until his death in 1900; a monument was unveiled in his honour in 2013. (He was not the only troublesome West African the French used Gabon as a penal colony for.) You can ask either at the auberge or down on the river about hiring a pirogue if you fancy an outing to the island or on the Ogooué.

Across the river, the **Saint-Michel de Ndjolé** Catholic Mission dates to 1897, but it's long been abandoned and is slowly being reclaimed by the forest. Ask in town for a guide if you'd like to visit; it's about 1 hour from Ndjolé by foot and pirogue.

Moyen-Ogooué NDJOLÉ

6

149

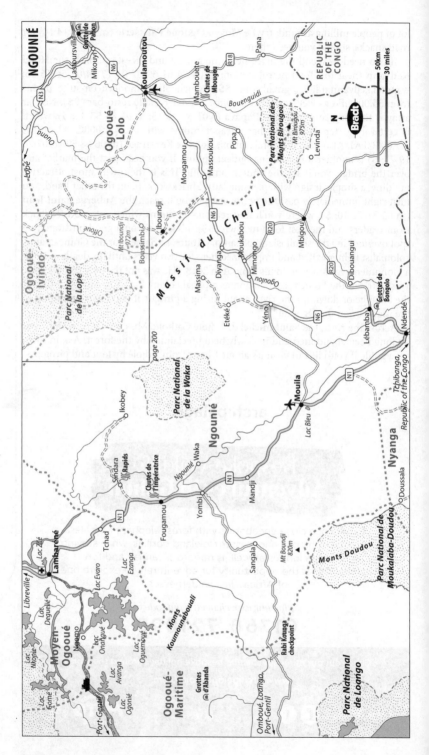

above left Gabon's forest-based communities (sometimes referred to as 'Pygmies') are renowned for their hunting and guiding expertise (SS) page 17

above Gabon's original inhabitants are known for their unique musical traditions (NG/A) page 19)

left Gabon's wooden masks, traditionally used in rituals, have inspired artists such as Picasso and Matisse (SC) page 22

below left & below Bwiti is the foremost secret society in Gabon, where initiates are taught generations-old knowledge of natural forces and spiritual powers (SS) page 18

above   Oil has been the mainstay of the Gabonese economy for nearly 60 years (AI/S) page 13

above left   Libreville's Saint-Michel de Nkembo Church attracts worshippers and wanderers alike to admire its intricate carvings and paintings (BS/S) page 104

left   Régab, the national beer of Gabon, is a hands-down favourite (SC) page 71

below   With nearly 900km of Atlantic coastline, Gabon is a legendary fishing hotspot for sport and subsistence alike (H/A) page 51

above The church at the Mission Sainte-Anne beside Lagune Fernan Vaz was designed by none other than Gustave Eiffel (H/A) page 128

right The 670km-long Transgabonais railway, completed in 1987, is the economic backbone of the country (SJ) page 66

below Just about everything can be bought and sold in Libreville's largest market, the Marché Mont-Bouët (GC/A) page 100

below right The Flamme de la Paix monument sits in central Libreville, on the staunchly Modernist boulevard Triomphal Omar Bongo Ondimba (SS) page 104

top   African skimmers frequent Parc National d'Akanda (SS) page 109

above left, above right, left & below   Lady Ross's turaco, African grey parrot, black-casqued hornbill and kingfisher are all well represented in Gabon's forests (VW/S), (P/S), (APL/A) & (SK/MP/FLPA) page 44

above　Keep an eye out for ornate monitor lizards near Gabon's rivers (SS) page 43

top right　Follow the tracks of Gabon's world-famous 'surfing hippos' in Parc National de Loango (NGIC/A) page 128

above right　The gaboon viper is Gabon's most famous snake (PI/A) page 43

right　The beach south of Mayumba boasts the highest density of leatherback turtle nests anywhere in Africa (WF/S) page 43

bottom　Central African slender-snouted crocodile inhabit many lagoons and rivers (SS) page 43

above left A *pirogue* journey on the black waters of the Ivindo River is the best way to explore the untouched wilderness of Parc National d'Ivindo (SJ) page 210

above The thrilling 365m cable bridge in Parc de la Lékédi offers a breathtaking perspective on the forest below (K/S) page 191

left Mont Brazza can easily be climbed in an afternoon and offers spectacular views over the surrounding forest and savannah (SS) page 204

below More than 1,500 Iron Age rock engravings have been found in and around Parc National de la Lopé (EL/NPL) page 205

above — Visitors to Parc National de la Lopé can now join researchers on mandrill-tracking excursions (EL/NPL) page 204

above right — Gabon's growing network of upmarket safari camps means exploring the wilderness can be done in comfort and style (SJ)

right — A knowledgeable guide is absolutely essential when it comes to exploring Gabon's seemingly endless forests (SS) page 27

below — Gabon's coastal patchwork of forest and savannah is prime territory for 4x4 safaris (t/i)

7

Ngounié

As with most of Gabon's regions, Ngounié takes its name from its main watercourse – in this case the Ngounié River – an important tributary of the Ogooué, which feeds the region's forests and lakes. It's home to just over 100,000 Ngounis and is also known as Mitsogo country, after the people who have traditionally lived here. To the south lies the Republic of the Congo; along the region's eastern flank rise the du Chaillu Mountains; and along its western flank the Monts d'Ikoundou (Ikoundou Mountains). Sandwiched between these forested mountains lies the grassy Ngounié Valley, location of the town of Ndendé.

Ngounié must be one of the least-visited regions of Gabon. If it welcomes any visitors they are invariably passing through on their way to either Tchibanga in Nyanga province or Dolisie in Congo; sometimes there's also a rare visitor making a brief southerly foray from Lambaréné to Fougamou and Sindara. Those who linger a while, however, and venture deeper into the province, are rewarded with the beauty of a deeply traditional corner of Gabon, where the Mitsogo (see box, page 152) inhabitants are renowned (and occasionally feared) for their talents at conjuring spirits from the world beyond. Indeed, Bwiti (see box, page 18) itself traces its origins to the secret societies of the Mitsogo, and iboga, the name given to the hallucinogenic root used in Bwiti ceremonies, is Tsogo for 'healing wood'.

The region's capital is the sleepy river town of Mouila, which sprawls astride Ngounié's namesake river. The area around the town has seen serious changes since the installation of the Singaporean company Olam (see box, page 15), which recently acquired rights to 50,000ha of land near the capital to grow oil palms for 50 years.

Ngounié is also home to Waka and Monts Birougou national parks, which theoretically have plenty to offer natural and cultural tourists, although both lack any infrastructure whatsoever and exploring them requires arranging a bespoke excursion with the ANPN or Gabon Untouched (page 51) well in advance.

The N1 cuts through Ngounié, leading travellers directly from Lambaréné to the Congolese border via Ndendé, from where the N6 leads southwest to Tchibanga and the coast and northeast to Koulamoutou and the mountains of the interior. The N1 is paved and in good shape as far as Ndendé, but reverts to laterite as it continues southbound towards Congo. The N6 is surfaced between Mayumba and Ndendé, but unsurfaced and very much 4×4 only for all but 35km of the 300km journey to Koulamoutou. The turn-off for the long and difficult 350km road to Port-Gentil (page 120) is also on the N1 at Yombi, 20km south of Fougamou.

$ ATMS

The only ATMs in Ngounié are in Mouila, where BICIG is represented. Otherwise, the nearest alternatives are in Lambaréné or Gamba.

The Mitsogo are thought to be among the first Bantu peoples to have migrated into the forests of Gabon, previously home to Babongo (Pygmy) people alone. Before the arrival of the French in their traditional homelands along the Ngounié River, they traded slaves for salt and other goods with peoples along the coast. The arrival of French concessionary companies, particularly the Compagnie de la Haute-Ngounié, and their brutal demands of forced labour, saw a determined anti-colonial resistance take root among the Mitsogo, under their freedom-fighter chief Mbombé in particular. Colonial forces put down several uprisings between 1903 and 1907, until the French succeeded in imprisoning the famous warrior. In 1913, chief Mbombé was executed in Mouila's prison – but only after being baptised.

MOUILA

Divided in two more or less equal halves by the Ngounié River, Mouila is the provincial capital, with a population of about 36,000. The N1 cuts through the west side of town, while the track leading towards the N6 and Koulamoutou enters on the east side of the river. All administrative and government buildings are on the east bank; most of the shops, hotels and restaurants are on the west bank.

Unsurprisingly, life on the region's rivers and lakes has always played a large part in Mouila (and Ngounié's) culture, and the town's coat of arms features a *sirène* (mermaid). Water spirits are traditionally worshipped here, with believers performing rituals to seek the spirits' beneficence and avoid their wrath.

GETTING THERE AND AWAY The **airport** is 2km north of town, but no-one was flying here at the time of writing.

There are multiple daily **minibuses** to Libreville (430km; 7hrs; 13,000CFA) via Lambaréné (195km; 3hrs; 8,000CFA), and **Sergio Transports** (m 04 81 01 07) is a recommended operator; early morning departures leave from their office just east of the main gare routière. It's best to drop by the office and get your ticket the day before you wish to travel as vehicles will sometimes be full with through traffic from Libreville. If you don't get a seat with them, other minibuses depart from the gare routière.

Heading north on the 100km leg between Mouila and Fougamou (covered by regular minibuses; 90mins; 4,000CFA) the road has fantastic views of mountains on both sides – to the west is the Massif de Koumounabouali (Koumounabouali Mountains) and far away to the east are the du Chaillu Mountains. Heading south, minibuses cover the 160km to Tchibanga via Ndendé in 2½ hours for 8,000CFA; you may have to change vehicles in Ndendé.

In either direction from Mouila, the N1 is surfaced and in good condition; the track leading 70km east to join the N6 at Yeno (⊕ -1.6742, 11.4856), from where you can eventually reach Koulamoutou, is 4×4 only.

GETTING AROUND For the most part, your options are either to **walk** or take a **taxi**, though if you're feeling intrepid you could also charter a **pirogue**. The pirogue launch up the street from La Métisse [map, opposite] is the place to negotiate for a piroguier to take you to Lac Bleu (page 154), about 5km or 2 hours away. (You can also walk to the lake (3.3km on foot; page 154), but it's not nearly as scenic as paddling there. Taxis charge 1,000–2,000CFA for a charter trip across town.

For a town of its size, Mouila is home to a fair selection of budget and mid-range accommodation options.

Le Doufoura (27 rooms); m 01 86 26 21/07 20 03 91/04 58 74 79; Residence Hoteliere Le Doufoura. A decent hotel but nothing special, with small AC rooms. *From 18,500CFA.* **$$**

Hôtel du Lac Bleu (75 rooms) West bank of the river; m 06 97 27 90; w hoteldulacbleu. com. The best hotel in town has a tennis court & swimming pool, as well as a comparatively pricey restaurant (**$$**) & bar. All rooms have AC, TV & en-suite facilities. The hotel also offers all-inclusive w/end deals, depending on the number of people booking. We've had reader reports of mis-totalled accounts here though, so check your bill before paying. **$$**

Résidence Hôtelière Mukab (12 rooms) m 07 31 37 37/05 12 62 15; e rhmukab9@gmail. com; Résidence Hôtelière Mukab Mouila. A former Gabonese politician, originally from Mouila, turned one of his garden villas into a nicely decorated motel, & today it's a reliable pick favoured by tour operators. *Fan rooms from 12,500CFA, AC from 20,500CFA.* **$$**

Hotel Dreamland (14 rooms) m 02 65 77 99/07 82 54 48/01 86 25 62. This basic hotel

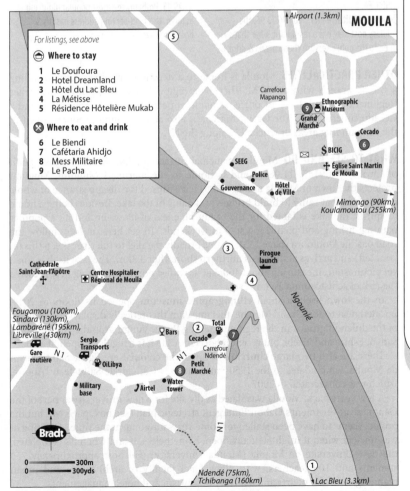

MOUILA

For listings, see above

⬭ **Where to stay**
1 Le Doufoura
2 Hotel Dreamland
3 Hôtel du Lac Bleu
4 La Métisse
5 Résidence Hôtelière Mukab

✖ **Where to eat and drink**
6 Le Biendi
7 Cafétaria Ahidjo
8 Mess Militaire
9 Le Pacha

Airport (1.3km)

Carrefour Mapango

Ethnographic Museum
Grand Marché
Cecado
BICIG
Église Saint Martin de Mouila

SEEG
Police
Gouvernance
Hôtel de Ville

Mimongo (90km), Koulamoutou (255km)

Pirogue launch

Cathédrale Saint-Jean-l'Apôtre
Centre Hospitalier Régional de Mouila

Fougamou (100km), Sindara (130km), Lambaréné (195km), Libreville (430km)

Gare routière   N1
Sergio Transports
OiLibya

Bars
Cecado
Total
Carrefour Ndendé
Petit Marché

Military base
Airtel
Water tower

Ngounié

N

Bradt

0 ———— 300m
0 ———— 300yds

Ndendé (75km), Tchibanga (160km)

Lac Bleu (3.3km)

offers cheap en-suite rooms with fan or AC & little balconies. There's a bar downstairs, so dreamland may or may not be a misnomer. **$**

🛏 **La Métisse** (16 rooms) West bank of the river; ☎01 86 18 06. Clean, friendly & good value. Large rooms with en-suite facilities & fan/AC. Good restaurant (**$$**) serving brochettes, grilled fish & several European dishes. **$**

✗ WHERE TO EAT AND DRINK *Map, page 150*

With the exception of the Hotel Dreamland, all of the hotels listed on page 153 serve food; these are the most reliable bets for a meal in Mouila. Otherwise, there are a few standalone eateries in town.

✳✗ **Cafétaria Ahidjo** Carrefour Ndendé; 📱 07 88 35 14; ⊕ 04.00–20.00 Mon–Sat, 04.00–10.00 Sun. This Cameroonian-run spot is popular at all hours, serving up belly-pleasing plates of rice, chicken, fish & more for a wallet-pleasing 1,500CFA. **$**

✗ **Mess Militaire** N1; ☎01 86 12 96. The military post here has a restaurant & bar that's open to the public serving cheap meals & drinks.

They also have a number of rooms with AC on offer from 15,000CFA (**$**). **$**

♀ **Le Pacha** Carrefour Mapango. Popular bar serving cold Régab. **$**

☆ **Le Biendi** Behind Notre Dame school; ☎07 35 29 45. Probably the most popular nightclub in town, this long-serving address has DJs & occasional live performances.

OTHER PRACTICALITIES Mouila is home to a decent array of services, including a BICIG branch with an ATM. There is a regional hospital (Centre Hospitalier Régional de Mouila), a post office, a couple of petrol stations, a police post and a Cecado supermarket. The Grand Marché is also active, selling produce grown in the surrounding areas or trucked in along the N1.

WHAT TO SEE AND DO Mouila's principal attraction, **Lac Bleu**, sits just south of town (⊕ -1.9145, 11.0633) and is home to the mermaid Mugumi. Mugumi protects the town of Mouila and is said to have caused the disappearance of whole expeditions that came to build bridges and dams in the lake. Besides being a home to spirits, the lake is famed for the bright blueness of its water and it's a popular bathing, fishing and picnicking spot at weekends. To get here on foot, follow the road past Le Doufoura (page 153); it runs broadly parallel to the river (keep this on your left) and arrives at the lake's northern shore after 3.3km. The lake itself is small yet picturesque, measuring about 400m at its widest point. Swimming here presents the risk of schistosomiasis, however.

In the town itself, a small **ethnographic museum** opened its doors in 2014. Located next to the Grand Marché, this museum theoretically displays pieces of art of the different groups in the region including Punu, Vungu, Apindji, Akélé, Tsogo, Sango, Eshira and Nzébi, but recent reports indicate it is irregularly open, if at all.

There are also two large **churches** in town: the colonial-era Église Saint Martin de Mouila, which dates to the 1950s; and the new Cathédrale Saint-Jean-l'Apôtre, which was consecrated in 2007.

A few years back, Mouila was slated as the site for a new **university** as part of the Gabonese government's Gabon Émergent strategic plan (see box, page 14), but the project seems to have been stalled for some years now and, at the time of writing, it was unclear when it might actually open. Nonetheless, if and when it's completed, the new Université de Mouila (Mouila University) will host approximately 750 students and 100 teachers, with plans for a faculty of architecture and urban planning, a faculty of arts and a faculty of tourism and hotel management.

SINDARA

About 17km south of Lambaréné, before arriving in Fougamou, there is a left turn leading to the pretty village of Sindara. To get here by **public transport**, you should wait on the N1 at the Sindara turn-off, from where the occasional clando will take you the remaining unsurfaced 15km into the village.

Sindara is worth a visit mainly because of its beautiful, peaceful **mission** (⊕ -1.0403, 10.6701; m 07 51 14 22/06 18 16 33; f Sanctuaire Notre Dame de L'Équateur et des Trois Epis; Our Lady of the Equator and the Three Ears – the latter being a reference to a 1491 apparition of the Virgin Mary holding three ears of wheat in Orbey, France). Alsatian missionaries founded the mission in 1899, in part as a memorial (Sindara was an active port during the slave trade, and many abductees were loaded on to boats here for eventual sale into slavery further down the Ngounié River). It is reached via a grand avenue lined with mango trees. The main building has arched colonnades on two levels and is built in brick and wood. Opposite is a small, whitewashed church, **Notre Dame de L'Équateur**, painted with touches of blue, making it look Greek in style. The library and church are still in use and well maintained, but the school – widely known for the quality of education on offer – unfortunately suffered a catastrophic fire in April 2019, and it will likely be some time before this is rebuilt. When you arrive at the mission, ask for a guide and you will be shown around.

About 3km east of the mission there's a set of surging rapids (⊕ -1.0417, 10.6962) in a horseshoe bend along the Ngounié; ask your guide at the mission to show you the way. Some say these are part of a husband-and-wife pair, with the larger rapids in Fougamou.

Sindara is also the jumping-off point for the 60km track to Ikobey, near the northern end of Waka National Park (page 158).

FOUGAMOU

Located along the N1 roughly equidistant between Mouila and Lambaréné, Fougamou (population 7,200) is a green and pretty place surrounded by forested hills. The town itself stretches for a couple of kilometres between the N1 and the west bank of the Ngounié. The mission, market, pharmacy, shops and places to stay and eat are all on the main street.

GETTING THERE AND AWAY Leaving town, Fougamou sees a fair amount of passing clandos and minibuses on the N1 in either direction, so it's just a question of hailing one and squeezing in. Heading north, it's 10km to the Sindara turn-off and 95km to Lambaréné, while southbound Mouila is 100km away.

WHERE TO STAY, EAT AND DRINK If you find yourself here overnight, the best place to stay is the **Ngôunié Hôtel** (10 rooms; centre-ville; m 07 54 43 99/94 30 79; **$$**), a large place with a fantastic view of the river and rooms from 21,000CFA. The **Auberge Tsamba Magotsi** (8 rooms; m 06 65 54 71; f L'auberge Tsamba magotsi; **$$**) or **Auberge du Rond Point** (m 02 04 10 74/04 20 85 71; **$**) are reliable options if they're full. Visitors are also welcome in one of the simple but clean rooms of the **Mission de la Sainte-Famille** (4 rooms; m 07 54 80 29; **$**).

WHAT TO SEE AND DO Sightseeing opportunities in Fougamou itself are rather thin on the ground, but it's hard to argue with the appealing views over the Ngounié. The peaceful **Mission de la Sainte-Famille** dates to the 1950s and merits a quick look if you're in town. There's also the option to stay overnight here (page 155). Outside town, some 5km to the north, are a set of **waterfalls** (✪ -1.1676, 10.5960), which some say are the husband to the supposed wife-rapids at Sindara (page 155). The falls are known either as the Chutes de Samba (Samba Falls), Chutes de Fougamou (Fougamou Falls) or, most commonly, as the Chutes de l'Impératrice (Empress Falls; the name given them by the explorer du Chaillu in the 19th century). To get here, take the eastbound turning in Kessi I, 2km north of the final roundabout in Fougamou, and continue for 3.5km along an unsurfaced road. There's an active proposal to build a hydroelectric dam here, so it could be a construction site by the time you read this; ask in Fougamou for the latest.

MASSIF DU CHAILLU

The area east of the N1 road is dominated by the du Chaillu mountain range, which can be seen as a continuation of the Crystal Mountains found north of the Ogooué River. The mountains are dissected northeast to southwest by two roads from Koulamoutou, the N6 and the R20, which eventually merge at Lébamba for the final stretch to Ndendé. The N6 is the primary route here, but even this is a generous description, as it's little more than an earthen track. Some claim these routes are among the country's prettiest because of the breathtaking scenery of mountains and valleys, but their beauty is well matched by their ruggedness and a 4×4 is essential in this area, particularly in the rainy season. As such, the area sees precious few visitors and travellers here should be prepared for basic, and often difficult, conditions.

NDENDÉ Ndendé (population 6,000) lies in an area of gentle hills, overshadowed from the northeast by the du Chaillu Mountains. It mainly functions as a crossroads for travellers, here to refill their petrol or stock up on provisions in the small market. It's also the last town before the border with Congo and the end of the surfaced portion of the N1, after which the remaining 50km to Congo are generally in quite rough shape.

There are several daily **minibuses** along the surfaced N1 to and from **Libreville** (500km; 8hrs; 15,000CFA) via **Mouila** (75km; 1hr; 3,000CFA) and **Lambaréné** (270km; 4hrs; 10,000CFA), and **Sergio Transports** (m 04 81 01 07) is a recommended operator with early morning departures. **Tchibanga** (85km; 1½ hrs; 5,000CFA) and **Mayumba** (190km; 3½hrs; 9,000CFA) are reached along the newly surfaced N6 to the southwest. Covering the 300km of N6 northeast to **Koulamoutou** is a considerably bigger challenge, however, as transport in this direction is irregular thanks to the dire state of the unsurfaced road; only the first 37km to Lébamba are paved. Occasional minibuses will cover the route between Ndendé and Lébamba but, for anything beyond, departures are considerably less frequent; ask around at the gare routière for the next vehicle; passing trucks may also sell seats in clando fashion. (Bring extra food and water in case you get stuck.) As with any of Gabon's unsurfaced routes, transport is easier and more frequent during the dry season. For information on what there is to see along this route, see opposite.

If you're on your way to or from the Congo border at Doussala, immigration formalities need to be done in Ndendé (see box, page 181). To spend the night, try **Hotel Divive** (✪ -2.4011, 11.3589; **$**), which is clean and popular with overlanders. The rundown **Motel Le Barbeque** (**$**) opposite the Total station is well past its prime, but could be useful as a fallback. For those bringing their own tents, the

Immaculée Conception de Ndéndé Catholic mission (**$**) may let you camp in their garden, if you turn up and ask nicely.

THE N6 FROM NDENDÉ TOWARDS KOULAMOUTOU
Leaving Ndendé and heading northeast on the N6, the road is surfaced for the first 35km to **Lébamba** (population 7,800), after which the real fun begins, with 270km of unsurfaced 4×4-only road between here and Koulamoutou. For further details on travelling this route, see opposite.

Lébamba's renowned 158-bed Bongolo Hospital (**w** bongolohospital.org), run by the American Christian and Missionary Alliance of Gabon, attracts patients from as far as Brazzaville. It has a busy outpatient department and laboratory, along with a HIV/AIDS treatment centre. The mission here can offer you a bed for the night (**$**) and connect you with a guide for an excursion to the nearby **Grottes de Bongolo** (Bongolo Caves), a couple of massive underground cave networks hollowed out by underground streams, the longest of which is nearly 2km. Although they are some of the most ancient caves on the planet (around 50 million years old), and evidence of human activity here dates back 7,000 years, scientists have only recently begun to explore them. If you want to visit the caves, make sure you are well prepared and in the company of one of the mission's experienced and trustworthy guides. Beware that the innumerable bats living in the caves are often carriers of ebola and HIV, so avoid being bitten.

CONIAMBIÉ: THE FABLE OF THE LEOPARD

Coniambié was a king who made an *orambo* (trap) in which a *ncheri* (gazelle) was caught. After it had been caught, it cried and called for its companion; then a *ngivo* (another gazelle) was caught. The ngivo cried, and a wild boar came and was caught; then an antelope came, and was caught; afterwards a bongo and a buffalo came, and all were caught, and all of them died in the trap. At that time Coniambié was in the mountains. A leopard was caught also, but did not die. Then came a turtle, who released the leopard from the trap. Then the leopard wanted to kill the turtle that had saved him. The leopard got hold of the turtle to kill it, but the turtle, seeing this, drew her head, legs, and tail inside her shell, but not before she had managed to get into the hollow of an old tree, with the leopard after her in the hollow, and he could not get away.

The tree is called *ogana*, and bears a berry on which monkeys are fond of feeding. So there came to the tree at this time, for the purpose of feeding, a *miengai*, or white-moustached monkey; a *ndova*, the white-nosed monkey; a *nkago*, the red-headed monkey; an *oganagana*, a blackish monkey; a *mondi*, which has very long black hair; a *nchegai* and a *pondi*, who all came to eat the berries. When the leopard heard the noise of the monkeys, he shouted, 'Monkeys, come and release me!' They came and helped the leopard out of the hole. But the leopard, instead of being grateful, fought with the monkeys, and ate the nkago and the ndova. Then the monkey called a mondi said, 'Mai! mai! That is so; that is so! You leopards are noted rogues. The leopard and the goat do not live together at the same place. We came to help you, and, as soon as you were helped, you began to kill us. Mai! mai! You are a rogue.'

Moral: the reason why the leopard wanders solitary and alone is on account of his roguery; he is not to be trusted. There are men who cannot be trusted any more than the leopard.

From *Lost In The Jungle*, Paul du Chaillu (1897)

Continuing northeast along the N6 for just over 80km, **Yéno** is the junction village for the 70km track heading west to Mouila. To the north of Yéno is a gold-panning area centred around the old mining village of **Etéké** (◈ -1.4947, 11.4771). It was a sizeable producer of alluvial gold some decades ago, though today **Massima** (◈ -1.4370, 11.5884), some 18km further northeast, is apparently the more active site. Moroccan mining firm Managem launched a feasibility study into reopening the mines at Etéké in 2018. Etéké is reached along a side track 25km north of Yéno, (and Massima 18km beyond that), though we've had reports that visitors are not encouraged to drop by uninvited, so it would be wise to ask in Yéno before setting out.

Back on the N6, it's a further 20km from Yéno to the large Mitsogo village of **Mimongo** (population 2,100; ◈ -1.6207, 11.6015). It's the most significant settlement along this stretch of the N6 (for what that's worth), and the large proportion of traditionalist Mimongo residents means the area is arguably the true cradle of Bwiti (see box, page 18) and Gabonese culture. Don't expect any ceremonies designed for a visitor, but if you stick around long enough to make some friends in town, you may be invited to one. Mimongo is also home to a *pont des lianes* (vine bridge) over the Ogoulou River, in regular use by villagers living on the opposite bank. There's little in the way of facilities, but travellers can stay in the basic *case de passage* here (**$**).

Continuing from here, it's about 75km to the bridge over the Offoué River, which marks the border between Ngounié and Ogooué-Lolo provinces; Koulamoutou (page 169) is a further 90km beyond.

MBIGOU AND THE R20 Even more difficult than the journey along the N6 between Lébamba and Koulamoutou (page 157) is the R20 that runs parallel to this route, bypassing the N6 between Lébamba and Moukabou via Mbigou. If you're on public transport, look for vehicles headed this way in Lébamba.

Heading out of Lébamba, it's worth stopping for a look at the ramshackle colonial-era Notre Dame de Lourdes (Our Lady of Lourdes) Church in tiny Dibouangui village after about 20km. Continuing northeast, after another 60km or so, you'll reach the small town of **Mbigou** (population 5,900; ◈ -1.8954, 11.9083), situated along the Louetsi River. Mbigou is the source of the eponymous soapstone favoured by Gabonese sculptors and found in craft markets around the country (page 74). You may find some artisans at work here, though today the stone is generally shipped to Libreville in its raw form and sculpted there instead, most notably at COOPAM (page 100).

From Mbigou, the R20 heads northwest and rejoins the N6 at Moukabou after 57km; Mimongo (see above) is 10km west of here. There's also, theoretically, a roughly 80km route continuing northeast from Mbigou to Popa (page 172) in Ogooué-Lolo province, passing north of the Birougou Mountains National Park, but it's unclear if this is at all passable, even in a 4×4. Another potentially impassable and profoundly remote route leads 80km southeast to Malinga, where there's a rarely used border crossing into Congo.

PARC NATIONAL DES MONTS BIROUGOU AND PARC NATIONAL DE LA WAKA The northern section of the du Chaillu range, between Fougamou and Lopé National Park, has been gazetted as the 107,000ha **Parc National de la Waka** (Waka National Park; entry 5,000/1,000CFA a day for foreigners/Gabon residents), home to rare endemic palm forests. Meanwhile the southern end is protected as the 69,000ha **Parc National des Monts Birougou** (Birougou Mountains National Park; entry

5,000/1,000CFA a day for foreigners/Gabon residents), which takes its name from the 975m Mont Birougou.

The whole of this area has plenty of both natural and cultural tourism potential, although at present there are no facilities, the parks remain undeveloped for visitors and are particularly difficult to access. In theory, though, it could be great walking country – there are footpaths throughout the du Chaillu Mountains – but as yet these are known only to locals; don't even consider setting out without a knowledgeable local guide. Furthermore, the region is poor and people depend heavily on hunting, which naturally poses a big threat to the park's wildlife.

Ngounié is home to a great deal of ethnic diversity; though the areas immediately around both parks are largely uninhabited, the region around the Birougou Mountains National Park is home to the **Nzébi people**, known for their ceremonies and secret societies. The area around Waka National Park is home to Eshira, Tsogo, Mitsogo, Babongo, Akélé, Evia and Apindi communities; the largest of these ethnic groups is the **Mitsogo**, traditional agriculturalists who grow manioc, bananas and other staples for trade with the Babongo. Owing to their early arrival in the area (see box, page 152), the Mitsogo claim to be the most Gabonese of all the ethnic groups living in Gabon and the original practitioners of Bwiti (see box, page 18).

The **Babongo** people, often derogatively referred to as Pygmies (see box, page 17), are known for residing in temporary domed shelters in the forest, but thanks to a series of (colonial and independent) government 'resettlement programmes', the vast majority of villages have moved to the roadsides, and the tradition is a disappearing practice. However, there are still villages in the forest that can only be accessed on foot.

For true adventurers, the profoundly isolated village of **Ikobey** (⊕ -1.0539, 10.9904) and several nearby Babongo settlements in the forests at the northern fringes of Waka National Park – including Tchibanga (⊕ -1.0410,11.0781), Tranquile (⊕ -1.032, 11.0541) and others – can be visited with Gabon Untouched (page 51). Trips here are not for the faint of heart, but give you unprecedented access to a natural and cultural world that few outsiders will ever lay eyes on. The 60km road to Ikobey begins just across the Ngounié River from Sindara. It is a difficult route of unmaintained earthen tracks and log bridges that may have to be rebuilt by hand as you go along.

If you have the chance to visit a Babongo village in the forest, remember that it is very important to pay respect to every village chief. Even if mostly a formality, initial greetings to the local chief are essential for a pleasant experience. Beware that there are many sacred and taboo sites in the forest and near villages. Streams and waterfalls are considered to be important homes for spirits. The Babongo have infinite traditional knowledge of forest resources, and much of this knowledge is sacred, only to be passed on to the properly initiated.

SEND US YOUR SNAPS!

We'd love to follow your adventures using our *Gabon* guide – why not tag us in your photos and stories via Twitter (🐦 @BradtGuides) and Instagram (📷 @bradtguides)? Alternatively, you can upload your photos directly to the gallery on the Gabon destination page via our website (w bradtguides.com/gabon).

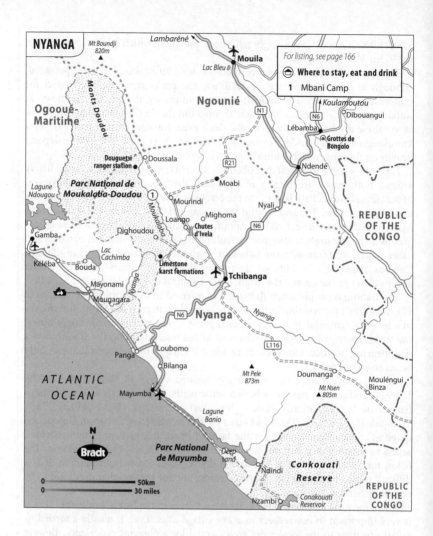

8

Nyanga

Wedged between Congo and the Atlantic Ocean in the far southwest of the country, Nyanga is Gabon's least-populous province, with just 52,000 resident Ninois. The steamy provincial capital Tchibanga is on the Nyanga River, nestled in a low-lying corridor between the Mayumba and Ikoundou mountains, paralleling the Ngounié Valley to the east. Tchibanga is the gateway to Moukalaba-Doudou National Park, a promising site for gorilla watching that is known for its high density of primates. A major advantage for the park's emergent ecotourism activities is that members of Nyanga's main ethnic group (the Bapounou, or Punu) do not hunt gorillas and chimps, as they see apes as a re-embodiment of their ancestors.

About 100km southwest of Tchibanga, at the northern point of an 80km lagoon, lies Mayumba, famous for its endless windswept beach. Remote Mayumba National Park is dedicated to the protection of marine life and is Africa's most important breeding site for the vulnerable leatherback turtle. Between November and February, up to 550 females may crawl ashore in a single night. From June to October, humpback whales pass through the park's waters on their annual migration to their breeding grounds. Unfortunately, up until now Mayumba National Park has been largely restricted to adventurous people with both time and money, as there are no organised tourist activities and the park lacks even basic tourist infrastructure. There are a couple of decent accommodation options in Mayumba town, though, and a new tarmac road from Tchibanga means that today access is easier than ever.

TCHIBANGA

Tchibanga is the capital of Nyanga province, which explains its number of government buildings. It's a town of about 30,000 residents and is surrounded by attractive countryside. Although it's a relaxed place to stop if you are not pressed for time, there is little to see or do as such. Approaching Tchibanga by road from the north offers a wonderful view of the town from the hills above, especially in the rainy season when the sky is clear. The market, shops and gare routière are all very close together in the commercial centre, which lies north of the administrative quarter of town.

GETTING THERE AND AROUND While Tchibanga does have an airport about 4km north of town on the road to Mourindi, no-one was flying there at the time of writing.

Nyanga TCHIBANGA

8

> ## $ ATMS
> There are no ATMs anywhere in Nyanga province, so bring enough cash to get you through. The nearest ATMs are in Mouila and Gamba.

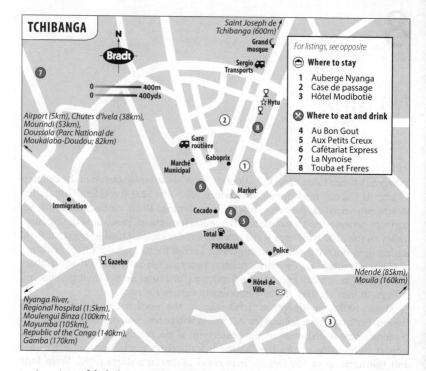

For listings, see opposite

Where to stay
1 Auberge Nyanga
2 Case de passage
3 Hôtel Modibotiè

Where to eat and drink
4 Au Bon Gout
5 Aux Petits Creux
6 Cafétariat Express
7 La Nynoise
8 Touba et Freres

A variety of daily **buses** and minibuses from PK8 in **Libreville** cover the 590km journey to Tchibanga in 9–10 hours, depending on how courageous, experienced or careless the driver is. **Sergio Transports** (m 04 81 01 07) is recommended for its reliable drivers. You should reserve a seat in advance (preferably the day before), either by phone or at their office in the northeast of town; their buses depart from the offices at 07.00 in either direction and a ticket will set you back 18,000CFA. The road is surfaced the entire way, with the exception of the last 15–20 kilometres as you enter Tchibanga.

A minibus between Tchibanga and **Mouila** (160km) via Ndendé takes about 2½ hours and costs 8,000CFA, with vehicles generally heading to Mouila around 07.00 and returning around 13.00. Vehicles to **Mayumba** (105km; 2hrs) and **Gamba** (170km; 3½hrs) operate on a similar schedule, charging 8,000CFA and 11,000CFA respectively. The road is now surfaced all the way to Mayumba, and to Gamba as far as the Mougagara–Mayonami ferry, after which it's 45km of well-maintained laterite.

A **taxi** around Tchibanga costs under 1,000CFA.

TOUR OPERATORS

Back to Roots Tours m 02 08 78 83/07 45 94 69; e ghislain.bouassa@gmail.com; f Ghislain Bouassa. Run by the Tchibanga-based Ghislain Bouassa, Back to Roots Tours has a lot of experience in the region & is well placed to arrange excursions to Moukalaba-Doudou, as well as anywhere else in Nyanga province & beyond.

PROGRAM [map, above] & [95 B3] L'association Protectrice des Grands Singes de la Moukalaba (Protector of the Great Apes of Moukalaba); offices in Tchibanga & Quartier Louis in Libreville, page 89; m 07 12 68 04/06 62 25 72; e ong.program@gmail.com/marieangele. program@gmail.com/zangobamerina@yahoo.fr; w association-program.com; f ong.program.

This should be the first stop in town for anyone planning a trip. Their focus is on community-based ecotourism & they organise all activities & practicalities within the Moukalaba-Doudou, including gorilla trekking & accommodation.

WHERE TO STAY *Map, opposite*

Tchibanga offers a couple of reasonably comfortable and well-priced accommodation options. The upmarket Hôtel Modibotiè is known for having one of the best restaurants in town, but don't count on efficient service. In the centre of town there are some cheaper auberges and a case de passage ($), the most basic option in town.

Hôtel Modibotiè (12 rooms) Quartier Ibanga, south of the town centre; m 06 04 20 49; f Complexe Hôtelier MODIBOTIÈ de Tchibanga. Modibotiè is the most luxurious hotel in town, & also the most expensive. Rooms have TV, AC & fridge, & there is a small pool. The restaurant serves grillades, pizzas & African dishes ($$).
$$$

Auberge Nyanga (20 rooms) Opposite Gaboprix; m 07 10 68 68/06 17 77 82/06 71 26 16/04 30 85 73. This no-nonsense Mauritanian-run place has well-kept en-suite rooms with hot water & Wi-Fi. Located on the main drag through town. *Fan/AC room from 10,000CFA/22,000CFA.*
$-$$

OTHER PRACTICALITIES In keeping with its status as a regional capital, Tchibanga is home to a couple of petrol stations, a post office, police post, Cecado and Gaboprix supermarkets, and a new regional hospital, located just outside of town towards Mayumba.

WHERE TO EAT AND DRINK *Map, opposite*

For breakfast, head to **Aux Petits Creux** (Centre-Ville; m 06 69 83 74/07 58 57 06; 07.00–afternoon, closed Sun; $) across the street from the Cecado supermarket, an ideal place for coffee with fresh pastries. Its tiny terrace is a popular place to check out what's going on in the street. It sits just behind **Au Bon Gout** (centre-ville; m 05 62 38 62; $$), which serves up a variety of Gabonese plates like *sanglier* (wild boar) and crocodile, as well as some more conventional options for 2,500–5,000CFA. Another good option for a snack is **Cafétariat Express** (on the way to the gare routière; 07.30–afternoon, closed Sun; $). Senegalese dishes are available at **Touba et Freres** (opposite the case de passage; $). A bit out of the centre, **La Nynoise** (closed Mon; m 07 37 31 23; $$) serves surprisingly good pizza in a homey setting for 6,000CFA.

Self-caterers can take their pick at one of Tchibanga's reasonably stocked supermarkets, including the omnipresent Cecado and Gaboprix. At the Marché Municipal you'll find many women selling fresh fruit and vegetables for low prices.

ENTERTAINMENT AND NIGHTLIFE For a sense of Tchibanga's nightlife, you'll find a few options on the road north of Auberge Nyanga; try the **Hytu** nightclub in the heart of the Quartier Commercial, an area packed with bars and food stalls selling grilled fish and brochettes at night. If that's a bit too much commotion for you, the outdoor **Gazebo Bar** west of the city centre is a good spot to sink a couple of Régabs in (relative) peace.

WHAT TO SEE AND DO Beyond scoping out the central market, enjoying the views over the Nyanga River at the N6 bridge south of town, and visiting the Saint Joseph de Tchibanga – an appealing church, built in 1954 and located to the north of town, there's not a whole lot to see.

If you have your own 4×4 transport (page 87), you can visit the **Chutes d'Ivela** (Ivela Falls; ☉ -2.6821, 10.8446), a series of small waterfalls over steep rocks deep in the pristine rainforest. Back to Roots (page 162) can arrange trips here.

Take the road towards Mourindi (4×4 required) and stop at the village of Loango (not to be confused with the national park; 1hr; ☉ -2.6701, 10.8190), where you should request permission from the chief to visit the falls (to find him, ask around the village). He will assign you a guide to take you to the falls on foot through the forest (about 1½hrs each way). There are no fixed costs, but a tip would certainly be appropriate. Alternatively, look for somebody in Loango to take you to the falls by pirogue.

Continuing a further 15km north by road from Loango, you'll reach the larger village of **Mourindi** (☉ -2.5584,10.7369), which is home to a small yet fetching chapel, the Notre Dame du Mont Carmel, which dates to the 1930s.

PARC NATIONAL DE MOUKALABA-DOUDOU

Gabon's third largest national park, the 503,000ha Moukalaba-Doudou is a rugged area with a diverse range of habitats, from tropical rainforest and grassy savannahs to papyrus swamps. Running between the Moukalaba River to the east and the Ndogo Lagoon to the west, the park also covers the Doudou Mountains. This is the largest mountain range in southwestern Gabon, reaching an altitude of approximately 700m. While the Doudou Mountains were logged from the 1960s until the 1980s, the area is now completely uninhabited.

With an estimated population of almost 5,000 chimpanzees and gorillas, Moukalaba-Doudou has some of the highest densities of primates in Gabon, making it one of the country's most promising gorilla-tourism sites. The best time of the year to see primates is during the dry season, between June and September. Former logging sites are now abundant with succulent *marantaceae* plants, a major food source for gorilla as well as forest elephant and other species. Furthermore, the savannahs near Doussala are the only place in Gabon where herds of common *cobe* (waterbuck) are found. The park is also a remarkable area for birders; more than 380 species (many of them unique) have been spotted here, including the vermiculated fishing owl, black-backed barbet, black-headed batis, fiery-breasted bush-shrike, brown twinspot and some rare swallows.

The 4km² of community-managed forest around the village of Doussala is home to several groups of gorilla. In collaboration with Kyoto University, the Institute for Research in Tropical Ecology (IRET), WWF and the ANPN, the local NGO PROGRAM (page 162) is in charge of the habituation of gorilla groups for tourism development, and the habituation rangers have their permanent base at Douguetsi ranger station (☉ -2.3683, 10.5600), about 6km southwest from Doussala. The project suffered a setback in 2017, when the primary habituation group's silverback, Gentil, disappeared, leaving the group leaderless and prone to splintering. (Gentil is presumed to have died, but his body is yet to be found.) Encouragingly, most of the group have now reorganised under another silverback, Marcial, and habituation work with this reformulated group of 13 continues. Gorilla trekking visits are possible and, while accessing the park is not exactly easy, they are well worth the effort.

VISITING THE PARK All excursions to the park depart from Tchibanga and must be arranged through one of the below-mentioned operators. Those who want to visit the park must be over 15, and trekking here requires good physical condition.

Local NGO **PROGRAM** [map, page 162] and [95 B3] (offices in Tchibanga & Quartier Louis in Libreville; **m** 07 12 68 04/06 62 25 72; **e** ong.program@gmail.com/marieangele.program@gmail.com/zangobamerina@yahoo.fr; **w** association-program.com; **f** ong.program; page 162) is the main contact point for the park and can facilitate all visits. Arrangements *must* be made in advance to ensure that staff are ready to receive you – you're likely to be the only visitors on any given day. The NGO's mission is to protect the park's great apes and support local communities in sustainable livelihood generation through community-based ecotourism. They organise gorilla trekking around Doussala and safaris to a camping site on the bank of the Mbani River, on the beautiful Mbani Plain (see below). Experienced guides take visitors on walking tours deep in the forests. The safari to Moukalaba-Doudou is one of the most authentic rainforest experiences one could wish for – and therefore is unsuitable for people uncomfortable with basic living conditions. (Accommodation in Doussala, however, is simple but reasonably comfortable).

As is often the case in Gabon, trips to Moukalaba-Doudou are not especially cheap, though you can save a fair amount, particularly on transport, by travelling in a group. Park **entry fees** begin at 15,000/5,000CFA a day for foreigners/Gabon residents. Otherwise, prices depend on the number of people and the season. As an estimate, however, a night in either of the accommodation options in Doussala or at Mbani Camp respectively cost 30,000/15,000CFA per person, plus an additional 20,000CFA a day per person for meals. Guiding fees for gorilla tracking and other hikes are 30,000CFA a day to go with only the trackers, while it's 50,000CFA a day to go with the trackers and an interpretive guide. A 10,000CFA donation to the village (if staying in Doussala) is also mandatory, but this payment is a one-off. All profits go to the development of communities and ecotourism activities. Unforgettable, all-night displays of fiery traditional dancing and ceremony (such as Bwiti, Bilomba, Madanji and Njembé) can also be arranged in Doussala for an additional 100,000CFA, and make for a spectacular and genuinely uncontrived way to cap off a visit to the park. For a full list of PROGRAM's offerings (in French) and prices, see **w** association-program.com/nos-forfaits-typiques.

Tchibanga-based **Back to Roots** (page 162) can also arrange all trips into the park, including gorilla tracking and other hikes, for broadly comparable prices.

GETTING THERE AND AROUND From Tchibanga, the 4×4 journey to either Mbani Camp (⊕ -2.5057, 10.5743; around 80km; 120,000CFA/vehicle) or Doussala (⊕ -2.3375, 10.5921; 100,000CFA/vehicle), arranged through one of the tour operators listed on page 162, takes around 2 to 3 hours and is a safari in itself.

En route **to Mbani Camp**, you cross the Moukalaba River on a car ferry near its confluence with the Nyanga, passing the mostly deserted village of Dighoudou (-2.7233, 10.6482), where the large elephant population destroyed houses and crops and forced many villagers to leave. Along the Nyanga River, just south of Dighoudou, wonderfully shaped ancient limestone karst formations remain where the once-surrounding land eroded away. A **4×4** can go some 30km past Dighoudou until you reach the bridge over the Mbani River close to Mbani Camp, where a quad bike awaits (unless it's broken, in which case you may have to walk) to transport visitors the last few kilometres to the camp.

Doussala is accessible from Tchibanga by 4×4 on 85km of earthen tracks that travel via Mourindi and pass through several semi-abandoned villages and a landscape of forest and savannah peppered with mushroom-shaped termite mounds; with a bit of luck, you can spot waterbuck and occasionally gorilla right from the road. While it is possible to reach Doussala in your own vehicle, the staff at either of the accommodation options (see below) will definitively not be prepared to receive anyone without advance warning; ensure you have arrangements in place before setting out.

In the rainy season, you can also travel along the Moukalaba River between Doussala and Mbani Camp in a traditional pirogue made by the inhabitants of Doussala (120,000CFA/boat; arranged with PROGRAM, page 162), opening up the possibility to complete a circular tour of the park, via Doussala, Mbani and Dighoudou.

 WHERE TO STAY, EAT AND DRINK All stays, both within the park and in Doussala, must be arranged in advance with one of the tour operators listed on page 162, where further information on prices and available excursions can also be found.

Crossing tree bridges, sleeping in igloo tents and bathing in a crystal-clear river in the middle of the jungle at PROGRAM's **Mbani Camp** [map, page 160] all contribute to a true into-the-wild experience. The guides provide decent local meals, and the sounds of the forest at night are a cacophony of life itself (bring plenty of insect repellent).

In Doussala, you now have two (equally priced) options: **Case Madre** is PROGRAM's guesthouse, formerly used by the logging companies but refurbished for visitors in 2018. It sleeps six people in three rooms (two with double beds and one with two singles). Local women provide traditional dinners.

Additionally, the **IRET Guesthouse** was built in Doussala for gorilla researchers in 2015 and, when not needed for the researchers, offers four rooms with single or double beds; the easiest way to book here would be through Back to Roots in Tchibanga (page 162).

MAYUMBA

The small town of Mayumba (population 5,500) is divided into two parts, straddling either side of the Lagune Banio (Banio Lagoon), with the town centre set on the narrow peninsula between this and the ocean. It is a somewhat rundown, sleepy place which, when the light hits it just right, can feel ever-so-slightly Caribbean. The ambience is pleasant enough regardless, and there is a great view of the ocean from the hospital on the hill. In 2010 France erected a 20m-high Croix de Lorraine (Cross of Lorraine) in memory of Commandant Parant of the Free French Forces, who seized Mayumba on 16 September 1940.

Talk of building a deep-water port on Gabon's southwestern coast near Mayumba has been going on since 1958 and though it's still likely a long way off, President Ali Bongo has continued to advocate for the project. The 2016 completion of a bridge over the lagoon, linking the two sides of town for the first time, may bring it one step closer to fruition.

The Gabonese will tell you that Mayumba has the best **beach** in the world. It's almost certainly the best in Gabon. It stretches for kilometres into the distance, in a slow curve of silky sand fringed with palm trees. Best of all, it is virtually deserted, which is undoubtedly an important factor in its popularity among nesting turtles. The NGO **Aventures Sans Frontières** (**f** AventuresSansFrontieres; page 35) has been conducting turtle surveys on this beach throughout the turtle season for many years. Their research, which shows that Mayumba has the largest concentration of nesting leatherback turtles on earth, was highly instrumental in the establishment of **Parc National de Mayumba** (Mayumba National Park), one of Africa's first marine parks, in 2002. In addition to turtles, this remote protected area (covering

800km² of coastal sea and a narrow 1km by 60km strip of beach) boasts 10% of the world's humpback whales, as well as the rare and threatened West African manatee. The lagoons, islands, channels and rivers support an exceptional wealth of fauna.

GETTING THERE AND AROUND Although there is an airport south of town, there were no flights to Mayumba at the time of writing. However, thanks to the completion of the lagoon bridge and 105km of tarmac road from Tchibanga, accessing Mayumba is no longer the slog it once was. **Minibuses** go in either direction between Tchibanga and Mayumba about twice daily, leaving the gare routière in each town at around 07.00 and returning around 13.00 (2hrs; 8,000CFA). There were no direct vehicles between Mayumba and Gamba at the time of writing, but with the increase in traffic thanks to the new road, you might have some luck finding a lift at the junction village of Loubomo, 35km north of Mayumba, rather than backtracking all the way to Tchibanga. This route also involves a trip on the Mougagara–Mayonami ferry.

Self-drivers should note that the piste heading southeast out of town past the airport and along the peninsula quickly turns into deep sand.

In town itself, taxis putter around charging the usual few hundred CFA for a trip. Those wanting to make a longer pirogue trip on the lagoon or one of the rivers that feeds it should ask around for a willing piroguier, starting at the lagoon landing stage below the market.

WHERE TO STAY, EAT AND DRINK Thanks to its appealing location, Mayumba is served by a better-than-average assortment of accommodation, with quality and prices to suit a variety of budgets. The hotels are also your best bet for meals, but for breakfast or snacks you could head to the main road to **Basse Banio** ($), one of the few eateries in town. More snack food, such as *beignets*, might be available at the market.

Likwale Lodge (20 rooms) On the continental side of the lagoon, next to the Catholic Mission; m 04 50 05 00; e likwale.lodge@yahoo. fr; w likwalelodge.com; ⨍ Likwale Lodge. Formerly the Safari Club, this sport-fishing lodge reopened under new management in 2016 & remains one of Mayumba's best options. The recently renovated AC bungalows are set in a large waterfront garden with a swimming pool. The terrace offers great views over the lagoon. **$$$**

Hôtel l'Ocean (5 rooms) Southern end of town, next to Mayumba airport; ☎ 01 83 51 27. Boasts lovely views over the sea. This small hotel, with AC en-suite rooms, is just next to the airport, which would be convenient if there were any flights. Not only are there no flights, it can be difficult to find a taxi here, too. There is a snack bar on the premises. **$$**

Motel Fabso (12 rooms) Quartier Bana; ☎ 02 93 59 59; m 07 93 59 59; e residencehotelierefabso@gmail. com/motelfabso11217@gmail.com; ⨍ ResidenceHoteliereFABSO. This new hotel is a clean, comfortable & well-managed option in the centre of town, offering en-suite rooms with either fan or AC. The resto-bar comes recommended ($–$$). *Room with fan from 12,000CFA/with AC from 17,000CFA.* **$–$$**

Motel La Banio (5 rooms) Next to the lagoon boat launch (former ferry port); m 07 58 04 70. This hotel has views of the lagoon & decent AC rooms with an attached resto-bar ($). **$**

WHAT TO SEE AND DO Though it's just about possible to skirt the northern edges of the terrestrial portion of the park from Mayumba (the park officially begins about 15km southeast of town), getting much deeper into **Parc National de Mayumba** is not exactly a stroll in the park as it lacks adequate infrastructure – there are neither roads in the park (the track that follows the coast southeast from Mayumba town quickly becomes an unmaintained stretch of deep sand, and thus only for 4×4s and drivers who know what they're doing), nor any co-ordinated way to arrange boat trips. However, the beach landscape visible before you enter the park is largely similar to that found within, and the turtles that come here to lay their eggs between October and March aren't particularly aware of the difference. Turtle lovers and whale-watchers with limited time and/or means should consider heading to the much more accessible Pongara National Park (page 113) near Libreville instead.

That being said, Likwale Lodge (page 167) should be your first port of call for trips out on to the water both in and around the park; they specialise in **fishing** but should be able to arrange **whale watching** and **sightseeing trips** as well. As for getting on the water without a motor, some Mayumba residents are now trying their hand at **surfing** – get in touch with **BanaBeach** (f VanOEKeysha) in Mayumba town if you'd like to give it a go, but beware of the heavy surf.

Some 4km to the southeast of town, you can also have a quick gawk at the tropical decay of Mayumba's overgrown and abandoned **airport terminal**, which has fallen into total disrepair.

Just across the water on the inland side of the lagoon, the **Sainte-Odile Catholic Mission** dates to 1888, and the complex is worth visiting for the rundown colonial architecture (including a sizeable cathedral) and views over the lagoon and ocean beyond. Senegalese holy man and founder of the Mouride Sufi brotherhood Ahmadou Bamba was imprisoned at the mission after the French exiled him to Gabon for seven years, fearing his growing influence in colonial Senegal. He spent five of those years at the mission in Mayumba.

Finally, if Mayumba isn't off the beaten track enough for your taste, **Ndindi** (population 1,100) sits some 75km southeast, at the far end of the Banio Lagoon near Gabon's southernmost point. There are irregular supply boats every few days from Mayumba, and it takes between 4 and 5 hours to make the crossing. From Ndindi it's just under 40km on unsurfaced roads to Congolese border controls at Nzambi. (There's a checkpoint in Ndindi, but Gabonese border formalities should be done before you leave Mayumba.) There's also basic accommodation (**$**) in Ndindi which is just as well, as you'll almost certainly be in for a wait when it comes to onward transport into Congo.

The Congolese village of **Nzambi** sits along the northern shore of the Conkouati Lagoon, from where it's a further 140km to Pointe-Noire (and 85km until you reach the tar road at Madingo-Kayes). The area here is also home to the Conkouati-Douli National Park, where you'll find the HELP Congo (Habitat Ecologique et Liberté des Primates; ◈ -3.9837, 11.31882; w help-primates.org; f) chimpanzee sanctuary just outside of Tandou Ngoma village on the south side of the lagoon. Here they can arrange simple accommodation in wooden cabins and trips to visit the orphaned chimps found on the lagoon's islands; advance reservation is required.

9

Ogooué-Lolo

Cut through by the Ogooué River and its tributary the Lolo River (hence the name), Ogooué-Lolo is Gabon's third least-populous province, home to just 65,000 Logovéens spread over more than 25,000km². A third important river, the Offoué, marks the natural border between Ogooué-Lolo and Ngounié provinces to the west. The neighbouring provinces are remarkably similar, taking in the rolling and remote green hills of the du Chaillu Mountains, where both the Offoué and Lolo rivers rise. The seemingly impenetrable primary forest, known along the N3 between Lopé and Lastoursville as the Forêt des Abeilles (Forest of Bees) is, as its name suggests, infamous for its phenomenal number of bees – and in turn famous for its excellent honey. The forest here has long attracted timber companies, and more recently scientists and conservationists. Besides them, not many visitors frequent the region and tourists are a bona-fide rarity.

The du Chaillu Mountains are rich in endemic species – just *how* rich remains unknown – but a host of primates including gorilla, chimpanzee, mandrill and the rare endemic sun-tailed monkey are all resident here. Straddling the border between Ogooué-Lolo and Ngounié, the **Parc National Monts Birougou** protects 690km² of their hill-studded habitats. Though the park itself is nearly inaccessible, requiring one or two days of fully self-sufficient walking through uninhabited bush just to reach the boundary (contact ANPN if you're interested in arranging an excursion; page 88), excursions on foot anywhere in the region practically guarantee encounters with a variety of primates and birds. Climbing the 972m Mount Iboundji represents the biggest challenge, but there are other, less strenuous, alternatives. The road heading south from the region's little-visited capital, Koulamoutou, leads to the remote village of Pana and the Congolese border beyond, but we've had no reports on the condition of this crossing.

KOULAMOUTOU

The regional capital since 1960, Koulamoutou is a small town built at the confluence of the Lolo River and its tributary the Bouenguidi and is home to about 26,000 residents (known as Koulois). Though it sits astride the N6 between Ndendé to the south and Lastoursville to the north, it remains a rather long way from anywhere and as such visitors here are few and far between.

> ### $ ATMS
>
> There are no ATMs anywhere in Ogooué-Lolo, so bring enough cash to get you through. The nearest ATMs are in Moanda, Franceville and Mouila.

Koulamoutou is divided in two by the Bouenguidi River, which is crossed by two bridges, conveniently referred to as the Ancien and Nouveau ponts (Old and New bridges; there's also a third bridge at the west end of town, crossing over the Lolo). On the west bank are the airport and the gare routière, while on the east bank are the administrative buildings and the market. All the streets are surfaced and there are hotels on both sides. Koulamoutou feels refreshingly green, no doubt the result of its fresh climate and the comparative lack of biting insects.

The town was once shaped significantly by the efforts and money of a former minister of tourism, Jean Massima, who was born in the nearby village of Popa. Massima was keen to promote Koulamoutou as a state-of-the-art, not-to-be-missed urban centre, but his successors had other interests and it wasn't long before Koulamoutou went back to the sleepy town it had always been.

GETTING THERE AND AROUND Afric Aviation flew between Koulamoutou and Libreville until they suspended operations in mid-2017. Should someone pick up the route again, the airport is 7km from town on the N6 towards Ndendé.

Koulamoutou's gare routière is next to the market. Reasonably regular clandos ply the 50km of surfaced road between Koulamoutou and Lastoursville to the northeast (1hr; 2,000CFA), but it's a considerably longer and harder slog on the difficult 4x4-only track that heads southwest to Ndendé (300km; 1 day) so ask about onward vehicles as soon as you get to town if you're headed this way and agree on a price. The 235km from Koulamoutou to Franceville – via Lastoursville – makes for a pleasant drive on tarred road; a handful of vehicles cover this route daily, though you may have to change en route in Lastoursville or Moanda. For more information on reaching Franceville from either of these destinations, see pages 173 and 186.

Central Koulamoutou is easily **walkable**, with most points of interest within a few hundred metres of one another, though you'll probably want to take a **taxi** (usually simple enough to find on the street) if you're staying in one of the further-flung hotels.

🏠 WHERE TO STAY, EAT AND DRINK *Map, page 172*

🏠 **Résidence-Hôtelière Bichi** (22 rooms) m 07 00 51 43. Located on an islet in the Lolo reached by a short liana bridge, this unusual hotel was known as a choice lodging for ministers & VIPs visiting Koulamoutou, but today it's anyone's guess as to whether or not you'll find it open. Most rooms are actually set in an annex 200m away on the mainland, where there's also a swimming pool. **$$$$**

🏠 **Hôtel Bouenguidi** (30 rooms) Close to Cecado; m 07 83 42 46. Koulamoutou's oldest & largest hotel, where the clientele are mostly Gabonese business travellers. It's showing its age these days & the pool has called it quits, but the resto-bar (**$$**) still functions. **$$–$$$**

🏠 **Hôtel Résidence Paul Ndama** (20 rooms) Airport rd; m 07 76 01 20. Set a few km from central Koulamoutou, this is newer & sharper than most options in town, with bungalows arranged around a central courtyard & parking area. There's a swimming pool & resto-bar (**$$–$$$**) on site. **$$–$$$**

🏠 **Motel Biki** (24 rooms) Near the Pont Nouveau; m 07 60 32 75. Popular & conveniently located, with a small pool on the premises. **$$**

🏠 **Notre-Dame de la Salette** (6 rooms) West of centre; m 01 65 51 59. Popular place to stay for those on a budget. It is worth a look not only for its striking red-brick church & tower that date from the mid 20th century, but also for the magnificent view of the river & town from its elevated position. **$**

✖ **Café Jacqueline** Riverside, just north of the Pont Nouveau; m 06 26 52 09; ⨍ Cafe Jacqueline Koulamoutou. Overlooking the river, a clean & bright resto-bar serving good grillades. There are also 5 rooms available here (**$$**). **$$**

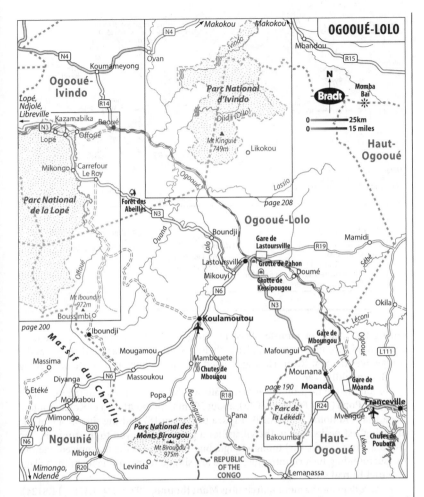

WHAT TO SEE AND DO Once upon a time (in the days of the former minister of tourism), Koulamoutou was very well catered for in terms of urban entertainment. Although it would be stretching things to say this now, the town still makes a good base from which to explore the surrounding countryside, thanks to its fetching location at the confluence of the Lolo and Bouenguidi. The bridges over either of these rivers make a fine place to watch the world go by. Or, even better, head up to the brick-built **church complex** at Notre-Dame de la Salette. Built in 1949, the views from here offer an expansive overview of the city. (Keep an eye out for the mansions across the river – no prizes for guessing the owners!) There are rooms available at the complex as well (see opposite).

Massif du Chaillu Setting off into the du Chaillu Mountains, the climate is noticeably fresher and cooler. About 40km southwest of town on the unsurfaced Popa road (4×4 only; no public transport), near the village of Mambouete, you can visit a succession of waterfalls, the **Chutes de Mbougou** (Mbougou Falls), on the Bouenguidi River. While not quite in the same league as the Migouli Falls (page 208), they were pounced on as the perfect opportunity for attracting tourists

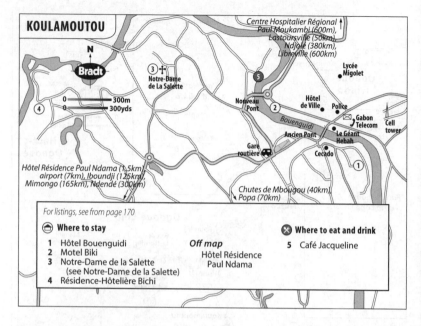

KOULAMOUTOU

N

Bradt

Notre-Dame
de La Salette

300m
300yds

Centre Hospitalier Régional
Paul Moukambi (600m),
Lastoursville (50km),
Ndjolé (380km),
Libreville (600km)

Lycée
Migolet

Nouveau
Pont

Hôtel
de Ville

Police

Gabon
Telecom

Cell
tower

Bouenguidi

Ancien Pont

Le Géant
Hebah

Gare
routière

Cecado

Hôtel Résidence Paul Ndama (1,5km),
airport (7km), Iboundji (125km),
Mimongo (165km), Ndendé (300km)

Chutes de Mbougou (40km),
Popa (70km)

For listings, see from page 170

🛏 **Where to stay**
1 Hôtel Bouenguidi
2 Motel Biki
3 Notre-Dame de la Salette
    (see Notre-Dame de la Salette)
4 Résidence-Hôtelière Bichi

Off map
Hôtel Résidence
Paul Ndama

✗ **Where to eat and drink**
5 Café Jacqueline

during the tenure of minister Massima (page 170). There's now a rudimentary access road through the forest, picnic shelters with rustic tables and chairs, and a bridge over the Sibi River. Having crossed this, it's a short walk to the falls along the Bouenguidi River.

Not taking the turn-off towards the falls will bring you instead to the mountain village of **Popa** (✛ -1.6040, 12.3046), about 70km to the southwest of Koulamoutou. Popa is a traditional centre of Bwiti (see box, page 18) and the site of one of the area's highest peaks. Ask in the village for a guide to take you to the summit. The climb is short (about 1hr) though tough, but the reward is the magnificent view of the surrounding lush countryside. There are simple rooms available in the village at **Motel Konadembe ($)**.

A more demanding mountain climb is **Mont Iboundji** (972m; ✛ -1.1787, 11.8124), a steep-sided plateau that's often – and erroneously – marked as Gabon's highest peak (an honour that in reality belongs to Mont Bengoué near Mékambo; page 211). Though it falls well short of the 1,575m taught to Gabonese schoolchildren, the summit here is probably best left to experienced walkers. You'll need a 4×4 to reach the base: head southwest out of Koulamoutou on the N6 towards Mimongo and turn right at Ngouassa (just before Mougamou; ✛ -1.4185, 12.0079), continuing for 40km until you reach the eponymous town of Iboundji (✛ -1.2212, 11.8225), where you can find basic rooms (**$**).

Hikes generally begin from the pinprick village of Boussimbi (✛ -1.1761, 11.8217), set directly opposite the mountain 7km beyond Iboundji. The chief here (again, ask around the village for him) will connect you with an obligatory guide (roughly 5,000CFA per day), who can take you either to the 100m-high waterfall round the back of the mountain (3hrs), or to the summit (5hrs). As the mountain is considered sacred, certain areas are off limits (even to locals), and you will be asked to pay for some food and drink as an offering to the spirits. All routes up the mountain are steep, rocky, slippery and densely forested. With the appropriate gear and permission from the chief, it would also be possible to camp in Boussimbi before or after the hike.

Lastoursville is the final major town (population 12,000) before the long trip through the Forêt des Abeilles (Forest of Bees) on what's known locally as the *route economique* (N3) towards Lopé. It is a sleepy, steamy, low-slung town that stretches for several kilometres along the Ogooué River, surrounded by dense forest. There are several small and densely forested river islands facing the town, one of which is known as L'Île Fétiche (Fetish Island); this was once an open-air prison for slaves awaiting shipment downriver to Lambaréné and is still avoided by people today.

This seemingly inauspicious settlement was known as Mandji until 1883, when Savorgnan de Brazza arrived to found a French outpost, rechristening it Maadiville, or 'oil town', after the many oil palms found growing in the area. However, the town took its current name just three years later, after a young French engineer, François Rigail de Lastours, died here from a severe bout of malaria. His tomb lies with those of other Frenchmen in a bamboo grove not far from the Hôtel Ngoombi. Today, the town is more commonly referred to by locals as 'Lozo'.

GETTING THERE AND AWAY Lastoursville is linked to Libreville and Franceville by the **Transgabonais railway** (page 66). Libreville-bound trains (11hrs; 42,400/35,600CFA Express/Omnibus train in 1st class) depart at around 19.30, and those headed for Franceville (3hrs; 14,400/12,100CFA express/omnibus train in 1st class) depart at around 04.15.

There are **minibuses** and clandos from Lastoursville to Koulamoutou (50km; 1hr) and to Moanda (125km; 2hrs) and Franceville (180km; 3hrs), leaving when full from the central gare routière; roads to all three towns are surfaced and in good shape.

Libreville is less than 600km away by roads to the northwest – starting with the N3 until Alembé (310km), then the N2 to Bifoun (95km) and the N1 into Libreville (165km). This is a long slog of a trip and the sparsely populated (even by Gabonese standards) 305km of N3 between Mikouyi and Alembé remains unsurfaced, rough and remote (4×4 required), despite the on-and-off presence of Chinese roadworkers here for several years. There is occasional public transport, but most travellers sensibly opt to take the train.

Whether self-driving or taking public transport, you might have (or want) to change vehicles or take a break at Ndjolé (350km). Better still, a stop at Lopé National Park (210km; page 197) is the most enjoyable way to break up the long journey. (Lastoursville and Lopé are also connected by train; 3½ hrs; 18,000/15,000CFA Express/Omnibus in 1st class).

WHERE TO STAY, EAT AND DRINK Formerly the most luxurious hotel in town, the **Hôtel Tchenga** (18 rooms; centre-ville; m 07 87 79 63; $) was recently described to us by a reader as 'appallingly rundown' and 'truly on its last legs'. Thus, while the Tchenga may offer beautiful views of the Ogooué, you'd be better off at the **Hôtel Ngoombi** (16 rooms; m 06 05 98 89; $–$$) nearby, which also has air-conditioned rooms, a restaurant ($$) and a nightclub (readers have reported that they like to play games with their pricing, so don't be afraid to bargain and always get a receipt). The cheapest place to stay is the **Catholic Mission of Saint-Pierre-Claver** (✆ 01 64 02 17; $; see below) just west of town.

WHAT TO SEE AND DO About 3km out of town on the Koulamoutou road is the **Mission Catholique Saint-Pierre-Claver** (Catholic Mission of Saint-Pierre-Claver; ✆ -0.8244, 12.7042), a complex of buildings with a beautiful towered church. Works began on the mission here in 1893 but were partially destroyed in a rebellion led by the Adouma, Ogooué-Lolo's major ethnic group, several years later. The Adouma resisted European incursions into their territory, and the mission's first attempt to make a home here in the 1880s was aborted after repeated attacks; it was only finally reinstated in the 1940s. The French administration received an equally frosty reception, being driven off in 1896, only returning to their post in 1909. Despite the fact that the rebellions continued, Lastoursville was then the most prominent town of the Ogooué-Lolo.

The leading figure of the Adouma revolts was Chief Wongo, a warrior who became the leader of protests against forced-labour requirements imposed by the French (page 6). In 1929 Wongo was captured and imprisoned by the French and subsequently deported to Bangui, Central African Republic; he was to die shortly after. Since 2004, Wongo's statue has enjoyed pride of place in Lastoursville's main roundabout.

Lastoursville is also known for its *grottes* (caves), carved into cliff sides at the edge of the forest above town. These are part of a vast subterranean world that spreads across the region, with nearly 35 caves identified over an area of 150km². Some of the oldest on the planet, most of these cavities were formed around 50 million years ago, and evidence of human activity in them, including the performance of sacred rites, has been dated as far back as 7,000 years ago. Stunningly, the caves remain a ritual site, playing host to Bwiti and other initiation ceremonies. In 2005, the Ministry of Culture and Arts proposed the caves for UNESCO World Heritage Status.

The most famous caves in this network are the Grotte de Kessipougou and the Grotte de Pahon, in which you can see traces of where prehistoric people prepared poisonous arrows and other hunting tools. The caves should ideally be visited in the dry season, and always with a guide. To find one, ask at the mission or the Hôtel Ngoombi (page 173). Pahon and several other caves (Lipopa 1, Lipopa 2 (also known as Missie), and Boukama) are all potentially within walking distance of town, while Lihouma and Kessipougou are further away (ask your guide about arranging transport). No matter which cave you plan to visit, wear boots with a good grip (preferably waterproof) and take a good torch, also waterproof. For more information, a team of speleologists surveyed the caves in 2015 and 2016 and published a detailed (French-language) account of their visit at w grottes-de-lastoursville.org. The Jean Lou Carnets de Voyages au Gabon website (w carnetsdevoyages.jeanlou.fr/Les_Grottes_du_GABON) is another excellent (French-language) resource on these and other caves in Gabon.

There are several **rapids** in the area, and a 140km stretch of the Ogooué upriver from Lastoursville has been recognised as a RAMSAR site since 2009, known as the Rapides de Mboungou, Badouma et Doumé. All these rapids in the area go a way towards accounting for the impressive navigational skill of the local piroguiers; it should not be too difficult to negotiate with one in Lastoursville if you wish to visit the Doumé rapids, which lie 30km upriver. These can also be reached by driving to the village of Doumé (✆ -0.8891, 12.9912), 50km from Lastoursville. Follow the N3 towards Moanda for 20km, then take a left-hand turn on to an unsurfaced road for a further 30km. Doumé is also home to a stop on the Transgabonais railway (page 66), but the trip by river is the most relaxing (and fun) option.

GABON ONLINE

For additional online content, articles, photos and more on Gabon, why not visit w bradtguides.com/gabon?

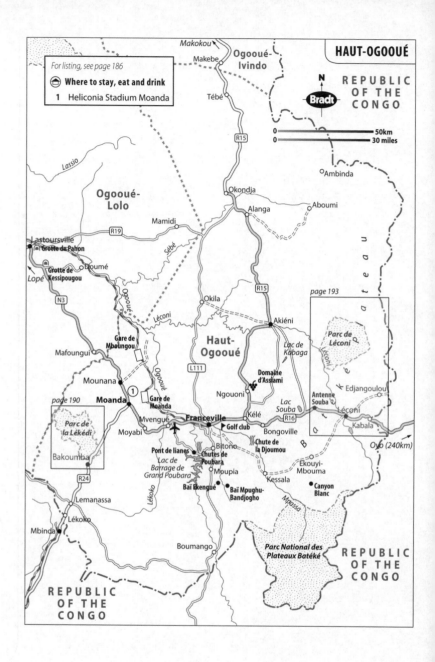

REPUBLIC OF THE CONGO

N

Bradt

| 0 | | 50km |
| 0 | | 30 miles |

For listing, see page 186

⊙ **Where to stay, eat and drink**

1   Heliconia Stadium Moanda

Makokou

Makebe

Ogooué-Ivindo

Tébé

Lassio

R15

○Ambinda

Ogooué-Lolo

Mamidi

Okondja

Alanga ○Aboumi

R19

Lastoursville
Grotte de Pahon

○Doumé

Sébé

R15

○Okila

Grotte de Kessipougou

Lopé

N3

Akiéni

page 193

Parc de Léconi

Léconi

Ogooué

Léconi

Haut-Ogooué

Lac de Kabaga

Gare de Mboungou

L111

Mafoungui

Ogooué

Domaine d'Assiami

Edjangoulou

Mounana

Antenne Souba

Léconi

① **Moanda**   Gare de Moanda

Ngouoni

Lac Souba

Kabala

page 190

Mvengué

Franceville   Kélé

R16

Oyo (240km)

Parc de la Lékédi

Moyabi

▶ Golf club

Bongoville

Bakoumba

Pont de lianes

Bitono

Chute de la Djoumou

R24

Lac de Barrage de Grand Poubara

Chutes de Poubara

Moupia

Ekouyi-Mbouma

Lemanassa

Baï Ekengué

Baï Mpughu-Bandjogho

Kessala

● Canyon Blanc

Lékoko

Lékoko

○Lékoko

Mpassa

Mbinda

Boumango

Parc National des Plateaux Batéké

REPUBLIC OF THE CONGO

REPUBLIC OF THE CONGO

10

Haut-Ogooué

Set in the far southeast corner of Gabon, the Haut-Ogooué (High Ogooué) province has historically been cut off from the rest of the country, so much so that it was even administered as a part of French Congo rather than French Gabon from 1925 to 1946. Even afterwards, it was to remain isolated from the other regions until the roads to Libreville and the airport (capable of taking jumbo jets) were built in the 1970s, followed by the Transgabonais railway and the Intercontinental Hotel in the 1980s.

The rich resources in the mining towns of Mounana and Moanda in the west of the region played an important role in ensuring that Franceville was brought closer to the capital, but arguably the most important factor was President Omar Bongo himself. Of all the peoples in the Haut-Ogooué – Ombaba, Bawoumbou, Banjabi and so on – the dominant group are the Batéké, the former president's people. Bongo hailed from Bongoville (originally named Lewai), a village lying between Franceville and Léconi. He was unceasingly committed to developing his region (and indeed today it's Gabon's second most populous, with some 250,000 Altogovéens in residence), but he never fulfilled his dream of transforming it into an important place on the international stage. The airport never handles international flights, and the (now former) Intercontinental is never full.

Nevertheless, the Haut-Ogooué remains well worth a visit, even if only to witness the stark contrast from the rest of Gabon. The capital Franceville is an excellent base for exploring the surrounding countryside, and the region's transport infrastructure is some of the best in the country. Poubara's waterfall and hand-woven liana bridge are a great source of Altogovéen pride, while the wide-open Batéké Plateaux in the southeast are a birder's paradise and a delightfully refreshing sight for forest-saturated eyes. Animal spotting is guaranteed in the Lékédi and Léconi parks, and the remote Léconi Canyons boast spectacularly eroded cliffs of pink, orange and black.

FRANCEVILLE

Franceville (often abbreviated as FCV in writing) is the capital of the Haut-Ogooué and the third largest town in the country, with a population of 110,000. It began life as Masuku (meaning waterfall), but its name was changed to Francheville by Savorgnan de Brazza in 1880 when he chose the site as a refuge for freed slaves.

> ### $ ATMS
>
> The only ATMs in Haut-Ogooué are in Franceville and Moanda, but there are several in both towns. Ecobank, BGFI, and BICIG are represented in Franceville, while BICIG, UGB, and BGFI are present in Moanda. Otherwise, the nearest alternatives are in Mouila or Lambaréné.

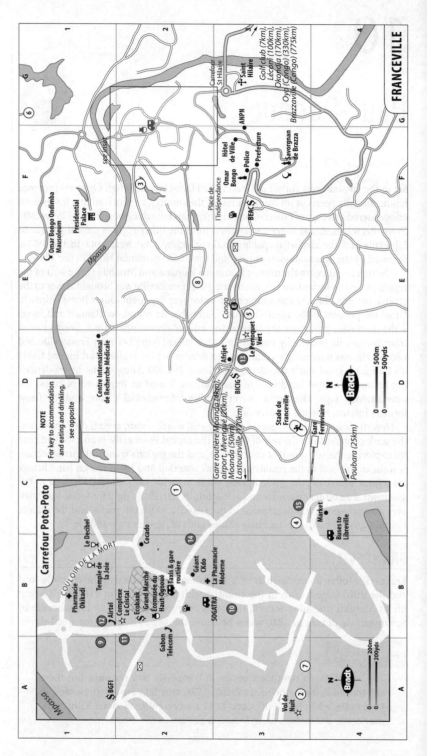

Carrefour Poto-Poto

Mpassa

COULOIR DE LA MORT
Pharmacie Okikadi
Temple de la Joie
Le Decibel
Cecado
Complexe Le Cristal
Airtel
Ecobank
Grand Marché
Écomusée du Haut-Ogooué
Gabon Telecom
Taxis & gare routière
Géant CKdo
SOGATRA
La Pharmacie Moderne
Vol de Nuit
Market
Buses to Libreville

BGFI

NOTE
For key to accommodation and eating and drinking, see opposite

Mpassa

Presidential Palace
Omar Bongo Ondimba Mausoleum

Centre International de Recherche Médicale

see inset

Carrefour St Hilaire
Saint Hilaire

Golf club (7km),
Léconi (100km),
Okondja (170km),
Oyo (Congo) (330km),
Brazzaville (Congo) (775km)

ANPN
Hôtel de Ville
Police
Prefecture
Place de l'Indépendance
Omar Bongo
BEAC
Savorgnan de Brazza

Afrijet
BICIG
Le Perroquet Vert

Congo

Stade de Franceville
Gare Ferroviaire

Gare routière Moanda (4km),
airport, Mvengue (20km),
Moanda (50km),
Lastoursville (170km)

Poubara (25km)

Buses to Libreville

0   200m
0   200yds

0   500m
0   500yds

Bradt

N

FRANCEVILLE

The French authorities wasted no time in amending this to Franceville, supposedly because of the region's likeness to certain parts of France.

Built over a series of hills and valleys, it can be quite difficult to get one's bearings here, although it helps to know that the Mpassa River cradles the town's northeastern shoulder. Much like other Gabonese towns, Franceville is a rather sprawling affair, and the closest thing to a town centre here is the bustling central market at Carrefour Poto-Poto or Potos (the streetsellers' roundabout) in the Mpassa Valley. The administrative centre (banks, airline agencies and post office) is on a hill to the south. The combination of green spaces between quartiers, pleasant hill views and friendly residents makes Franceville a widespread yet relaxed place to be.

Franceville's landmarks include the golden **statue of Omar Bongo** [178 F3] that stands in place de l'Indépendance, adjacent to the police station and government offices. There is also a **commemorative bust of Savorgnan de Brazza** [178 F3] (who seems to have lost his nose) just after the mosque as you leave the square behind you and head down the hill to Carrefour Poto-Poto. Architecturally speaking, the town's most interesting building is the church of **Saint Hilaire** [178 G3], which was founded in 1899. It's a vast red-tiled building with an improvised football pitch in front at the east end of town.

Also of interest is the **Centre International de Recherche Médicale** (CIRMF) [178 D1] (☎ 01 67 70 92/96/85; e lecirmfgabon@gmail.com; w cirmf. ga; ⏹ aidealasantepubliquerechercheformation), which accounts for the sizeable expat community in Franceville, for the most part French scientists. It was founded in 1979 by the Gabonese government with support from Total Gabon to study primates and apply these findings to help fight against diseases such as AIDS, ebola and malaria. It is the only facility of its type in equatorial Africa. The centre is active in the fields of Parasitology, Virology and Tropical Ecosystems. Visits here are possible, but only by advance arrangement; call or email to set up an appointment.

CIRMF has long hosted a primate centre with nearly 400 individuals, including chimpanzee, gorilla, mandrill, and vervet monkey, but is in the process of releasing these populations into wilderness reserves and national parks in partnership with the ANPN (page 88). The last three gorillas were released to the Fernan Vaz Gorilla Project (page 128) in 2013. More than 60 CIRMF mandrills have been released in Lékédi Park, and a management plan for future chimpanzee release is in development. The centre will continue to take in young primates orphaned by poaching, keeping them for a secure quarantine period before transferring them to other shelters.

Preparations for the Africa Cup of Nations (CAN), hosted by Gabon in 2012 (with Equatorial Guinea) and again in 2017, boosted construction activities in town. Next to the train station, the 35,000-seat Stade de Franceville was built for the occasion, and Gabon took home the CEMAC cup here in 2013. An associated programme of works on the roads, pavements and plumbing means Franceville is looking sharper today than it has for many years past.

10

GETTING THERE AND AROUND Afrijet (📞 02 00 90 01 (Libreville)/02 29 93 93 (Franceville); w flyafrijet.online; page 66) runs daily **flights** from Libreville to Mvengué, 20km west of town on a surfaced road, with two flights per week continuing on to Brazzaville in Congo. Count on 5,000CFA per person for a shared taxi between the airport and the centre of town. One-way tickets start at about 80,000CFA (but can and do go up in price) from Mvengué to either Libreville or Brazzaville. La Nationale (NRT) (📞06 66 90 86; e infos@nrtgabon.org; w nrtgabon. org; f NationaleRegionaleTransport; page 66) also serves Mvengué (from Libreville) four times weekly. Tropical Air (page 66) runs the same route twice per week. Snacks are available at the airport, and there's a nice terrace overlooking the landing strip.

Car rental is available at the airport from EGCA-SATRAM (📞01 72 23 68/70; e info@satram.ga; w satram.ga) and also from Gesparc (📞07 08 28 05), with 4×4s starting at around 100,000CFA a day.

There are six **trains** a week connecting Owendo (Libreville) and Franceville, departing from Owendo early evening and arriving in Franceville the next morning (see page 84 for details and prices).

By **road**, Libreville is a gruelling 750km overnight ride (vehicles often break for the night in Ndjolé) from Franceville via the N3, passing Lastoursville and Lopé en route. Driving in Haut-Ogooué is a breeze by Gabonese standards, with surfaced roads connecting Franceville to most major towns in the region: the route to Libreville is surfaced between Franceville and Mikouyi (190km), unsurfaced between Mikouyi and Alembé (300km), and surfaced once again between Alembé and Libreville (260km). Lampassa Voyage (m 07 05 35 14/06 83 84 62) runs daily buses on this route from the east end of town at 06.30 for 25,000CFA. They also serve Makokou via Okondja on Wednesdays and Saturdays (10hrs; 20,000CFA), also departing at 06.30 in either direction. Now that the road is surfaced, Sogatra (w sogatra.ga) also runs midday buses as far north as Okondja (170km) from Carrefour Poto-Poto. Heading towards Moanda, Sogatra buses run from Carrefour Poto-Poto, while other vehicles depart from the Gare Routière Moanda (⊕ -1.6362, 13.5386) at the far western edge of Franceville.

To get around Franceville, the usual **taxi** rates apply (page 68). The town's commercial centre around the Carrefour Poto-Poto is manageable, and best appreciated, **on foot**.

TOURIST INFORMATION ANPN [178 F3] has an office in town that is responsible for the Plateaux Batéké National Park, though in practice any trips here should be arranged with the office in Libreville (page 88) first.

For other trips, **Batrho Tour** (m 06 23 48 18/07 54 40 22; e batrhotour@yahoo.fr) is a Franceville-based agency that can arrange excursions throughout Haut-Ogooué, to anywhere mentioned in this chapter at a fixed price of 100,000CFA per person per day, including all transport, lodging, meals and guide fees.

WHERE TO STAY One of the few places in Gabon where you can find decent accommodation for under 20,000CFA a night, Franceville is home to a range of decent-to-good budget hotels.

Léconi Palace [178 G1] (formerly Intercontinental Hotel; 96 rooms) North of the city centre; 📞01 67 74 16/17/18. Once the most luxurious place to stay in Franceville, Léconi Palace doesn't deserve its 4 stars today. The rooms are comfortable enough (if dated) with satellite TV & large baths, but the service is minimal (perhaps unsurprisingly, as salaries are often delayed; recent years have seen several strikes). The hotel has a bar & nightclub, which is popular on Fri

There's now a good tarmac road (the R16) connecting Franceville to the Republic of the Congo and continuing on to Brazzaville and Ouésso (in different directions). Opened in 2014, it represents the first time the two countries have been linked by tarmac road. It's still not marked on most maps, but departs Gabon some 30km east of Léconi and continues a further 200km through Congo's Cuvette Department via Leketi, Okoyo, and Boundji (the latter two having basic guesthouses), and finally connecting to the N2 trunk road at Obouya, near Oyo.

Despite this being the most comfortable route between the two countries, the road traverses a great deal of sparsely populated territory, and transport options are slim indeed. In late 2018, we were advised that only one public vehicle was making the trip into Congo weekly, theoretically on Saturday mornings, but unscheduled private cars making the trip will often sell vacant seats – either ask around in Franceville or aim for Léconi and look for passing traffic there. If you plan to go this way, it would be wise to start asking about upcoming departures near the bus terminal in Franceville as soon as you get into town. It's also possible to do the journey in stages, hiring motorcycle taxis from one small town to the next.

Southwest of Franceville, there are also two laterite roads to Congo via either Bakoumba or Boumango, but don't expect much transport and self-drivers should use a 4×4. From Bakoumba, it's possible to continue for 45km to Lekoko (Gabon) and Mbinda (Congo), the terminal stop for a branch of the Chemin de fer Congo-Océan (Congo-Ocean Railway), which connects on to Pointe-Noire and Brazzaville. It supposedly runs about once a week, to no set schedule. Get your exit stamp in Bakoumba.

In Franceville, the Congolese Consulate [178 E3] (01 67 17 39; e consulatcgfcv@gmail.com) sits opposite the Hôtel Masuku and visa applications are possible.

& Sat nights. Non-guests can use the pool for a small fee. **$$$**

Residence Lyz'Aurore [178 E2] (36 rooms) Opposite the CIRMF turn-off; 02 59 22 52. In an unmissable green building with a popular resto-bar (**$$**) & large swimming pool (1,500CFA for non-guests) out front, this newish business hotel has modern AC rooms & apartments with balconies overlooking the city. **$$$**

Evoula Palace [178 A3] (50 rooms) Carrefour Léconi; m 06 45 46 19/07 75 87 83. Formerly known as the Beverly Hills, this place was fully remodelled for CAN 2017 & today is among town's smarter options. The restaurant has floor-to-ceiling windows overlooking a wide, green valley & rooms are modern with AC & satellite TV. There's a swanky nightspot attached, but the pool was out of service when we visited. **$$**

Hôtel Masuku [178 E3] (30 rooms) Close to pl de l'Indépendance; 02 05 30 00. Done up in purple & white, the retro-chic Masuku has been open for years & remains a reliable option. There is a large & well-maintained pool (1,500CFA for non-guests), surrounded by *paillottes* (grass huts) & overlooked by the terrace restaurant Le Masuku Plus (**$$**). **$$**

Hôtel Apily [178 F2] (25 rooms) Near the Mpassa River; 01 67 72 84; m 06 64 38 75/07 52 70 40; e hotelapily@yahoo.fr; w hotelapily. com. This well-kept & long-serving hotel offers comfortably equipped AC rooms in a quiet location across from the river & not far from the centre. There is a terrace bar-restaurant (**$$**). **$-$$**

Complexe Buké Buké [178 C2] (25 rooms; e ndounoujules@gmail.com; f Hôtel Buke-Buke Franceville) Along the Mpassa River, 400m from Carrefour Poto-Poto; m 06 24 52 86/07 29 55

40. This is an old favourite along the riverfront, with good-value AC rooms & a well-loved terrace restaurant overlooking the water (though the service leaves something to be desired). **$**

🏠 **Hotel La Djoue** [178 C3] (18 rooms) m 02 06 05 52/07 75 45 96. On the way to Carrefour St Hilaire, this is a fine budget option offering neat & trim cold-water rooms with AC & TV. There's a small sitting area with drinks available on site, but for food you'll have to go to the (good) Senegalese joint next door (see below). **$**

🏠 **Motel Le 40 Pieds** [178 A3] (26 rooms) m 07 72 46 46. Just downhill from the Evoula Palace, this is a rather grim-looking encampment of converted shipping containers on stilts. Rooms are small & feel quite jerry-built, but they nonetheless come with TV, AC & (supposedly) hot water for the price. No food or drink. **$**

✗ **WHERE TO EAT AND DRINK** There are a number of places to eat in the area surrounding Carrefour Poto-Poto, from roadside grills along the rue de la soif (also known for its nightlife, see below), to a few smarter sit-down options.

✗ **Africando** [178 B3] Carrefour Poto-Poto; m 06 95 22 61/03 00 10 11; ⏰ 09.00–midnight daily. This is a popular spot in the centre, serving pizzas, grills & beer, with mains starting at about 5,000CFA. **$$**

✳︎✗ **Complexe Buké Buké** [178 C2] On the riverbank; m 06 24 52 86/07 29 55 40. One of the best restaurants in town, serving excellent fish, gambas or steak, with fried bananas, French fries, papaya gratin or courgette gratin. Sun lunchtimes the tables are full of Franceville's expats. **$$**

✗ **Le Gourmet** [178 D3] ✆ 02 18 88 88; 🅕 Le Gourmet Restaurant-bar; ⏰ 11.00–23.00 daily. Though it's a little out of the way, this is a trim & comfortable resto-bar with a diverse menu stretching from grills & burgers to Lebanese specialties (& shisha pipes too). Mains *4,000– 8,000CFA*. **$$**

✗ **Le New Garage** [178 B2] Quartier Poto-Poto; m 06 61 33 88. Popular place to have a beer, a snack (sandwiches, pizzas, hamburgers) or a proper meal. It serves both local & European dishes & does grillades in the evening. The tables on the nice terrace look on to the hustle & bustle of the street. **$$**

✗ **La 5ième Dimension** [178 A1] Carrefour Poto-Poto; ✆ 01 21 65 72/98 66. May look a bit ramshackle from the street, but the food is good. It serves a bit of everything – salads, fish, steaks – but specialises in local dishes that include smoked chicken & saltfish. **$**

✳︎✗ **Les Délices de Masuku** [178 B1] Carrefour Poto-Poto; ✆ 02 21 66 19. A great place to have coffee & pastries in the morning. **$**

✳︎✗ **La Teranga** [178 C3] Towards Carrefour St Hilaire; m 07 34 35 32/02 68 99 53; ⏰ 07.00– 22.00 Mon–Sat. With a friendly proprietor & hearty Senegalese plates like *thiéboudiène* (stewed rice & fish), *mafé* (peanut sauce), & *yassa* (onion-lemon sauce) starting around 2,000CFA, this little place on the 1st floor next to Hotel La Djoue is a winner. **$**

🍷 **Au Bord de Mer** [178 A2] Carrefour Poto-Poto. Not only a lively bar playing a mixture of popular African & Western music, it also serves the best pizza in town. **$$**

ENTERTAINMENT AND NIGHTLIFE At night, la rue de la soif (Thirsty Street), also known (more ominously) as le couloir de la mort (Death Row), in Poto-Poto is where things happen. Past the market are *les maquis*, small bar-eateries that look like nothing during the day but are transformed by night, when doors and bottles are cracked and dozens of grills appear, perfuming the street with freshly grilled meats. Plenty of the bars here can't be bothered with stuffy formalities like names, but some better-known addresses include **Temple de la Joie** [178 B1] and **Le Decibel** [178 B1]. More established nightclubs can be found around the corner at **Complexe Le Cristal** [178 B2] (Quartier Poto-Poto, behind Airtel; m 06 67 06 70), or about 1km further from the centre at the stylish new **Vol de Nuit** [178 A3] (m 06 90 20 24; ⏰ 22.30–06.00) attached to the Evoula Palace hotel (page 181). Uphill from here, in the administrative quarter of town, **Le Perroquet Vert** [178 D3] (m 06 88 20 23; ⏰ 18.00–late daily) is another popular option.

Dedicated dancers should also check out the **Haut-Ogooué Salsa Social Club** (f HeliconiaSocialClub), which puts on salsa nights every Tuesday at Hôtel Masuku (page 181), as well as other one-off dance events in Franceville and Moanda.

OTHER PRACTICALITIES The best place to go **shopping** in town, whether for fresh produce or clothes, is the Grand Marché [178 B2] at Carrefour Poto-Poto, where West African and Lebanese sellers are in the majority. A large new market hall was being built here at the time of writing. There is also a massive Géant CKdo [178 B2] supermarket across the street.

The best **pharmacy** in town is La Pharmacie Moderne [178 B2], on the Carrefour Poto-Poto.

If you are looking for an **ATM**, Ecobank [178 B2] and BGFI [178 A1] both have agencies near Carrefour Poto-Poto, while BICIG [178 D3] is represented in the administrative quarter.

Franceville is also home to several petrol stations, a post office [178 E3], and agencies for both Airtel [178 B1] and Gabon Telecom (Libertis) [178 B2].

WHAT TO SEE AND DO The only real bespoke tourist attraction in town is the sorely neglected **Écomusée du Haut-Ogooué** [178 B2] (Haut-Ogooué Ecomuseum; m 07 15 09 60/02 69 06 67; ⊕ 08.00–15.30 Mon–Sat; entry 1,000CFA). The disorganised collections here run to a handful of dusty traditional crafts and a series of French-language informational panels on the region's ecology, with a few crafts for sale.

Though it's not open to casual visitors, the **Omar Bongo Ondimba Mausoleum** [178 E1] on the north side of the Mpassa was inaugurated here in 2014; the enormous white-marble complex boasts a mosque, church, library, and museum of the former president's personal effects. Ask around locally if you are particularly interested in getting inside.

Otherwise, there's a **golf club** [178 G3] (w fggolf.org) 8km from the city towards Léconi. It's also possible to use the **swimming pools** at a couple of the hotels in town (Léconi Palace, page 180; Masuku, page 181) for a small charge or the cost of a meal. Essentially, though, after a couple of good nights on the town, Franceville is best understood as a base for visits to the surrounding countryside and there is little in particular to detain visitors here for long.

Chutes de Poubara et Pont de lianes (Poubara waterfalls and liana bridge; ⊕ -1.7622, 13.5450; m 04 17 84 25/06 69 34 79/02 80 35 46; e site. touristiquepoubara@yahoo.fr; w moussikoue-jojo.e-monsite.com; f mypoubara. fr) These falls are essentially the emblems of the Haut-Ogooué region, and have been for many years. When Savorgnan de Brazza arrived in the Haut-Ogooué in the late 1870s, he and his companions were amazed at how developed the societies were, in particular in the spheres of agriculture and the building of bridges from liana vines.

Getting there and away The falls are about 25km south of Franceville, and **excursions** here can be organised by most of the larger hotels, or Franceville-based operator Batrho Tour (page 180). Alternatively, a local **taxi** will take you there and back (including waiting time) for a negotiable 25,000CFA.

Self-drivers have two possibilities: the most direct route starts from the Franceville's Gare Ferroviaire (train station), from where it follows the Boumango road for 18.5km. About 2.5km after passing through Bitono village, take the right-hand turning and continue for 7.5km until you reach Poubara. Though shorter, this route is unsurfaced and could require a 4x4 after rain; this can be organised by Batrho Tour (page 180) or hired from the airport (page 180).

Alternatively, the route via Mvengué is about 50km from Franceville overall, but it's all on surfaced roads, as this is the main access road for the Grand Poubara Dam (see below). Entering Mvengué from the main roundabout, keep right at the fork where you would otherwise enter the airport and continue for 27km.

What to see and do Today, both the bridge and the falls are well worth the entrance fee (5,000CFA per person). The bridge is 52.5m long and hangs 6m above fast-flowing water. It has to be replaced every year, a process that takes three months. The new bridge is built above the existing bridge, which is only cut down when it's time to start the whole process again. The result is that there are in fact two bridges, and crossing while the new bridge is in the early stages of construction can feel a bit precarious.

To get to the falls, turn right after the bridge, walk through the little village and follow the road up the hill. About halfway up there is a small track leading off to the right into the forest. From here it takes about 15 minutes to walk to the falls. Since 2016, there has been a stilted open-air restaurant next to the bridge, offering meals, drinks, and views over the river (**$$**).

Though it's not open to the public, the 160-megawatt **Barrage de Grand Poubara** (Grand Poubara Hydroelectric Dam) opened here in 2013; it sits just over 2km upstream from the liana bridge.

Baïs de Moupia Continuing south along the Boumango road, a set of two *baïs* (forest clearings) are accessible as a day trip from Franceville. **Baï Ekengué** (✪ -1.9049, 13.6424) and **Baï Mpughu-Bandjogho** (✪ -1.9224, 13.6780) are collectively known as the Baïs de Moupia, thanks to their (relative) proximity to Moupia village (✪ -1.817522, 13.605721).

The main turn-off (✪ -1.9194, 13.5885) for both baïs is 45km south of Franceville and 25km south of the turn-off for Poubara. From here, travel 5–10km east on unmaintained bush paths that certainly require a 4×4 and may even necessitate walking (come prepared with all supplies). As such, and even though the baïs aren't particularly far from the road, a guide is imperative. Fortunately, the cost of one is included in the entry fee (Baï Ekengué: 20,000CFA; Baï Mpughu-Bandjogho: 30,000CFA) levied in Moupia village. Batrho Tours (page 180) can also arrange trips here.

Known as a gathering place for elephant, the two baïs are infrequently visited, but are today home to a nascent ecotourism project managed by the **Association M'pughu-Bandjogo de Moupia** (m 07 88 67 48/06 65 38 48/07 11 73 38; e jmokokolipandi@yahoo.fr; **f** M'pughu-Bandjogho); they built a viewing platform here several years ago. For a detailed (French-language) trip report and photos, see **w** bit.ly/bais-de-moupia.

MOANDA

Nestled between two mountains, Mount Boudinga and Mount Moanda, is the bustling town of Moanda, with a population of about 60,000. More industrial centre than tourist attraction, Moanda is the manganese capital of Gabon and the third largest manganese producer in the world, after South Africa and Australia. As such, there are few (if any) true tourist attractions here, but there are plenty of services for travellers and the town has the energetic, bustling vibe of a successful

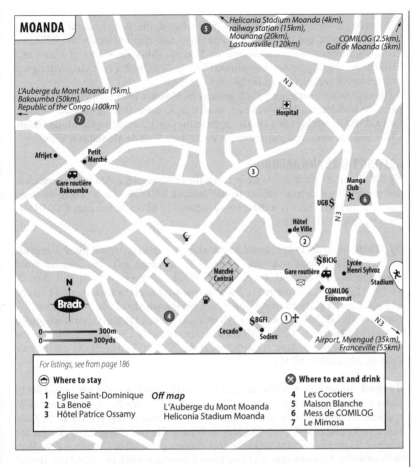

MOANDA

Heliconia Stadium Moanda (4km),
railway station (15km),
Mounana (20km),
Lastoursville (120km)

COMILOG (2.5km),
Golf de Moanda (5km)

N3

L'Auberge du Mont Moanda (5km),
Bakoumba (50km),
Republic of the Congo (100km)

7

Hospital

Afrijet ●   Petit
              Marché

Gare routière
Bakoumba

3

Manga
Club

6

UGB $

N3

Hôtel
de Ville

2

$ BICIG   Lycée
Gare routière   Henri Sylvoz

Marché
Central

COMILOG
Economat

Stadium

N

Bradt

4

0   300m
0   300yds

Cecado ● $ BGFI   1 ✝
            $
            Sodiex

N3

Airport, Mvengué (35km),
Franceville (55km)

For listings, see from page 186

🛏 **Where to stay**

1 Église Saint-Dominique   *Off map*
2 La Benoë   L'Auberge du Mont Moanda
3 Hôtel Patrice Ossamy   Heliconia Stadium Moanda

✖ **Where to eat and drink**

4 Les Cocotiers
5 Maison Blanche
6 Mess de COMILOG
7 Le Mimosa

commercial centre. The company that made it all happen here is the Compagnie Minière de l'Ogooué (COMILOG), a subsidiary of the French company Eramet, which has been mining manganese in the area since 1957.

COMILOG's offices perch symbolically on a hill above the town centre: it's clear that the company rules here, both economically and socially. It is the beating heart of the region and its influence is visible in every aspect of daily life. From infrastructure, public transport, shops and houses to schools, hospitals and churches, everything is owned and managed by them, and their logo is omnipresent. COMILOG is also responsible for the installation of the town's electricity and water grids, supplying these amenities to residents for free. The company's input into Moanda has even stretched to a nice, nine-hole golf course, managed by Le Manga Golf Club.

As part of the Emerging Gabon master plan (see box, page 14), the Gabonese government is encouraging the domestic processing of raw materials and subsequent export of high value-added products. For manganese this involves the promotion of 'downstream mineral processing' (the transformation of ore into semi-processed products). To this end, the €240 million Complexe Métallurgique de Moanda (Moanda Metallurgical Complex) opened here in 2015, enabling the local processing of manganese ore, which can now be converted into higher-value manganese metal and silico-manganese in Moanda rather than abroad.

Haut-Ogooué   MOANDA

10

In order to bridge the significant gap between the skilled labour needed at the new complex and the quality of education and training locally available, the École des Mines et de la Métallurgie de Moanda (Moanda School of Mines and Metallurgy; w e3mg.ga) was inaugurated here in 2016, with a curriculum designed to train senior technicians and engineers.

Though most people only stick around in Moanda long enough to fill up on petrol or withdraw cash, if you've got some time in town, there are several facilities for COMILOG workers that are also open to the public, including the **Manga Club**, where you can swim and play tennis, or the 18-hole **Golf de Moanda** (w fggolf.org).

GETTING THERE AND AROUND

By air There are daily flights from Libreville to Mvengué, 35km to the southeast. See page 180 for details. Expect to pay around 9,000CFA for a taxi to Moanda from the airport. There is technically an airstrip in Moanda, but only COMILOG charters (page 185) fly here.

By train Moanda is the penultimate stop on express trains from Libreville to Franceville, which run three times a week (page 84). The journey from Libreville to Moanda (60,500/53,000/39,500CFA Express VIP/1st/2nd class & 44,500/31,500CFA Omnibus 1st/2nd class) is scheduled to take about 12 hours, and you'll arrive early morning. The train from Franceville (5,000/4,000/3,000CFA Express VIP/1st/2nd class & 3,500/2,500CFA Omnibus 1st/2nd class) is scheduled to arrive in Moanda at 20.30. Moanda's train station is 15km out of town to the east, but you can buy your train tickets at the SETRAG office in the centre-ville (✆01 66 20 74/04 30 87 35).

By road To get between Moanda and **Franceville** requires a journey of just 50km along the surfaced N3, passing the largely defunct Africa No. 1 shortwave radio transmitters at Moyabi en route. Clandos and minibuses drop you off at the Gare Routière Moanda (✪ -1.6362, 13.5386) in **Franceville** and charge 2,000CFA for the journey. Sogatra buses also make the trip, dropping you off at Carrefour Poto-Poto in Franceville. **Lastoursville** is 120 surfaced kilometres north of Moanda on the N3 (2hrs; 4,000CFA), passing Mounana on the way. Clandos to here leave less frequently than those to Franceville. Moanda's main gare routière is at the southern end of town.

To get around Moanda, the usual **taxi** rates apply (page 68). The town's commercial centre around the gare routière and Marché Central is manageable, and best appreciated, **on foot**.

🏠 **WHERE TO STAY, EAT AND DRINK** *Map, page 185, unless otherwise stated*
In addition to the below, there are plenty of identikit resto-bar-clubs in the centre of Moanda – just follow your nose.

🏠 **L'Auberge du Mont Moanda** (7 rooms) 5mins from Moanda on the Bakoumba road (R24), in the village of Doumai; ✪ -1.5735, 13.1742; ✆02 21 36 00; 🄵 Mont Moanda Auberge-Restaurant. This charming rural hotel is beautifully decorated with Gabonese masks & paintings. Rooms are comfortable & carefully furnished, & it makes an ideal base to explore the region. The hotel organises tours to Lékédi,

Poubara & the Plateaux Batéké. Rate includes b/fast & Wi-Fi. **$$$**

🏠 **Heliconia Stadium Moanda** [map, page 176] (50 rooms) ✆03 31 58 27. Set next to the stadium 4km north of town, this is Moanda's most luxurious option. Built for CAN 2012 & renovated for the 2017 tournament, the business-oriented rooms here are comfortable if sterile, & there's a swimming pool & restaurant on site. **$$$**

🏠 **La Benoë** (20 rooms) Close to the Hôtel de Ville; 📞 01 66 20 24. Clean & well-maintained AC rooms. **$$**

🏠 **Hôtel Patrice Ossamy** (formerly Hôtel du Mont Boudinga) centre-ville; 📞 01 66 19 93. Large & well kept with en-suite facilities & AC as standard. Non-residents can use the swimming pool & children's playground at a small charge. There's a nightclub. **$$**

🏠 **Église Saint-Dominique** (10 rooms) centre-ville; 📱 07 38 14 77/06 79 96 60; 📧 diocesefcv@gmail.com/jeanpat518@gmail.com. Another cheap & convenient option with AC rooms. You can see the enormous roof of the church from afar. **$**

🍴 **Les Cocotiers** Quartier Fumier; 📱 06 04 30 45. Moanda's most upmarket restaurant located in a nice villa serves good grillades & pizzas. **$$$**

🍴 **Le Mimosa** Quartier Alliance; 📱 07 43 18 92. This is a popular address keeping long hours & serving barbecue pork & cold beer in the evenings. **$$**

🍴 **Maison Blanche** Situated on the N3. Tasty food in a nice environment. **$**

🍴 **Mess de COMILOG** In cité COMILOG; 📞 01 66 41 04. It won't surprise anyone that COMILOG also runs a restaurant, though it's a rather indifferent canteen. The attached **Manga Club** offers athletic facilities. **$**

OTHER PRACTICALITIES Thanks to its commercial importance, Moanda boasts better-than-average services for a town of its size. For banking, BICIG, UGB, and BGFI are all represented in town with ATMs. Packaged foods can be purchased at Cecado or the COMILOG Economat, and fruit and veg are readily available at the Marché Central.

MOUNANA

Moanda's twin mining town is Mounana, a smaller place of around 5,000 inhabitants. It lies 25km to the northwest on the N3. Mounana's equivalent of COMILOG was the Compagnie des Mines d'Uranium de Franceville (COMUF), a subsidiary of the French firm Areva, which was founded in 1958 to mine the local uranium deposits. It did so until a combination of factors – a decline in world demand, increased competition and, ultimately, much smaller yields – forced it to close in the late 1990s.

The town's population has been declining ever since, and its future remains somewhat uncertain, with few new sources of employment on the horizon. The land around Mounana and Moanda is fertile, however, and large-scale agricultural projects such as growing sugarcane, fruit and vegetables may provide some hope for the future.

According to local NGOs, though, radioactive residues from the mines have contaminated the area's waterways and soils, and continue to cause environmental and medical problems. They claim radioactive waste was poured directly into the river during the mine's first 15 years.

Aside from taking a wander around some of the **ruined COMUF facilities** like the old recreation centre and bar, there's little reason to linger in Mounana, but should you need to spend the night, the quality **Auberge du Lac** (📞 01 62 03 14; **$$**) is a beautifully located chalet at the lake, with 13 clean and attractive rooms and a good restaurant (**$$**).

BAKOUMBA AND PARC DE LA LÉKÉDI

Like everything in the small town of **Bakoumba** (population 4,000), the 13,000ha **Parc de la Lékédi** (Lékédi Park; 📱 04 28 51 90/07 58 14 48; 📧 sodepal@gmail.com; 🌐 parcdelalekedi.com; 📘 lekedi.parc) owes its conception and creation to the mining company COMILOG (page 185), which decided to set up the park in 1990. The park is just a 15-minute drive from Bakoumba itself, where visitors typically

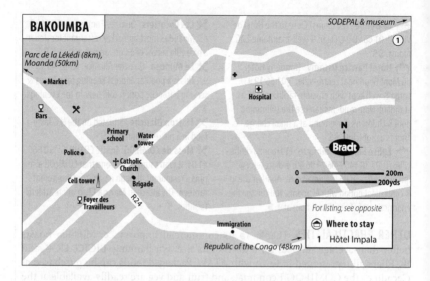

SODEPAL & museum

Parc de la Lékédi (8km),
Moanda (50km)

Market

Bars

Primary
school

Water
tower

Police

Catholic
Church

Cell tower

Brigade

Foyer des
Travailleurs

R24

Hospital

N

Bradt

0 ——————— 200m
0 ——————— 200yds

For listing, see opposite

⊖ **Where to stay**

1 Hôtel Impala

Immigration

Republic of the Congo (48km)

stay. Bakoumba is also the place to complete immigration formalities if you're headed to or from Mbinda in Congo (see the box on page 181 for details).

By 1959, COMILOG had started work on the construction of a 76km téléphérique (cableway) designed to transport manganese from Moanda to Mbinda in the Congo. From Mbinda a train carried the manganese to waiting boats at Pointe-Noire, but after just 30 years of operation the cableway (and its hundreds of workers) became redundant, due to the arrival of the Transgabonais railway in 1986. The manganese could now be directly transported to the Gabonese coast, which was obviously preferable. As Station F of the cableway and the location of the command and maintenance stations, the little town of Bakoumba was hit hard by the closure. As compensation and an alternative source of income, COMILOG created the Société d'Exploitation du Parc de la Lékédi (SODEPAL).

The first aim was to provide work for former COMILOG cableway employees, albeit at a reduced wage. The second was to breed animals for consumption: notably fish, antelope, buffalo and bush pigs. As part of this process, impala and ostrich were flown in from Namibia and three fisheries were set up. The third aim was to create a park where tourists could see animals, including primates, in a protected environment, and where eventually sports hunters could shoot animals on foot (primarily buffalo and antelope). Aside from the fish, the humid and hot climate did the newly imported animals no good: the ostriches all died and just a few brave impalas survived this hostile environment. Tourism itself never really got off the ground either.

Luckily for them, gold was found in the nearby mine of Bakoudou in 2008, and many of Bakoumba's inhabitants subsequently found jobs with Moroccan mining firm Managem. Bakoumba's ups and downs seem set to continue, however, as Managem was in discussions with the Gabonese government about wrapping up operations at the mine at the time of writing.

Today the most important functions of **Lékédi Park** are the fisheries and the protection and research of primates. Resident primates include a group of 120 habituated mandrills, several orphaned gorillas (three of which were released into the Plateaux Batéké National Park in 2017; page 191), and a number of chimpanzees living on an island in Lac Lékédi. Buffalo and antelope (including the occasional sitatunga) also roam the area. Lékédi is often sold as a park where visitors will certainly encounter the wildlife that is otherwise so difficult to spot. This is certainly true, as the animals simply cannot hide: the park is divided into three separately fenced modules (access is through 18 different gates – the main ones are mapped on page 190), which gives an impression of an enormous zoo. There is also a saddening compound where some red river hogs are kept.

VISITING THE PARK From **Moanda** (page 184), the park base at Bakoumba is just over an hour's drive away. The road is unsurfaced, but can still be tackled in a 2WD (though best to ask if it's rained recently before setting out). The Hôtel Impala (see below) offers transfers for 15,000CFA (Moanda) and 20,000CFA (Mvengué) per person. Alternatively, a clando from Moanda's Gare Routière Bakoumba to here costs 1,000CFA.

From Franceville, it's a 110km drive along mostly surfaced road, via Moanda.

Within the park, a 4×4 is required; it is not permitted to drive or walk in the park unguided, so if you come with your own vehicle you will be assigned a guide to accompany you (included in the excursion cost; for more information on excursions on offer and the costs of these, see page 190). Unfortunately, not all guides seem equally enthusiastic about their work or convinced of the need of wildlife conservation.

The park can be visited at any time, but the **best months** are probably May and June. In July and August, the park is much drier, but animal spotting can be somewhat trickier as they tend to spend more time in the forest. What's more, large groups of schoolchildren come for visits of up to three weeks during these months, funded by Total and COMILOG, so it can get rather crowded.

WHERE TO STAY, EAT AND DRINK Set 9km away from the park in Bakoumba, the **Hôtel Impala** [map, opposite] (m 04 28 51 90/07 58 14 48; f Hotel Impala Bakoumba; **$$**) is under the same management as Lékédi Park itself. It occupies buildings that were once the houses of COMILOG's foreign workers, plus its biggest maintenance and command stations. The buildings have changed little and are not particularly well maintained, which accounts for the hotel's dilapidated charm. However, the price/quality ratio is not bad for Gabonese standards: Lékédi is certainly the cheapest park to visit. The package price of 61,000CFA per person includes accommodation, full board and two excursions per day. For more information on these excursions, see page 190. Booked separately, there are six double rooms at 18,000CFA and ten bungalows sleeping four to six adults plus children for 36,000 to 50,000CFA. Rooms are spacious, more or less air conditioned and sparsely furnished. There is running (hot) water in the mornings and evenings. Meals are served under a paillotte overlooking the neglected swimming pool and tennis court. Breakfast is 3,500CFA; lunch or dinner 8,000CFA (**$$**). There is a huge bar where a beer will set you back 1,000CFA. Alternatively, there is no lack of bars and small eateries in town, including the popular **Foyer des Travailleurs**.

A little further (40km) from the park, and just 5 minutes from Moanda on the Moanda–Bakoumba (R24) road, lies **L'Auberge du Mont Moanda** (⊕ -1.5735, 13.1742; ✆ 02 21 36 00; f Mont Moanda Auberge-Restaurant; **$$$**; page 186) in the village of Doumai, which could make a more comfortable base for a trip to Lékédi, booked either directly through the park or through the Hôtel Impala.

WHAT TO SEE AND DO Module 1 is 650ha (entry gate: ⊕ -1.7987, 13.0200), Module 2 is 1,750ha (entry gate: ⊕ -1.7940, 12.9941) and Module 3 is a massive 11,600ha (entry gate: ⊕ -1.7675, 12.9571).

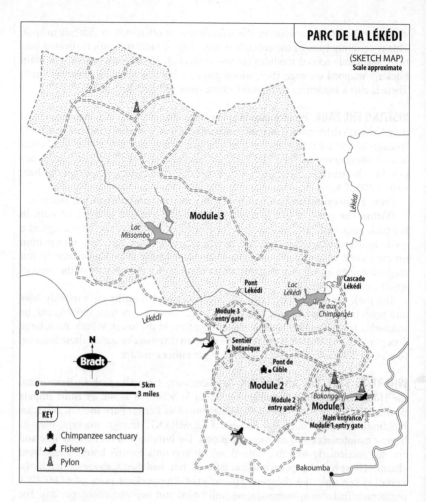

Module 3

Lac Missombo

Lékédi

Pont Lékédi

Lac Lékédi

Cascade Lékédi

Module 3 entry gate

Île aux Chimpanzés

Lékédi

Sentier botanique

N

Pont de Câble

Module 2

Lac Bakongo

Module 2 entry gate

Module 1

Main entrance/ Module 1 entry gate

0 ——————— 5km
0 ——————— 3 miles

Bakoumba

KEY

🐾 Chimpanzee sanctuary
🎣 Fishery
⛏ Pylon

All **excursions** must be arranged and paid for either at the park's main entry gate (⊕ -1.7987, 13.0200; ⊕ 06.00–18.00 daily), 9km from central Bakoumba and 1.4km from the main Moanda–Bakoumba (R24) road, reachable from a signposted turn-off at ⊕ -1.7972, 13.0295, or at the Hôtel Impala (page 189). They can also be arranged in advance by calling **m** 04 28 51 90/07 58 14 48. Visitors are offered a choice of excursions, and in two full days can go on four (two per day), which is about the right amount for really getting the measure of the park. Excursions are made on foot in the forest, by boat on one of the lakes, or 4×4 across the savannah. They cost 10,000CFA per person per activity, including park entry, guiding fees and transport from Bakoumba, and begin at 08.00 and 16.00. Visits can also be booked as part of a package with the Hotel Impala (page 189).

It's quite spectacular to see the group of 120 semi-wild mandrills frolic in the forest on a **mandrill-tracking excursion**, best done in the morning. The park's mandrill population was boosted through reintroduction. In 2003, an experimental group of 36 captive-born mandrills, previously kept at the nearby CMRF, was released into the reserve. The animals successfully mixed with a group of wild mandrills. Several have been radio-collared; they are constantly followed by researchers from the Mandrillus Project (w projetmandrillus.com), who collect data for a study into the social behaviour of the group.

Another exciting excursion involves crossing the thrilling **pont de câble** (cable bridge; ✪ -1.7844, 12.9786), which stretches for 365m above the forest canopy of the Mioula Valley. It is made up of ten cables, a direct attempt to re-use the skills of COMILOG workers in setting up the park. From this bridge you have a great view of the **chimpanzees** that roam the sanctuary below. Although visitors should be aware that some smart chimps have discovered how to access the bridge and use these skills to have a good look at the visiting tourists. In part because of their tendency to escape, after they reach a certain age these chimpanzees are moved from the sanctuary to the Île aux Chimpanzés (Chimpanzee Island; ✪ -1.7573, 12.9971) in Lac Lékédi. Boat safaris to see them weren't running at the time of writing, but may restart again in the future.

The park has long been home to a **gorilla rehabilitation project**, preparing orphaned gorillas for eventual reintroduction to the wild. To that end, three gorillas from Lékédi were released into the Plateaux Batéké National Park in 2017, with more reintroductions planned for the future. At the time of writing, the park was home to only one young orphan gorilla: Jojo, a victim of the bushmeat industry who can sometimes be seen in the sanctuary near the cable bridge.

Not far to the east of Lac Lékédi, the impressive **Cascade Lékédi** (Lékédi Waterfall; ✪ -1.7493, 13.0085) is accessible just outside the southeastern corner of Module 3. The forested descent to get here is steep, but a cable banister has been rigged up to help prevent skidding, especially likely in the rainy season. The hike is under 1km and takes roughly 30 minutes each way.

Finally, there is another atmospheric walk to be had at the 2km **sentier botanique** (Botanical Trail; ✪ -1.7761, 12.9650), where numerous species of trees and plants are labelled along the route. It was under renovation at the time of writing, but will hopefully be open by the time you read this.

Back in Bakoumba, you can also take a tour of the various SODEPAL activities taking place in the vicinity of the hotel, namely the vivarium, the mushroom project, the cane rat breeding centre and the small **museum**. If you're staying at the hotel, this tour does not count as one of your daily excursions, and there will be an additional fee if you wish to take it. The museum is in the former control room of the cableway, and displays various pictures of cableway equipment, bits of pottery found in the area and a couple of charts.

EAST OF FRANCEVILLE

Tucked away in the far southeastern corner of Gabon, as you head east from Franceville along the new road to Congo, is a landscape different from any other that the country has to offer. Spanning both Congo and Gabon, the Batéké Plateau is the source of the Ogooué River and the homeland of the Batéké, President Bongo's people. At the height of their power in the 11th century, the Batéké-led Anzico Kingdom was feared for their mythical deadly axes and famous for their distinctive raffia palm cloth. In 1880, Batéké king Makoko signed a treaty with Savorgnan de Brazza, placing his region under French protection (page 6).

Today, the area is sparsely populated and home to several natural attractions, including the spectacular eroded landforms of the Léconi Canyons, the savannahs of the privately administered Léconi Park, and the uninhabited and untamed Plateaux Batéké National Park, straddling the Congo border in the far southeast.

THE ROAD TO LÉCONI Leaving Franceville, the first settlement of any size you'll encounter is **Bongoville**, about 50km east of Franceville and halfway down the surfaced road to Léconi. Originally known as Lewai, Bongoville was renamed to honour President Omar Bongo, who was born here (as Albert-Bernard Bongo) in 1935. This small roadside village has benefited from the presidential connection with better-quality housing than neighbouring villages, a large stadium and the three-star **Heliconia Hôtel** (m 06 51 72 69/07 09 81 45/06 00 20 22; **$$**). Occassional clandos serve Bongoville (usually en route to Léconi) from Franceville (1hr; 2,000CFA).

Continuing east from here, you suddenly emerge from the forests, entering a landscape of endless, gently undulating plains of **open grassland**. The most remarkable feature of this new landscape is the almost total absence of trees. On the north side of the road as you exit Bongoville, the town cemetery offers fabulous views in both directions. The first 5 to 10km of this route is also renowned as a place to spot the black-headed bee-eater.

Before reaching Léconi (see below), the road passes through Souba, where **Lac Souba** (◈ -1.4773, 14.0808) – just over 10km down the small left turn before the Souba antenna – is worth a visit because of its amazing blue colour. It's possible to camp and fish here, but a 4×4 is essential. The equally scenic but rarely visited **Lac de Kabaga** (◈ -1.3486, 13.9328) sits some 25km further along the piste to Akiéni.

LÉCONI AND SURROUNDS The small town of Léconi (population 7,300) sits just east of its namesake Léconi River (home to a good spot for swimming; page 194). Though somewhat notable as being home to Andza, Gabon's only mineral water company, Léconi is above all a convenient base from which to visit the Léconi Canyons (eroded sand escarpments) and Léconi Park. It is also the last place of tourist interest before the border with Congo, and immigration and customs are based here.

Getting there and away Léconi is 100km east of Franceville along the R16, a good tarred road that continues into Congo (see box, page 181). For further information on what to see and do along this route, see above. Several clandos run between Franceville and Léconi daily (2hrs; 4,000CFA), leaving Léconi from the big tree on the main road by the turn-off to the Hôtel de Léconi. Alternatively, and if you don't have your own transport, you could contact the Léconi Park (via Hôtel de Léconi; page 194) to see if a lift would be possible from Franceville or Moanda (they can also arrange special transfers). There's an airstrip in Léconi, but no-one was flying here at the time of writing.

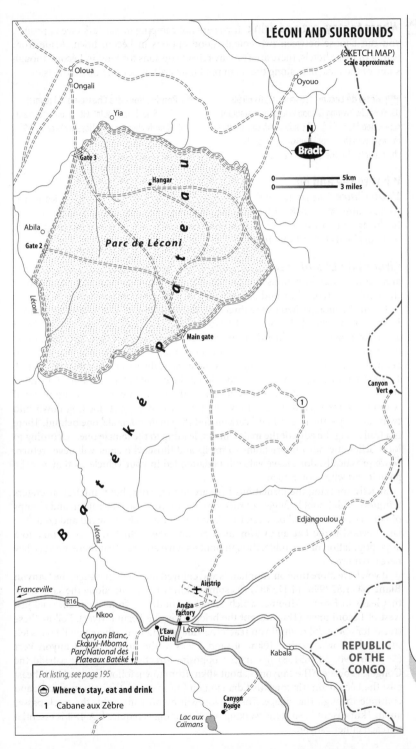

LÉCONI AND SURROUNDS

(SKETCH MAP)
Scale approximate

Oloua
Ongali
Oyouo
Yia

N
Bradt

0 ——— 5km
0 ——— 3 miles

Gate 3

Hangar

Abila
Gate 2

Parc de Léconi

Léconi

Main gate

B a t é k é   P l a t e a u

Canyon Vert

1

Edjangoulou

Léconi

Franceville
R16
Nkoo

Airstrip

Andza factory

L'Eau Claire
Léconi

Canyon Blanc,
Ekouyi-Mboma,
Parc National des
Plateaux Batéké

Kabala

REPUBLIC
OF THE
CONGO

For listing, see page 195

◉ **Where to stay, eat and drink**
1 Cabane aux Zèbre

Canyon Rouge

Lac aux
Caimans

10

🏠 **Where to stay, eat and drink** If you are not camping in the park (see opposite), you can choose between two equally good options in Léconi town. Aside from eating in these hotels, there aren't many reliable options for food in Léconi, though some of the local bars along the main road may grill something up on occasion.

🏠 **Hôtel de Léconi** (30 rooms) ☏ 01 69 90 03. Friendly, inviting & good value. The restaurant serves good food ($$). The hotel staff can arrange excursions to the Léconi Canyons, or a car & chauffeur to visit the general area. **$$**

🏠 **Rendez-Vous des Chasseurs** (4 rooms) m 07 96 48 48. Family hotel with good restaurant ($$). Slightly cheaper than Hôtel de Léconi. **$$**

What to see and do

L'Eau Claire The stretch of the Léconi River just west of Léconi itself is known as L'Eau Claire (◈ -1.58484, 14.24479) for its startlingly clear waters. The area just off the bridge into town makes a great spot to take a dip and is unsurprisingly popular with local kids for just that reason.

Cirques de Léconi (Léconi Canyons) There are three named canyons in the area, collectively known as the Léconi Canyons, and individually named after their colours (red, white and green).

By far the most visited of the three, the **Canyon Rouge** (also known as Canyon Rose or the Cirque de Lékoni; ◈ -1.6446, 14.2875) is easily accessible from Léconi and is fortunately said to be the prettiest of the three. It sits less than 10km southeast of Léconi town, though the last 5km are on a sandy track, so a 4×4 is required. To get here, drive 5km towards Congo and take the right-hand turning at ◈ -1.6147, 14.2902, continuing for another 3.5km. It may be useful to have a guide in the rainy season (just ask at your hotel). After 3.5km, the track emerges at the lip of a cliff without warning (so drive carefully), and you'll find yourself looking down into twin canyons – the larger 'male' canyon and the smaller 'female' one behind. There is a trail along the edge of the male canyon, leading to the female one. According to local belief, the canyons are home to spirits and those who enter will never return. More prosaically, don't leave valuables unattended in your vehicle, as they may be gone if and when you return.

Strictly speaking the formations here are not canyons, but semicircular craters (*cirques*), with knobbly fingers of rock poking up from the crater floor, and clumps of tall trees interspersed between them. At sunset the rocks glow red and gold. The lake beyond is the **Lac aux Caïmans** (Caiman Lake), which was once home to a large population of crocodile, though hunters have ensured that there are very few here anymore.

If you have more time on your hands and enjoyed the Canyon Rouge, the **Canyon Blanc** (◈ -1.828996, 14.175383) sits some 35km from Léconi along the sand track that leads to Ekouyi-Mboma, which branches southwest from the main road just west of Léconi town (1km west of the bridge over the Léconi River). Follow these tracks for about 25km until you reach the village of Léwou, where you'll take a left turn and follow a further 10km of sand tracks to the canyon. The **Canyon Vert** (◈ -1.369390, 14.465108) lies in the opposite direction, sitting just astride the Congolese border. The canyon is about 40km from town; follow the track northeast past the Léconi airstrip towards Edjangoulou (more or less the halfway point), and continue through the village. The canyon will be on your right; the track passes about 1km east of it, so some walking or off-roading is required. A 4×4 is essential to reach either canyon.

PARC DE LÉCONI About 20km north of Léconi town, Léconi Park is a private reserve that was founded in 1997 and is administered by the Société des Plateaux Bateké (SPB; m 07 15 14 81; e spb.direction@gmail.com; w parcdeleconi.ga; f parcdeleconi). It covers some 28,000ha, of which 70% is grass savannah and 30% scattered patches of rainforest. For many visitors, the open and undulating savannah scenery is its greatest attraction (and a jarring contrast to much of Gabon). Moreover, in a single afternoon you are almost guaranteed to see zebra, oryx, eland, great kudu, impala and springbok. All of these animals were originally imported from Namibia, but today most are born in the park (the 14 original oryx, for example, have now given rise to a population of over 300). There are also populations of jackal, civet and bush pig, but these typically require a bit of luck to spot. A couple of days spent camping in the park is the best way to take advantage of the beautiful landscape and serenity. The pistes, or tracks, are colour-coded to make driving around easier.

Visiting the park The park can be visited year-round, but a particularly good time to visit is June, when the new grass is shooting through the charred ground left by the annual savannah fires, and the animals are out. From October to January the orchids are in flower on the plateau.

The **main entry gate** (⊕ -1.423335, 14.280871) sits 18km north of Léconi, reachable from a left-hand turning on the Edjangoulou road after the Andza bottled water factory and just before you reach the airport. Visitors to the park can use their own car, with or without a park driver/guide, but the sandy roads must be taken with care and a bit of skill. If you don't have your own vehicle, **driving safaris** are easily arranged with the Hôtel de Léconi (see opposite); they have several safari vehicles and driver-guides with experience in the park.

The **entry charge** is 5,000CFA per person and hiring a car and driver costs an additional 15,000CFA. Drivers should be tipped at the end.

To **camp** in the park (in designated areas) costs 5,000CFA per tent, plus 5,000CFA per car. You can also spend the night at the rustic bamboo-built **Cabane aux Zèbre** (Zebra Cabin; ⊕ -1.3469, 14.3239) where you'll find barbecue facilities, firewood and a cooker, along with a shower and mattresses. The cost is 15,000CFA per night (**$$**). Book a stay by calling SPB (see above), or just turn up. Take a sleeping bag and all provisions – bear in mind that food shopping is best done in Franceville, before arriving in Léconi.

PARC NATIONAL DES PLATEAUX BATÉKÉ The uninhabited southern part of the Batéké Plateau, along the Congolese border, has been designated as the 205,000ha Plateaux Batéké National Park because of its beautiful rolling savannah landscape and its exceptional bird diversity.

Practically speaking, Plateaux Batéké is not set up for casual visitors, but if you'd like to try and arrange a trip (10,000/5,000CFA daily entry for foreigners/residents), contact the ANPN (page 88) well in advance to make arrangements. As for getting to the park itself, the tiny village of Ekouyi-Mbouma (⊕ -1.7922, 14.0644) is the jumping-off point for access, from where it is a rough 30km ride south in a 4×4 across sand to the *embarcadère* (pirogue launch; ⊕ -1.9767, 14.0043), followed by a 3-hour pirogue trip along the Mpassa. This leads to the Aspinall Foundation's **Projet Protection des Gorilles** (Gorilla Protection Project; w aspinallfoundation.org), which acclimatises young gorillas to live in the wild, in areas with no remaining wild populations, through a reintroduction programme. They have reintroduced more than 60 western lowland gorillas since they began operations in both Gabon and Congo in the 1990s, with more than 30 new babies born to returnees in the wild since then.

Birders travel to the park to see open-country species including Stanley bustard, Congo moor chat, Angola batis, black-collared bulbul, black-chinned weaver, Finsch's francolin and 'téké cisticola' (the latter two species are found only here on the Batéké Plateau). Huge flocks of storks also migrate through the area.

The **grasslands**, found all over the park, are the only place in Gabon to see the rare Grimm's duiker and there is also buffalo, antelope, elephant, gorilla and chimpanzee. These animals appear in low numbers, though researchers have returned encouraging results in recent years. Sightings include **spotted hyena** captured on camera traps in 2017 – the first time since the 1990s – and even a solitary lion (also the first to be seen here in two decades) that has been resident in the park since 2015, making him quite literally Gabon's one and only **lion**. Discussions on introducing a potential mate and re-establishing a local lion population in the park are ongoing.

The November 2018 declaration of a new national park just across the border in Congo is another hopeful sign for Plateaux Batéké; the 350,000ha Ogooué-Leketi National Park will further strengthen wildlife protection in and around the new transboundary protected area, which now covers more than half a million hectares.

OKONDJA

Set along the road between Franceville and Makokou to the north, the only reason you're likely to end up in the deep forest town of Okondja (population 10,800) is if you're travelling between the two.

The recent surfacing of the road to Franceville has opened up access to what has long been one of Gabon's most isolated towns. There's now a midday Sogatra bus covering the 170km from Franceville in the south (page 206) to Okondja. Continuing north from here, the 260km road to Makokou remains unsurfaced and can be difficult; ask around in town for transport headed this way.

The array of services on offer here can be rather limited, but petrol is available, and both Cecado and Gaboprix supermarkets are represented. To spend the night, try either the **Mission Catholique Christ Roi d'Okondja ($)** or the **Auberge des Miniers** (↘07 80 61 99; **$**).

There's not much in the way of sightseeing to be done in Okondja itself, but if you've got some time in town, the ponts de liane (vine bridges; ✪ -0.5691, 13.8383 & -0.5779, 13.8497) along the Sébé River in Ambinda village (sometimes mapped as Lekadouba) are 25km away and would make a worthwhile day trip. It's 21km on a rough road to get here, reachable from an eastbound turning 4km south of Okondja. For a full trip report, see w bit.ly/ponts-de-liane.

11

Ogooué-Ivindo

Set in the country's far northeast, Ogooué-Ivindo is Gabon's largest province by area, but its second least populous, counting barely 63,000 Ogivins, spread out over an area of 46,000km². It is traversed by the Ogooué and Ivindo rivers, as well as the N3 and N4 main roads. The regional capital is the small town of Makokou, which sprawls along the banks of the Ivindo. East of the river, the N4 passes through a clutch of diminutive villages before arriving in Mékambo, the furthest town before the road splits and deteriorates rapidly on its way to the Congolese border. Away from the roads, the region is largely inaccessible and uninhabited, except for forest-based Baka communities (often referred to as 'Pygmies'; see box, page 17) living along the length of the Ivindo, and the gold panners sifting through the small streams around the Nouna River. The other peoples living in the province are mostly Fang, Kwélé and Kota, all of whom largely live a subsistence lifestyle, growing, fishing and hunting their food.

There are promising iron deposits around Mont Bélinga that the government is eager to develop, but several years of low global ore prices mean a suitable investor is yet to be found. The environmental consequences of mining in this area – one of the country's richest in terms of flora and fauna – could be profound.

Indeed, so uniquely rich is the environment here that Ogooué-Ivindo includes no fewer than three national parks. Thanks to a direct train connection, the enchanting Lopé National Park is very accessible for tourists: from those in search of the little-known Dja River warbler or rare species of orchid, to those interested in mandrill tracking or a 'gorilla experience'. Southwest of Makokou is Ivindo National Park, home to the impressive Koungou, Migouli and Djidji falls, and the famous Langoué Baï, brought to public attention by Dr Mike Fay's Megatransect (page 28); today it is among the preeminent wildlife-viewing destinations in the country. Continuing east from Makokou, between the Lodié and Louayé rivers, is the nearly inaccessible Mwagna National Park, known for its baï which is among the largest in the country. Mwagna and its surrounding forests represent one of Africa's last frontiers, almost uninhabited. As such, it is an area of pristine rainforest, full of elephants, birds, monkeys and other wildlife.

PARC NATIONAL DE LA LOPÉ

Lopé National Park is a vast expanse totalling 485,000ha. Bordered by the majestic Ogooué to the north, the Offoué to the east, the du Chaillu Mountains in the south and the Mingoué River to the west, more than 1,500 plant species have been recorded here, of which 40 represent new species for Gabon. Lopé is also home to 412 of the 700 species of birds recorded in the country, including seven kinds of hornbill, three forest kingfishers and the vulnerable grey-necked picathartes. The largest known wild primate gathering – 1,350 mandrills in one great foraging group

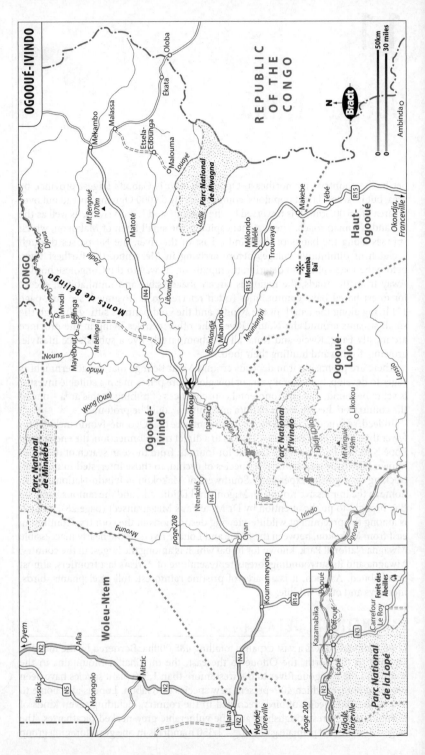

– was recorded here in 1996. Mandrills are particularly visible in the dry season (Jul–Aug), when they hang around in the north of the reserve for up to two weeks at a time. No-one knows why they gather in such large groups.

Besides mandrill, there are large gorilla and chimpanzee populations. The Station d'Études des Gorilles et Chimpanzés (Centre for Gorilla and Chimpanzee Studies; SEGC), co-managed by CIRMF and CWS, has made Lopé well known in the scientific field.

The first thing to strike you as you arrive at Lopé is the dramatic patchwork landscape of open savannah and dense rainforest. The explanation for this landscape lies in the last ice cap in northern Europe, 18,000 years ago (page 25), when the cooler, drier climate caused great stretches of tropical rainforest to disappear. When the Ice Age ended about 12,000 years ago, the forest recolonised the open savannah. The forest that you find in Lopé, therefore, is relatively young compared with some of Gabon's truly ancient forests. There are still areas of savannah along the northern and eastern borders of the reserve, which have survived because here the average annual rainfall is just 1,500mm – insufficient for the forest to take root. The Lopé region has one of the driest climates in Gabon and therefore the most fragile rainforest.

Another reason for the survival of Lopé's savannah areas is down to humans. Archaeological findings including early Stone-Age pebble tools, Stone-Age arrowheads and Iron Age petroglyphs indicate that people have been present in the Ogooué Valley for 400,000 years. Lopé is one of the oldest archaeological sites in Africa and remains of numerous prehistoric villages are still visible on savannah hilltops. It is likely that fire was a key tool for these early inhabitants to control their environment and that by regularly burning the savannah areas, the encroachment of the forest was stalled. Burning is still used each dry season by the Ministère des Eaux et Forêts (page 104) to ensure that the limits between forest and savannah are maintained.

It's thanks to its unique archaeological and natural landscape that Lopé and its surrounding areas – the Écosystème et paysage culturel relique de Lopé-Okanda (Ecosystem and Relict Cultural Landscape of Lopé-Okanda; w pmlope.org; 🛐) – was recognised as a UNESCO World Heritage Site in 2007.

WHEN TO VISIT The park (and the Lopé Hôtel; page 202) is open all year, but the best time to visit to see wildlife and plants in flower is during the rainy season (Feb–May & Oct–Nov). At this time of year, animals are easier to track if you are on foot in the forest and there is more to see if you are on a game drive in the savannah. Mandrill can now be tracked between May and December. For a detailed chart of more than 20 activities and their optimal timings, see w pmlope.org/accueil/infos-pratiques, and for information on excursions, see page 204.

GETTING THERE AND AWAY Thanks to its proximity to the Transgabonais railway line, Lopé is one of the easier national parks to get to. There is also a small landing strip just across from the Lopé Hôtel, but it was out of service at the time of writing.

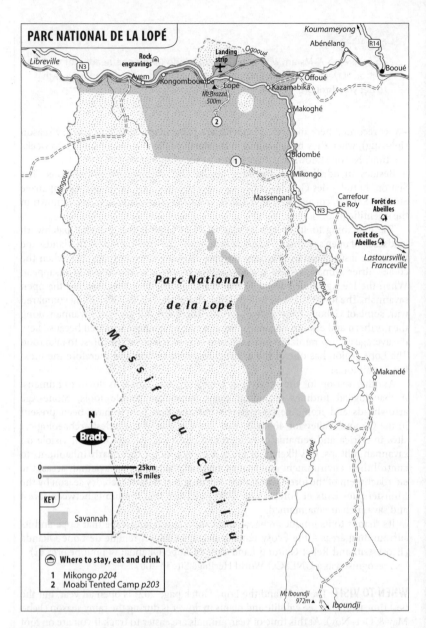

PARC NATIONAL DE LA LOPÉ

Koumameyong
Abénélang   R14
Libreville   N3   Boooué
        Ayem   Kongomboumba   Landing   *Ogooué*
                               strip
        Rock   Lopé   Offoué
        engravings   Mt Brazzd   Kazamabika
                        500m
                                    Makoghé
                            (2)
                            Bidombé
                            (1)
                            Mikongo
                    Massengani   Carrefour   **Forêt des**
                                      Le Roy   **Abeilles**
                                         N3
                                              Forêt des
                                              Abeilles

                                              Lastoursville,
                                              Franceville

Parc National

de la Lopé

                                                    Makandé

N

Bradt

0 ————————— 25km
0 ————————— 15 miles

KEY

    Savannah

⌖ **Where to stay, eat and drink**
1 Mikongo *p204*
2 Moabi Tented Camp *p203*

                                        Mt Iboundji
                                        972m ▲ *Iboundji*

By train Though the **Transgabonais railway** is by far the easiest way to reach the park, all trains run at night, which is a shame as the landscape is amazing. A daytime tourist train was proposed in 2019, though it wasn't yet running at the time this book went to print – see the box on page 85 for further details.

Trains to Lopé leave **Libreville** six times a week at 17.30 (30,000/26,000/19,000CFA Express VIP/1st/2nd class & 22,000/15,000CFACFA Omnibus 1st/2nd class) and take roughly 8 hours, arriving in Lopé at any time from 01.30 (see page 84 for further details); trains coming from **Franceville**

(35,000/31,000/23,000CFA Express VIP/1st/2nd class & 26,000/18,000CFA Omnibus 1st/2nd class) depart at about 17.00, arriving in Lopé after 6 hours at around 23.00; keep in mind delays are very common in either direction.

To reach the regional capital, **Makokou**, you can pick up the Transgabonais for the short hop to Booué (1 stop on the Express train/2 on the Omnibus; 1hr; 4,500CFA/3,600CFA), from where there's road transport covering the 195km to Makokou (page 206).

GETTING BETWEEN LOPÉ AND IVINDO

Though it seems like the logical next step if you were looking to park-hop around the country, continuing on from Lopé to Ivindo National Park is, like so many things in Gabon, not as simple as one might hope, and lack of transport and difficult timings make this something of an awkward journey.

The 'best' way to do this is to pick up the **Transgabonais** for the journey between Lopé and Booué (1 stop on the Express; 5,000/4,500/3,300CFA VIP/1st/2nd class, or 2 stops on the Omnibus; 3,600/2,500CFA 1st/2nd class; 1hr). Once in Booué, the next step depends on where in Ivindo you're heading.

Booué itself (or the nearby Gare d'Ivindo) is the jumping-off point for trips to Langoué Baï; for the Chutes de Koungou and surrounds you need to aim for Makokou first. Daily minibuses cover the road to Makokou, departing from Booué's railway station at around dawn and taking 4–5 hours. Whichever way you're headed, you can break your journey at the surprisingly decent **Hotel Splendeur de l'Equateur** (200m west of the railway station; **$**), which has air-conditioned and fan rooms and a restaurant ($).

Night departures can make this a rather bleary-eyed trip, with eastbound trains officially running from Lopé to Booué between 01.00 and 02.00 (although in reality they are often much later). As such, doing the journey in reverse may be more pleasant, with westbound trains officially covering this stretch between 22.00 and 23.00 (although the caveats about punctuality still apply).

Going **by road**, you can also theoretically backtrack the 105km from Lopé to Alembé on the N2 and look for onward road transport towards Makokou there, but transport on this route is very rare indeed, and vehicles passing are likely to be full (the latter also applies when you get to Alembé), so we don't recommend it.

Finally, if you have your own 4x4, there is a thoroughly scenic and little-used route between Lopé and Booué, departing the N3 10km east of Lopé village at Kazamabika (✛ -0.1201, 11.6955). It continues for 60km from here, crossing a bridge over the Offoué River and branching to the right after about 11km, just before Offoué village (✛ -0.1013, 11.7760; which is also home to a stop on the Transgabonais). From here, it follows a rough and winding 4x4 track through uninhabited forest and savannah until re-emerging along the shores of the Ogooué opposite Booué (✛ -0.1146, 11.9489), where there is, at least in theory, a car ferry that can take you across to Booué and the river's north bank. Note well, however, that the ferry is renowned for being out of service for months at a time, so be sure to ask for the latest conditions in Lopé if you're considering this route. For an excellent trip report (in French), see: **w** carnetsdevoyages.jeanlou.fr/La_Piste_OFFOUE/.

The night departures (leaving Lopé between 01.00 and 02.00) can make this a tiring journey; it would be a bit more pleasant to travel in the opposite direction, from Booué to Lopé, as this runs between 22.00 and 23.00.

If you book your stay with Lopé Hôtel or its annex (see below), a car will meet you at the station (included in the price of your stay). The same car will drop you here around 01.30 on the morning of your departure – regardless of the direction of your train. Otherwise, nothing in Lopé village is more than 1km from the station.

By road The 365km drive **from Libreville** to Lopé takes around 8 hours in a 4×4. The road is currently surfaced for the first 260km to Alembé, but the remaining 105km of N3 are poorly maintained laterite and slow going. Owing to the difficult conditions on the last stretch of road, the majority of visitors without their own 4×4 arrive in Lopé by train (page 200).

Before reaching Bifoun, the road passes numerous villages punctuated with makeshift stalls of old oil drums displaying coconuts, bananas and palm wine, along with dead monkeys suspended from poles by their tails. There are occasional restaurants en route, on the left-hand side of the road as you drive through Ekouk, for example, but the best place to stop for a breather is probably the halfway point, Ndjolé (page 148). From here to Lopé there are occasionally stunning views of the river.

Be careful on the Ndjolé–Alembé stretch, particularly after dark. The twisting, turning road and the impatience of logging trucks heading for an overnight stop at Ndjolé accounts for a high number of vehicles run off the road here.

GETTING AROUND It is not permitted to drive or walk in the park unguided. All treks, game drives and pirogue trips must be arranged and paid for at the Lopé Hôtel (see below), or in advance via a travel agent (see opposite).

WHERE TO STAY, EAT AND DRINK With the exception of Mikongo Vision (for information on staying here, see page 204), which operates its own facility 50km to the southeast, and the new Moabi Tented Camp, all park lodging is in Lopé village. Barely 2km from the park's entry gate, this is where all activities originate. If Mbeyi Motel (see opposite) is out of your budget, there are also a couple of cases de passage in town. **Motel Lopé Okanda** (m 07 55 51 09/06 51 19 52; $) sits about 200m east of the railway station, and there's another on the main road through town. There's not much to choose between them, and both have rooms for around 10,000CFA. There are a few **shops** selling tinned food and local restaurants on the village's main drag, and some small bars at the train station.

Accommodation and tour options within the park itself are soon set to expand when Gabon Wildlife Camps by ANPN opens the Moabi Tented Camp (see opposite), which will be located deep within the park.

Lopé Hôtel [map, opposite] (25 rooms) m 07 44 68 11/06 33 37 35; e hotellope@yahoo. fr; f LHGabon. Perched on a bend of the Ogooué River west of Lopé village, this long-serving hotel is the undisputed hub of tourism in Lopé. It enjoys a magnificent location, with stunning views of the river, best enjoyed from the swimming-pool terrace or the restaurants & chalets 9B & 10B. All the comfortable chalets have AC & hot water. To save energy, power is off from 09.00 to 17.00, when most guests will be on safari or relaxing at the pool. Good (though pricey; $$$–$$$$) meals are served in an open-sided restaurant-bar overlooking the water, where some board games are available if you get tired of the view (unlikely). There were plans to introduce overnight tented camping trips in 2019; ask at the hotel & check w bradtupdates.com/gabon to see if this has moved forward. The hotel also has a booking office in Libreville (page 89). *62,000/65,000CFA*

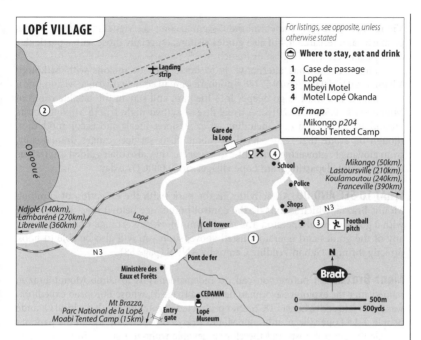

For listings, see opposite, unless otherwise stated

🏠 **Where to stay, eat and drink**

1 Case de passage
2 Lopé
3 Mbeyi Motel
4 Motel Lopé Okanda

Off map
Mikongo *p204*
Moabi Tented Camp

LOPÉ VILLAGE

Landing strip

Ogooué

Gare de la Lopé

School

Police

Shops

N3

Football pitch

Mikongo (50km), Lastoursville (210km), Koulamoutou (240km), Franceville (390km)

Ndjolé (140km), Lambaréné (270km), Libreville (360km)

Lopé

N3

Cell tower

Ministère des Eaux et Forêts

Pont de fer

CEDAMM

Mt Brazza, Parc National de la Lopé, Moabi Tented Camp (15km)

Entry gate

Lopé Museum

N

Bradt

0 ——— 500m
0 ——— 500yds

---

sgl/dbl standard chalet; 70,000/73,000CFA sgl/dbl superior; 105,000/108,000CFA sgl/dbl junior suite; 110,000/113,000CFA sgl/dbl VIP suite, all rates B&B & inc transfer from the train station. Discounts may be possible for multi-day direct bookings. **$$$**

🏠 **Mbeyi Motel** [map, above] (10 rooms) N3, centre-ville; m 07 47 18 18. A cheaper option is Lopé Hôtel's annex, the Mbeyi Motel. It's set in the heart of Lopé village, & although the view is not as spectacular, the comfort level is good & there's a considerable difference in price & a good attached restaurant (**$$**). Park excursions & transfers to

& from the train station (5,000CFA for a round trip) are carried out by the hotel, where motel guests can also swim for an additional 3,000CFA. *35,000/40,000/55,000CFA standard/superior/ suite.* **$$**

⛺ **Moabi Tented Camp** [map, page 200] (5 tents) On a hilltop in the northern half of the park; m 04 41 65 69; e info@gabonwildlifecamps. com; w gabonwildlifecamps.com. This camp should be open by the time you read this. Expect comfortably equipped standing tents with private ablutions, & an associated range of hikes & activities originating in the camp. **$$$$**

CHOOSING AND BOOKING YOUR SAFARI As of early 2019, visitors could choose between two **safari companies**, but with the imminent arrival of Gabon Wildlife Camps by ANPN (page 88), you should have three options by the time you read this (see w bradtupdates.com/gabon for updates). The biggest part of the market is in the hands of the **Lopé Hôtel** (see opposite), which charges 30,000CFA for a full day (with one morning and one afternoon excursion), or 20,000CFA for a half day (one excursion). All excursions take place in the north of the park. Morning excursions start at 07.30, returning around 11.00. The afternoon excursion runs from 16.00 to 19.00. The guides that work with the Lopé Hôtel receive mixed reports. While some obviously have a passion for wildlife and love to share their knowledge on the park and its inhabitants, others mistake big rocks for elephants. The English-speaking **Remy Nkombe** (m 02 26 03 83/07 05 49 26; e nkomberemy. tour@yahoo.fr; w nkomberemytour.simplesite.com; f nkomberemy.tourgabon) is recommended for his knowledge and professionalism. Holding a PhD in ecology,

11

Vianet Mihindou (e vianet.mihindu7@gmail.com; f vianet.mihindou) works primarily as a researcher, but also guides visitors, especially those with a particular ecological interest, in English or French.

A more adventurous alternative is to book your excursions with **Mikongo Vision** (m 07 74 03 97/06 79 57 69; e ndjibadi@gmail.com; w mikongo-vision.info), especially if you want to go deeper into the park and stay in the satellite camp of Mikongo (⊕ -0.3065, 11.7018). A usual three-day/two-night trip to Mikongo costs around 107,000CFA a day, including all excursions, meals and accommodation, though be aware that reader feedback about their services ranges dramatically, from glowing to glowering, with little in between. They also offer guided excursions (see opposite), departing from Lopé village, for 50,000CFA a day.

WHAT TO SEE AND DO All activities in the park (with the exception of climbing Mount Brazza, which is outside the control points; see below) must be arranged with a guide or local operator. The most common way to arrange visits is through any of the guides and operators listed above; soon you will also be able to book directly through Gabon Wildlife Camps by ANPN (page 88).

Mont Brazza
An outing you can do independently is to climb Mount Brazza, named after the explorer Savorgnan de Brazza (page 5), whose European expedition was the first to arrive here in 1875, after protracted negotiations with the local Okandé people. Like Lopé village, although Mount Brazza is technically within the park, it's outside the control posts and therefore accessible without a guide. To reach it, just follow the N3 southwest from the village to the base of the mountain.

Alternatively, the Lopé Hôtel will take you by car and provide a guide for the price of a standard excursion (page 203). Other local guides (page 203) will be happy to do the same.

The actual ascent isn't especially strenuous, taking about an hour to the antenna at the top. The climb is best done in the afternoon, when you've got a higher chance of enjoying expansive views over the Ogooué and the forest-savannah patchwork of the park below. (Mornings often find the summit shrouded in mist.) The pond at the foot of the mountain attracts numerous **birds**.

Safari game drives and forest walks
The turn-off to the park entrance is just a few minutes' drive from the Lopé Hôtel. The wooden houses immediately to the right are lived in by the employees of the Ministère des Eaux et Forêts and their families. Just beyond on the left are some beds of orchids and the small **Lopé Museum**, exhibiting findings from the prehistoric sites and information about the flora and fauna. The Wildlife Conservation Society's training centre, the Complexe Educatif Dr Alphonse Mackanga Missandzou (CEDAMM), is also located here.

The designated 4x4 safari route largely sticks to the savannah, with brief forays into patches of forest, where an exploration on foot is possible. The horizon backdrop alternates between mountains and forest. August and September is the time when elephant, buffalo, sitatunga, monkey and gorilla are most visible. Take some binoculars so that you can identify between the groups of mangabeys, putty-nosed monkeys and moustached monkeys that you will no doubt see crashing through the treetops.

Mandrill tracking
The newest activity at Lopé is mandrill tracking and this is one of the only places in the world where it is possible. Visitors can now join researchers based in Lopé village, who have tagged several members of a 1,000-strong troupe

on a tracking mission, conducted in 4×4s and on foot. Contact the ANPN (page 88) well in advance to make arrangements. You can also contact the tracking project directly (m 02 63 07 03; e mandrill.lope.anpn@gmail.com). The morning journey (150,000CFA per person; departing from Lopé village) requires several stops to put up the radio antenna and triangulate their location, and makes for an utterly thrilling encounter when you finally meet.

Rock art In addition to its natural riches, Lopé is the location of several of Gabon's most important archaeological sites. About 15km (40mins) downriver by motorised pirogue from the Lopé Hôtel (where this excursion can be arranged), Kongomboumba is the landing point for a walking tour of rock engravings that attest to man's presence here in the Iron Age (2200–1800BC).

Once on the river, you can really appreciate the strength of the majestic Ogooué, where an experienced captain is essential. The river seems calm but is nonetheless merciless; the simple memorial to a French army officer next to the swimming pool is proof. He went swimming in the waters in front of the hotel and drowned; his body was never found. According to staff, the seemingly feminine rock in front of the hotel could be partly responsible, as it's believed to be a mermaid.

Found in a small savannah area of great beauty on the banks of the Ogooué, the reason for the engravings is difficult to guess at, although it's possible that they, and the hollows carved in some of the rocks, have a sacred significance. Of the 1,500 rock engravings discovered in and around the reserve between 1987 and 1993, three-quarters are **abstract and symbolic designs**. The concentric circular designs in particular, also found elsewhere in Africa, are typically Bantu. **Animal representations** account for 8% of the engravings, although none of the carvings here are of large mammals, such as elephant and buffalo, which feature so prominently in the archaeological finds of southern Africa. Engravings of drying civet hides probably point to their importance in the Bwiti initiation ceremony (see box, page 18), while the significance of lizards is less clear, but probably somehow linked to mystical beliefs. Weapons and tools account for 6% of the engravings.

Mikongo Mikongo was established 20-odd years ago as both a gorilla research station and a tourist camp (see opposite). Conditions here today are quite basic (one might even say run down), but it still functions as a satellite camp in Lopé National Park, even if research no longer takes place here. It's so deep in the forest you needn't even leave camp to see a fair amount of animal and birdlife (or be eaten alive by insects). Trees tower over the tents and the noises of the jungle are louder than ever.

Mikongo Vision will **transfer** you to Mikongo in a 4×4, a journey that takes about 2 hours from Lopé, and potentially a lot longer during or after heavy rain. The route travels 40km south, along the N3, where banana and manioc plantations can be seen alongside the terracotta-red laterite road that snakes through the grassy savannah, making for a really scenic drive. After crossing the Obidi River you'll take a right into the bush for a bumpy and slippery 10km drive on an old forestry road. If the vegetation hasn't been cut back for a while – it needs to be cropped about twice a month – then you'll be crashing through the undergrowth, a fitting beginning to your arrival deep in the forest.

If you have time for only one full day's trekking and want to make the most of every minute, you can arrange for a guide to meet the car just before you arrive. You'll end up approaching the camp on foot after an easy introductory walk of about 1½ hours through fairly light and open marantatia forest. A perfect ending to a sweaty trek is to bathe in the river below camp (black leopard are sometimes seen here).

Excursions from camp come in the form of **walks**; tourists are taken into the forest in the hope of seeing primates, forest elephants and birds. The wildlife is exactly that, wild, so sightings can be sporadic, although keen birdwatchers will be interested to know that there are seven known nesting sites for the rare picatharte rock-fowl within reach of camp. This gawky, timid bird is habitat-specific, favouring large, leaning rocks near small rivers. As, at any given time, you're likely to be the only people at the camp, routes can be totally personalised to suit the individual or group.

A lot of the tourists who come here are primarily interested in **gorillas**, but habituation is a labour- and funding-intensive activity requiring daily contact with the animals, and programmes were no longer running in 2019. Thus, gorilla sightings, while not uncommon, cannot be relied upon in the same way that they now can be at Yatouga in Loango National Park (page 133) or Doussala in Moukalaba-Doudou. Nonetheless, Mikongo Vision rightfully stresses the broader appeal of the forest and offers a genuine wilderness experience.

MAKOKOU

Makokou (sometimes abbreviated as MKK) is a small town on the banks of the Ivindo; the Bouinandjé and Liboumba rivers join it here. With just 21,000 inhabitants it's the smallest of Gabon's nine regional capitals and, unsurprisingly, there's not much in the way of an established tourist infrastructure. Still, you could easily while away a day or two here, relaxing after an excursion into nearby Ivindo National Park. The usual services are present (post, petrol and nightclubs, primarily, although there are no ATMs), but the real attractions, of course, lie outside town.

GETTING THERE AND AROUND There's an airstrip in Makokou but no-one was flying here at the time of writing.

To drive the 630km **from Libreville** to Makokou takes at least 10 hours – if you have a 4×4. It's all tarmac until Ovan, and a deeply corrugated dirt road for the last 100km. Take particular care crossing the bridges. Buses cover this route daily (10–12hrs; 17,000CFA), travelling between the PK8 in Libreville and the gare routière in central Makokou.

Alternatively, it may be preferable to travel by train from Libreville to **Booué** (for more information on rail travel, see page 66), where you can hop on a minibus to cover the remaining 195km to Makokou (4hrs). FIGET/Gabon Right Routes (page 209) can arrange a private car to bring you from Booué station to your hotel in Makokou for 100,000CFA.

Travellers coming **from Franceville** should head north on the newly surfaced 170km road to Okondja (page 196), where you may want to spend the night and break up the trip, as it's a rough onward journey along 260km of dirt (4×4 only).

Lampassa Voyage (m 07 05 35 14/06 83 84 62) runs vehicles between Makokou and Franceville via Okondja on Wednesdays and Saturdays (10hrs; 20,000CFA), departing at 06.30 in either direction. Now that the road is surfaced, Sogatra (w sogatra.ga) also runs midday buses as far as Okondja.

Like many Gabonese towns, Makokou is a sprawling affair, and as such you may want to grab a **taxi** from time to time. You shouldn't pay more than 1,000–2,000CFA for a chartered trip across town.

WHERE TO STAY, EAT AND DRINK Makokou has a couple of reasonably priced, pleasant hotels, a mission and at least one good restaurant.

🏠 **Hôtel Belinga Palace** (25 rooms) centre-ville; m 07 62 18 28. Long-serving hotel with spacious rooms & AC. The staff went on strike in 2017 over non-payment of wages, but the situation seems to have been resolved since then. There's a restaurant ($$). **$$**

🏠 **Hôtel Wamy Residences** (15 rooms) Quartier Espassendje; m 07 24 44 28/07 66 00 38/06 23 63 31; e lajorita@yahoo.fr; 📱. The AC rooms here are colourful, well kept, & probably the newest in town. *17,000 dbl.* **$$**

🏠 **Paroisse Notre-Dame des Victoires** (10 rooms) centre-ville. Simple visitors' rooms in a compound overlooking the Ivindo River on the west bank of the river. **$**

✖️ **Pao Rosa** centre-ville; m 07 50 23 61/06 68 08 21; 📱 Le Bar Restaurant Pao-Rosa Makokou. This is undoubtedly the best place to eat, serving Gabonese favourites for b/fast, lunch & dinner. A good meal has its price, though. **$$$**

☆ **Complexe Minkebe** Near the Trésor public; 📞04 84 87 27; 📱. With disco lights & drinks aplenty, this is the happening spot for a night out in Makokou.

WHAT TO SEE AND DO Makokou has not traditionally been a tourist haunt and almost all visitors here are on their way to Ivindo National Park. Nonetheless, it's a calm and (unsurprisingly) green city, with plenty of views over the Ivindo River to be had. There are a handful of colonial-era buildings scattered around town, many in some stage of disrepair. The most notable is probably the mid-century **Cathédrale Notre-Dame des Victoires**, built from heavy laterite stones along the east bank of the Ivindo. Beyond having a wander through Makokou's meandering streets and chatting to the townsfolk, the best way to spend a day here is to get out on the **river**. It is relatively easy to find a *piroguier* in Makokou willing to head upriver, easier in fact than it is to head downriver, as the waters are wide and calm to the north, with none of the rapids that are found to the south. The chief of the remote fishing village of **Mayébout** (✪ 1.1143, 13.1112), some 100km up the Ivindo from here, is happy for visitors to set up camp in his village and go walking in the surrounding forest (but be sure to ask for him when you arrive!).

PARC NATIONAL D'IVINDO

Traversed in the north by the black waters of the Ivindo River – the Ogooué's largest tributary – and by the little-explored Djidji (Dilo) and Langoué rivers to the south, the 300,000ha of Ivindo National Park are among Gabon's wildest and most spectacular. Southwest of Makokou, the Ivindo's strikingly dark, tannic waters widen and break up into a labyrinth of channels and rapids flowing around hundreds of rocky islets, culminating in the phenomenal display of the **Chutes de Koungou** (Koungou Falls): a complex of waterfalls nearly 2km wide, broken up into four levels and three separate sets of cascades. These impressive falls, with a drop of over 50m, are the highest in equatorial Africa and of great spiritual value to local people. Intensely vegetated islands dot the river here, with some as small as individual trees that seem to grow directly out of the falls.

Several years ago, Koungou Falls were threatened by the proposed construction of a hydroelectric dam to supply power for iron ore mining at Bélinga, some 100km upstream. Had it been fully constructed, the dam would have flooded large areas of forest, risking the displacement of local communities and opening up the park to increased poaching and illegal logging. A successful pressure campaign saw the project shelved in 2009.

A pirogue trip (arranged with FIGET; page 209) through the forest to the Koungou Falls provides an exhilarating introduction to the wilderness, with plenty of opportunities to glimpse birds, monkeys and hippos (see box, page 210). More than 430 species of bird, including large concentrations of African grey parrots, are recorded as living in the Ivindo Basin, making it one of the most rewarding bird-spotting regions in Africa. Indeed, more than 350 species have been recorded in the area immediately surrounding the IRET research station alone. Underwater, the Ivindo's ichthyological fauna changes significantly above and below the falls, as most fish are unable to cross the natural barrier formed by the rapids.

Further downstream, near the park's western border, the wide and dramatic **Chutes de Migouli** (Migouli Falls; ✛ 0.2228, 12.3606) see the Ivindo drop 43m and the powerful **Chutes de Djidji (Dilo)** (Djidji (Dilo) Falls; ✛ 0.0111, 12.4484) crash for 60m; both waterfalls are difficult to access and see precious few visitors – contact FIGET (see opposite) if you'd like to be one of them.

The park includes the 10,000ha **Ipassa Reserve**, one of Africa's first protected areas, located directly southwest of Makokou and recognised as an Important Bird Area since 2001. Incredibly, logging has never been allowed in the Ipassa

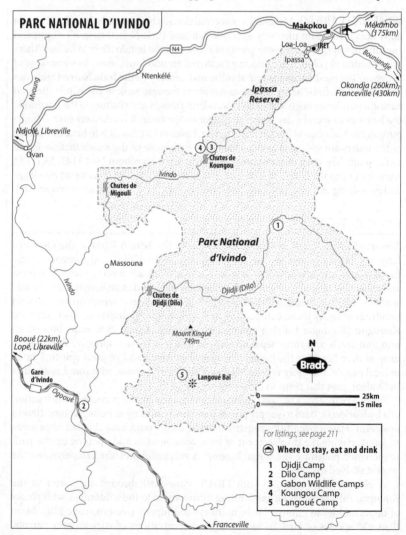

PARC NATIONAL D'IVINDO

For listings, see page 211

🍽 **Where to stay, eat and drink**

1 Djidji Camp
2 Dilo Camp
3 Gabon Wildlife Camps
4 Koungou Camp
5 Langoué Camp

Reserve (though hunting remains an issue). The Institute for Research in Tropical Ecology (IRET) has been here since the early 1970s, and at its peak there were 100 researchers. Research still continues today, but on a much smaller scale.

Around 50km south of the Koungou Falls (as the crow flies) is **Langoué Baï** (✪ -0.1872, 12.5597), a place of unparalleled beauty. The baï, which is the Pygmy word for forest clearing, is approximately 1km by 300m wide. It was brought to public attention in 2000 by biologist Mike Fay during his epic Megatransect (page 28) and now houses the Langoué Baï camp, established by the Wildlife Conservation Society, which monitors wildlife in the park. Langoué Baï's mineral waters lure animals, above all elephants, out from under the cover of the forest to feed on the nourishing saline soil. The elephants keep the baï clear and maintained by digging in its mineral-rich soils, creating a magnet for gorilla and other mammals, including sitatunga, red river hog, buffalo, monkey and mangabey. Along with the habituated population in Loango (page 133), the baï is the most reliable place in Gabon to see gorilla, and chances are highest in the dry season (Dec–Jan & May–Jul). There is now an observation tower overlooking the baï, where visitors have commanding views over the surroundings; it's possible to contact FIGET (see below) and arrange to spend the night here.

Outside of the park, FIGET also arranges trips to the little-known **Momba Baï** (✪ 0.0272, 13.4234), lost deep in the forests some 25km to the west of the Makokou–Okondja (R15) road. See w gabonrightroutes.org/en/itineraries/momba-bai for details on how to visit.

TOUR OPERATORS Created in May 2000 upon request of the Gabonese government, the **Fondation Internationale du Gabon pour l'Eco Tourisme** (FIGET; now also marketed as **Gabon Right Routes**; m 07 90 55 13/06 06 82 47/06 07 56 80; e okoui_joseph@yahoo.fr/info@gabonrightroutes.org; w gabonrightroutes.org) is the only organisation that's authorised to organise tours in the park. You can contact Dr Joseph Okouyi Okouyi at FIGET directly (see above) or book your stay via any of the travel agencies in Libreville (page 88). **Gabon Wildlife Camps** (page 88) may soon begin arranging trips here as well, when they open their planned camp in the park.

A typical three-day/two-night trip to the Koungou Falls costs 320,000/220,000/180,000CFA per person for groups of one/two/three to six, including excursions. Park entry costs an additional 5,000CFA per person. Shorter, longer, and custom trips can also be arranged, and die-hard completists (those in good physical condition, anyway) can cross the entire park by foot and pirogue, taking in both the Koungou Falls and Langoué Baï, in nine days (800,000/650,000/550,000/450,000CFA pp for groups of one/two/three/four to six). A fuller set of pre-planned itineraries can be found at w gabonrightroutes. org/en/itineraries.

HOW TO VISIT Depending on whether you're aiming for the Koungou Falls or Langoué Baï, there are two different modes of access from opposite sides of the park; both are arranged through FIGET (see above). The Koungou Falls (✪ 0.2894, 12.5743) are reached by pirogue from the IRET research station's pier in Loa-Loa, a little fishing village 12km south of Makokou. Theoretically you could quite easily arrange a taxi or pirogue to get to the dock, but as you are only allowed into the park when you're on a tour accompanied by FIGET guides, FIGET will likely pick you up at your hotel in Makokou. Trips to Koungou Falls usually last three days, including two visits to the falls themselves, as well as hiking in the

A PIROGUE EXPEDITION TO KOUNGOU CAMP AND THE KOUNGOU FALLS

Stuart Jarvis (w stujarvis.com)

At the Ipassa ranger station near the frontier town of Makokou, I boarded a long and narrow motorised pirogue, along with three rangers, ready to embark on a three-day expedition downriver to the Koungou Falls. The initial part of the journey took us to Koungou Camp, adjacent to the falls; over the course of around 3 hours I sat, mesmerised by the vista of the wide dark-brown Ivindo River, which cut the only navigable path through impenetrable flanks of thick, verdant forest.

The journey was not without hazard. On occasion, the river entered the shallows, where its pace quickened dramatically, rushing between large protruding boulders. There were nervous looks on the rangers' faces as our boatman picked a zig-zag course through narrow channels, avoiding the rougher white waters. There were odd glancing blows and scrapes, and we took on a little water, but nothing that we couldn't bail out again; furthermore, nothing capsized us or cracked the hull of the pirogue, which was our main concern.

Koungou Camp is an array of a dozen simple, yet very substantial, wooden huts, nestled beneath the high forest canopy. Adjacent to the camp is a small promontory, from where you can view the falls. Here, the calm waters of the Ivindo burst to life, cascading over grassy slopes and sheer drops. Relentlessly, the water tumbled over the edge, creating a collage of frothy white tumult.

Later that afternoon, the rangers led a walk out of camp. Over the course of a few hours, we picked our way along forgotten forest tracks, before emerging at the foot of the falls. Only there could I start to appreciate their width and incessant power. One of the rangers took to a pirogue to, very successfully, catch fresh fish for dinner.

Day two consisted of a much longer walk: down to the foot of the smaller falls, back into the pirogue to cross the river and then up to the head of the larger falls (Bouila N'a Ngonde). The latter part of the route was completely encased in vines and virtually impenetrable. The rangers hacked through jungle so dense it clad even the uneven rocks beneath our feet.

The roar of the larger falls grew louder until we emerged at their head. They were fairly typical in their form, with water pouring over precipices on three sides before being slammed in a swirling cauldron far below. We all sat, taking in a spectacle that only nature can provide.

With our appetite for the brutish falls sated, we slowly retreated to the camp. The third (and final) day of the expedition took us back upriver.

---

surrounding forests. Journey times are 4 to 5 hours' sailing downriver on day one, and 5 to 6 hours upstream back to Makokou on day three.

Langoué Baï, on the other hand, is most directly accessed from Booué or Gare d'Ivindo (Ivindo station; ◉ -0.1973, 12.1992) on the Transgabonais railway line. From Ivindo station it's 40km as the crow flies to the baï, a distance that FIGET covers using a combination of pirogue, 4×4, quad bike, and foot power, with a possible stop at Dilo Camp on the way out or back.

The Migouli and Djidji (Dilo) falls are infrequently visited, but custom trips here can be planned in consultation with FIGET.

WHERE TO STAY, EAT AND DRINK *Map, page 208*

There are several rustic camps in and around the park. These largely consist of a few wooden cabins with terrace and shared or private bathroom, although no electricity or hot water (or often just a river shower). All accommodation must be arranged through FIGET (page 209). All the camps are very similar – which one you stay in depends purely on which excursions you want to take. For more information on the cost of staying here, see page 209.

Inside the park, **Koungou Camp** sits adjacent to the Chutes de Koungou, **Langoué Camp** is roughly 3km from Langoué Baï, and **Djidji Camp** is a basic bivouac site along the Djidji (Dilo) River.

Outside the park to the west, **Dilo Camp** sits next to a Transgabonais rail bridge and overlooks the confluence of the Djidji (Dilo) and Ogooué rivers.

The **meals** provided at all three camps are simple (rice, beans, potatoes and fish), but tasty and filling.

At the time this guide went to print, Gabon Wildlife Camps (page 88) was in the process of developing camps at several sites in Ivindo. Upmarket tented camps at both Langoué Baï and the Chutes de Koungou were planned for 2020, with a potential further outpost at the Chutes de Djidji (Dilo) to be developed after that. Once open, these will be by far the most upmarket options in the park, offering comfortably equipped standing tents with private hot-water ablutions and commanding views.

MÉKAMBO

If you brave the unsurfaced N4 for 175km east of Makokou, you'll wind up 740km from Libreville in one of Gabon's most isolated towns: **Mékambo**. (You'll also pass just south of Gabon's highest peak, **Mont Bengoué** (◉ 0.9544, 13.6860; 1,070m), after about 140km.) Nicknamed 'Meroe' locally, Mékambo is a typically sprawling and sleepy Gabonese town of 7,000, set along the Zadié River. The built-up area follows a handful of meandering earthen roads, and the town sits surrounded on all sides by the incredibly dense forests typical of Ogooué-Ivindo. Short of simply having a penchant for the faraway, there aren't many reasons why you'd end up out here, but the languorous tropical vibe is enjoyable enough, and there's some pretty mid-century brick architecture to be seen, including a **hospital** and the **Notre-Dame-du-Rosaire Cathedral**, which dates to the 1950s.

In travel terms, Mékambo is something of a dead end, with few **transport** options beyond vehicles shuttling back and forth to Makokou (6hrs; 7,000CFA). Would-be overlanders should note that both routes continuing into Congo from here (towards either Ékata or Mazingo) are in detestable condition (with the Mazingo route reportedly completely impassable). This is not a practical route across the border unless you've got your own 4×4 and some considerable skills using it. (See the following trip report on the Ékata route if you think we're being overdramatic: **w** bit.ly/gabon-ekata.) If you do attempt this route, immigration formalities are completed in Mékambo.

Mékambo is also the theoretical jumping-off point for the profoundly remote **Parc National de Mwagna** (Mwagna National Park), but this 115,500ha park is largely inaccessible and there is currently no tourist development planned for this little-known region. Regardless, the closest road access to the park is approximately 55km south of Mékambo in Malouma village (◉ 0.6755, 13.8776), which is 35km down a dirt track reached from a turn-off (◉ 0.8953, 14.0418), about 20km towards Ékata. From Malouma, it's some 11km further south on foot until the park boundary at the Louayé River. If visiting ever does become an option, you will need to contact ANPN (page 88) well in advance to arrange an excursion.

🏠 **WHERE TO STAY** To spend the night in Mékambo (if you make it all the way out here you'll almost surely have to), the Conseil Départemental de la Zadié (Zadié Departmental Council) runs a basic **auberge ($)**, alternatively, the considerably more modern **Complexe Hôtelier Franck Atabi Bokamba** (22 rooms; m 07 87 40 02/02 36 93 53/05 51 20 00; **$$**) opened here in 2016 with AC rooms and a bar-restaurant.

12

Woleu-Ntem

Gabon's northernmost region takes its name from two large rivers, the Woleu and the Ntem. It's a frontier region, separated from Cameroon to the north by the Ntem River, and wrapping around Equatorial Guinea to the west; the Crystal Mountains form the border with Estuaire province to the south. The regional boundaries were created by the French in the early 20th century (page 6). Woleu-Ntem fell under German colonial control between 1912 and 1915 – the German legacy lives on in the cocoa they planted – but today the region thrives on cross-border trade, and most of the fruit, veg, and other Cameroonian produce eaten throughout Gabon will pass through here en route. As such, the region is a draw for immigrants from Equatorial Guinea, Cameroon and beyond, making the 155,000-strong population of Woleu-Ntemois among the most diverse in Gabon.

This cross-border movement mushroomed in the early 1990s, when government-owned Hévégab carved more than 8,000ha of *hevea* (rubber tree) plantations into the forest near Bitam and Mitzic. Owing to the region's higher altitude, the weather tends to be colder than in most of the rest of the country, with a longer rainy season: the perfect conditions for these trees. Hévégab's work opportunities not only meant less of a youth exodus from Woleu-Ntem compared with other, less wealthy regions of Gabon, but also acted as a magnet for jobless young men from across the borders. Today, Hévégab has been absorbed into the Belgian-run Siat Gabon (**w** siatgabon.com).

In 2012, the Singapore-based Olam Gabon took on a highly controversial 37,000ha concession for rubber tree planting between Bitam and Minvoul. As of 2019, 11,000ha have been planted and a further 25,000ha are being managed for conservation purposes. Although the project creates jobs (Olam Gabon is in fact the largest private-sector employer in the country), NGOs and local populations remain concerned about the ongoing destruction of primary rainforest.

Thanks to all this economic activity, Woleu-Ntem is one of Gabon's wealthiest provinces. Entering Gabon from Cameroon, you immediately notice the difference: a beautifully surfaced main road awaits, which allows all that Cameroonian produce to quickly make its way to Libreville. Other striking differences are the lack of hawkers and street food, and the significant increase in prices.

Woleu-Ntem is the heartland of the Fang, Gabon's largest ethnic group. The Fang are widely known for the *mvet* musical tradition, played on an eponymous harp-like instrument made from bamboo and calabash gourds. There are also villages of Baka

$ ATMS

The only ATMs in Woleu-Ntem are in Bitam and Oyem. UGB is represented in both locations, while Oyem is also home to Ecobank.

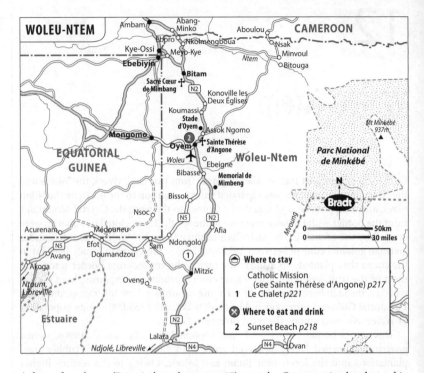

WOLEU-NTEM

Ambam · Abang-Minko · Aboulou · **CAMEROON**
Ebbro · Nkolmengboua · Nsak
Kye-Ossi · Meyo-Kye · Minvoul
Ebebiyin · Bitouga
Ntem
Bitam
Sacré Cœur de Mimbang · N2 · Konoville les Deux Églises
Koumassi
Stade d'Oyem · Assok Ngomo · *Mt Minkébé 937m*
Mongomo · ② · **Oyem** · Sainte Thérèse d'Angone · *Parc National de Minkébé*
EQUATORIAL GUINEA · *Woleu* · Ebeigné · **Woleu-Ntem**
Bibassé · Memorial de Mimbeng
Bissok
Nsoc · N5 · N2 · Afia
Acurenam · Médouneu · **Bradt**
N5 · Efot · Doumandzou · Sam · Ndongolo · 0 ———— 50km
Avang · 0 ———— 30 miles
Akoga · ① · Mitzic
Ntoum, Libreville · Oveng
Estuaire
N2
Lalara ·
Ndjolé, Libreville · N4 · N4 · Dvan

🛏 **Where to stay**
  Catholic Mission
  (see Sainte Thérèse d'Angone) *p217*
  1 Le Chalet *p221*

✕ **Where to eat and drink**
  2 Sunset Beach *p218*

(often referred to as 'Pygmies'; see box, page 17) near the Cameroonian border and in the forests in the east, including the village of Bitouga near Minvoul, widely known for its traditional medicine.

Seen from the sky during a flight to Oyem, the region's overwhelming feature is the impossibly dense forest, broken only by the dramatic inselbergs and the occasional roads lined with pinprick villages dotted with avocado, mango and banana trees. The uninhabited northeastern corner of the region, and the country, is part of the largest wilderness area left in equatorial Africa and consists of nearly impenetrable forest, broken only by massive granite outcrops puncturing the thick green carpet below. Part of this ancient place is Minkébé National Park; though cross-border poaching has yet to be brought under control here, the park remains one of the most important forest reserves for elephants in Africa.

OYEM

The 60,000 inhabitants of Gabon's fifth largest city form a diverse and well-integrated mixture of people from Gabon, Cameroon and Equatorial Guinea, and the central market bustles and babbles along in a mix of French, Fang, Spanish, and even a bit of English from time to time.

Oyem is the most significant town along the well-travelled route between Cameroon and Libreville, so there is a good variety of services on offer here, and it makes a logical and relaxed place to break the overland journey between the two countries. The town sprawls over a series of gently rolling hills (note the presidential palace with pride of place on Mont Miyele), with the marshy Lac Mvet at its centre. There's little in the way of a prescribed tourist itinerary here, but it makes a fine place to soak up some international hustle and bustle nonetheless.

www.gabonuntouched.com

A place to discover, a place to preserve

TRAVEL BETWEEN GABON, CAMEROON AND EQUATORIAL GUINEA

The tri-border area at the northwest corner of Woleu-Ntem is a hotspot for international trade and transport, but the formalities can get a little tricky for foreigners, so it pays to know what to expect in advance.

There are two crossings from **Cameroon** here, with the most popular being at the north end of the N2 between Eboro (Gabon) and Abang-Minko (Cameroon), and a lesser-used but still busy crossing between Meyo-Kye (Gabon) and Kye-Ossi (Cameroon). Both are 25 to 30km away from Bitam and accessed on surfaced roads. Your passport and visa will be examined at the border checkpoint, but you still must formalise your stay with a passport stamp from immigration in Bitam. Note also that as of 2018, Gabonese immigration checkpoints demand a *valid* hotel reservation in order to enter the country; they will phone the hotel to check. Rather perplexingly, the booking can be made with a hotel in Libreville and dated for when you expect to reach the capital.

There is also a remote third border crossing 20km north of Minvoul between Nsak (Gabon) and Aboulou (Cameroon). Currently, only pirogues cross the Kom River border here, but longstanding plans to construct a bridge and cross-border market facility in Aboulou were revived in 2018, so this may change. As it stands, Aboulou's weekly market is held on Sundays; expect rough roads and precious little transport if you head this way. Formalities would again take place in Bitam.

To **Equatorial Guinea**, there's a surfaced road from Bitam to Ebebiyín (25km), which sits at the tri-point border just opposite Kye-Ossi in Cameroon, and a laterite route between Oyem and Mongomo (40km). There's public transport on both routes, but reports indicate that non-CEMAC (Communauté Économique et Monétaire de l'Afrique Centrale; Economic and Monetary Community of Central Africa) foreigners were not allowed to cross into Equatorial Guinea by land at the time of writing, so have a backup plan if you're refused entry by the Equatoguinean authorities, or enquire further at the Equatorial Guinea consulate (m 04 33 59 53) in Oyem near Carrefour Mekaga.

GETTING THERE AND AWAY

By air NRT (La Nationale; ✆06 66 90 72) flies three times a week (Mon, Wed & Fri) **between Oyem and Libreville** (flights return from Libreville on the same three days). Tropical Air (page 66) runs the same route on Mondays and Fridays. The 45-minute journey will set you back 80,000CFA. The airport is about 8km south of the city centre; a taxi here costs 3,000CFA for *une course* or you can always try and flag down a passing vehicle.

By road The N2 runs 300km through Woleu-Ntem, from Eboro on the Cameroonian border down through Bitam (30km) and Oyem (105km), and continues on to Mitzic (215km) and Lalara (270km; junction for the N4 and Makokou), passing through Moyen-Ogooué en route to Ndjolé. There's basic accommodation in Lalara at **Hotel Entre Nous ($)**, if you need to break your journey.

It's a beautifully surfaced road, making travel quick and painless, and **shared taxis** taking four or five passengers shuttle between major towns along the route. Taxis leave Oyem's gare routière intermittently throughout the day until about 17.00, for Bitam (75km; 1½hrs; 2,500CFA) in the north and Mitzic (110km; 2hrs; 3,000CFA) in the south.

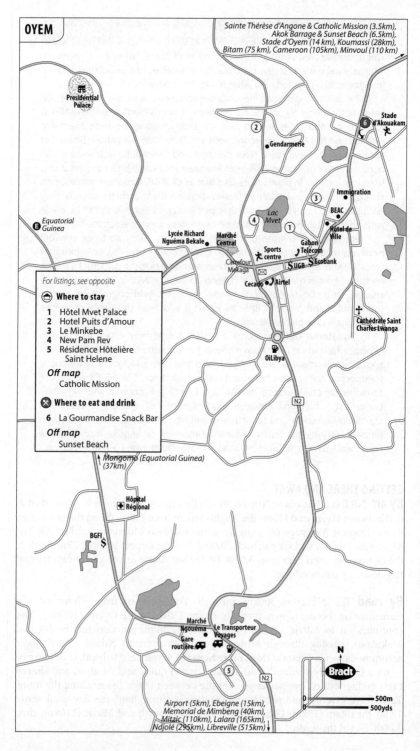

OYEM

Sainte Thérèse d'Angone & Catholic Mission (3.5km),
Akok Barrage & Sunset Beach (6.5km),
Stade d'Oyem (14 km), Koumassi (28km),
Bitam (75 km), Cameroon (105km), Minvoul (110 km)

Presidential Palace

Gendarmerie

Stade d'Akouakam

Equatorial Guinea

Immigration

BEAC

Lac Mvet

Hôtel de Ville

Lycée Richard Nguéma Bekale

Marché Central

Gabon Télécom

Sports centre

Carrefour Mekaga

UGB

Ecobank

Cecado

Airtel

Cathédrale Saint Charles Lwanga

OiLibya

N2

For listings, see opposite

Where to stay
1 Hôtel Mvet Palace
2 Hotel Puits d'Amour
3 Le Minkebe
4 New Pam Rev
5 Résidence Hôtelière Saint Helene

Off map
Catholic Mission

Where to eat and drink
6 La Gourmandise Snack Bar

Off map
Sunset Beach

Mongomo (Equatorial Guinea) (37km)

Hôpital Régional

BGFI

Marché Ngouéma

Le Transporteur Voyages

Gare routière

N2

N

Bradt

0 — 500m
0 — 500yds

Airport (5km), Ebeigne (15km),
Memorial de Mimbeng (40km),
Mitzic (110km), Lalara (165km),
Ndjolé (295km), Libreville (515km)

Regular **minibuses** charge 12,000CFA to bring you to Libreville in around 9 hours. Le Transporteur Voyages (**m** 06 40 15 30/07 13 08 08/05 94 33 33/06 34 33 33; **e** transporteurvoyages@yahoo.com) may be your best bet as they have reliable drivers and promise guaranteed departure from their offices next to Oyem's gare routière. Buses come with air conditioning and a TV screen. They run between one and four departures to and from their terminal in Libreville daily, departing between 05.30 and 10.30.

GETTING AROUND While the town centre is manageable **on foot**, the town as a whole is quite spread out and **taxis** come in handy (around 1,000–2,000CFA for a ride). It's possible to negotiate with taxi drivers to take you out of town too, although this is obviously easier if you have your own transport.

OTHER PRACTICALITIES Oyem is equipped with the usual assortment of services you would expect to find in a provincial capital, including a hospital, petrol station, post office, fruit and veg market, Cecado supermarket, mobile-provider offices and two ATMs.

There's an **Equatoguinean consulate** (**m** 04 33 59 53) here, too, though border crossings may be restricted (see box, page 215).

WHERE TO STAY, EAT AND DRINK *Map, page 216, unless otherwise stated*
Though it's got a fairly good selection of accommodation, Oyem isn't known for its dining opportunities and it's not easy to find a decent place to eat, so beyond a few chop houses serving barbecued food along the main roads, your most reliable bet is at one of the hotels below.

Hôtel Mvet Palace (70 rooms) Centre-Ville; ☎01 98 61 72; **m** 07 95 04 90. This has long been an Oyem landmark on the marshy shore of Lac Mvet, but recent reader reports indicate the 'palace' moniker may no longer be so á propos. Regardless, the prices at least seem to have dropped alongside the standards & it has a bar-restaurant (**$$**), souvenir shop & a noisy nightclub on Thu. The setting's not bad either, as many of the AC rooms overlook gardens & a lake. **$$**

Hotel Puits d'Amour (17 rooms) **m** 07 91 74 88; ⨍ Puits d'amour. This somewhat budget-friendly, pastel-hued digs comes warmly recommended for its trim AC rooms & tasty meals (**$$**). **$$**

Le Minkebe (40 rooms) **m** 02 39 69 89. The town's best hotel, the newly opened Le Minkebe sits in a 5-storey building just down the road from the Mvet Palace (see above) & has modern AC rooms, plus a large swimming pool & restaurant-bar (**$$$**). *From 35,000CFA.* **$$**

Résidence Hôtelière Saint Helene (17 rooms) Near the gare routière; ☎01 98 63 23; **m** 06 68 75 34/04 14 34 04; ⨍ SteHeleneR2H. Another well-managed choice with neat rooms &

a reliable restaurant (**$$$**) on the south side of town; it's a bit removed from the city centre but convenient for the gare routière. *20,000CFA dbl.* **$$**

New Pam Rev Hotel (20 rooms) ☎01 21 47 27. This hotel backs on to Lac Mvet & has en-suite rooms. There's no restaurant, but there is the New Pam Club (🕐 from 23.00 Thu–Sat). **$–$$**

☀**Catholic Mission** [map, page 214]
A few km out of town, behind the hospital; ⊕ 1.6176, 11.6085; ☎01 98 60 11/01 98 63 20. Located next to the large Sainte Thérèse d'Angone Cathedral (constructed by a French priest between 1949 & 1953), passers-by are always welcome to drop in here for a chat, or to stay overnight; it's a popular place with overlanders. The mission is home to the Frères St Gabriel & the Sœurs Ste Marie. They have a dormitory of 6 beds, 1 dbl room & a little kitchen. The mission's patch of lawn will be of particular interest to travellers with vehicles &/or tents, as there is room for both, & access to hot water. Rates are negotiable for those without means. There is a small workshop where the artistic creations of the female students can be bought (mostly pottery); the standard is very

good. *Around 5,000CFA per bed & 3,000CFA pp in a tent or camper van.* **$**

♀ La Gourmandise Snack Bar Akouakam; m 07 58 36 18/02 29 75 15. Though mostly known as one of Oyem's most popular bar-nightclubs, pizzas & other simple meals have been served here since 2018. The mirror-walled (& AC) nightclub really gets going at w/ends, with DJs, theme nights & plenty of Régab. **$$**

♀ Sunset Beach [map, page 214] About 5km north of town in Akok Barrage; m 07 23 29 91. For drinks or a relaxing afternoon, head here. Zanzibar it ain't, but the green gardens with tables under paillottes is about the closest you'll get to a beach feeling in Oyem. It's next to a little stream where you can swim.

WHAT TO SEE AND DO Oyem itself is rather short on sightseeing opportunities, but its position as the main settlement of the tri-border region with Cameroon and Equatorial Guinea (see box, page 215) means that its markets, particularly the **Marché Central** and **Marché Ngouéma**, are especially active, with fruit, veg, and all the everyday knick-knacks you can shake a stick at. There's also (naturally) a **presidential palace**; it's not open to the public, but you can see it atop the 700-odd-metre Mont Miyele on the northwest side of town. Otherwise, the **Cathédrale Saint Charles Lwanga**, just southeast of the centre, dates to 1967 but is of limited architectural interest, particularly when the lovely **Sainte Thérèse d'Angone** (⊕ 1.6176, 11.6085), a beautiful red-brick church complex surrounded by dense forest, is nearby, 1.5km north of the Sobraga bottling plant on the road to Bitam.

Travelling between these two churches, you'll pass the Stade d'Akouakam, where football fans can enjoy a match. Union Sportive d'Oyem is the home team here; they play in the Gabonese first division, though they've never managed to take home a title.

Continuing north from Sainte Thérèse d'Angone, keep an eye out on your left for the thoroughly unexpected (and thoroughly white-elephantish) 20,500-capacity **Stade d'Oyem**, which was built for the 2017 Africa Cup of Nations and sits 15km north of town at Assok Ngomo, just past the turn-off for Minvoul.

About 15km further on is the village of **Koumassi**. The village is impossible to miss, or rather its inselberg with its iron cross on top is (*koum* means 'mountain' in Fang). Stop at the village and ask for the chief, who will provide you with a guide. It's easily less than an hour to the top and the views are more than worth the effort. Just north of Koumassi, and halfway between Oyem and Bitam, you'll pass through the aptly named village of **Konoville les Deux Églises**, which is home to – you guessed it – two churches: one Catholic and one Protestant.

Finally, just 2km before you arrive in Bitam, you'll find the mid-century **Sacré Cœur de Mimbang Church** (⊕ 2.0664, 11.4930), where there is a small museum of religious art and Fang traditions, though recent reader reports indicate the man with the key is often nowhere to be found.

Travelling southbound between Oyem and Mitzic, you might want to stop 15km from town at the **leprosy village of Ebeigne**, to buy raffia baskets, chairs or lamps. Another 25km towards Mitzic brings you to the **Memorial de Mimbeng** (⊕ 1.2789, 11.6883), a small monument and cemetery where a number of soldiers, mostly **Tirailleurs sénégalais** (colonial infantry corps in the French army), were buried after losing their lives fighting for colonial France against the German invasion from Cameroon during World War I.

BITAM

This is the northernmost town in Gabon, just 30km south of the border with Cameroon. Though reasonably large (by Gabonese standards, anyway) with 28,000 inhabitants, almost everything is concentrated in a small central area – the market, the hotels, the post office, the petrol station, the bank, the pharmacy and even the airport (not in use at the time of writing) are all within easy walking distance.

If you arrive overland from Cameroon, you have to get your passport stamped in Bitam. There's a copy shop right across the street from the police station to make the necessary copies of your visa and passport. If you're leaving Gabon via this route, don't forget to get your exit stamp at the same office of immigration. Officials at the border will certainly send you back if your documents aren't properly stamped.

GETTING THERE AND AWAY The airport is right in town, 500m from the market, but there were no flights at the time of writing.

Buses from Libreville through Oyem take about 10 hours and cost 14,000CFA for the 590km journey. Le Transporteur Voyages (m 06 40 15 30/07 13 08 08/05 94 33 33/06 34 33 33; e transporteurvoyages@yahoo.com) runs between one and three departures between their terminal in Libreville and their office in central Bitam daily, departing between 04.30 and 09.30. For further information on travelling between Oyem and Bitam, see page 215.

If you've just **crossed the Cameroonian border** (see box, page 215), you can board one of the shared taxis waiting on the Gabonese side to take you to Bitam for 1,000CFA.

WHERE TO STAY, EAT AND DRINK

Hôtel Benedicta (53 rooms) Mengomo; m 07 00 25 25/06 06 09 09; **f** BenedictaHotel. Luxurious hotel with pool & Wi-Fi, located about 2km off the main road. Benedicta is a popular place with cyclists during La Tropicale Amissa (Gabon's biggest cycle event; page 72). Good value. **$$–$$$**

L'Auberge des Voyageurs (20 rooms) Marché Central; \01 96 80 20. A couple of blocks off the main road & close to the market, L'Auberge spreads across 2 buildings, 1 on either side of the road. It has rooms at many different rates. The cheapest is a room with fan & shared bathroom & the most expensive is a large en-suite room with AC. Meals can be cooked by arrangement (**$**) & there is a nightclub that opens very occasionally. The hotel is owned by a friendly & helpful couple, Mr & Mrs Hauger, who are committed to developing tourism in their little-visited region. *5,000–16,000CFA.* **$–$$**

NORTH OF BITAM

EBORO The border village, Eboro, is 30km north of Bitam along the N2, and just a short bridge crossing over the Ntem from Cameroon (see box, page 215). On Wednesdays and Saturdays there is a massive market on the Cameroonian side, 5km beyond the border, and many Gabonese shop here to resell their wares on their side of the border.

MINVOUL To get to Minvoul – the most remote settlement in the region right in the heart of the forest – entails a much longer, more arduous journey. Overloaded shared taxis or minibuses can take you there in 3 hours or so from Oyem (115km; 4,000CFA) or Bitam (110km; 4,000CFA). **From Oyem**, the turn-off is 15km north along the N2 at Assok Ngomo, while **from Bitam** it's 20km north along the N2 at Nkolmengboua. After leaving the N2 on either route, the roads are not tarred, which makes travel here very difficult in the rainy season.

To get between Minvoul and Libreville, Le Transporteur Voyages runs direct vehicles from their central office every Wednesday and Saturday at 08.00 for 20,000CFA.

Explorer and anthropologist Paul Belloni du Chaillu (1831-1903) was the first foreigner to confirm the existence of 'Pygmies' (see box, page 17) in the remote interior of Africa. Eager to bring a Pygmy skeleton back home with him, he asks his Ashango guides to lead him to the village's burial grounds, which they tactfully refuse.

'People say that there are dwarfs living in the forest. Is it so, Ashangos? How far are they from Niembouai?''At no great distance from this spot,' said the chief, 'there is a village of them; but, Oguizi, if you want to see them you must not go to them with a large number of attendants. You must go in a small party. Take one of your Commi men, and I will give you my nephew, who knows the dwarfs, to go with you. You must walk as cautiously as possible in the forest, for those dwarfs are like antelopes and gazelles; they are shy and easily frightened. To see them you must take them by surprise. No entreaty of ours could induce them to stay in their settlements if they knew you were coming. If you are careful, tomorrow we shall see them, for as sure as I live there are dwarfs in the forest, and they are called Obongos.'

[…]

'A dwarf!' I shouted, as the little creature came out. 'A woman!' I shouted again – 'a Pygmy!' The little creature shrieked, looking at me. 'Nchendé! Nchendé! Nchendé!' said she. 'Oh! oh! oh! Yo! yo! yo!' and her piercing wail rent the air. What a sight! I had never seen the like. 'What!' said I, 'now I do see the dwarfs of Equatorial Africa – the dwarfs of Homer, Herodotus – the dwarfs of the ancients.'

[…]

Then I said to the Ashango interpreter, 'Ask the little Obongos where they bury their dead.' I wanted to know, though I did not tell him why. I wanted the skeleton of an Obongo to bring

Small, isolated and profoundly remote, Minvoul's deep-forest setting will not disappoint fans of out-of-the-way places and end-of-the-road vibes. Remoter still (both physically and culturally), some of the Baka villages in the area, particularly **Bitouga** (5km south of Minvoul), are widely known as pilgrimage sites for people from all over Gabon seeking treatment with Baka traditional medicines. Bitouga is only accessible via a combination of hiking and pirogue, and you'll have to arrange a guide in town; your hotel should be able to help you find one. For a fascinating in-depth ethnolinguistic study of the Baka in Bitouga, see w ddl.cnrs.fr/fulltext/ Paulin/Paulin_2007_FEL.pdf. There's also an excellent French-language trip report at w carnetsdevoyages.jeanlou.fr/Les_Pygmees_de_BITOUGA.

 Where to stay, eat and drink To spend the night in Minvoul, the new three-storey **Hotel Jean Nkea** (m 06 48 03 96; **$$**) is surprisingly sharp, with AC rooms from 15,000CFA. A cheaper night's stay in the village can be had at the **Motel Akoulou** (**$**).

MITZIC

This is essentially a one-road town with an estimated 9,000 residents, although the number of unofficial immigrants makes it hard to be sure. Most people pass through Mitzic without a second glance, so visitors are greeted with a great deal of curiosity.

GETTING THERE AND AROUND Shared taxis do the run between the centre of Mitzic and **Oyem** several times a day if there's the demand (110km; 2hrs; 3,000CFA), and home, and I would have been willing to give a thousand dollars for one. 'Don't ask such a question of the Obongos,' said he. 'And why?' I inquired. 'Because,' he answered, 'they would be so frightened they would all run away. Even we ourselves, the Ashangos, who are their friends, know not where they bury their dead, and I will tell you why: they are afraid that the Ashangos would steal the skulls of the dead people for fetiches, and if they could procure but one they would always know where the Obongos were in the forest.'

'Tell me,' said I, 'how they bury their dead.' 'When an Obongo dies,' said my Ashango friend, 'there is great sorrow among the Dwarfs, and the men are sent into every part of the forest to find a tall tree which is hollow at the top. If they find one, they come back to the settlement and say, "We have found a tree with a hollow." Then the people travel into the forest guided by the man who has found the hollow tree, and taking with them the body of the dead Obongo. When they have reached the spot, some of them ascend the tree, carrying with them creepers to be used as cords for drawing up the body, and the corpse is then drawn and deposited in the hollow, which is immediately filled with earth, and dry leaves, and twigs of trees.'

'But,' said I, 'big hollow trees, such as you have been speaking of, are not found every day. If they do not find one, what then?' 'It is so, Oguizi. Sometimes they cannot find a big hollow tree,' said my Ashango guide, 'so they wander into the forest, far from paths and villages, in search of a little stream, which they turn from its natural bed, and then dig in it a big, deep hole, wherein they bury the body of the Obongo, after which they bring back the water to its own bed again, and the water forever and ever runs over the grave of the Obongo, and no one can ever tell where the grave of the Obongo is.'

From *The Country of the Dwarfs* (1871)

any minibus heading **from Libreville** to Oyem or Bitam can also drop you here (405km; 8hrs; 10,000CFA). Vehicles **from Booué** (165km) arrive in Mitzic about 09.00 and depart again around 14.00. Heading to Booué, the route is surfaced for the first 115km, but conditions deteriorate after the turn-off at Koumameyong, from where there are 50km of dirt roads, likely to require a 4×4.

Within the town itself, there are no taxis and no need for them either, as it's possible to **walk** from one end of the town to the other in a leisurely 10 minutes, barring impromptu conversations, of course.

WHERE TO STAY, EAT AND DRINK Accommodation choices are very limited, so the best place in town is probably the friendly **Catholic Mission ($)**, but **Hotel Bel-Air ($)** and the long-serving **Hotel Ngue ($$)** also come recommended by overlanders; both are set along the main road through town.

With your own transport, hotel-restaurant **Le Chalet** [map, page 214], 12km out of town on the Oyem road, is preferable. Here you'll find air-conditioned rooms (about 17,000CFA; **$$**), good food (**$$$**) and a small animal park with a few antelope.

PARC NATIONAL DE MINKÉBÉ

The area north of the N4 and east of the N2 – encompassing parts of both Ogooué-Ivindo and Woleu-Ntem – is known as the **Massif Forestier de Minkébé** (Minkébé Forest Massif). This forest is part of the major tri-national Dja-Odzala-Minkébé forest (TRIDOM), spreading 150,000km² over northern Gabon, southeastern Cameroon and northwestern Congo.

Minkébé National Park is at the centre of a vast uninhabited area covering 32,000km² of dense rainforest, broken only by marshy clearings and impressive grassy inselbergs: domed granite mountains piercing the canopy, which emerged millions of years ago. Great forest trees, many hundreds of years old, soar upward 50m, some crowned with wild orchid and fern gardens, or supporting huge twining lianas.

Though also home to sizeable populations of bongo, leopard, giant pangolin, mandrill and buffalo, the park is best known for its high – but acutely vulnerable – population of forest elephant. Gorilla and chimp populations are relatively low here, due to an outbreak of ebola in the 1990s, which is estimated to have killed upwards of 90% of the park's great apes. (Globally, ebola-related mortality rates for gorillas and chimpanzees are estimated at a devastating 95% and 77%, respectively.)

Perhaps more so than in any other park in Gabon, poaching and hunting are out of control here, and represent a grave threat to the park's future. Despite the fact that President Ali Bongo has adopted a 'zero tolerance policy' for wildlife crime (page 35) and a rotating detachment of 120 soldiers is now semi-permanently based at Minkébé to protect the remaining elephants, studies carried out by WWF, WCS and ANPN show that nearly 80% of the park's elephants – a staggering 25,000 individuals – vanished between 2004 and 2014. ANPN estimated that at its peak, 50 to 100 elephants were being killed daily; today that number is closer to 12. Asian demand for ivory for use in jewellery and ornamental items sadly seems inexhaustible, and Gabonese elephants have the 'extra-hard pinkish ivory' that is considered especially valuable.

GETTING THERE AND AWAY While the park is rich in tourist possibilities, no visits were possible at the time of writing owing to the presence of armed poachers and general lawlessness in the park. To find out more about whether or not it may be possible to arrange a visit, contact FIGET (page 209) or the ANPN in Libreville (page 88).

Even at the best of times, Minkébé is one of Gabon's most isolated parks and therefore seriously difficult to reach. There are no roads leading to it and the only way to enter is by river from Makokou in Ogooué-Ivindo (as well as via hundreds of elephant paths). Theoretically, when park access is possible, FIGET can organise trips by pirogue departing from Loa-Loa pier at the Ipassa research station, 12km south of Makokou. They will tailor a personalised trip for you so you should negotiate the price, but count on a minimum cost of 100,000CFA a day.

Should the opportunity to visit become available again, don't even consider going without a knowledgeable guide or you may get lost – forever.

Appendix 1

LANGUAGE

French is the official language in Gabon and, as English is not widely spoken at all, you will need some basic French to get around. However, there's no need to be intimidated by the language barrier, as any efforts will be highly appreciated. Many young Gabonese are eager to practise their English.

Politeness is very important, although as a foreigner you'll be quickly forgiven any mistakes.
- Adults use *tu* (you) to children, but children use *vous* (you) to all adults
- Adults use *tu* to adults they know well, *vous* to other adults they do not know very well

Besides one official language, Gabon has some 40 African languages. The principal indigenous language is **Fang**, a West Bantu language that is also spoken in southern Cameroon, Equatorial Guinea and the Republic of the Congo. The best-known song in Fang is probably 'Zamina mina zangalewa' (Come! Come! Who has called you?) by the Cameroonian group Golden Sounds, and sampled by Shakira in her 2010 World Cup anthem 'Waka Waka' (This Time For Africa).

FANG BASICS

English	Fang
Hello (for one person)	*M'bolo*
Hello (for many people)	*M'bolani*
How are you?	*Y'o num vah?*
I'm fine	*M'a num vah*
Thank you	*Akiba*
I don't speak Fang	*Ma kobe ki Fang*

FRENCH

English	French
Greetings	
Good morning	*Bonjour*
Good evening	*Bonsoir*
Good night	*Bonne nuit*
Goodbye	*Au revoir*
See you later	*A plus tard*
How are you?	*Comment allez-vous (polite)/ça va (informal)/ Comment tu vas (informal)?*
I'm fine	*Je vais très bien/ça va bien*

Basics

yes	*oui*
no	*non*
please	*s'il vous plaît*
thank you	*merci*
thank you very much	*merci beaucoup*
you're welcome	*de rien/je t'en prie*
excuse me	*excusez-moi, pardon*
I would like…	*Je voudrais…*
there	*là*
here	*ici*
stop	*arrêtez*
Help!	*Au secours!*
Do you speak English?	*Parlez-vous Anglais?*
I don't understand	*Je ne comprends pas*
I don't speak French	*Je ne parle pas Français*
A bit	*Un peu*
Where is…?	*Oú est…?*

Health

chemist	*la pharmacie*
doctor	*le médecin*
hospital	*l'hôpital*
malaria	*palu/paludisme*
mosquito net	*moustiquaire*

Accommodation

toilet	*la toilette, le WC*
How much is it?	*C'est combien?*
It is too much!	*C'est trop cher!*
hotel	*l'hôtel* (all sorts of accommodation), *l'auberge* (inexpensive), *le case de passage* (cheapest)
air conditioning	*climatisé*
May I see the room?	*Puis-je voir la chambre?*

Food

restaurant	*le restaurant, le maquis (small, informal eatery)*
market	*le marché*
bakery	*la boulangerie*
supermarket	*le supermarché*
some food	*de la nourriture/quelque chose à manger?*
breakfast	*le petit-déjeuner*
lunch	*le déjeuner*
supper	*le diner*
bread	*le pain*
butter	*le beurre*
sandwich	*un sandwich*
vegetables	*les légumes*
meat	*la viande*
beef	*le bœuf*
pork	*le porc*

chicken	le poulet
fish	le poisson
grilled meat/fish	les grillades
I don't eat meat/fish	je ne mange pas de viande/poisson
bushmeat	la viande de brousse
only vegetables	juste des légumes
eggs	les œufs
fruit	les fruits
apple	le pomme
peanuts	les arachides
drinking water	l'eau potable
soft drink	le jus
fruit juice	le jus de fruits
beer	la bière
wine	le vin
coffee	le café
tea	le thé

On the menu

crushed, fermented odika seeds	sauce au chocolat
antelope, porcupine, monkey, snake or any other wild animal	la viande de brousse
hot sauce made of peppers	piment

Getting around

car	la voiture
bus	le bus
bus/taxi station	la gare routière
four-wheel-drive (4x4)	le quatre-quatre
bush taxi	le clando (from clandestine – illegal) or le taxi-brousse
private taxi	le dépot
aeroplane	l'avion
boat	le bateau
canoe (dug-out or larger narrow fishing boat)	la pirogue
boatsman	le piroguier
Is it very far?	C'est très loin?
What time?	A quelle heure?
morning	le matin
afternoon	l'après-midi
evening	le soir
petrol/gas	l'essence
roundabout	le rond-point
street	la rue
road	la route
police	la police
post office	la poste
forest	la forêt
city, town	la ville

Appendix 2

FURTHER INFORMATION

BOOKS

Historical interest Mary Kingsley wrote several works about Africa (see box, page 146), but the best one to start with is her *Travels in West Africa* (Phoenix, 2001), which is fascinating and often funny. A good biography of Mary Kingsley is Dea Birkett's *Mary Kingsley: Imperial Adventuress* (Macmillan, 1992). Caroline Alexander's *One Dry Season: In the Footsteps of Mary Kingsley* (Bloomsbury, 1989) tells of Alexander's determined and resourceful attempts to recreate Mary Kingsley's 1895 journey a century on.

Of Paul B du Chaillu's writings, the most accessible is *Explorations and Adventures in Equatorial Africa* (London, 1861), a personal account of his explorations from 1856–59.

As far as I know there is no Pierre Savorgnan de Brazza in English translation. His first journey, 1875–77, is described in *Au Coeur de l'Afrique* (Paris, 1992). Monte Reel's *Between Man and Beast: An Unlikely Explorer and the African Adventure that Took the Victorian World by Storm* (Anchor, 2013) describes how du Chaillu's 20 preserved gorilla skins, trophies of his search in the Gabonese jungle, went from objects of wonder to key pieces in an all-out intellectual war about Darwin's evolution theory.

There is no shortage of works by Albert Schweitzer, of which the best one to start with is probably *From My African Notebook* (Bradford and Dickens, 1938). This book gives a valuable insight into the running of the hospital at Lambaréné and Schweitzer's vision of Africa (see box, page 144).

There is also the sensationalistic *Trader Horn*, a record of tales Aloysius 'Trader' Horn told to a South African writer in 1926.

Academic (and often in French)

Aicardi de Saint-Paul, Marc *Gabon: The Development of a Nation* (translated into English 1989, Routledge). Some useful background information, if a little outdated now.

Bernault, Florence *Colonial Transactions: Imaginaries, Bodies, and Histories in Gabon* (Duke University Press, 2019). An anthropological analysis of the colonial encounter in Gabon, relating to the imagined characteristics Africans and Europeans ascribed to one another.

Casteran, Christian *Bongo: Confidences d'un Africain* (SA, 1994). A collection of transcripts from interviews with Omar Bongo.

Dedet, Christian *La Mémoire du fleuve: L'Afrique aventureuse de Jean Michonet* (Paris, 1985). Tells the story of Jean Michonet, who among other things is an initiate of Bwiti.

Fernandez, James W *Bwiti: An Ethnography of the Religious Imagination in Africa* (Princeton, 1982). A comprehensive study of Bwiti.

Gray, Christopher *Colonial Rule and Crisis in Equatorial Africa: Southern Gabon, c. 1850-1940* (University of Rochester Press, 2002). A political and cultural history of southern Gabon as it came under French domination.

Heilbrunn, John R *Oil, Democracy and Development in Africa* (Cambridge University Press, 2014). A rather optimistic analysis of the continent's oil-producing states.

Jean-Baptiste, Rachel *Conjugal Rights: Marriage, Sexuality, and Urban Life in Colonial Libreville, Gabon* (Ohio University Press, 2014). A history of marriage and partnerships in colonial Libreville.

Mpenga, Annie and Hubert, Jacques *Culture Gabonaise: Annuaire des auteurs de 1950 à 2010* (Libreville, Gabon: Fondation Raponda-Walker, 2010). This excellent bibliography of over 1,000 works is a good list of Gabonese authors. Many of these references are only available in Gabon.

Oslisly, Richard *Archéologie dans le Parc National de la Lopé: site mixte nature culture du patrimoine mondial* (RD Éditions/ANPN/Ecofac, 2010). A 40-some-page work on the archaeology of Lopé National Park.

Raponda-Walker, André *Rites et Croyances des Peuples du Gabon* (Paris, 1962). A study of the beliefs of the different peoples of Gabon. Also of interest is his *Contes Gabonais* (Paris, 1967), a collection of Gabonese fables.

Rich, Jeremy *A Workman is Worthy of His Meat: Food and Colonialism in the Gabon Estuary* (University of Nebraska Press, 2009). A study of food culture and colonialism in Libreville.

Toman, Cheryl *Women Writers of Gabon: Literature and Herstory* (Lexington Books, 2016). The only critical text on Gabonese literature in English, including analysis of numerous modern female authors.

Yates, Douglas A *Historical Dictionary of Gabon*, 4th ed (Rowman & Littlefield, 2017). The most comprehensive bibliography of Gabon, covering work in the natural sciences, the humanities and the social sciences written in English and French. It also provides a wide range of short entries on major events and historical figures in Gabonese history.

Yates, Douglas A *The Rentier State in Africa: Oil Rent Dependency and Neocolonialism in the Republic of Gabon* (Africa World Press, 1996).

Natural history

Borrow, Nick and Demey, Ron *Birds of Western Africa* (Princeton University Press, 2014). The newest and most comprehensive guide. Each colour plate is accompanied by essential extra information of the bird's biology and behaviour.

Christy, Patrice and Clarke, William V *Guide des oiseaux de la Reserve de la Lopé* (Ecofac, Libreville, 1994). A colour-illustrated field guide published in French. Bird names in the body text at least are given in English and Latin as well.

Fossey, Dian *Gorillas in the Mist* (Boston, 1983). Part scientific report, part personal account of her remarkable 13-year study of four gorilla groups living in the Virunga Mountains that span the Zaire (now the DRC), Rwanda and Uganda. These mountain gorillas (*Gorilla gorilla beringei*) are a different subspecies from the lowland gorillas (*Gorilla gorilla gorilla*) found in Gabon, but Fossey's in-depth knowledge of gorilla behaviour makes it well worth the read.

Kingdon, Jonathan *The Kingdon Field Guide to African Mammals* (Harcourt, 1997). The definitive guide.

Raponda-Walker, André *Les Plantes Utiles de Gabon* (Libreville-Paris, 1995). A rundown of the different plants in Gabon and their properties.

Vande weghe, Gaël R *Les Papillons du Gabon* (Wildlife Conservation Society, 2010). Information about the butterflies of Gabon.

White, Lee and Abernethy, Kate *A Guide to the Vegetation of the Lopé Reserve Gabon* (Multipress-Gabon, Libreville, 1997). Excellent, and relevant way beyond Lopé.

National parks The Wildlife Conservation Society has published a series of beautiful full-colour books, all written by Jean Pierre Vande weghe, covering each of Gabon's national parks. All are 200-odd pages long and, while English translations do exist, the French original versions are easier to find.

Akanda et Pongara (2011)
Le delta de l'Ogooué (2017) Edited by Tariq Stévart.
Ivindo et Mwagna (2009)
Loango, Mayumba et le bas Ogooué (2013)
Lope, Waka et Monts Birougou (2017)
Minkébé (2013)
Monts de Cristal (2008)
Moukalaba-Doudou (2008)
Plateaux Batéké (2008)

Gabonese literature and novels set in Gabon

Bessora, Sandrine *Cuillez-moi jolis messieurs* (Editions Gallimard, 2004), *Les taches d'encre* (J'ai lu, 2002). Novels by Gabon's foremost prize-winning author; the former won the Grand prix littéraire d'Afrique noire in 2007. Both in French.

Bessora, Sandrine and Barroux *Alpha: Abidjan to Gare du Nord* (Bellevue Literary Press, 2018). Graphic novel telling the story of an Ivorian migrant to France. One of the few Gabonese novels available in English.

Divassa Nyama, Jean *La Vocation de Dignité* (Ndze, 2008). Another prize-winning Gabonese author.

Emane, Augustin *Albert Schweitzer, une icône africaine* (Fayard, 2013). In French, about the work of Albert Schweitzer in Gabon.

Mengara, Daniel *Mema* (Heinemann, 2004). One of the only Gabonese novels available in English, about the role of women in a changing society.

Ndongo, Donato *Shadows of your Black Memory* (Swan Isle Press, 2016). Though the author and setting are both Equatoguinean, its focus on Fang traditional life in Río Muni has many parallels with Gabon. In English.

Simenon, Georges *Tropic Moon* (NYRB Classics, 2005). English translation of Simenon's 1933 novel *Coup de Lune*, which take place in colonial Libreville.

Travel writing

Brokken, Jan *The Rainbird: A Central African Journey* (Lonely Planet, 1997). An entertaining and historically rich account of his travels through the jungles of Gabon, brought to life by anecdotes about the first explorers and missionaries, as well as the people he meets on the way.

Drummond, Titus *Pangolin with Vin Rouge: Five Weeks on a Motorbike in Gabon* (Amazon, 2018). Recent travel memoir of a British motorcyclist who travelled more than 4,000km across Gabon.

Gray, Jason *Glimpses through the Forest: Memories of Gabon* (Peace Corps Writers, 2013). Memoir of a Peace Corps volunteer stationed in Gamba for three years.

Meijer, Darcy Munson (ed) *Adventures in Gabon: Peace Corps Stories from the African Rainforest* (Peace Corps Writers, 2011). Stories and anecdotes written by former Peace Corps volunteers based in Gabon between 1962 and 2005.

Other Central Africa guides For a full list of Bradt titles, see w bradtguides. com/shop.

Becker, Kathleen *São Tomé & Príncipe* (Bradt, 2020)
Rorison, Sean *Congo Democratic Republic, Republic* (Bradt, 2012)
Scafidi, Oscar *Angola* (Bradt, 2019)
Scafidi, Oscar *Equatorial Guinea* (Bradt, 2015)
West, Ben *Cameroon* (Bradt, 2011)

MAPS There are currently three Gabon country maps in print. The first is a 1:1,000,000 Gabon map, with a 1:50,000 inset of Libreville, the work of the Institut Geographique National, the French government mapping agency (Paris, 2009). The second is a 1:980,000 map of Cameroon and Gabon produced by International Travel Maps and Books (Vancouver, 2009). The third is a Cameroon and Gabon map by the German Reise Know-How Verlag GmbH (2013).

TRAVEL MAGAZINES AND PHOTO BOOKS
National Geographic (w nationalgeographic.com) regularly runs articles on Gabon. Most famous are the series of pieces on Mike Fay's Megatransect, the epic 3,200km journey on foot with the objective of bringing the last pristine forest in Central Africa to the world's attention (several issues, 2001) (page 28).
The Edge of Africa, with photographs by Carlton Ward Jr and text by Michelle Lee (Hylas Publishing, 2003), is a stunning coffee table book with spectacular photographs.
Travel Africa (w travelafricamag.com) has consistently the best coverage of African destinations, with articles written by African specialists.

WEBSITES
Government travel advice
w **fco.gov.uk** British Foreign and Commonwealth Office
w **travel.state.gov** US Department of State Travel Advisory Department
w **dfat.gov.au** Australian Department of Foreign Affairs
w **dfait-maeci.gc.ca** Canadian Department of Foreign Affairs

News from Africa
w **allafrica.com** Daily news from over 130 African news organisations
w **africadaily.com** Broad range of online content
w **bbc.com/news/world/africa** BBC World Service on Africa
w **panapress.com** Site of the Pan African News Agency PanaPress

Gabon news sites
w **agpgabon.ga** Agence Gabonaise de Presse (Gabonese Press Agency), website of Gabon Matin
w **union.sonapresse.com** Website of L'Union
w **gabonews.com** Newssite of Gabonese press agency Gabonews
w **gabonreview.com** News site of Gabonese press agency ACI Presse
w **infosgabon.com** News site of Gabonese press agency Infosgabon
w **gaboneco.com** News site of Infosgabon

Gabon official sites The portal of the Gabonese government is **w** gouvernement. ga. President Ali Bongo's office can be found at **w** presidence.ga, **f** PresidenceGabon, or **🐦** @presidentabo. ANPN can be found at **f** PARCSGABON, which is kept up to date.

w gabonmagazine.com Website of the *Gabon Magazine* by Forbes Custom Magazines, a slick PR bureau in the UK, commissioned by the Gabonese government. In English and French.

Other useful sites

w lepriveonline.com Annually updated guide (not very complete) with practical addresses in Gabon. Also available in print.

w lepratiquedugabon.com Website of annually updated pocket publication with listings for Libreville and Port-Gentil covering all sorts of practical information, from banks and couriers to schools and hospitals.

NOTES

Index

Page numbers in **bold** indicate main entries, those in *italics* indicate maps.

INDEX OF ADVERTISERS